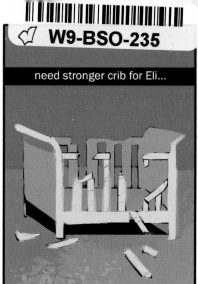

need stronger crib for Eli...

MY NAME IS ELI FRANKLIN, I'M FIFTEEN, AND I DON'T THINK I'M LIKE MOST GIRLS IN HELENA, MONTANA.

I'M ADOPTED. MY PARENTS ALWAYS SAY THE STORK DROPPED ME OFF IN THE WHEAT FIELDS.

WHICH ISN'T TRUE, BUT IT KINDA EXPLAINS *HOW* I'M DIFFERENT FROM OTHER GIRLS.

OTHERWISE MY LIFE HAS BEEN KINDA SUPER NORMAL.

EVEN WHEN MY FAMILY HAS TO DEAL WITH ME BEING...SUPERNORMAL.

THOUGH IT ALSO MEANS KEEPING QUIET ABOUT MY STRUGGLES.

BUT MOM ALWAYS FIGURES OUT SOME SOLUTION.

DAD WORKS FOR THE WHITE HOUSE AND SAYS IT'S HIS JOB TO KEEP WHAT I CAN DO A SECRET FROM PEOPLE.

WHICH IS WHY I'M NOT ALLOWED TO POST ANYTHING COOL--HE'D BE REALLY MAD IF HE SAW THIS.

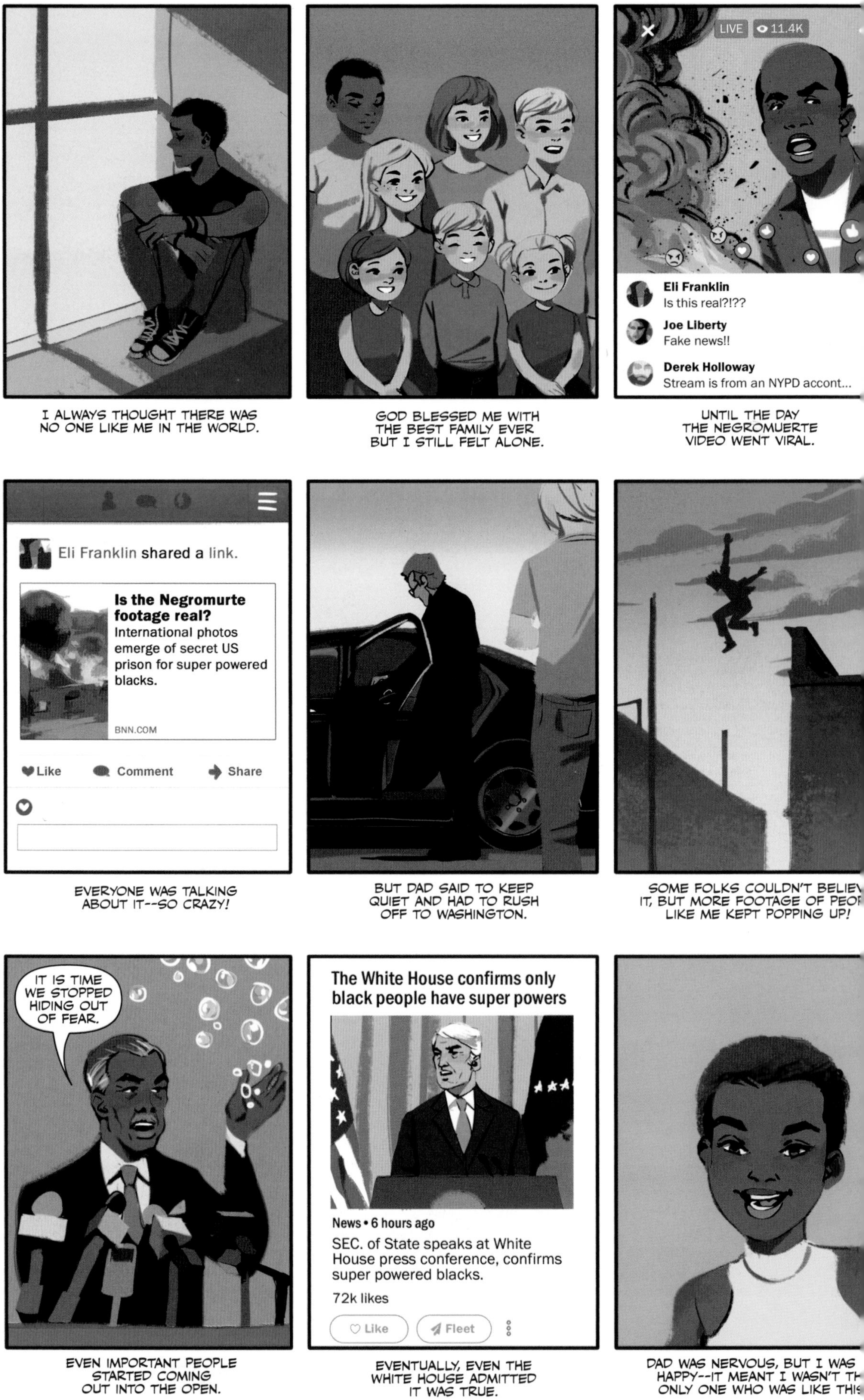
I ALWAYS THOUGHT THERE WAS NO ONE LIKE ME IN THE WORLD.
GOD BLESSED ME WITH THE BEST FAMILY EVER BUT I STILL FELT ALONE.
LIVE
11.4K
Eli Franklin
Is this real?!??
Joe Liberty
Fake news!!
Derek Holloway
Stream is from an NYPD accont...
UNTIL THE DAY THE NEGROMUERTE VIDEO WENT VIRAL.
Eli Franklin shared a link.
Is the Negromurte footage real?
International photos emerge of secret US prison for super powered blacks.
BNN.COM
Like
Comment
Share
EVERYONE WAS TALKING ABOUT IT--SO CRAZY!
BUT DAD SAID TO KEEP QUIET AND HAD TO RUSH OFF TO WASHINGTON.
SOME FOLKS COULDN'T BELIE
IT, BUT MORE FOOTAGE OF PEO
LIKE ME KEPT POPPING UP!
IT IS TIME WE STOPPED HIDING OUT OF FEAR.
EVEN IMPORTANT PEOPLE STARTED COMING OUT INTO THE OPEN.
The White House confirms only black people have super powers
News • 6 hours ago
SEC. of State speaks at White House press conference, confirms super powered blacks.
72k likes
Like
Fleet
EVENTUALLY, EVEN THE WHITE HOUSE ADMITTED IT WAS TRUE.
DAD WAS NERVOUS, BUT I WAS
HAPPY--IT MEANT I WASN'T T
ONLY ONE WHO WAS LIKE THI

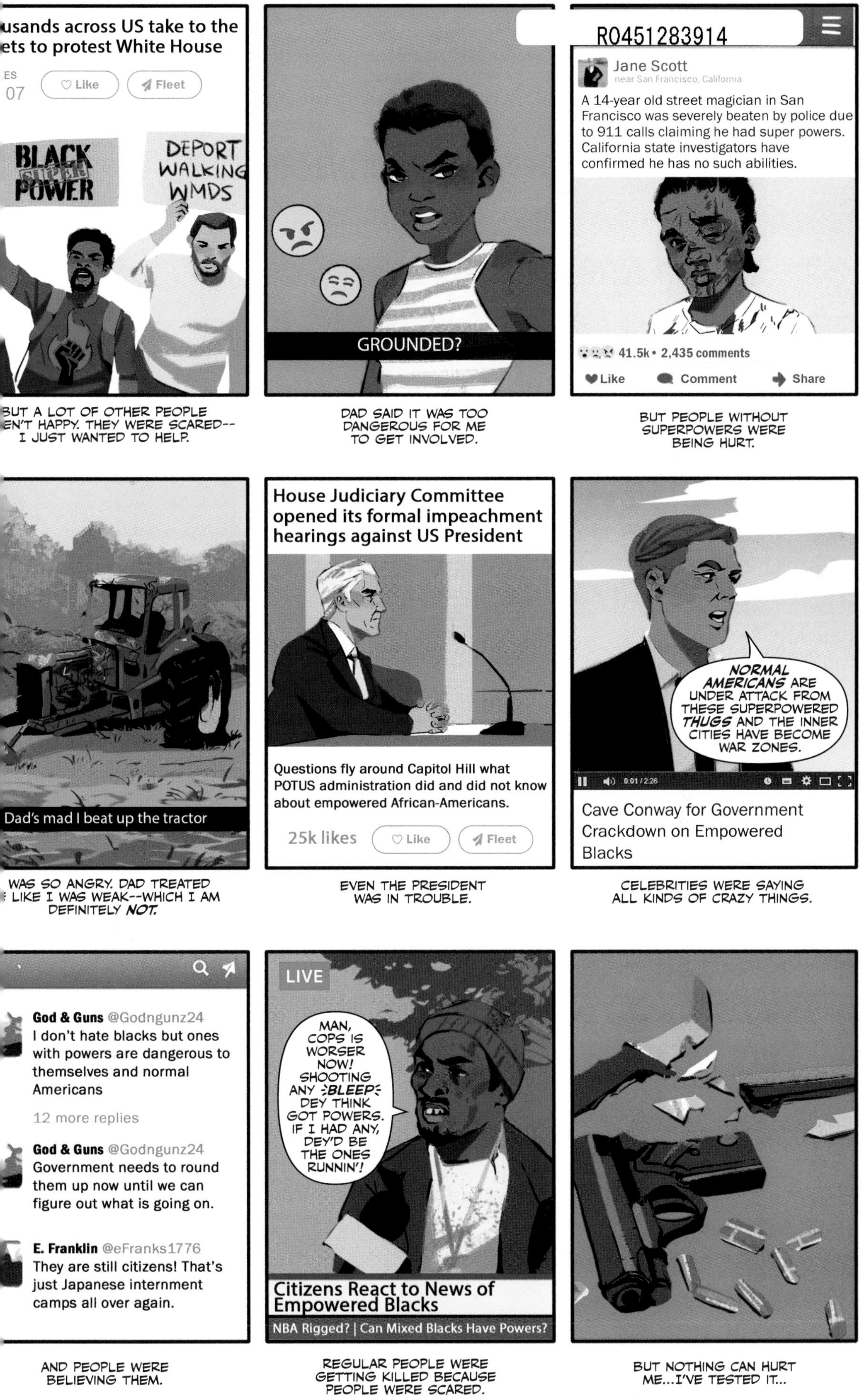
usands across US take to the
ets to protest White House
ES
07
Like
Fleet
BLACK
POWER
DEPORT
WALKING
WMDS
BUT A LOT OF OTHER PEOPLE
EN'T HAPPY. THEY WERE SCARED--
I JUST WANTED TO HELP.
GROUNDED?
DAD SAID IT WAS TOO DANGEROUS FOR ME TO GET INVOLVED.
Jane Scott
near San Francisco, California
A 14-year old street magician in San Francisco was severely beaten by police due to 911 calls claiming he had super powers. California state investigators have confirmed he has no such abilities.
41.5k • 2,435 comments
Like
Comment
Share
BUT PEOPLE WITHOUT SUPERPOWERS WERE BEING HURT.
Dad's mad I beat up the tractor
WAS SO ANGRY. DAD TREATED
LIKE I WAS WEAK--WHICH I AM
DEFINITELY *NOT.*
House Judiciary Committee opened its formal impeachment hearings against US President
Questions fly around Capitol Hill what POTUS administration did and did not know about empowered African-Americans.
25k likes
Like
Fleet
EVEN THE PRESIDENT WAS IN TROUBLE.
NORMAL AMERICANS ARE UNDER ATTACK FROM THESE SUPERPOWERED *THUGS* AND THE INNER CITIES HAVE BECOME WAR ZONES.
0:01 / 2:26
Cave Conway for Government Crackdown on Empowered Blacks
CELEBRITIES WERE SAYING ALL KINDS OF CRAZY THINGS.
God & Guns @Godngunz24
I don't hate blacks but ones with powers are dangerous to themselves and normal Americans
12 more replies
God & Guns @Godngunz24
Government needs to round them up now until we can figure out what is going on.
E. Franklin @eFranks1776
They are still citizens! That's just Japanese internment camps all over again.
AND PEOPLE WERE BELIEVING THEM.
LIVE
MAN, COPS IS WORSER NOW! SHOOTING ANY *BLEEP* DEY THINK GOT POWERS. IF I HAD ANY, DEY'D BE THE ONES RUNNIN'!
Citizens React to News of Empowered Blacks
NBA Rigged? | Can Mixed Blacks Have Powers?
REGULAR PEOPLE WERE GETTING KILLED BECAUSE PEOPLE WERE SCARED.
BUT NOTHING CAN HURT ME...I'VE TESTED IT...

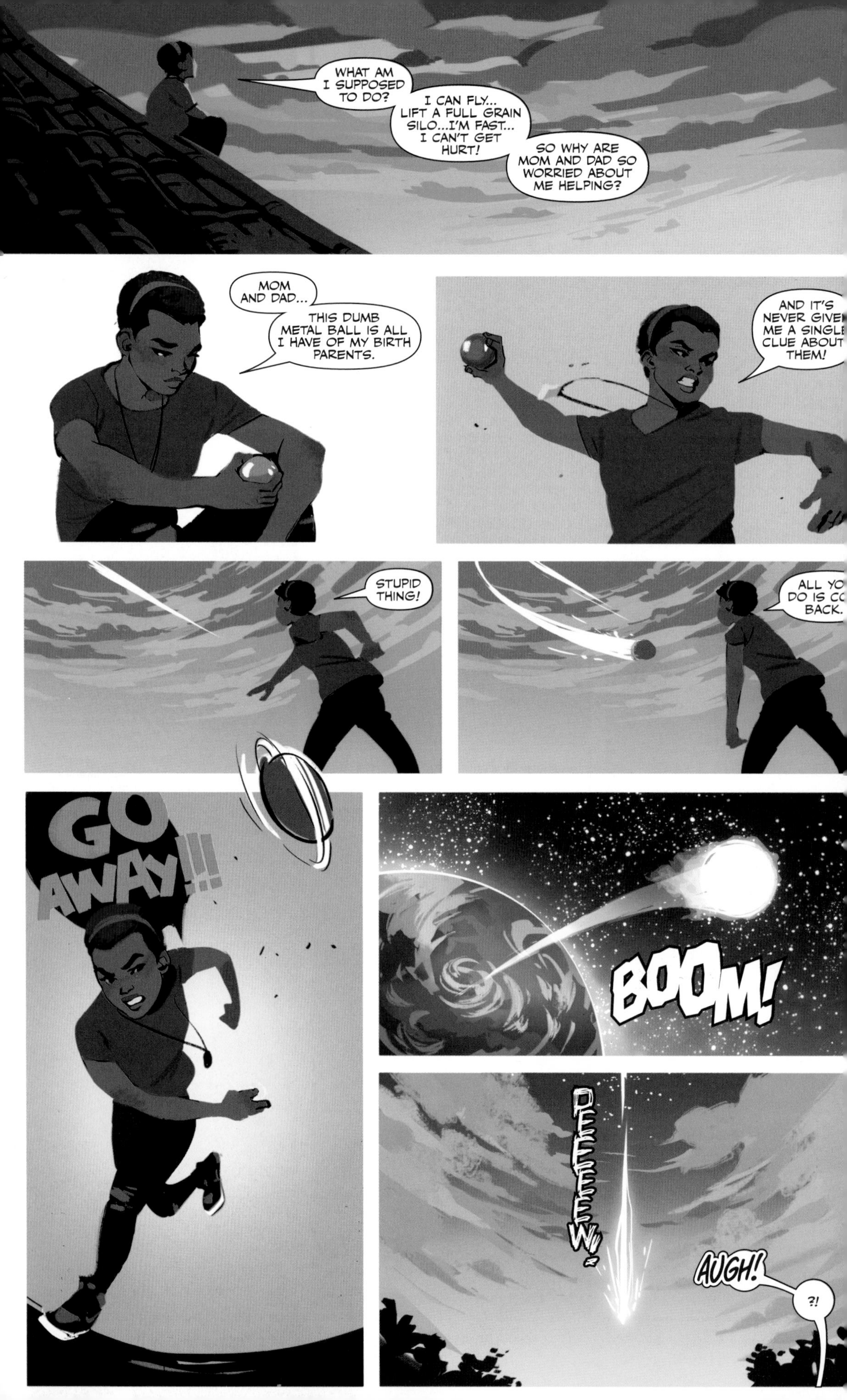
WHAT AM I SUPPOSED TO DO?
I CAN FLY... LIFT A FULL GRAIN SILO...I'M FAST... I CAN'T GET HURT!
SO WHY ARE MOM AND DAD SO WORRIED ABOUT ME HELPING?
MOM AND DAD...
THIS DUMB METAL BALL IS ALL I HAVE OF MY BIRTH PARENTS.
AND IT'S NEVER GIVE ME A SINGL CLUE ABOUT THEM!
STUPID THING!
ALL YO DO IS CO BACK.
GO AWAY!!!
BOOM!
DEEEEEEW!
AUGH!
?!

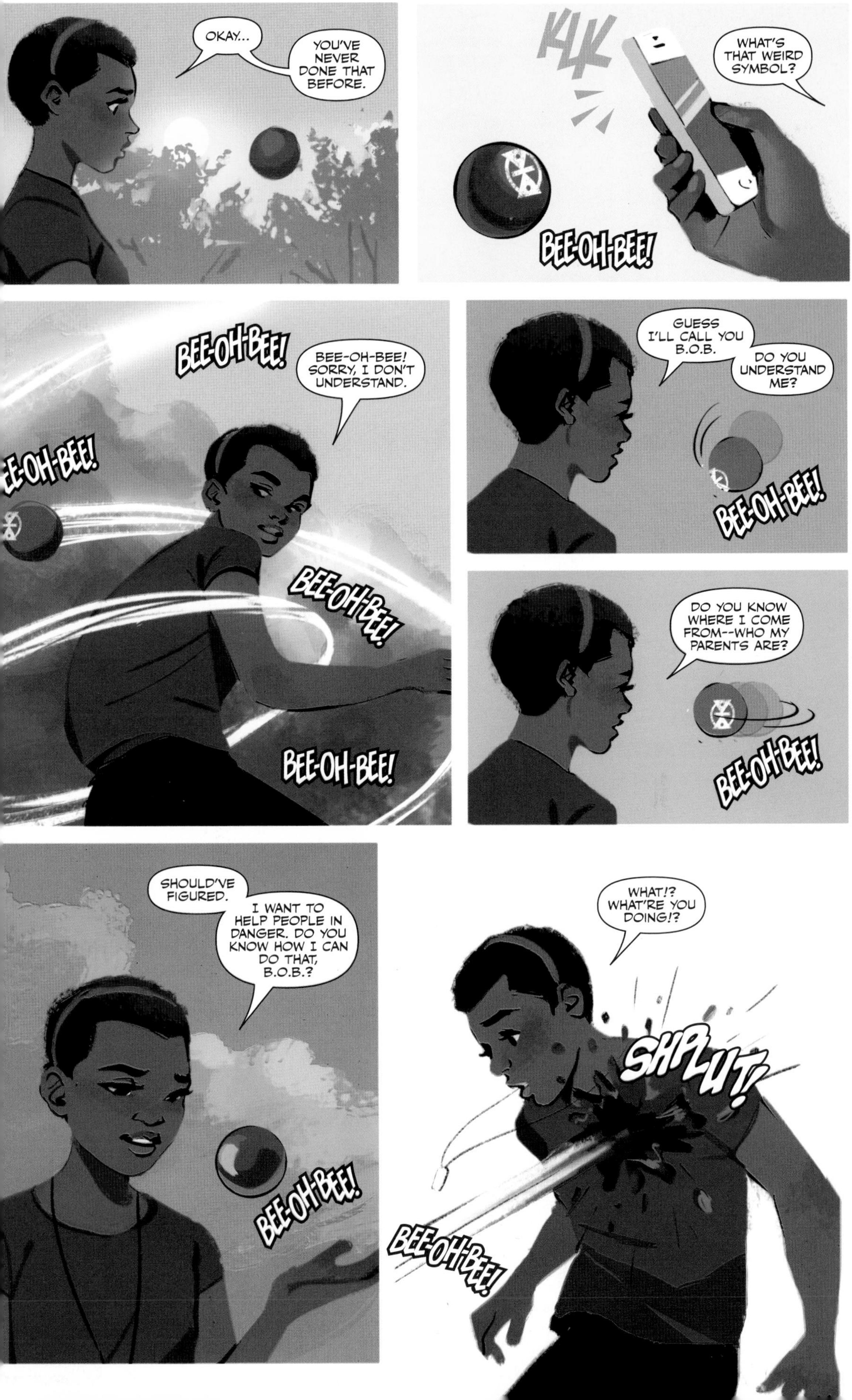
OKAY...
YOU'VE NEVER DONE THAT BEFORE.
KLIK
WHAT'S THAT WEIRD SYMBOL?
BEE-OH-BEE!
BEE-OH-BEE!
BEE-OH-BEE! SORRY, I DON'T UNDERSTAND.
EE-OH-BEE!
BEE-OH-BEE!
BEE-OH-BEE!
GUESS I'LL CALL YOU B.O.B.
DO YOU UNDERSTAND ME?
BEE-OH-BEE!
DO YOU KNOW WHERE I COME FROM--WHO MY PARENTS ARE?
BEE-OH-BEE!
SHOULD'VE FIGURED.
I WANT TO HELP PEOPLE IN DANGER. DO YOU KNOW HOW I CAN DO THAT, B.O.B.?
BEE-OH-BEE!
WHAT!? WHAT'RE YOU DOING!?
SHPLUT!
BEE-OH-BEE!

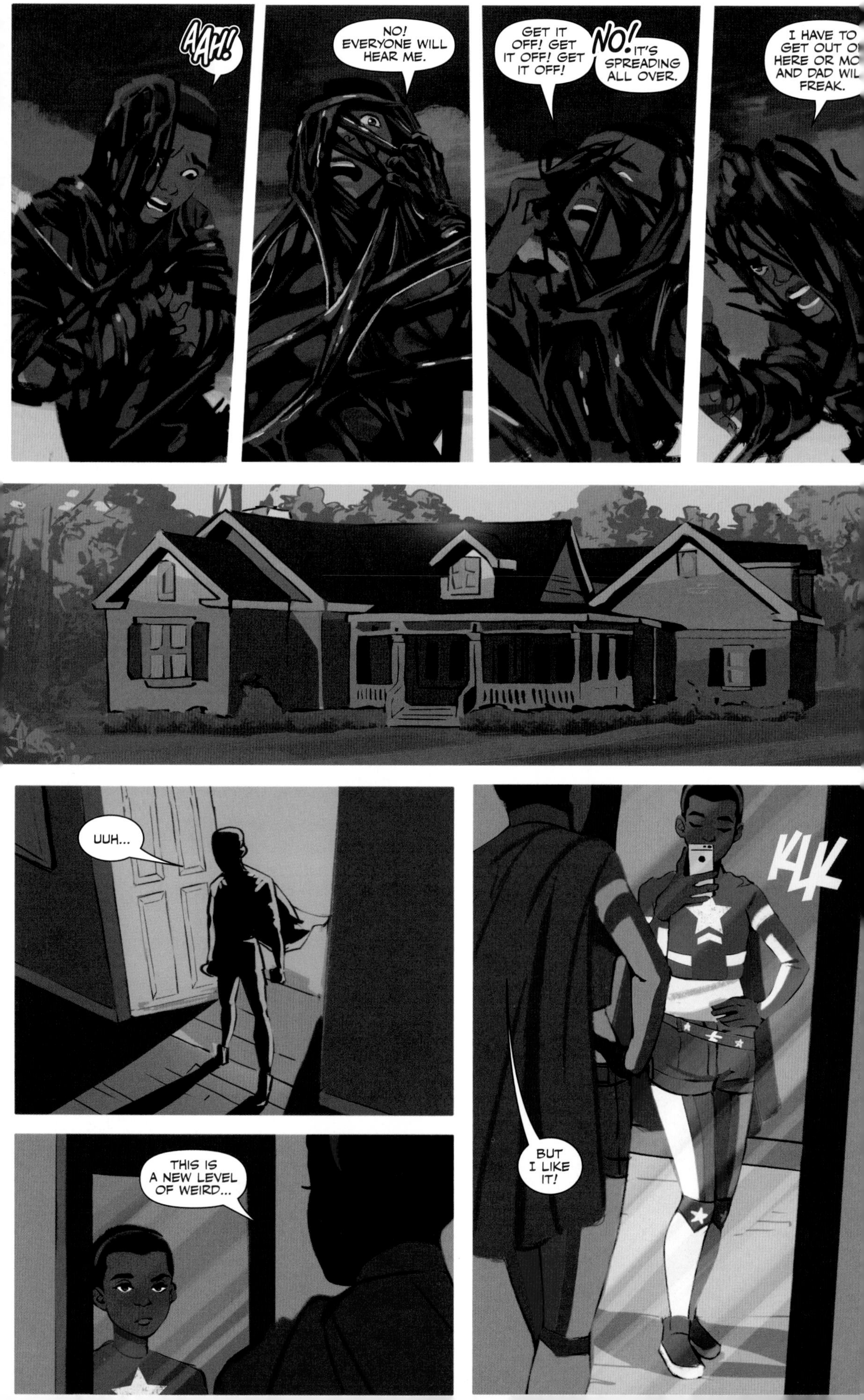
AAH!
NO! EVERYONE WILL HEAR ME.
GET IT OFF! GET IT OFF! GET IT OFF!
NO! IT'S SPREADING ALL OVER.
I HAVE TO GET OUT O HERE OR MO AND DAD WIL FREAK.
UUH...
THIS IS A NEW LEVEL OF WEIRD...
BUT I LIKE IT!
KLIK

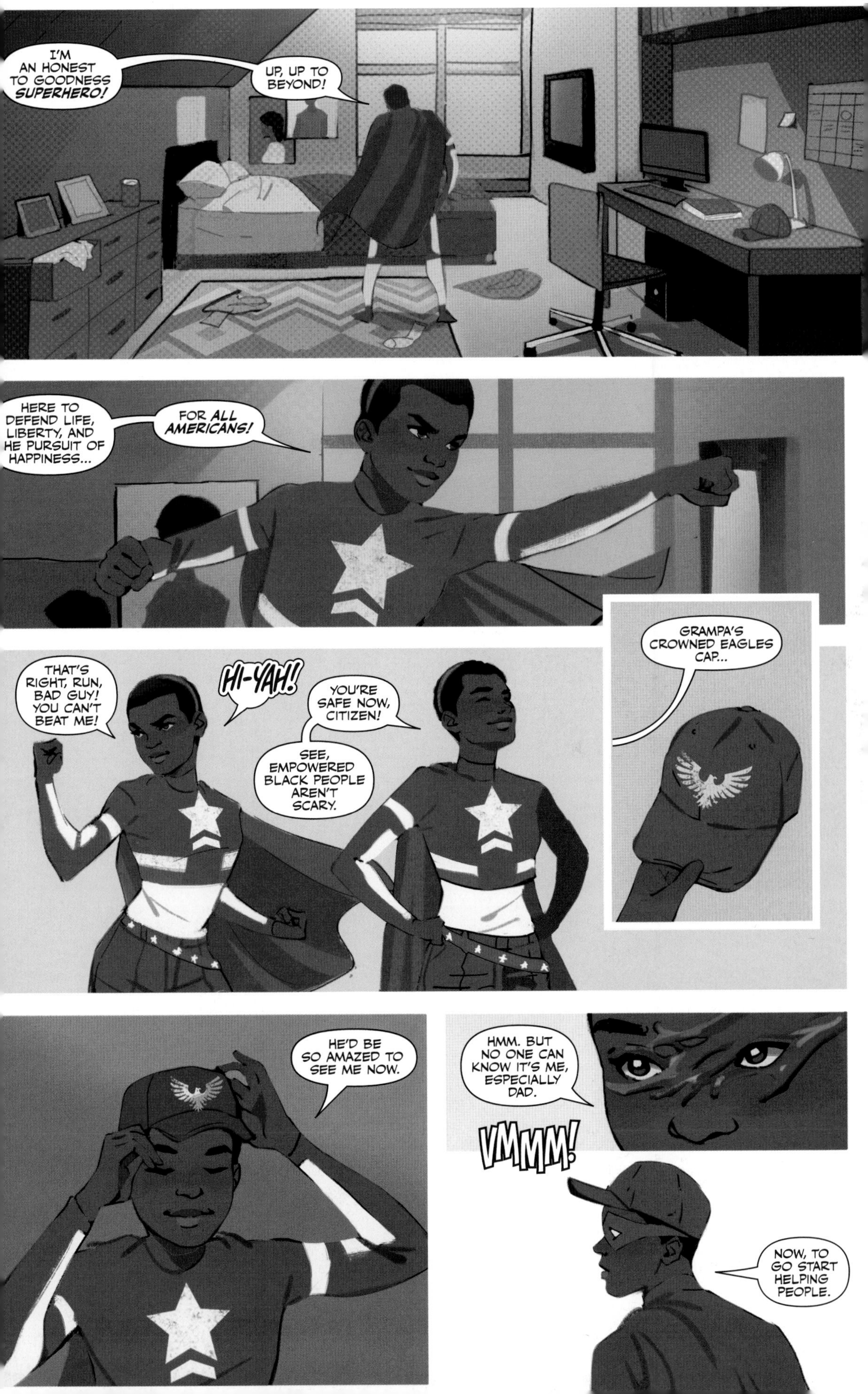
I'M AN HONEST TO GOODNESS SUPERHERO!
UP, UP TO BEYOND!
HERE TO DEFEND LIFE, LIBERTY, AND HE PURSUIT OF HAPPINESS...
FOR ALL AMERICANS!
THAT'S RIGHT, RUN, BAD GUY! YOU CAN'T BEAT ME!
HI-YAH!
YOU'RE SAFE NOW, CITIZEN!
SEE, EMPOWERED BLACK PEOPLE AREN'T SCARY.
GRAMPA'S CROWNED EAGLES CAP...
HE'D BE SO AMAZED TO SEE ME NOW.
HMM. BUT NO ONE CAN KNOW IT'S ME, ESPECIALLY DAD.
VMMM!
NOW, TO GO START HELPING PEOPLE.

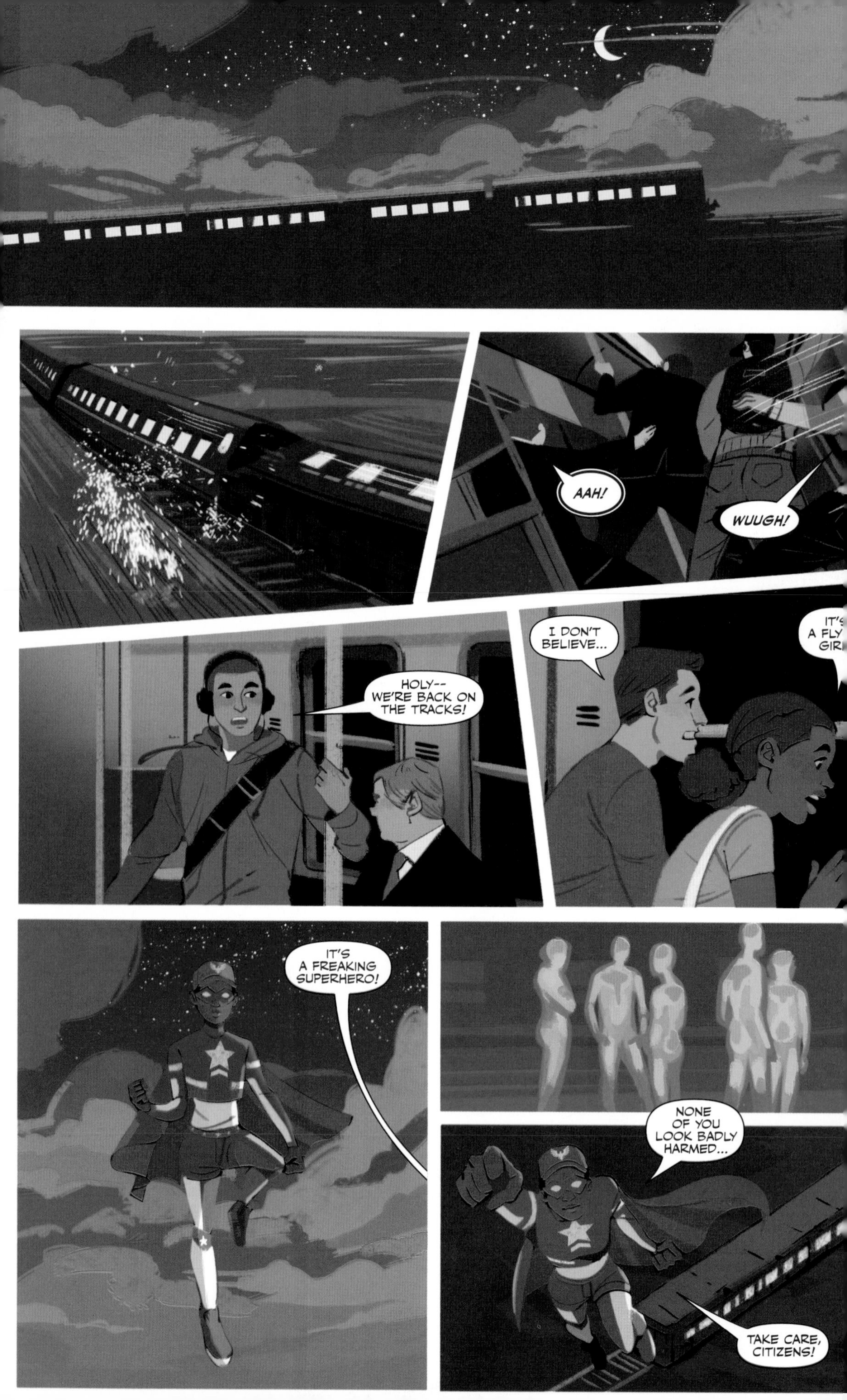
AAH!
WUUGH!
HOLY-- WE'RE BACK ON THE TRACKS!
I DON'T BELIEVE...
IT'S A FREAKING SUPERHERO!
NONE OF YOU LOOK BADLY HARMED...
TAKE CARE, CITIZENS!

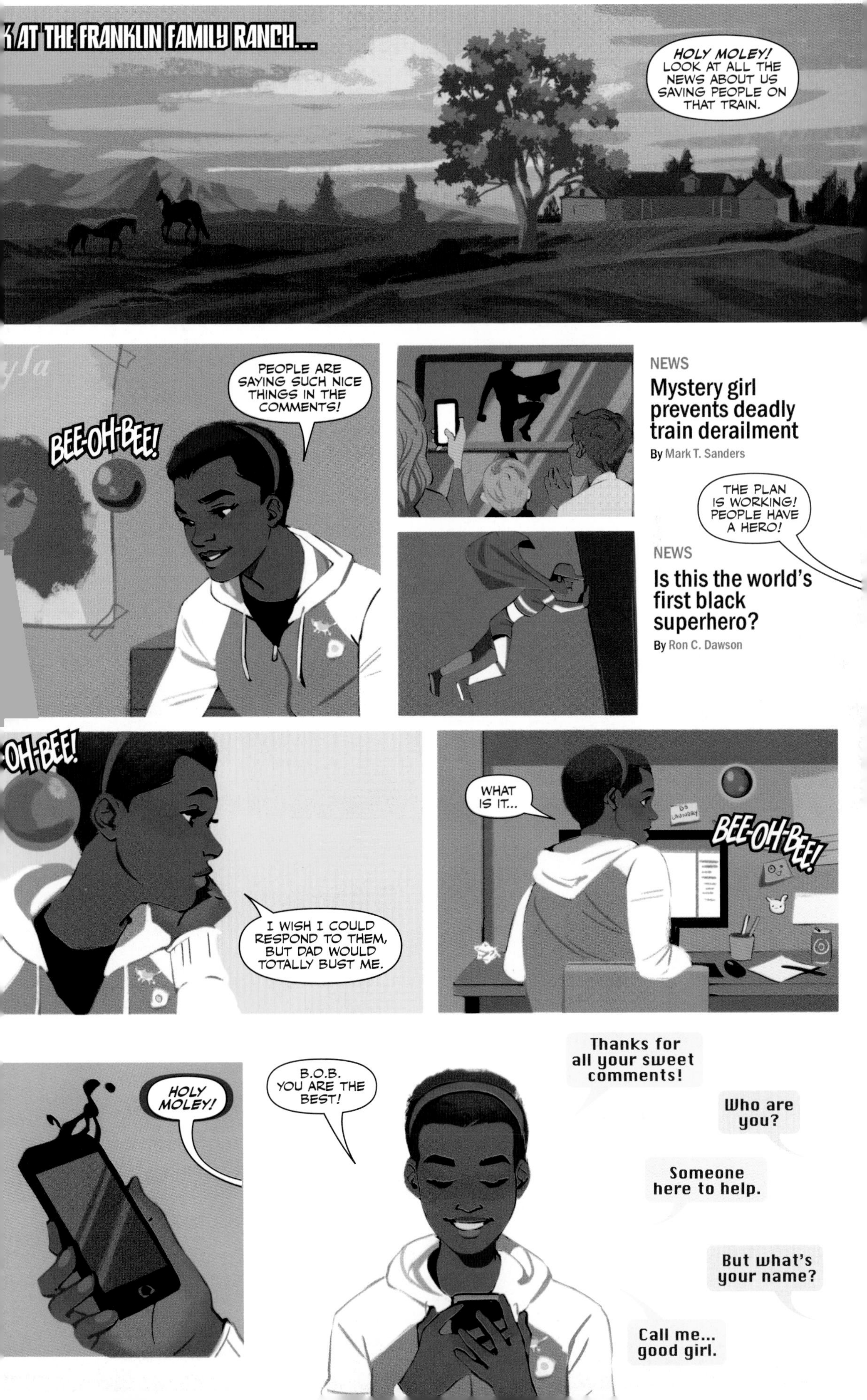
K AT THE FRANKLIN FAMILY RANCH...
HOLY MOLEY! LOOK AT ALL THE NEWS ABOUT US SAVING PEOPLE ON THAT TRAIN.
BEE-OH-BEE!
PEOPLE ARE SAYING SUCH NICE THINGS IN THE COMMENTS!
NEWS
Mystery girl prevents deadly train derailment
By Mark T. Sanders
THE PLAN IS WORKING! PEOPLE HAVE A HERO!
NEWS
Is this the world's first black superhero?
By Ron C. Dawson
OH-BEE!
I WISH I COULD RESPOND TO THEM, BUT DAD WOULD TOTALLY BUST ME.
WHAT IS IT...
BEE-OH-BEE!
DO LAUNDRY
HOLY MOLEY!
B.O.B. YOU ARE THE BEST!
Thanks for all your sweet comments!
Who are you?
Someone here to help.
But what's your name?
Call me... good girl.

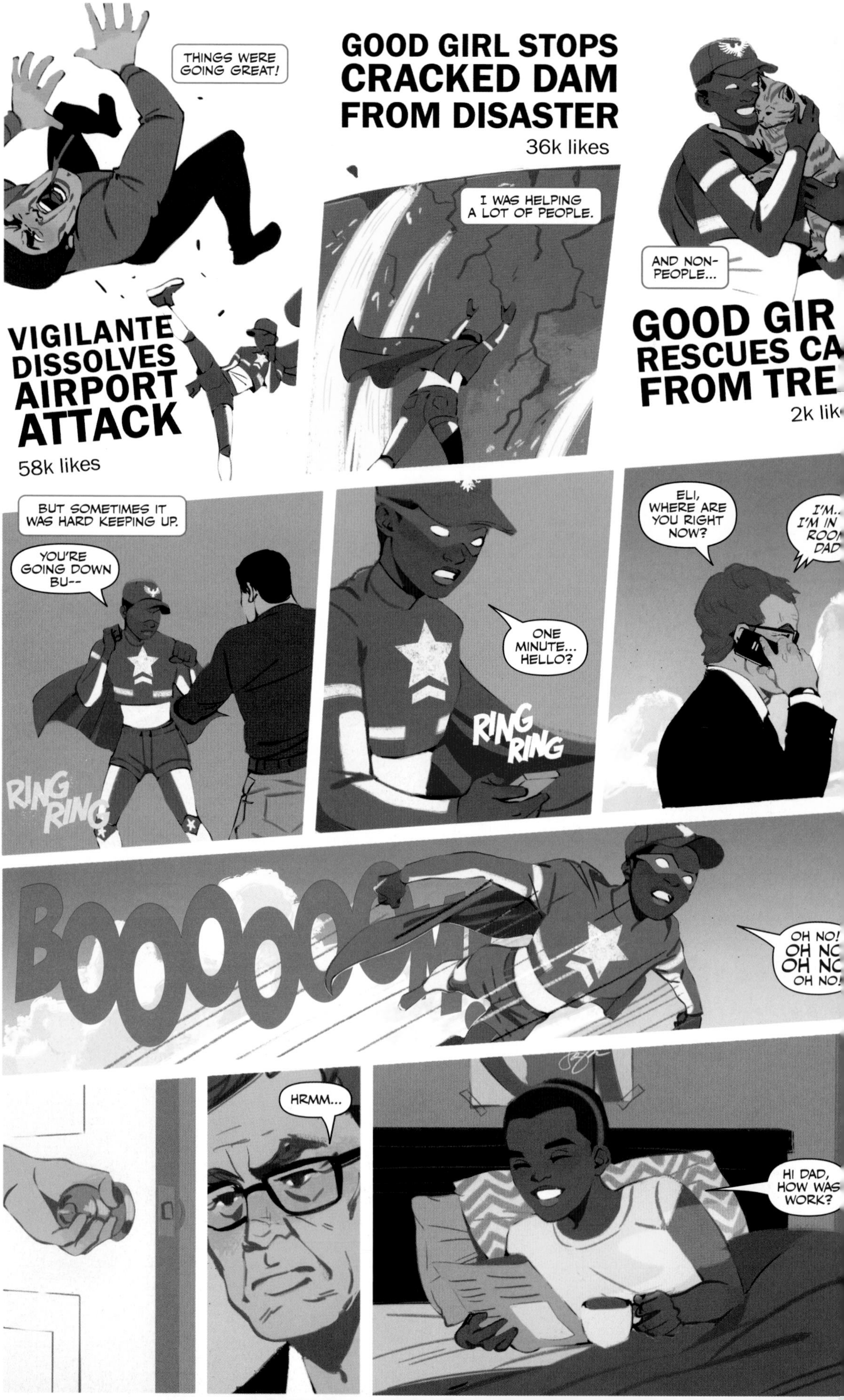
THINGS WERE GOING GREAT!
GOOD GIRL STOPS CRACKED DAM FROM DISASTER
36k likes
I WAS HELPING A LOT OF PEOPLE.
AND NON-PEOPLE...
VIGILANTE DISSOLVES AIRPORT ATTACK
58k likes
GOOD GIR
RESCUES CA
FROM TRE
2k lik
BUT SOMETIMES IT WAS HARD KEEPING UP.
YOU'RE GOING DOWN BU--
RING RING
RING RING
ONE MINUTE... HELLO?
ELI, WHERE ARE YOU RIGHT NOW?
I'M.. I'M IN ROO DAD
BOOOOOOM
OH NO! OH NO OH NO OH NO!
HRMM...
HI DAD, HOW WAS WORK?

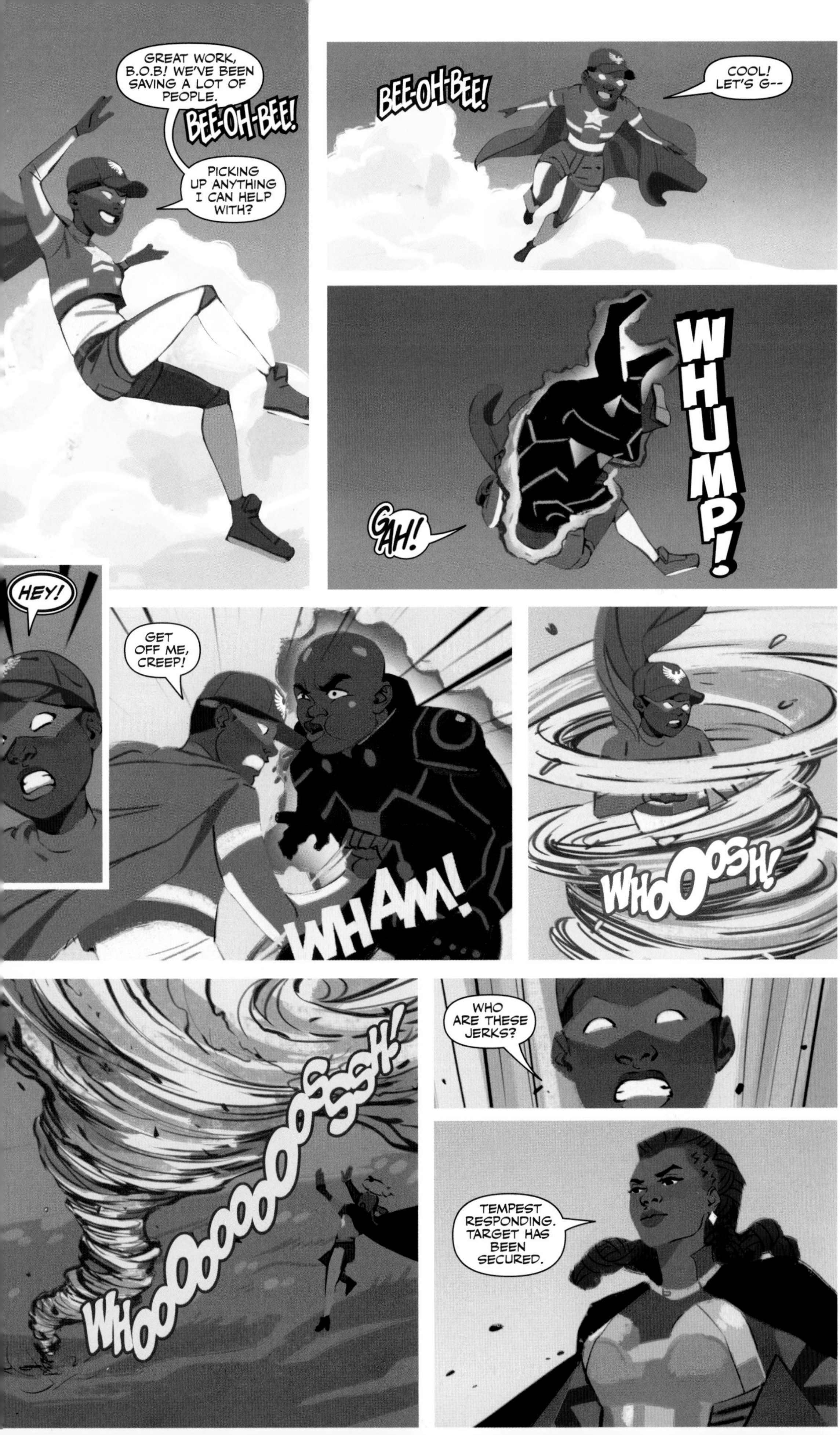
GREAT WORK, B.O.B! WE'VE BEEN SAVING A LOT OF PEOPLE.
BEE-OH-BEE!
PICKING UP ANYTHING I CAN HELP WITH?
BEE-OH-BEE!
COOL! LET'S G--
WHUMP!
GAH!
HEY!
GET OFF ME, CREEP!
WHAM!
WHOOOOSH!
WHOOOOOOOOOOOSSSH!
WHO ARE THESE JERKS?
TEMPEST RESPONDING. TARGET HAS BEEN SECURED.

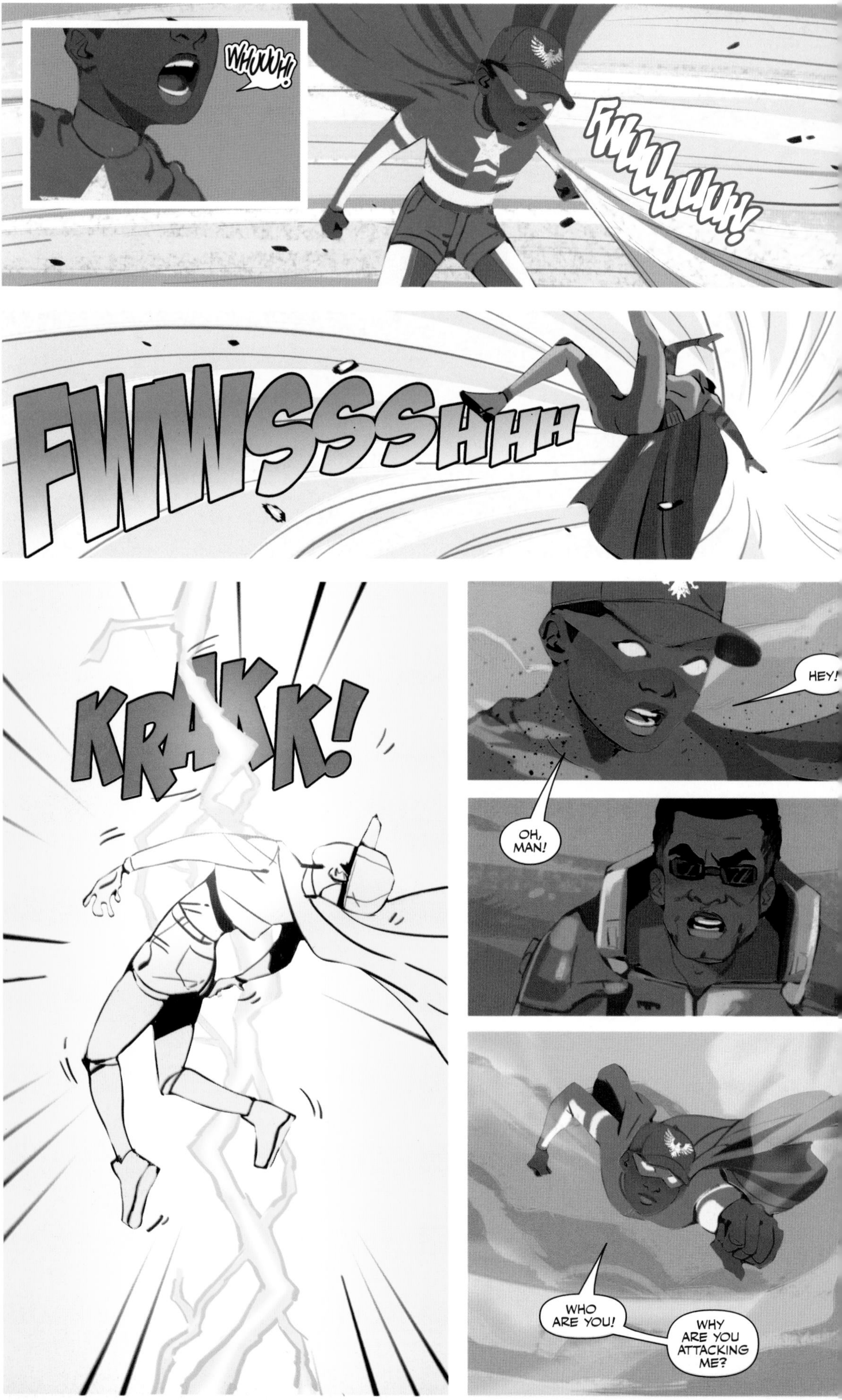
WHUUUH!
FWUUUUUH!
FWWSSSHHH
KRAKK!
HEY!
OH, MAN!
WHO ARE YOU!
WHY ARE YOU ATTACKING ME?

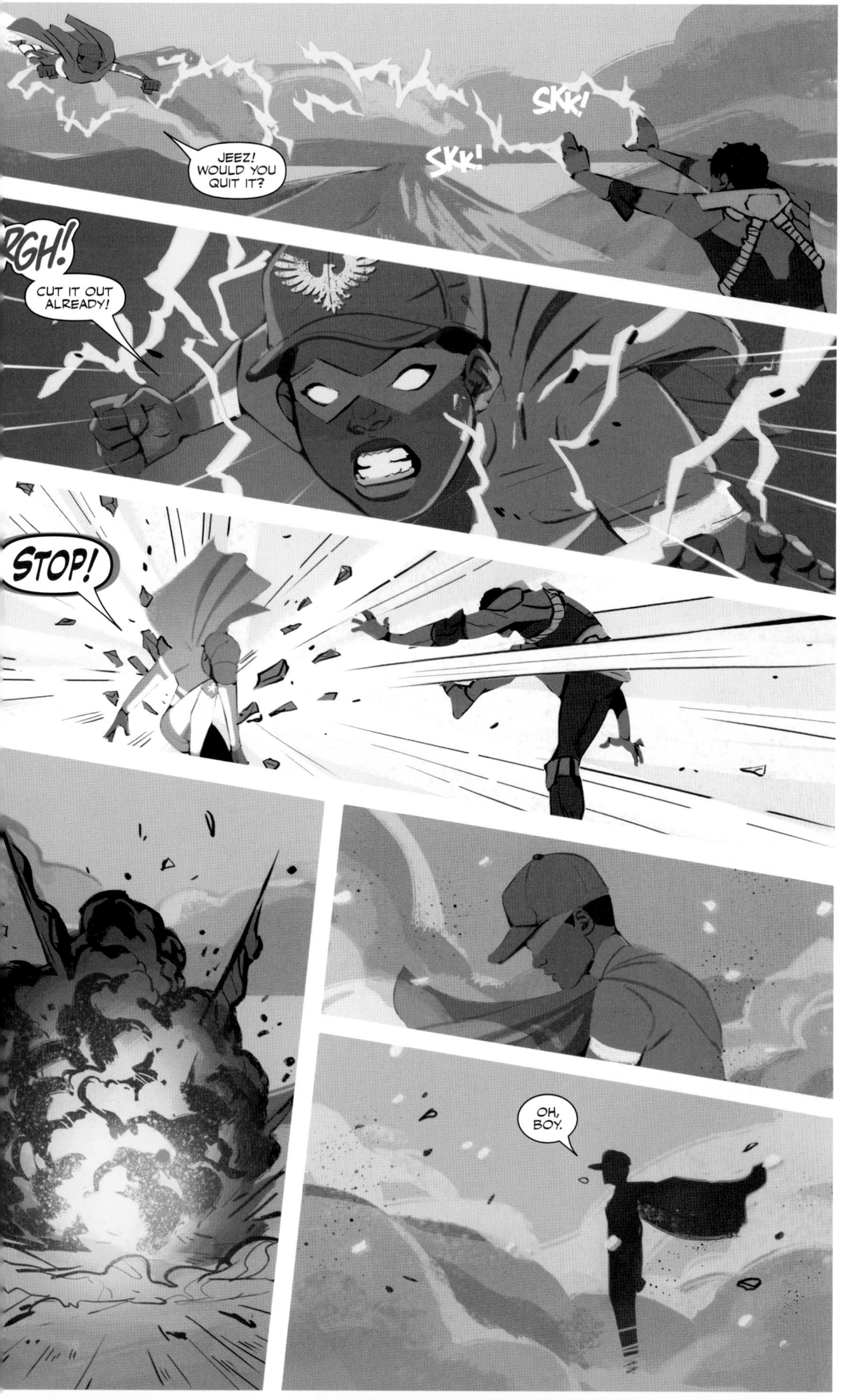
JEEZ! WOULD YOU QUIT IT?
SKK!
SKK!
RGH!
CUT IT OUT ALREADY!
STOP!
OH, BOY.

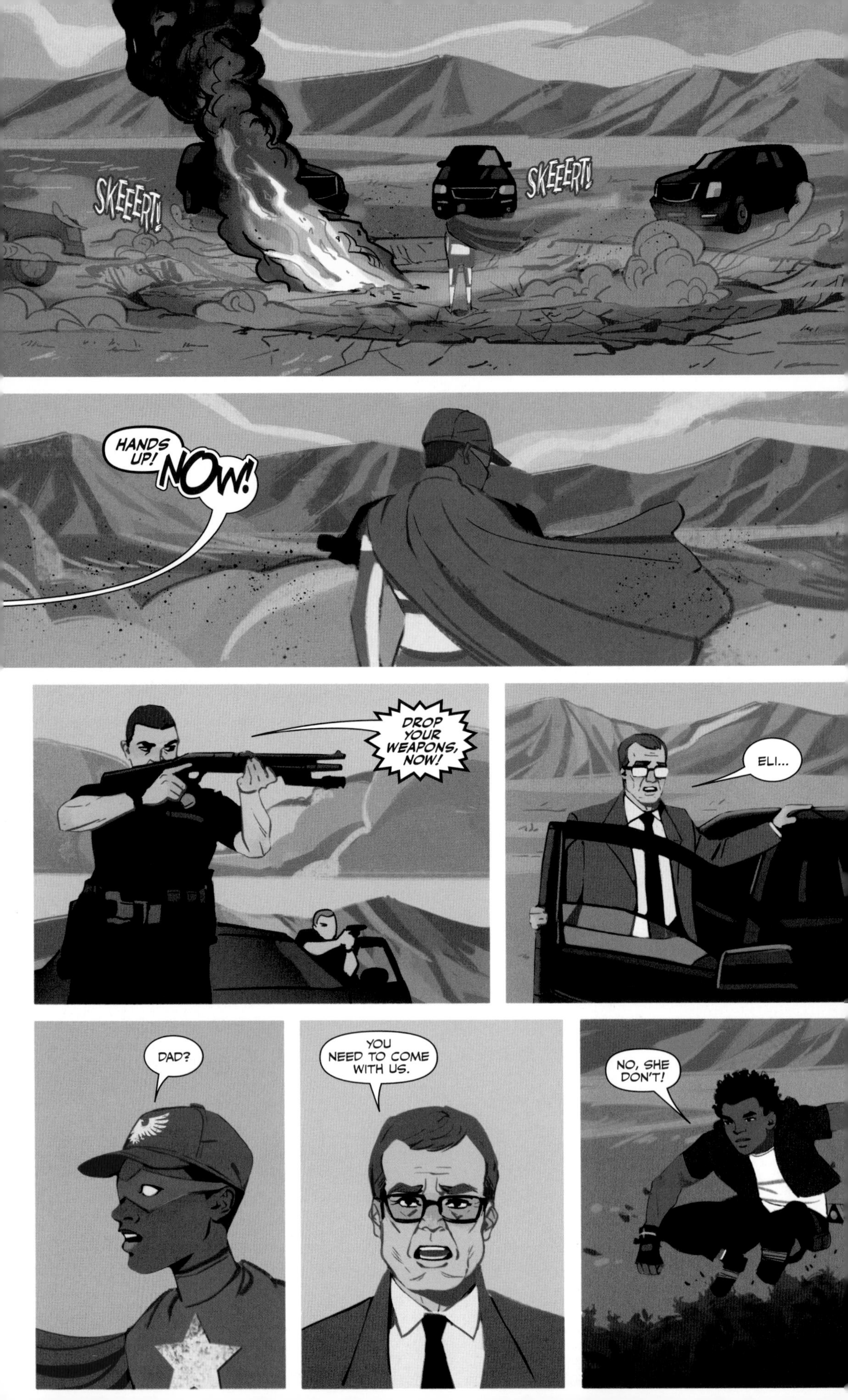
SKEEERT!
SKEEERT!
HANDS UP! NOW!
DROP YOUR WEAPONS, NOW!
ELI...
DAD?
YOU NEED TO COME WITH US.
NO, SHE DON'T!

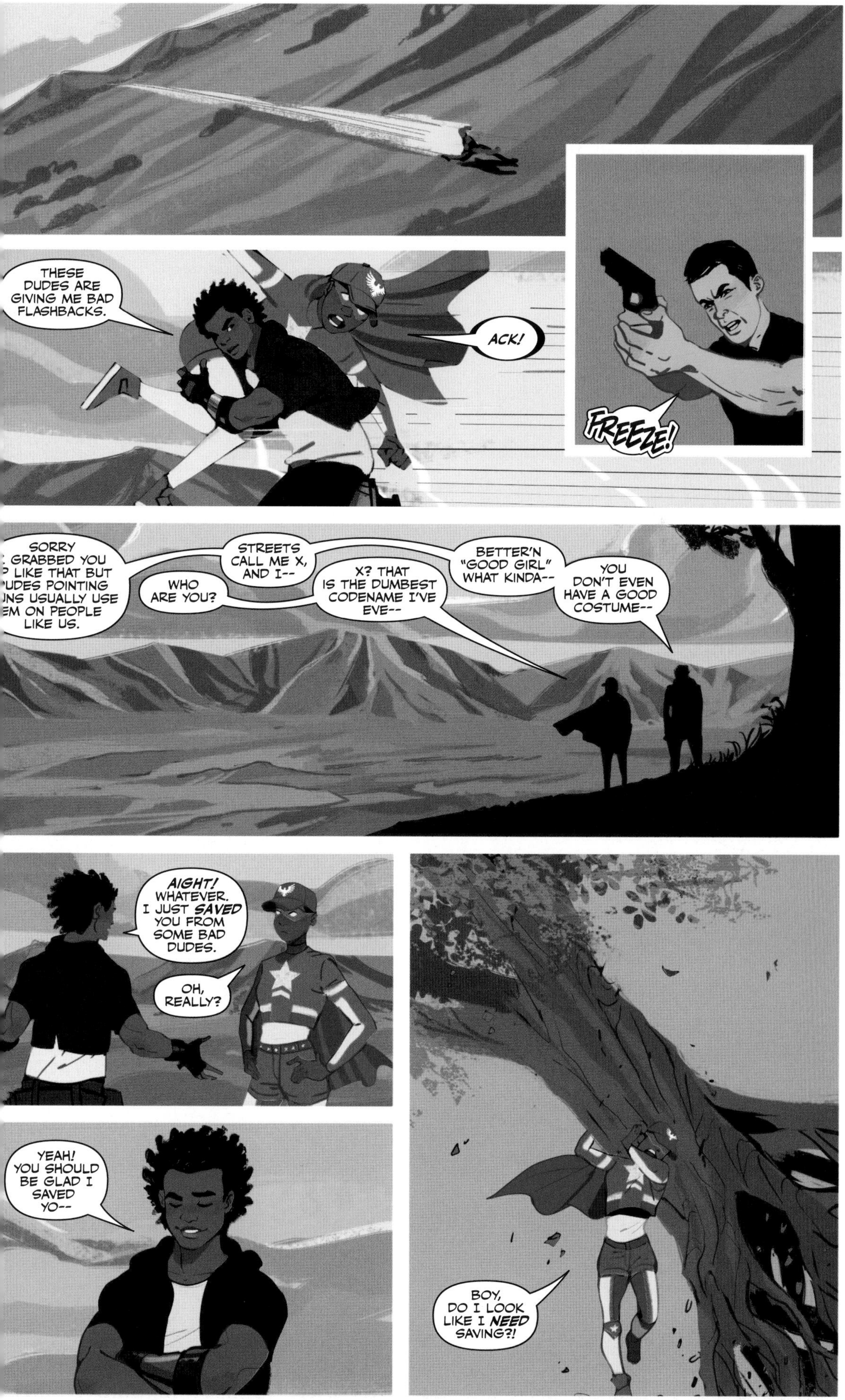
THESE DUDES ARE GIVING ME BAD FLASHBACKS.
ACK!
FREEZE!
SORRY GRABBED YOU P LIKE THAT BUT UDES POINTING UNS USUALLY USE EM ON PEOPLE LIKE US.
WHO ARE YOU?
STREETS CALL ME X, AND I--
X? THAT IS THE DUMBEST CODENAME I'VE EVE--
BETTER'N "GOOD GIRL" WHAT KINDA--
YOU DON'T EVEN HAVE A GOOD COSTUME--
AIGHT! WHATEVER. I JUST SAVED YOU FROM SOME BAD DUDES.
OH, REALLY?
YEAH! YOU SHOULD BE GLAD I SAVED YO--
BOY, DO I LOOK LIKE I NEED SAVING?!

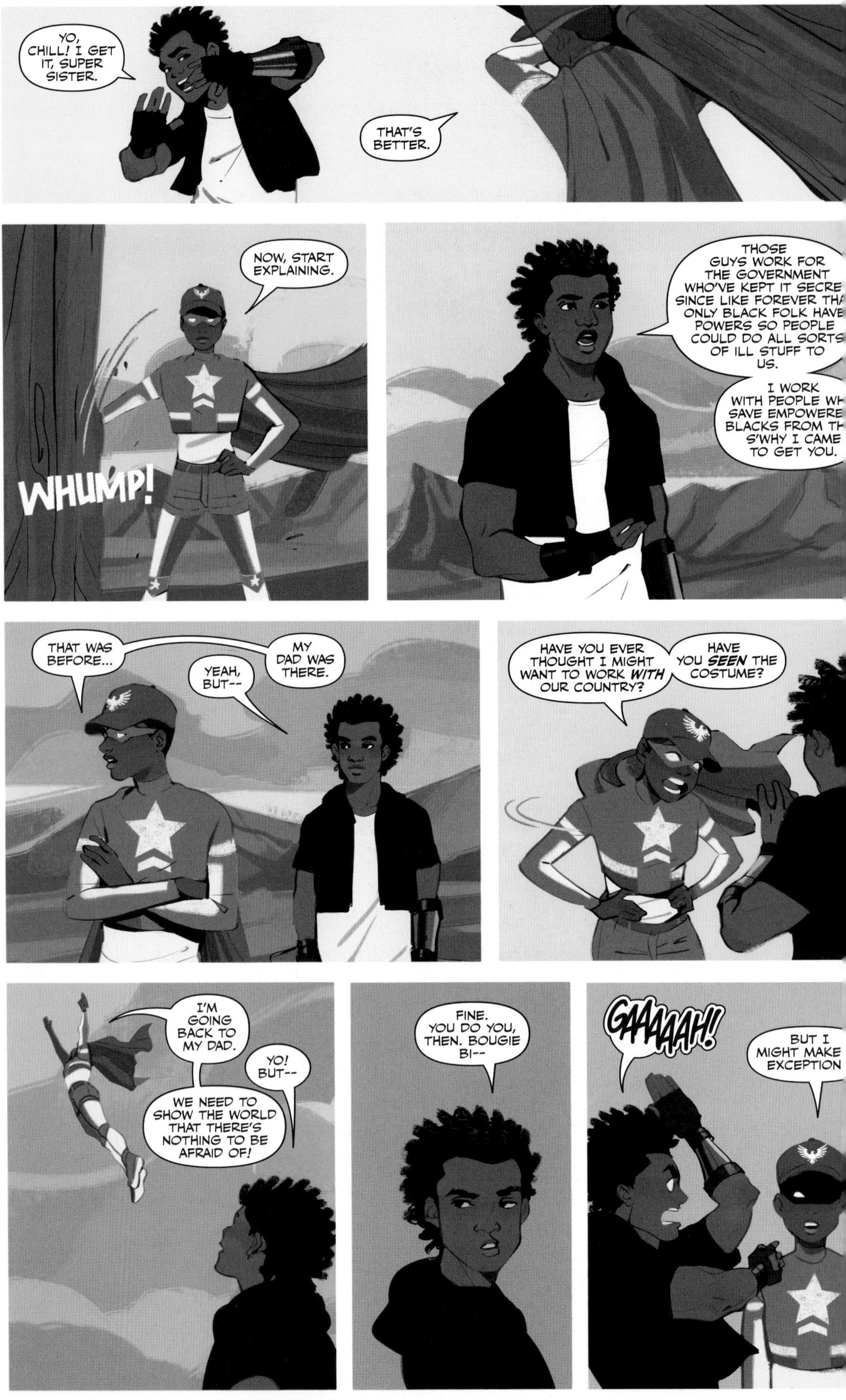
YO, CHILL! I GET IT, SUPER SISTER.
THAT'S BETTER.
NOW, START EXPLAINING.
WHUMP!
THOSE GUYS WORK FOR THE GOVERNMENT WHO'VE KEPT IT SECRE SINCE LIKE FOREVER TH ONLY BLACK FOLK HAVE POWERS SO PEOPLE COULD DO ALL SORTS OF ILL STUFF TO US.
I WORK WITH PEOPLE WH SAVE EMPOWERE BLACKS FROM TH S'WHY I CAME TO GET YOU.
THAT WAS BEFORE...
MY DAD WAS THERE.
YEAH, BUT--
HAVE YOU EVER THOUGHT I MIGHT WANT TO WORK *WITH* OUR COUNTRY?
HAVE YOU *SEEN* THE COSTUME?
I'M GOING BACK TO MY DAD.
YO! BUT--
WE NEED TO SHOW THE WORLD THAT THERE'S NOTHING TO BE AFRAID OF!
FINE. YOU DO YOU, THEN. BOUGIE BI--
GAAAAAH!
BUT I MIGHT MAKE EXCEPTION

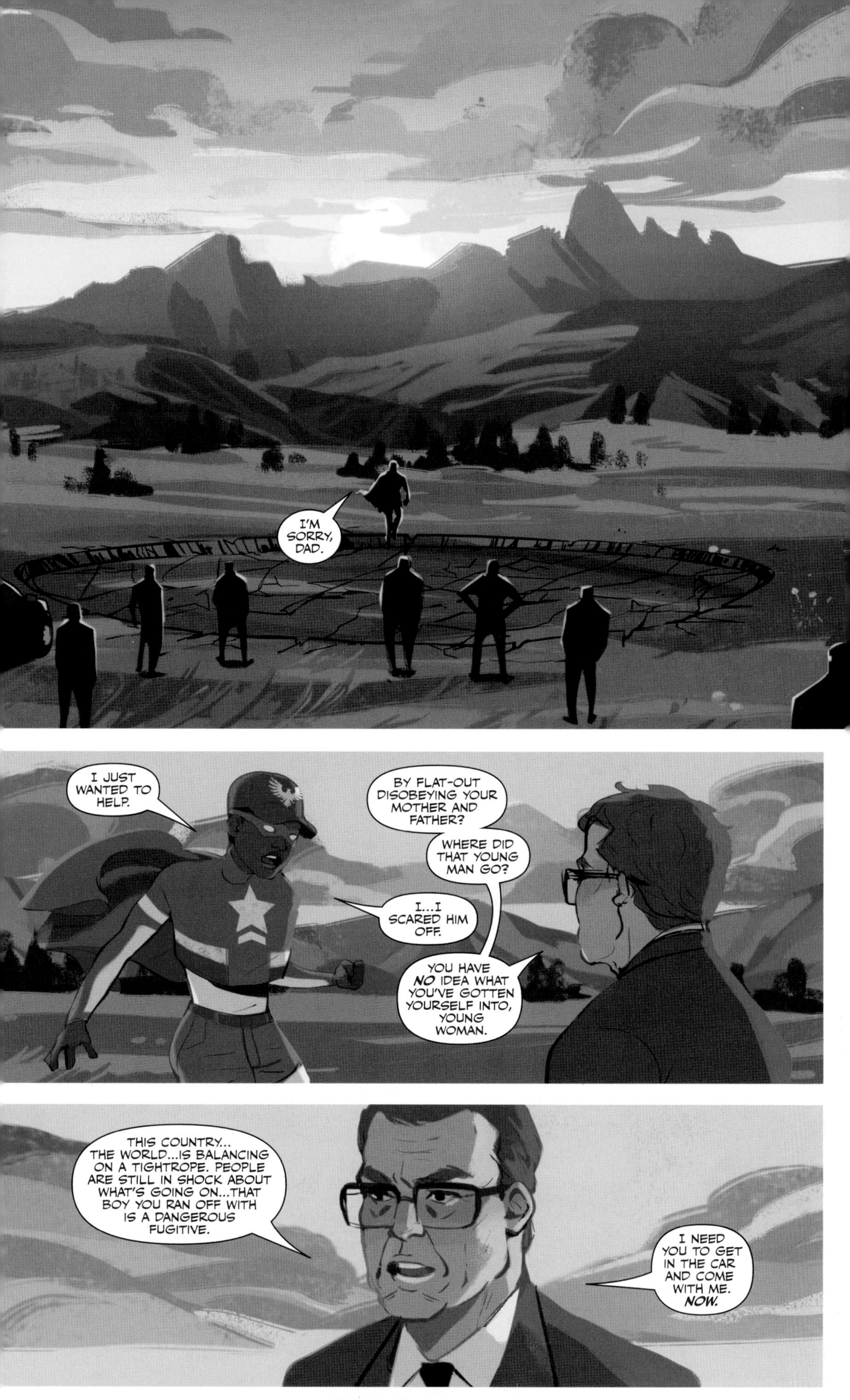
I'M SORRY, DAD.
I JUST WANTED TO HELP.
BY FLAT-OUT DISOBEYING YOUR MOTHER AND FATHER?
WHERE DID THAT YOUNG MAN GO?
I...I SCARED HIM OFF.
YOU HAVE ***NO*** IDEA WHAT YOU'VE GOTTEN YOURSELF INTO, YOUNG WOMAN.
THIS COUNTRY... THE WORLD...IS BALANCING ON A TIGHTROPE. PEOPLE ARE STILL IN SHOCK ABOUT WHAT'S GOING ON...THAT BOY YOU RAN OFF WITH IS A DANGEROUS FUGITIVE.
I NEED YOU TO GET IN THE CAR AND COME WITH ME. ***NOW.***

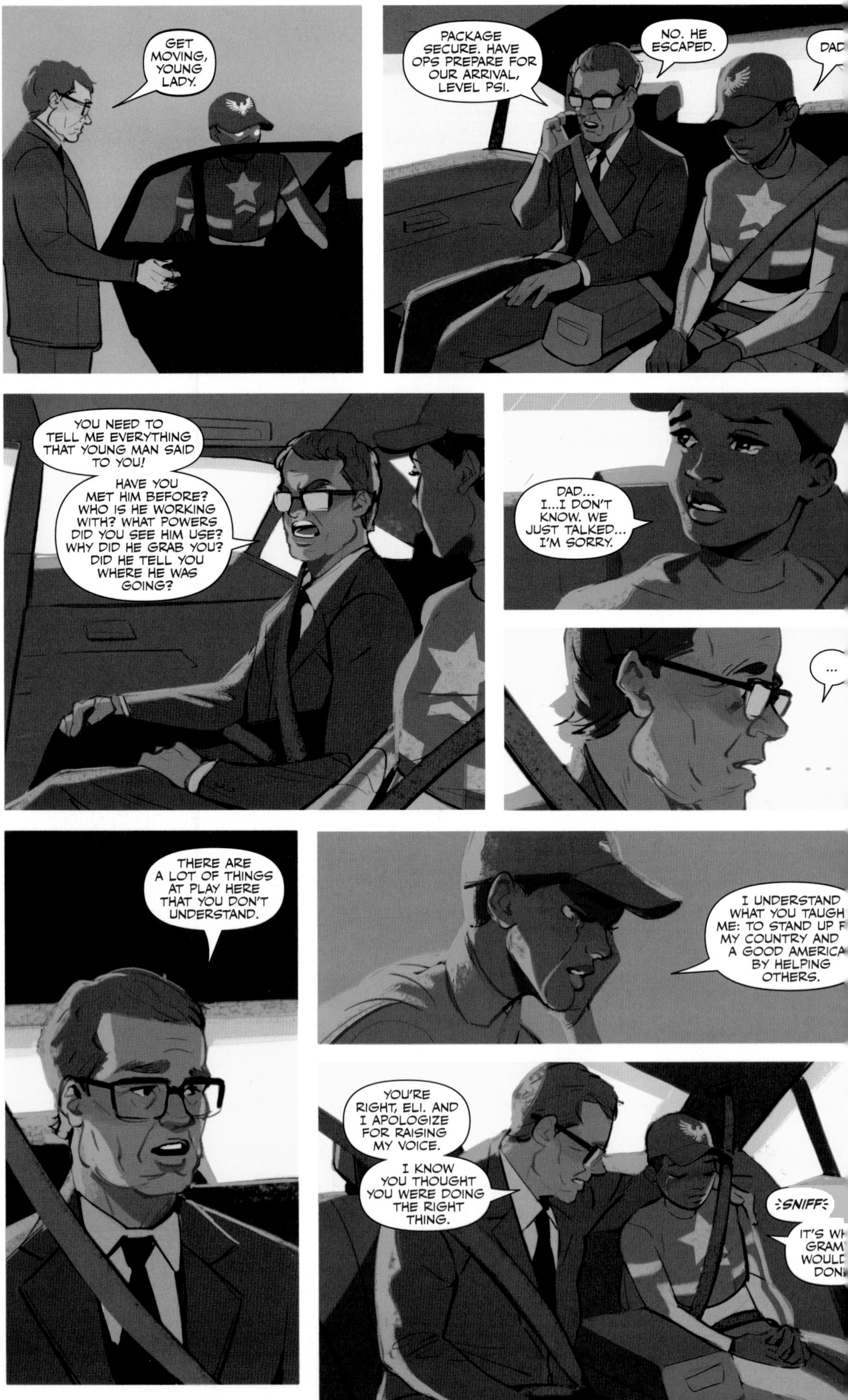
GET MOVING, YOUNG LADY.
PACKAGE SECURE. HAVE OPS PREPARE FOR OUR ARRIVAL, LEVEL PSI.
NO. HE ESCAPED.
DAD
YOU NEED TO TELL ME EVERYTHING THAT YOUNG MAN SAID TO YOU!
HAVE YOU MET HIM BEFORE? WHO IS HE WORKING WITH? WHAT POWERS DID YOU SEE HIM USE? WHY DID HE GRAB YOU? DID HE TELL YOU WHERE HE WAS GOING?
DAD... I...I DON'T KNOW. WE JUST TALKED... I'M SORRY.
...
THERE ARE A LOT OF THINGS AT PLAY HERE THAT YOU DON'T UNDERSTAND.
I UNDERSTAND WHAT YOU TAUGH ME: TO STAND UP F MY COUNTRY AND A GOOD AMERICA BY HELPING OTHERS.
YOU'RE RIGHT, ELI. AND I APOLOGIZE FOR RAISING MY VOICE.
I KNOW YOU THOUGHT YOU WERE DOING THE RIGHT THING.
SNIFF
IT'S WH GRAM WOULD DON

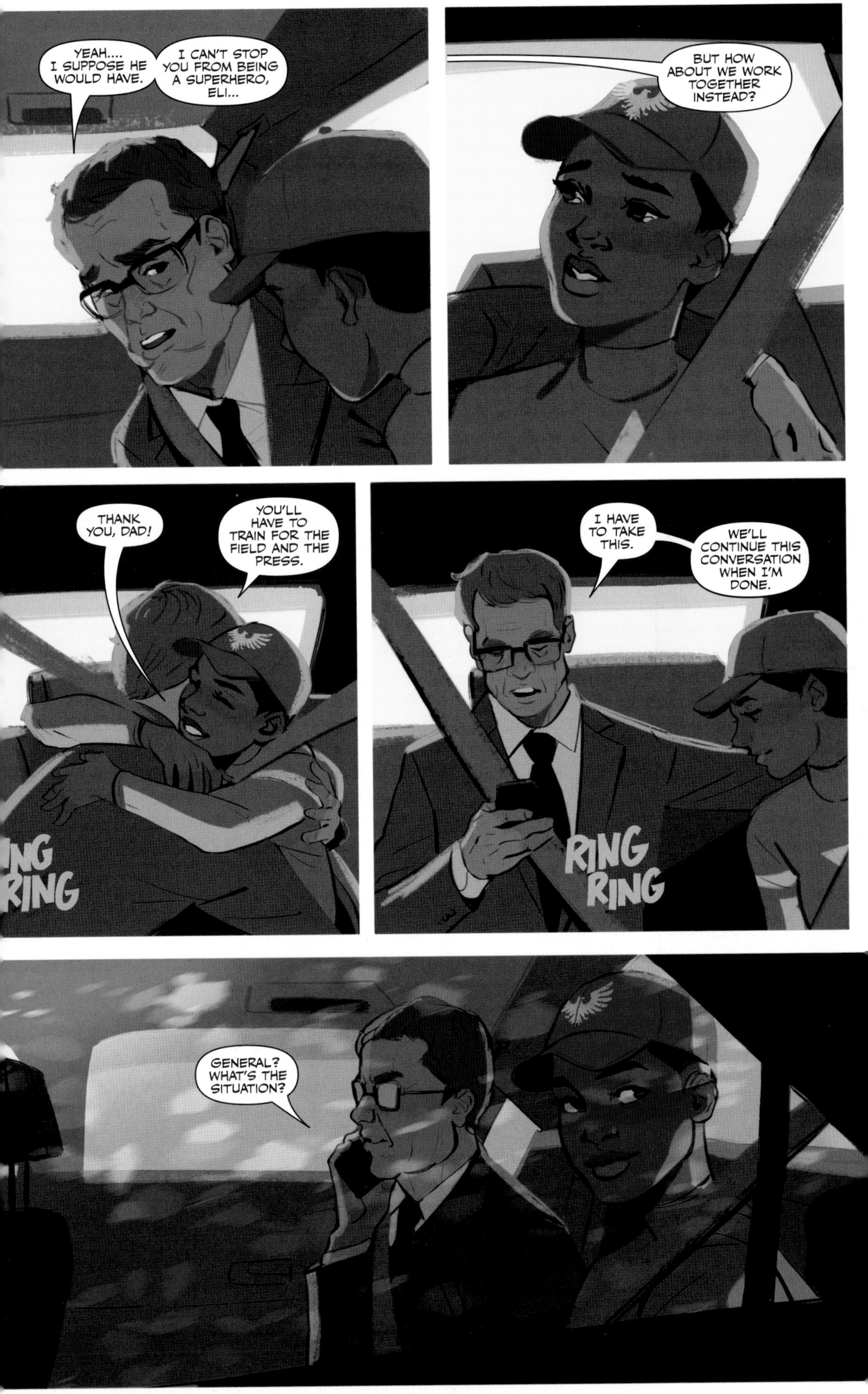
YEAH.... I SUPPOSE HE WOULD HAVE.
I CAN'T STOP YOU FROM BEING A SUPERHERO, ELI...
BUT HOW ABOUT WE WORK TOGETHER INSTEAD?
THANK YOU, DAD!
YOU'LL HAVE TO TRAIN FOR THE FIELD AND THE PRESS.
RING
I HAVE TO TAKE THIS.
WE'LL CONTINUE THIS CONVERSATION WHEN I'M DONE.
RING RING
GENERAL? WHAT'S THE SITUATION?

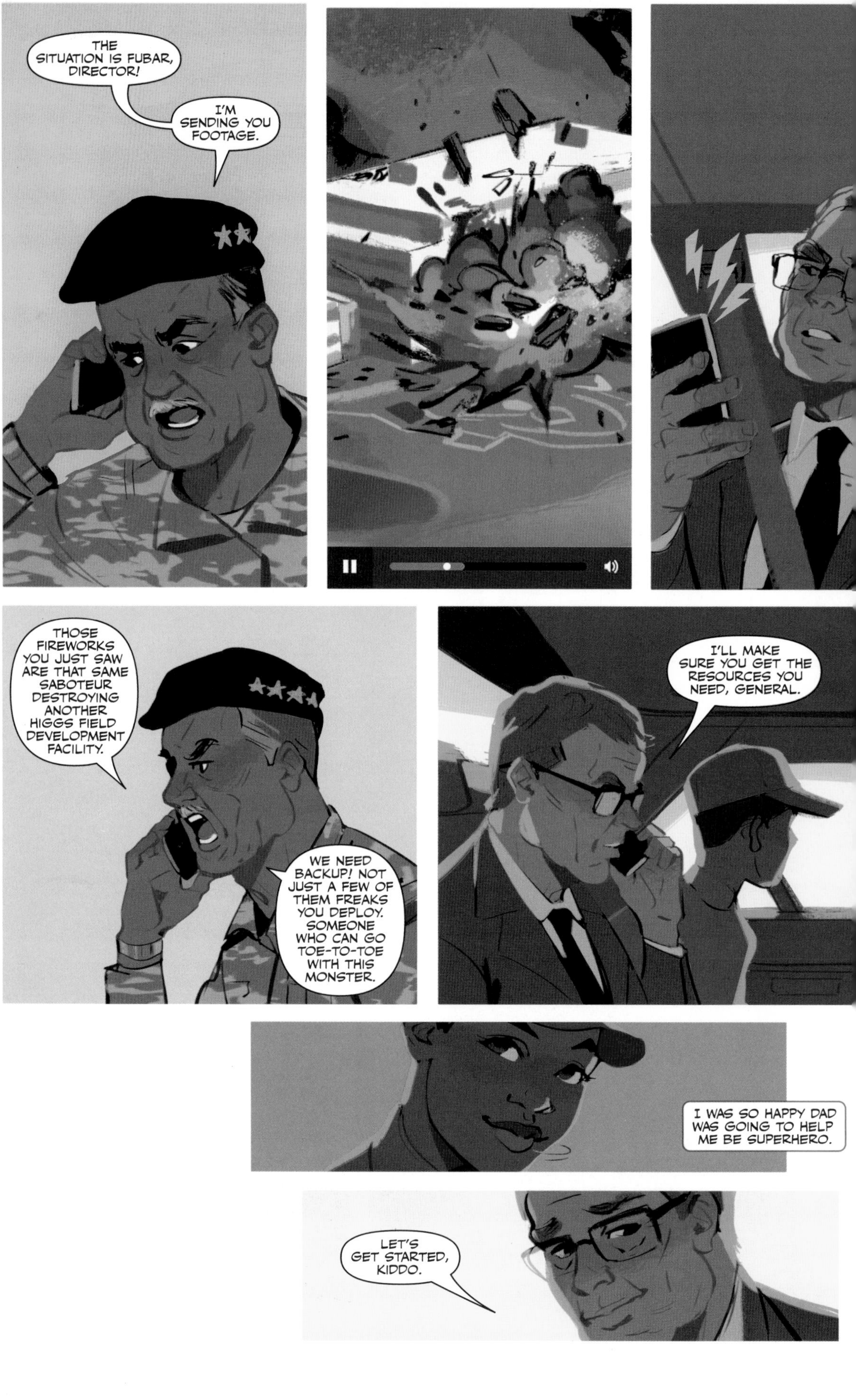
THE SITUATION IS FUBAR, DIRECTOR!
I'M SENDING YOU FOOTAGE.
THOSE FIREWORKS YOU JUST SAW ARE THAT SAME SABOTEUR DESTROYING ANOTHER HIGGS FIELD DEVELOPMENT FACILITY.
WE NEED BACKUP! NOT JUST A FEW OF THEM FREAKS YOU DEPLOY. SOMEONE WHO CAN GO TOE-TO-TOE WITH THIS MONSTER.
I'LL MAKE SURE YOU GET THE RESOURCES YOU NEED, GENERAL.
I WAS SO HAPPY DAD WAS GOING TO HELP ME BE SUPERHERO.
LET'S GET STARTED, KIDDO.

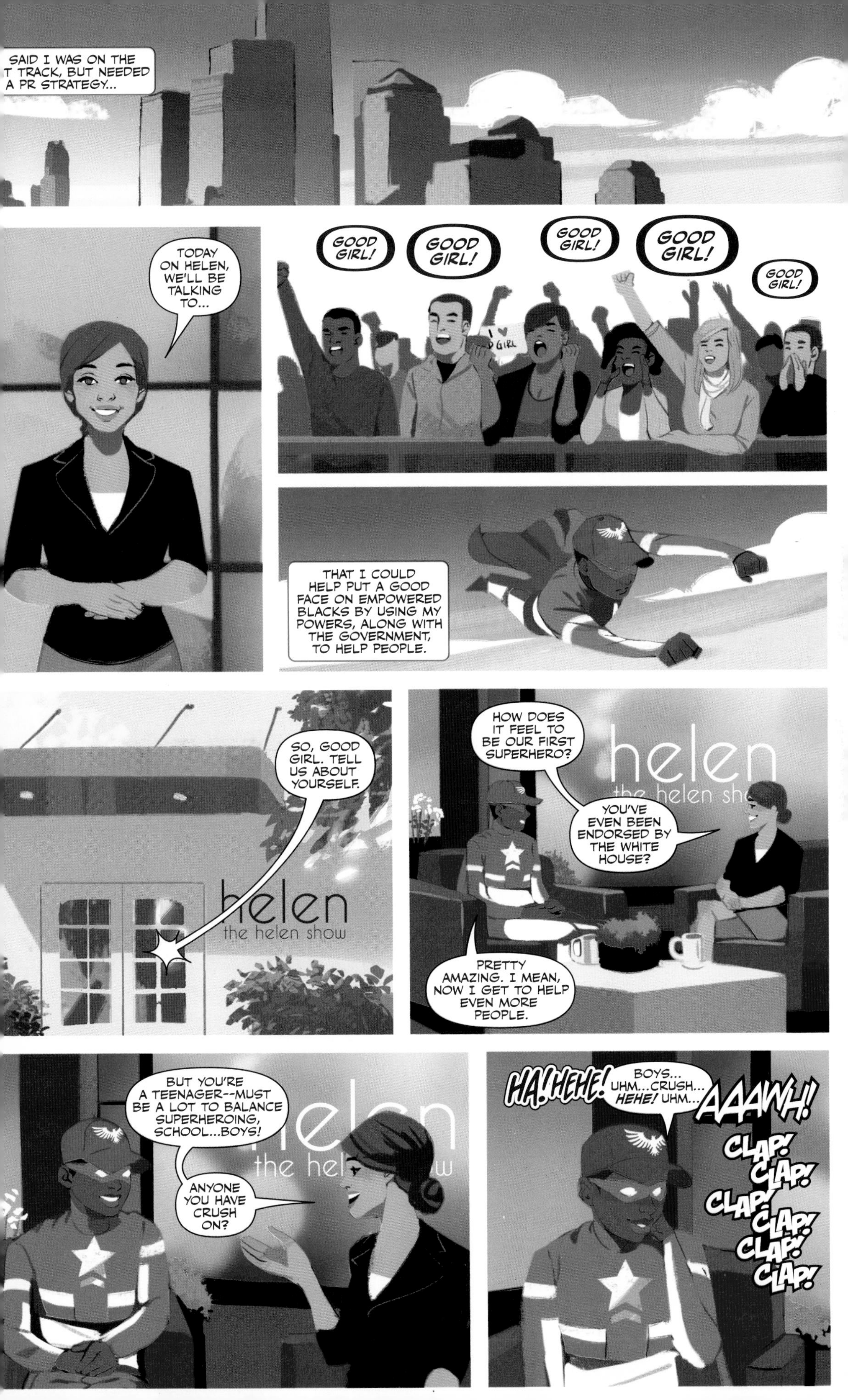
SAID I WAS ON THE
T TRACK, BUT NEEDED
A PR STRATEGY...
TODAY ON HELEN, WE'LL BE TALKING TO...
GOOD GIRL!
GOOD GIRL!
GOOD GIRL!
GOOD GIRL!
GOOD GIRL!
THAT I COULD HELP PUT A GOOD FACE ON EMPOWERED BLACKS BY USING MY POWERS, ALONG WITH THE GOVERNMENT, TO HELP PEOPLE.
helen
the helen show
SO, GOOD GIRL. TELL US ABOUT YOURSELF.
HOW DOES IT FEEL TO BE OUR FIRST SUPERHERO?
helen
the helen show
YOU'VE EVEN BEEN ENDORSED BY THE WHITE HOUSE?
PRETTY AMAZING. I MEAN, NOW I GET TO HELP EVEN MORE PEOPLE.
BUT YOU'RE A TEENAGER--MUST BE A LOT TO BALANCE SUPERHEROING, SCHOOL...BOYS!
ANYONE YOU HAVE CRUSH ON?
HA! HEHE!
BOYS... UHM...CRUSH... HEHE! UHM...
AAAWH!
CLAP! CLAP! CLAP! CLAP! CLAP! CLAP!

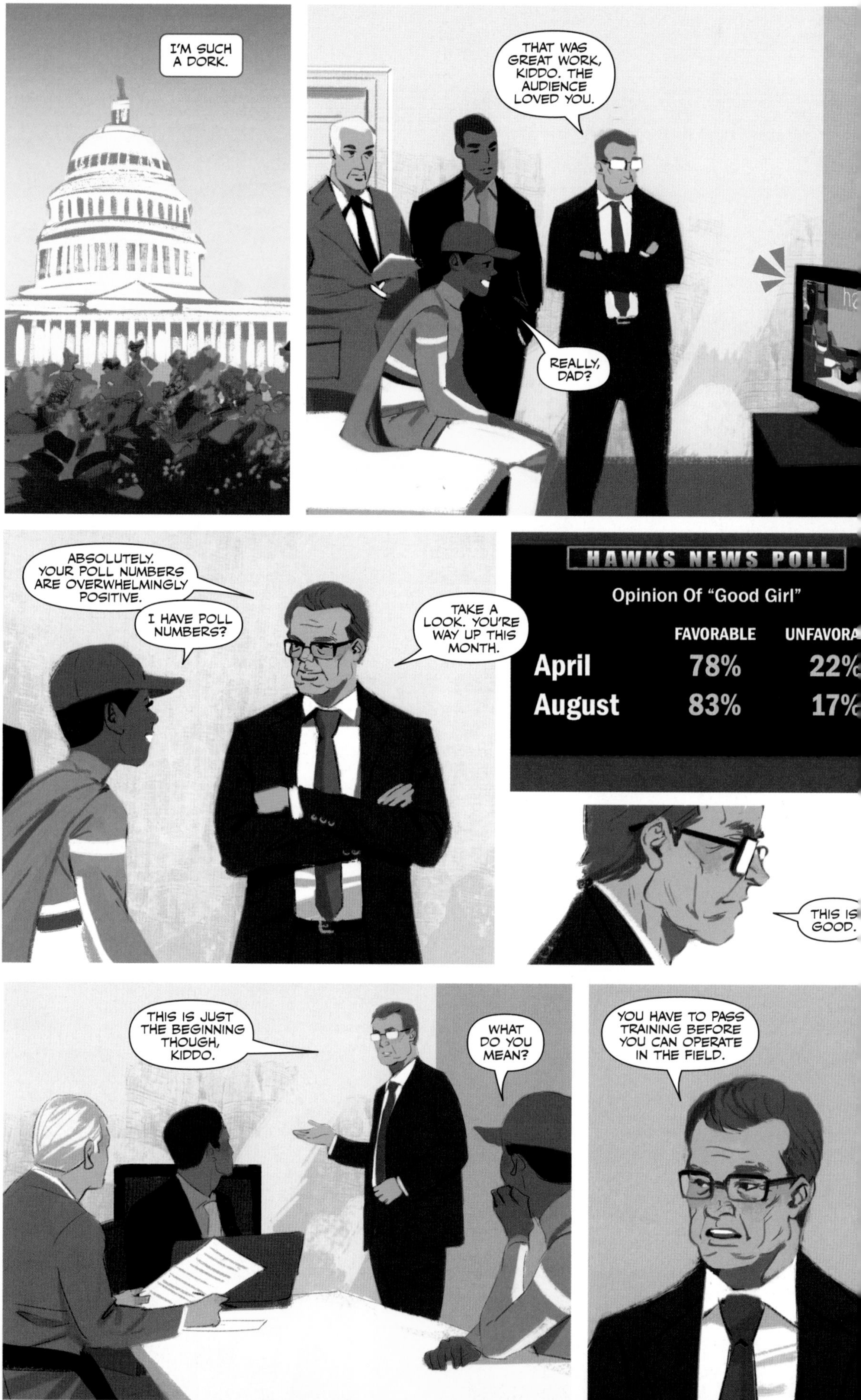
I'M SUCH A DORK.
THAT WAS GREAT WORK, KIDDO. THE AUDIENCE LOVED YOU.
REALLY, DAD?
ABSOLUTELY. YOUR POLL NUMBERS ARE OVERWHELMINGLY POSITIVE.
I HAVE POLL NUMBERS?
TAKE A LOOK. YOU'RE WAY UP THIS MONTH.
HAWKS NEWS POLL
Opinion Of "Good Girl"
FAVORABLE UNFAVORA
April 78% 22%
August 83% 17%
THIS IS GOOD.
THIS IS JUST THE BEGINNING THOUGH, KIDDO.
WHAT DO YOU MEAN?
YOU HAVE TO PASS TRAINING BEFORE YOU CAN OPERATE IN THE FIELD.

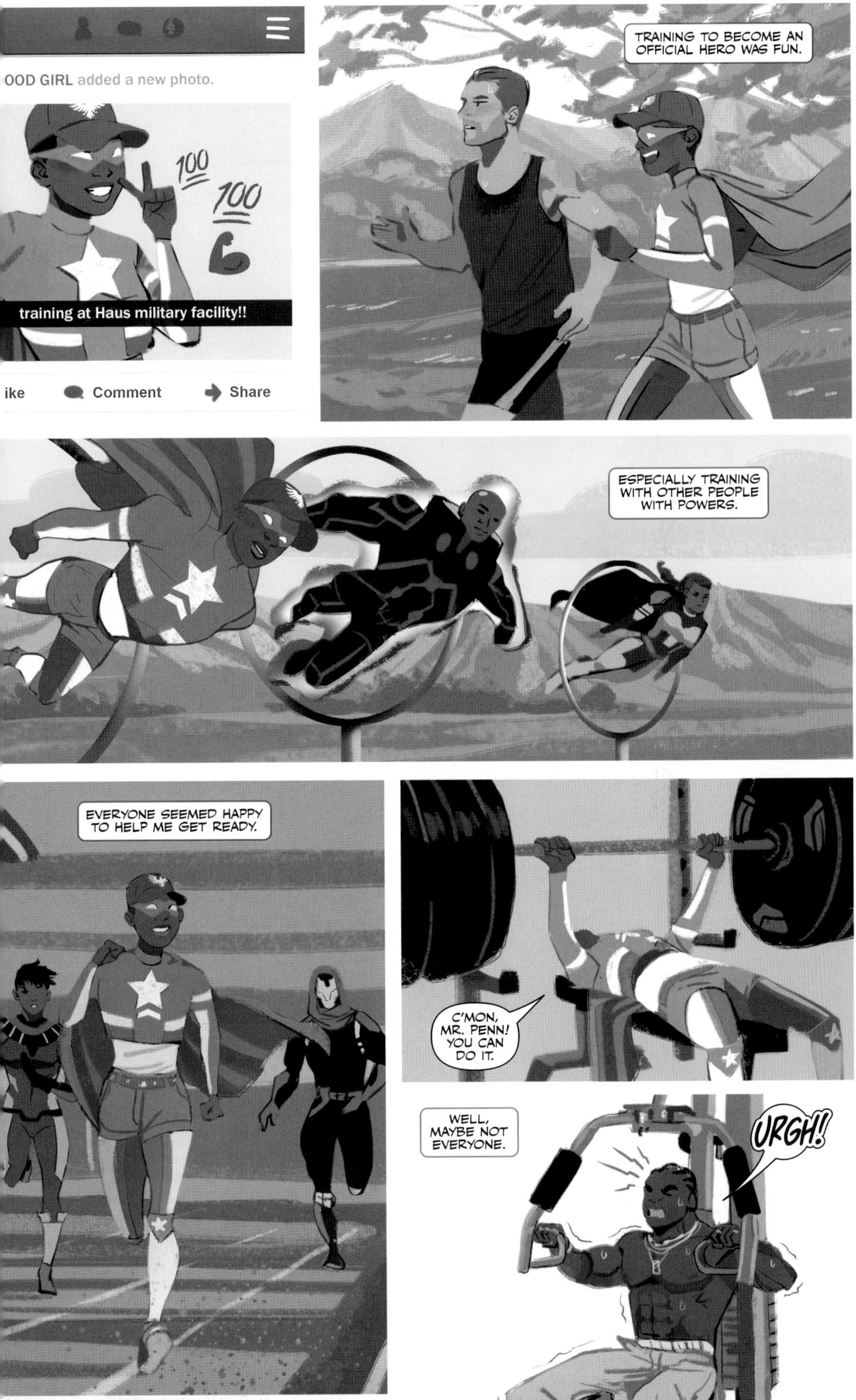

OOD GIRL added a new photo.
100
100
training at Haus military facility!!
ike
Comment
Share
TRAINING TO BECOME AN OFFICIAL HERO WAS FUN.
ESPECIALLY TRAINING WITH OTHER PEOPLE WITH POWERS.
EVERYONE SEEMED HAPPY TO HELP ME GET READY.
C'MON, MR. PENN! YOU CAN DO IT.
WELL, MAYBE NOT EVERYONE.
URGH!

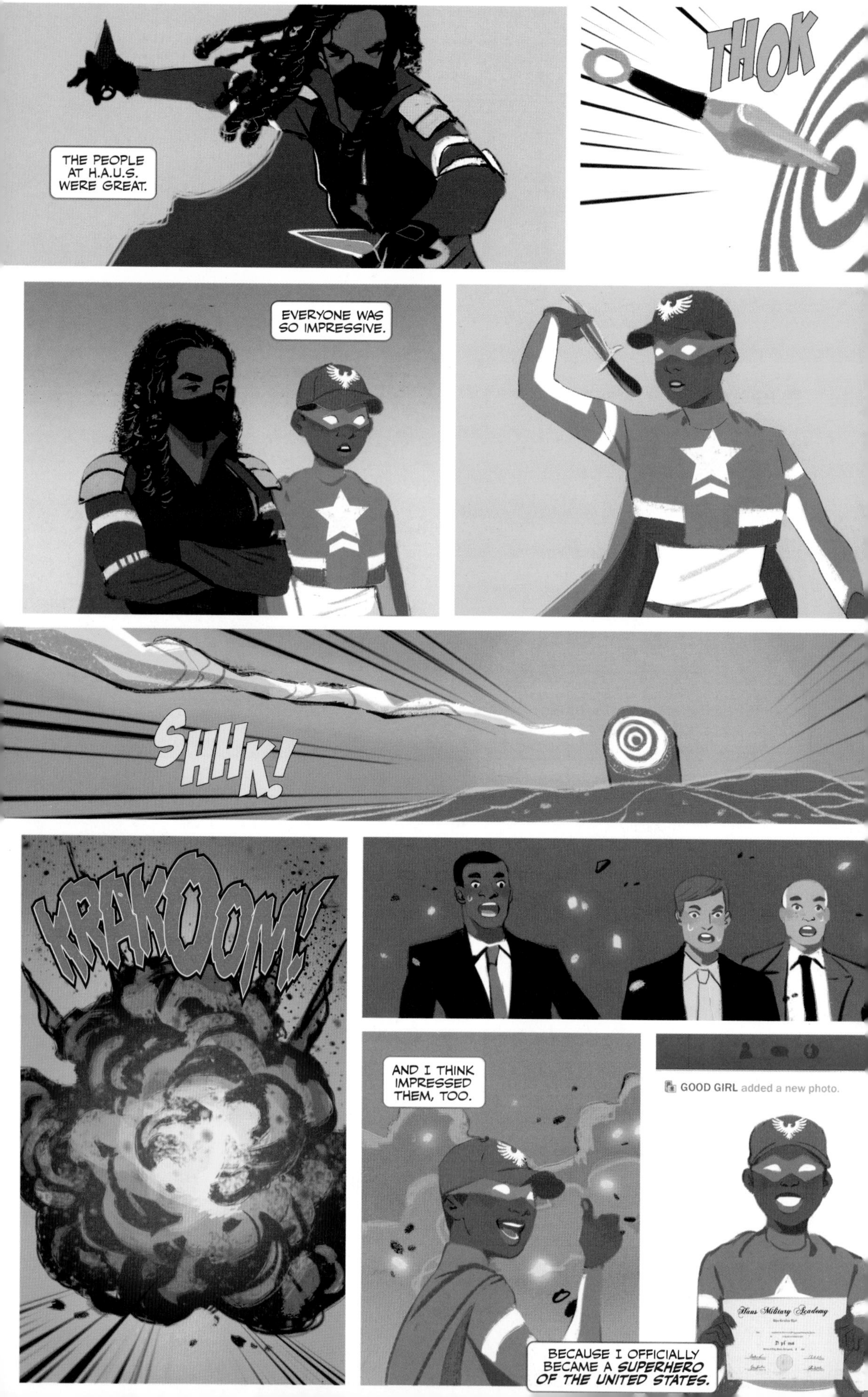
THE PEOPLE AT H.A.U.S. WERE GREAT.
THOK
EVERYONE WAS SO IMPRESSIVE.
SHHK!
KRAKOOM!
AND I THINK IMPRESSED THEM, TOO.
GOOD GIRL added a new photo.
Haus Military Academy
BECAUSE I OFFICIALLY BECAME A SUPERHERO OF THE UNITED STATES.

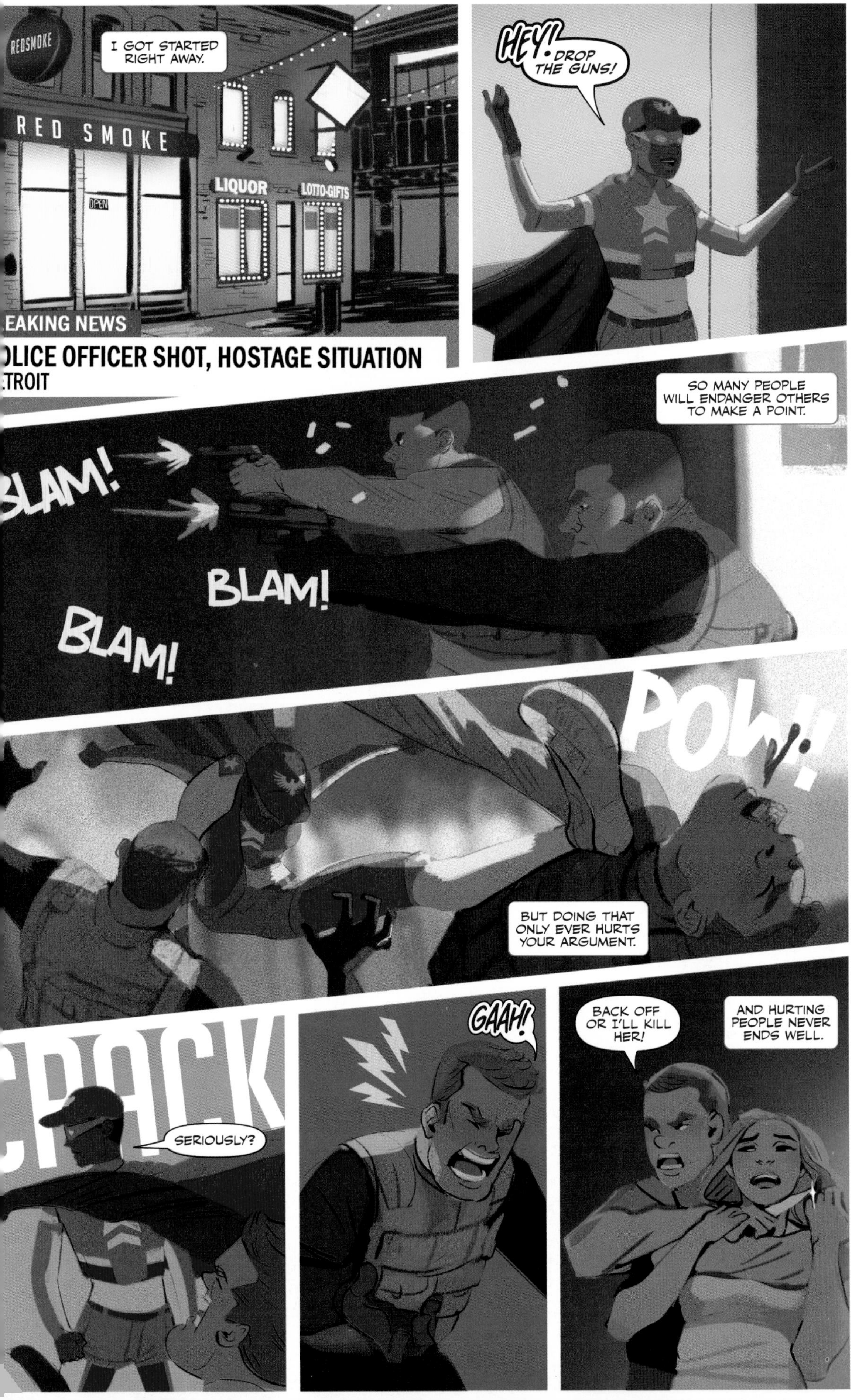

REDSMOKE
I GOT STARTED RIGHT AWAY.
RED SMOKE
OPEN
LIQUOR
LOTTO-GIFTS
EAKING NEWS
OLICE OFFICER SHOT, HOSTAGE SITUATION
TROIT
HEY! DROP THE GUNS!
SO MANY PEOPLE WILL ENDANGER OTHERS TO MAKE A POINT.
BLAM!
BLAM!
BLAM!
POW!
BUT DOING THAT ONLY EVER HURTS YOUR ARGUMENT.
CRACK
SERIOUSLY?
GAAH!
BACK OFF OR I'LL KILL HER!
AND HURTING PEOPLE NEVER ENDS WELL.

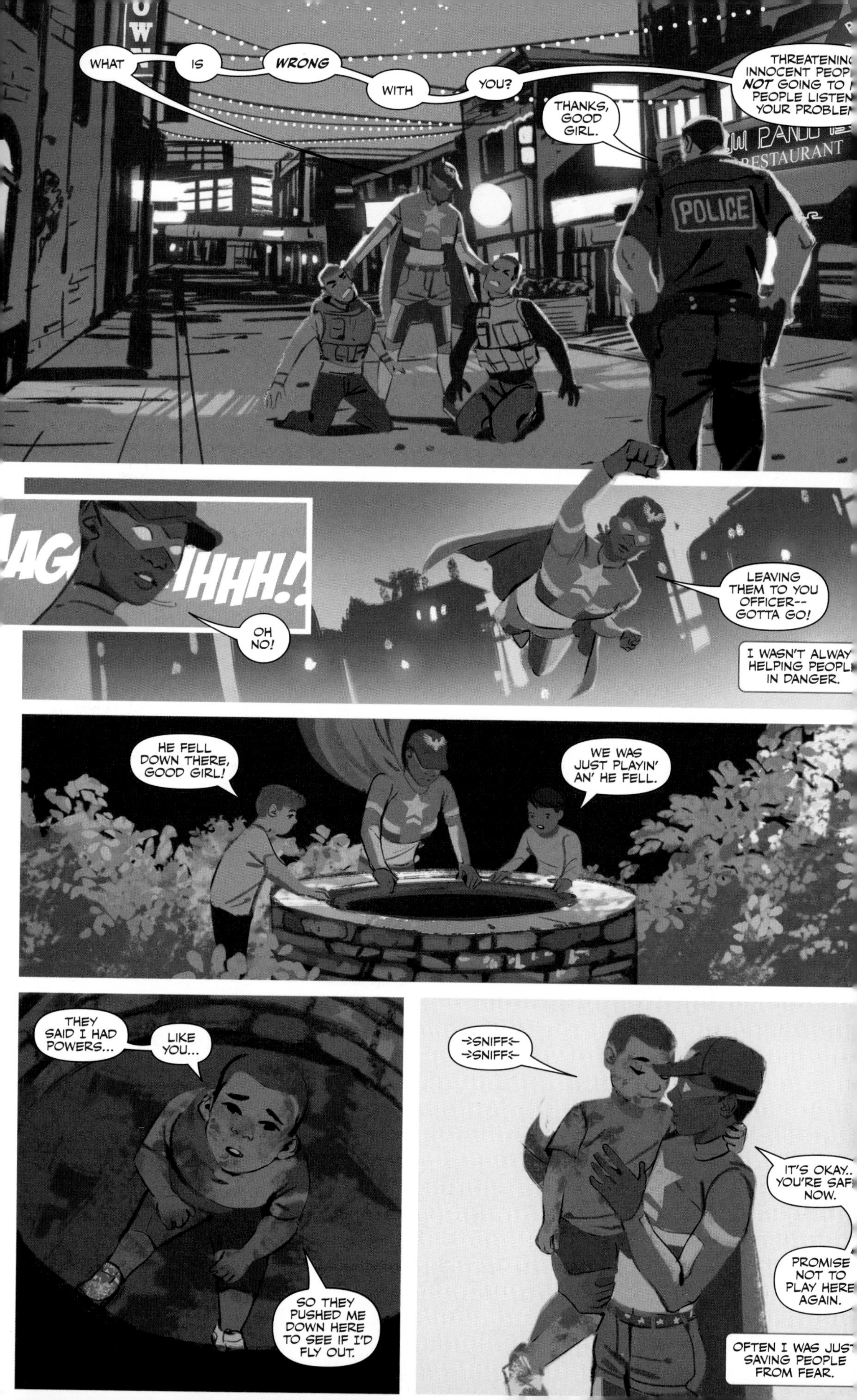
WHAT IS WRONG WITH YOU?
THREATENING INNOCENT PEOP NOT GOING TO PEOPLE LISTEN YOUR PROBLEM
THANKS, GOOD GIRL.
RESTAURANT
POLICE
AG HHHH!!
OH NO!
LEAVING THEM TO YOU OFFICER-- GOTTA GO!
I WASN'T ALWAY HELPING PEOPL IN DANGER.
HE FELL DOWN THERE, GOOD GIRL!
WE WAS JUST PLAYIN' AN' HE FELL.
THEY SAID I HAD POWERS...
LIKE YOU...
SO THEY PUSHED ME DOWN HERE TO SEE IF I'D FLY OUT.
>SNIFF< >SNIFF<
IT'S OKAY.. YOU'RE SAF NOW.
PROMISE NOT TO PLAY HERE AGAIN.
OFTEN I WAS JUS SAVING PEOPLE FROM FEAR.

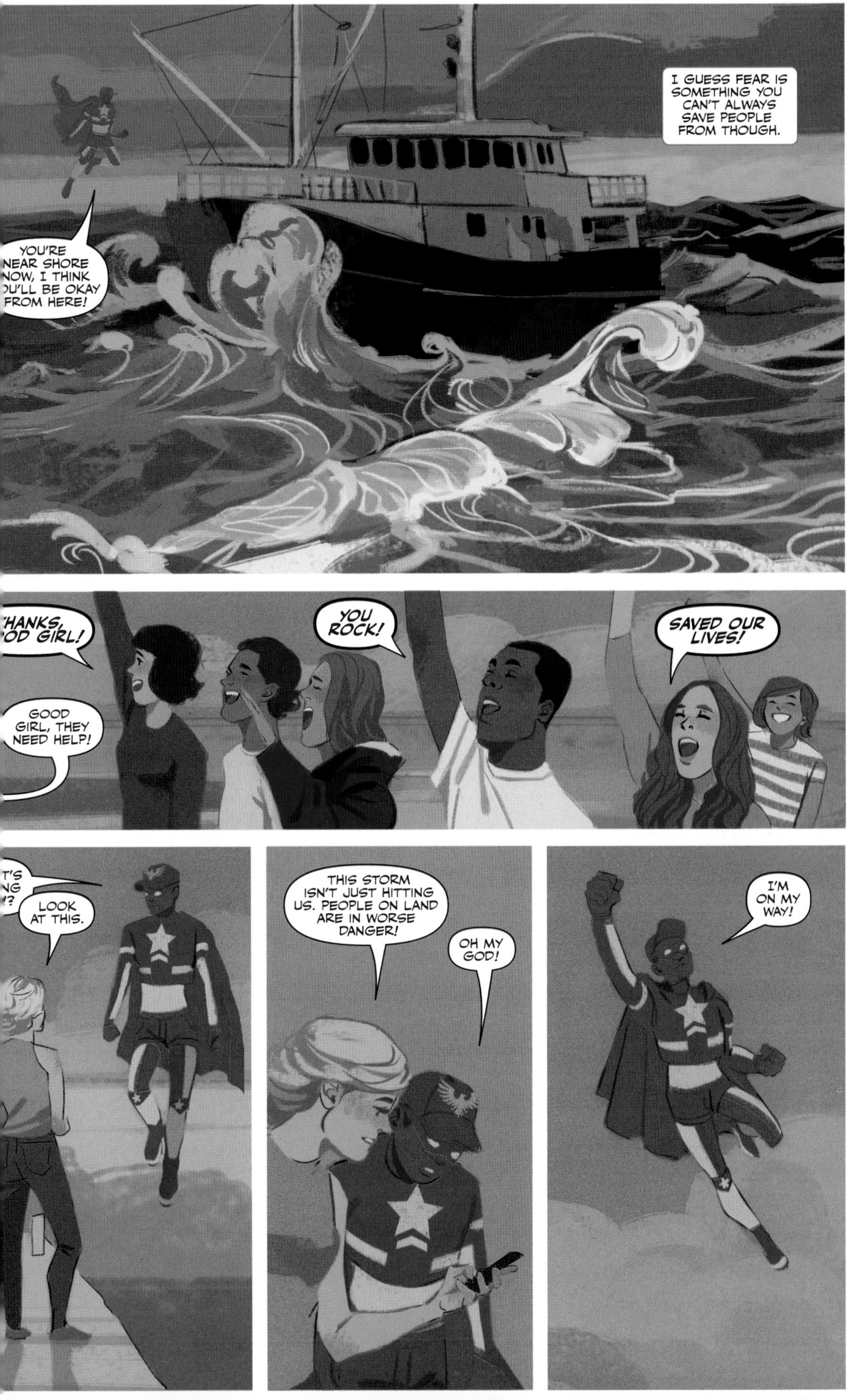
I GUESS FEAR IS SOMETHING YOU CAN'T ALWAYS SAVE PEOPLE FROM THOUGH.
YOU'RE NEAR SHORE NOW, I THINK OU'LL BE OKAY FROM HERE!
YOU ROCK!
SAVED OUR LIVES!
GOOD GIRL, THEY NEED HELP!
LOOK AT THIS.
THIS STORM ISN'T JUST HITTING US. PEOPLE ON LAND ARE IN WORSE DANGER!
OH MY GOD!
I'M ON MY WAY!

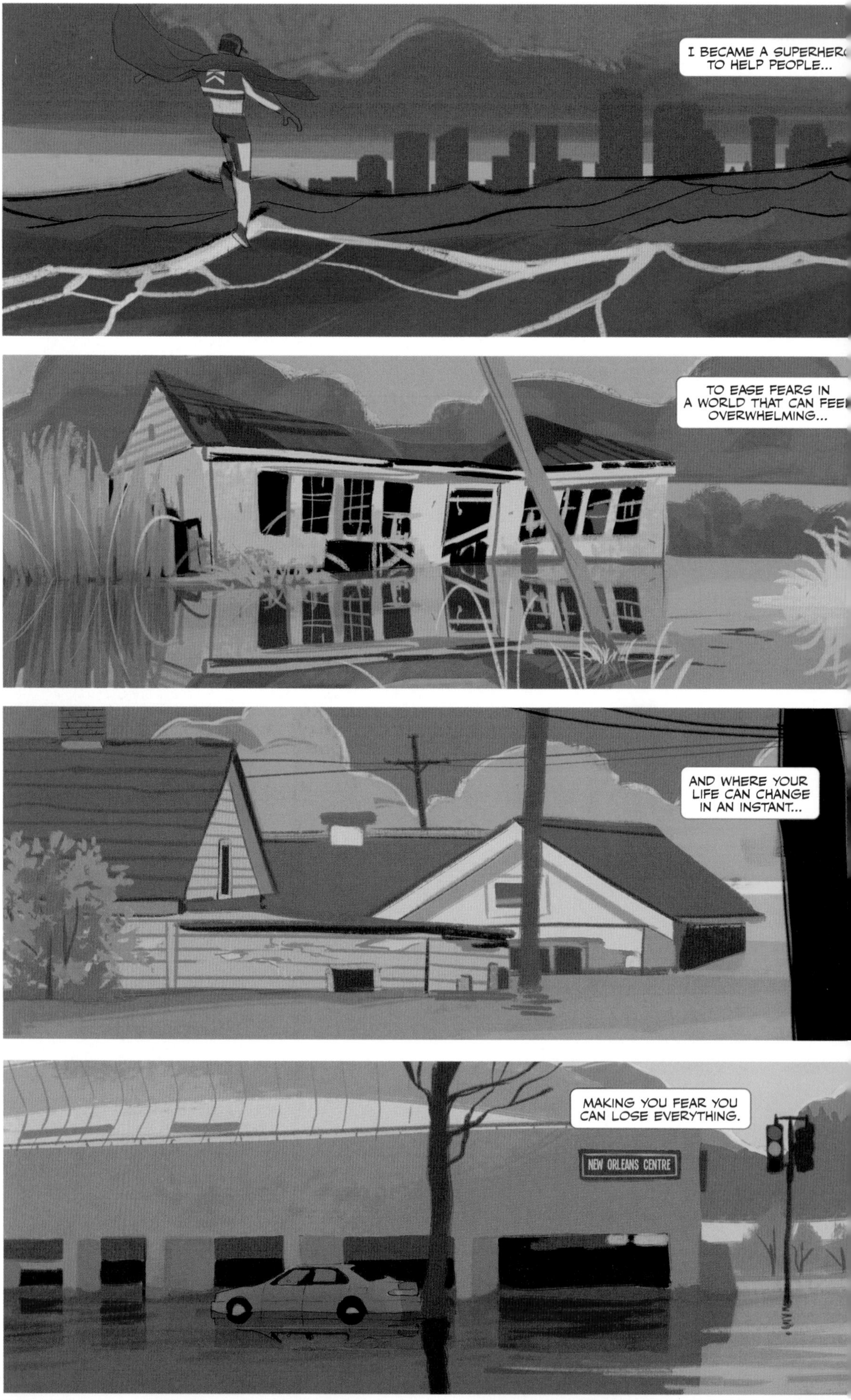
I BECAME A SUPERHERO
TO HELP PEOPLE...
TO EASE FEARS IN
A WORLD THAT CAN FEEL
OVERWHELMING...
AND WHERE YOUR
LIFE CAN CHANGE
IN AN INSTANT...
MAKING YOU FEAR YOU
CAN LOSE EVERYTHING.
NEW ORLEANS CENTRE

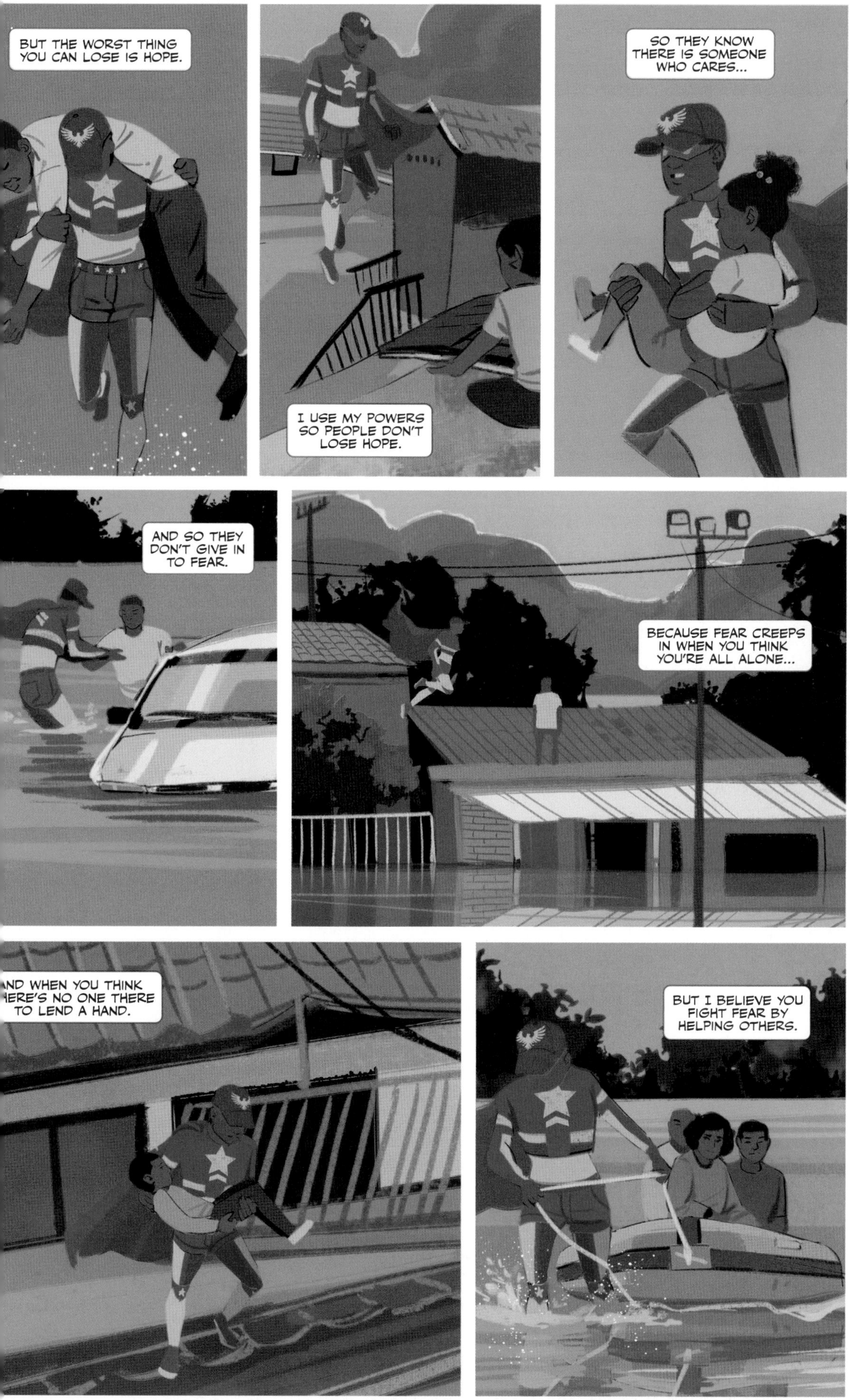
BUT THE WORST THING YOU CAN LOSE IS HOPE.
I USE MY POWERS SO PEOPLE DON'T LOSE HOPE.
SO THEY KNOW THERE IS SOMEONE WHO CARES...
AND SO THEY DON'T GIVE IN TO FEAR.
BECAUSE FEAR CREEPS IN WHEN YOU THINK YOU'RE ALL ALONE...
ND WHEN YOU THINK HERE'S NO ONE THERE TO LEND A HAND.
BUT I BELIEVE YOU FIGHT FEAR BY HELPING OTHERS.

FEAR ISN'T SOMETHING YOU CAN PUNCH IN THE FACE...

SPLASH!

ESPECIALLY WHEN YOU'RE DROWNING IN IT.

YOU HAVE TO TRY TO REDIRECT FEAR BEFORE IT BECOMES HATE...

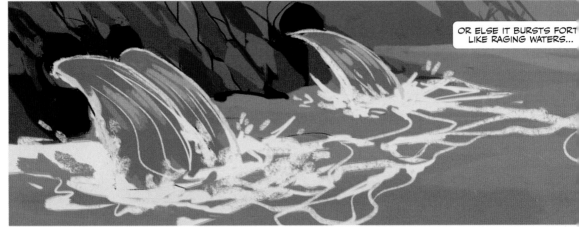

OR ELSE IT BURSTS FORT LIKE RAGING WATERS...

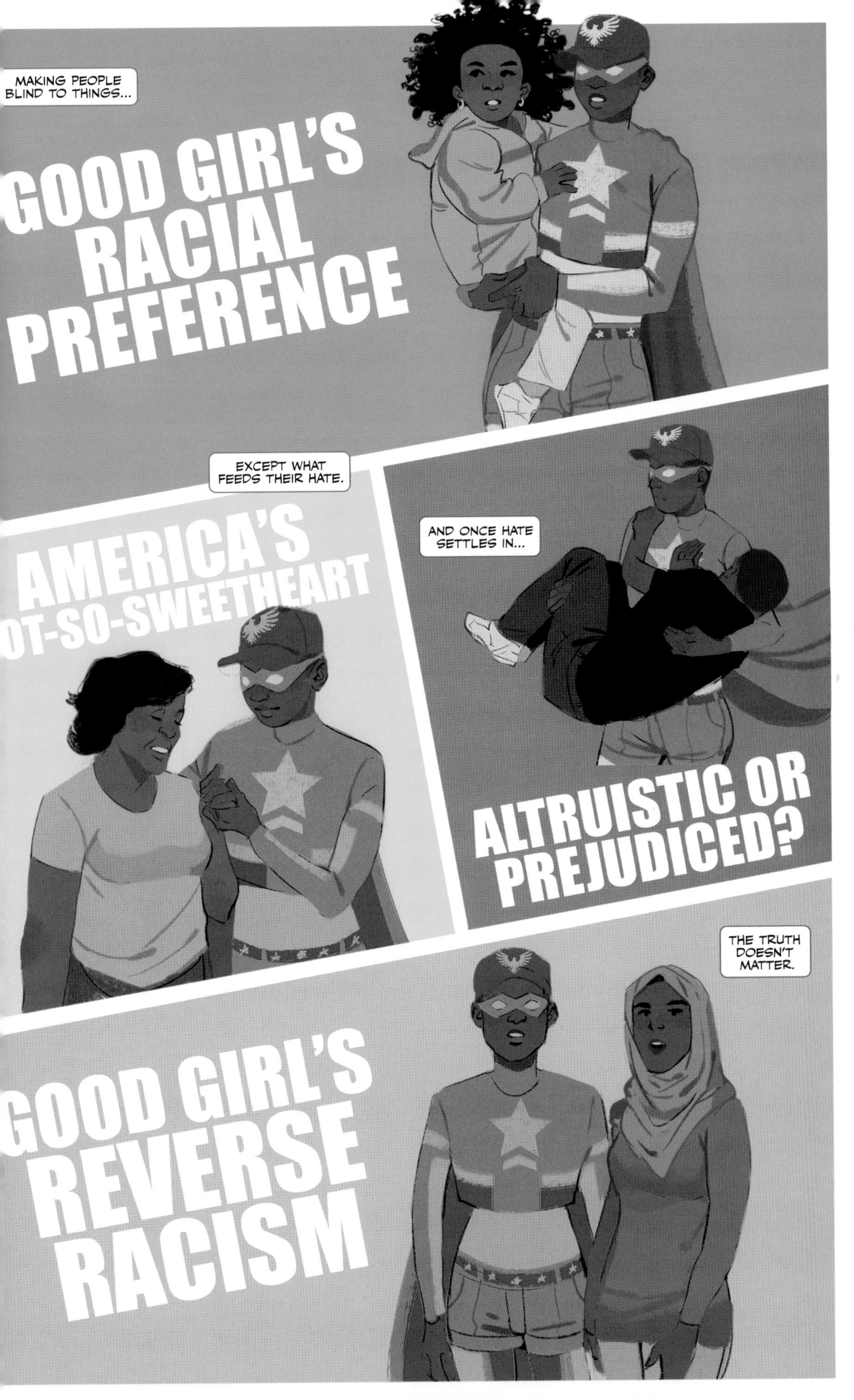
MAKING PEOPLE BLIND TO THINGS...
GOOD GIRL'S RACIAL PREFERENCE
EXCEPT WHAT FEEDS THEIR HATE.
AMERICA'S
OT-SO-SWEETHEART
AND ONCE HATE SETTLES IN...
ALTRUISTIC OR PREJUDICED?
THE TRUTH DOESN'T MATTER.
GOOD GIRL'S REVERSE RACISM

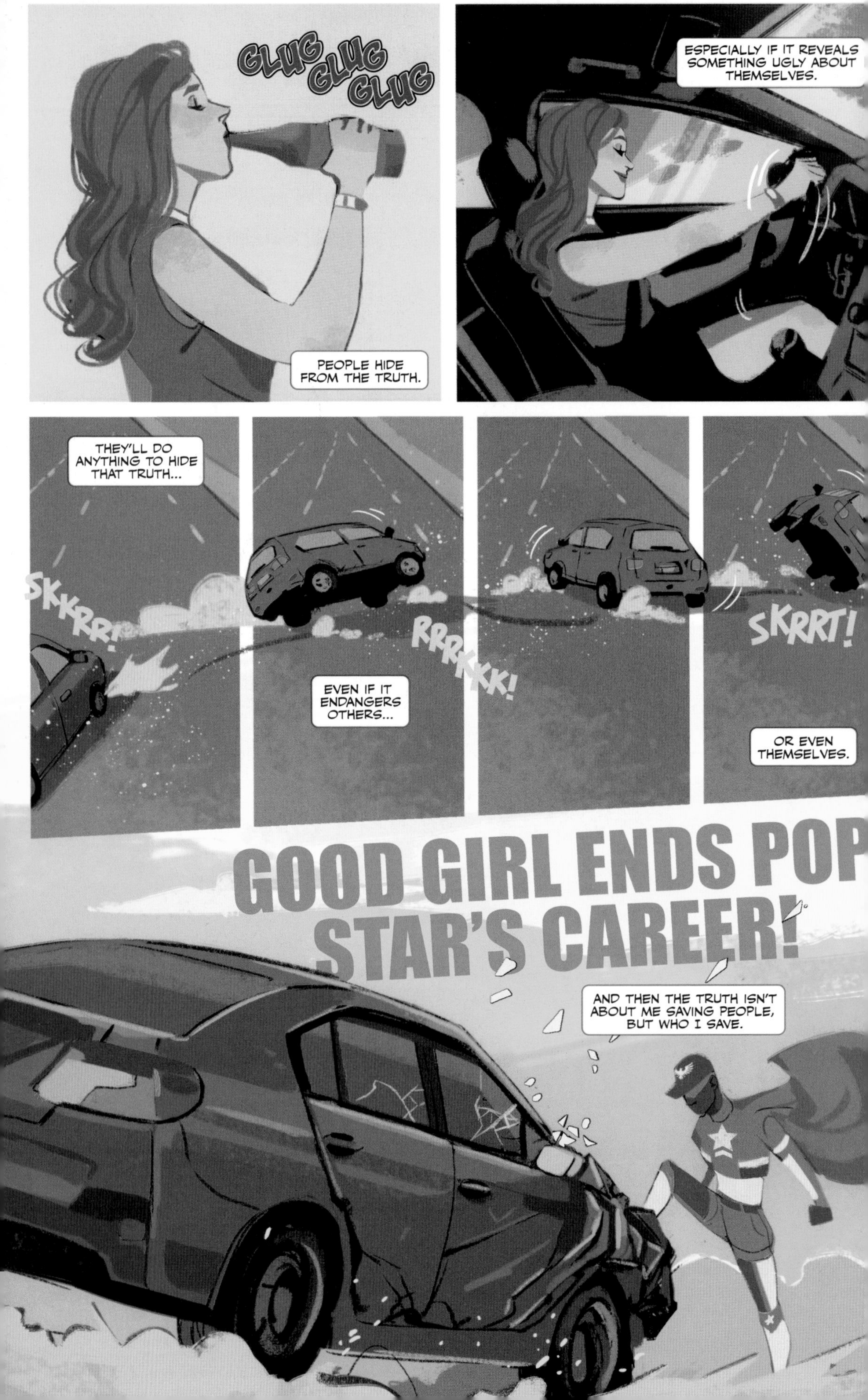
GLUG GLUG GLUG
PEOPLE HIDE FROM THE TRUTH.
ESPECIALLY IF IT REVEALS SOMETHING UGLY ABOUT THEMSELVES.
THEY'LL DO ANYTHING TO HIDE THAT TRUTH...
SKKRR!
RRRKKK!
EVEN IF IT ENDANGERS OTHERS...
SKRRT!
OR EVEN THEMSELVES.
GOOD GIRL ENDS POP STAR'S CAREER!
AND THEN THE TRUTH ISN'T ABOUT ME SAVING PEOPLE, BUT WHO I SAVE.

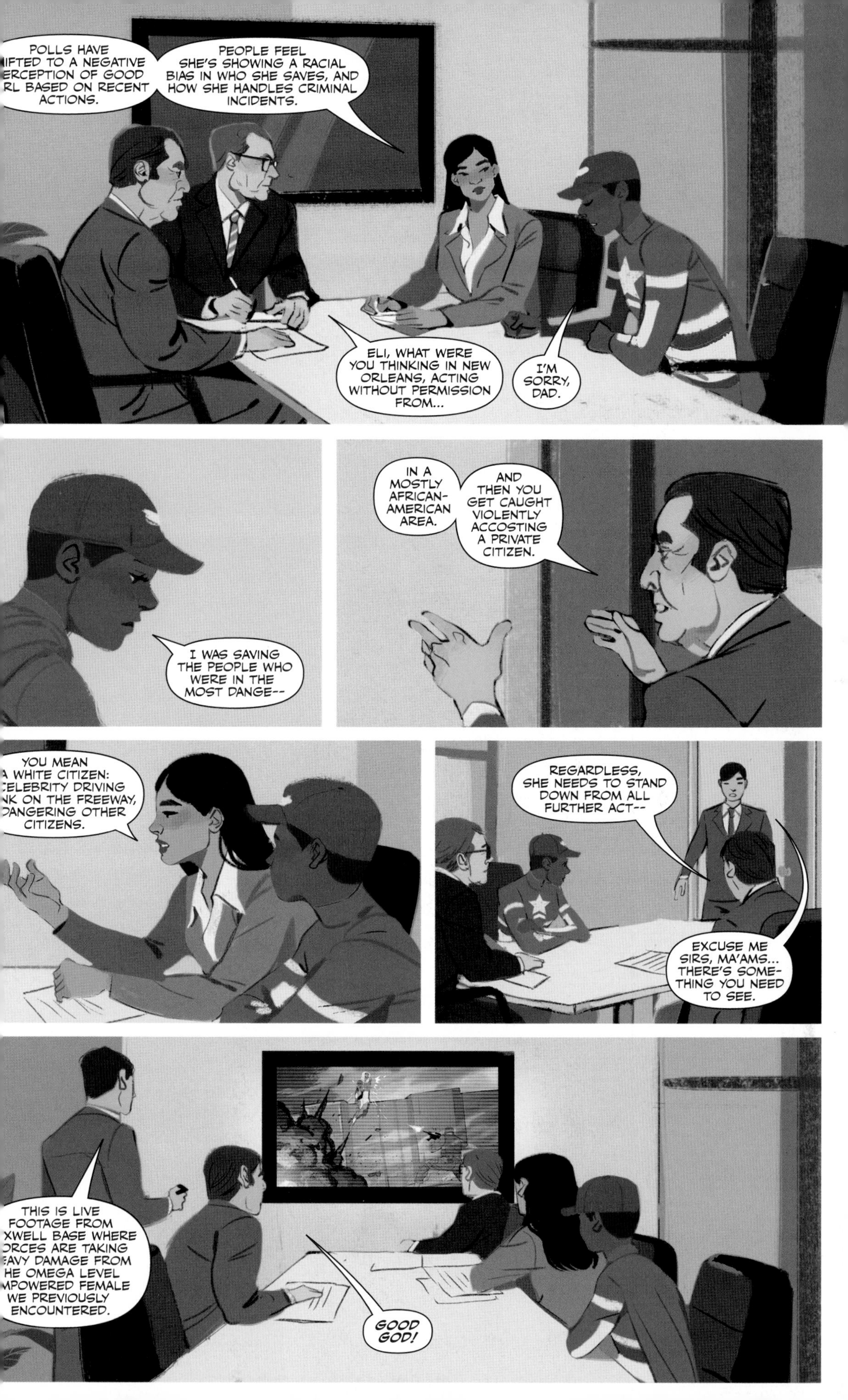
POLLS HAVE
IFTED TO A NEGATIVE
ERCEPTION OF GOOD
RL BASED ON RECENT
ACTIONS.
PEOPLE FEEL SHE'S SHOWING A RACIAL BIAS IN WHO SHE SAVES, AND HOW SHE HANDLES CRIMINAL INCIDENTS.
ELI, WHAT WERE YOU THINKING IN NEW ORLEANS, ACTING WITHOUT PERMISSION FROM...
I'M SORRY, DAD.
I WAS SAVING THE PEOPLE WHO WERE IN THE MOST DANGE--
IN A MOSTLY AFRICAN-AMERICAN AREA.
AND THEN YOU GET CAUGHT VIOLENTLY ACCOSTING A PRIVATE CITIZEN.
YOU MEAN
A WHITE CITIZEN:
CELEBRITY DRIVING
NK ON THE FREEWAY,
DANGERING OTHER
CITIZENS.
REGARDLESS, SHE NEEDS TO STAND DOWN FROM ALL FURTHER ACT--
EXCUSE ME SIRS, MA'AMS... THERE'S SOME-THING YOU NEED TO SEE.
THIS IS LIVE
FOOTAGE FROM
XWELL BASE WHERE
ORCES ARE TAKING
EAVY DAMAGE FROM
HE OMEGA LEVEL
MPOWERED FEMALE
WE PREVIOUSLY
ENCOUNTERED.
GOOD GOD!

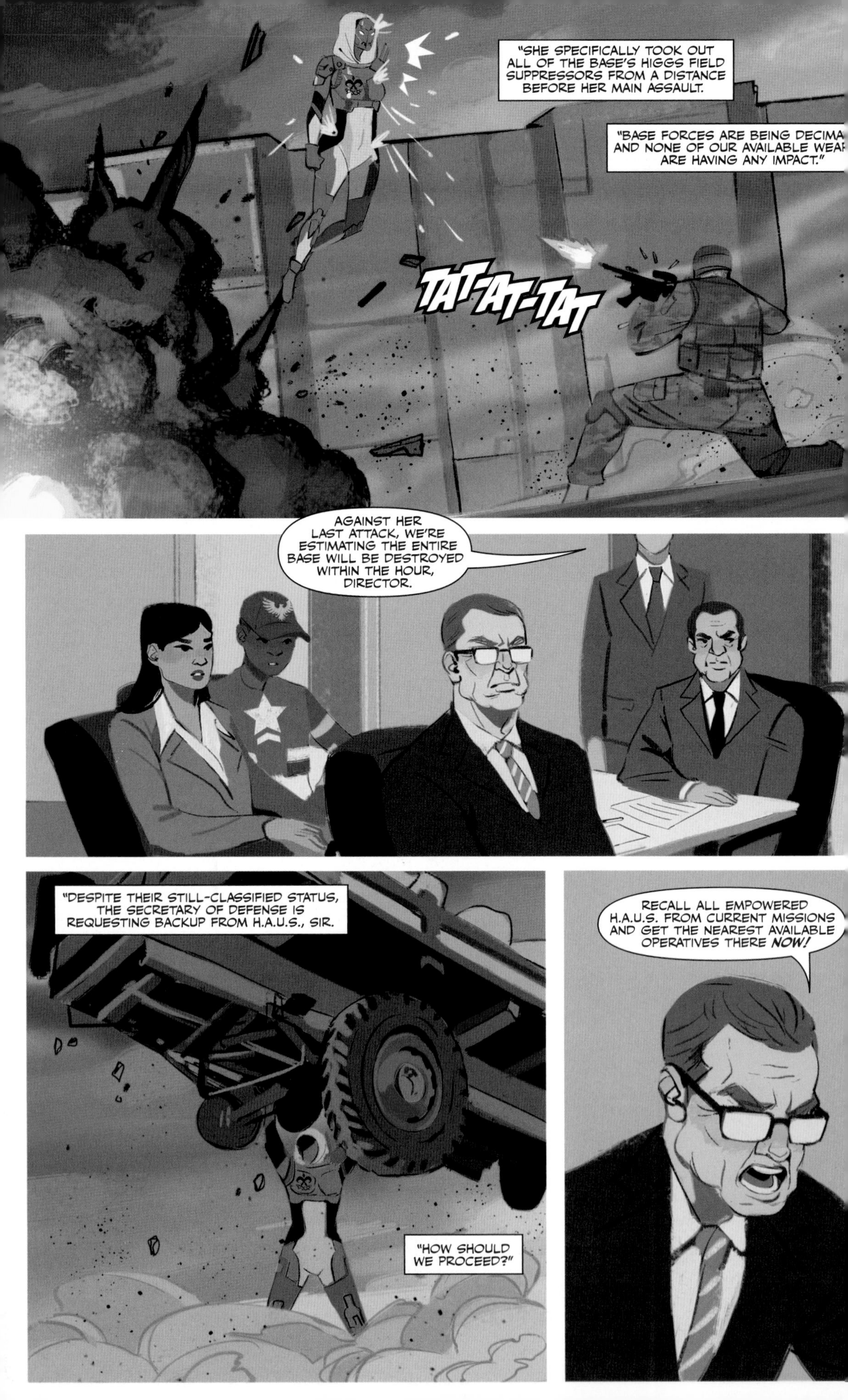

"SHE SPECIFICALLY TOOK OUT ALL OF THE BASE'S HIGGS FIELD SUPPRESSORS FROM A DISTANCE BEFORE HER MAIN ASSAULT.
"BASE FORCES ARE BEING DECIMA AND NONE OF OUR AVAILABLE WEAP ARE HAVING ANY IMPACT."
TAT-AT-TAT
AGAINST HER LAST ATTACK, WE'RE ESTIMATING THE ENTIRE BASE WILL BE DESTROYED WITHIN THE HOUR, DIRECTOR.
"DESPITE THEIR STILL-CLASSIFIED STATUS, THE SECRETARY OF DEFENSE IS REQUESTING BACKUP FROM H.A.U.S., SIR.
"HOW SHOULD WE PROCEED?"
RECALL ALL EMPOWERED H.A.U.S. FROM CURRENT MISSIONS AND GET THE NEAREST AVAILABLE OPERATIVES THERE *NOW!*

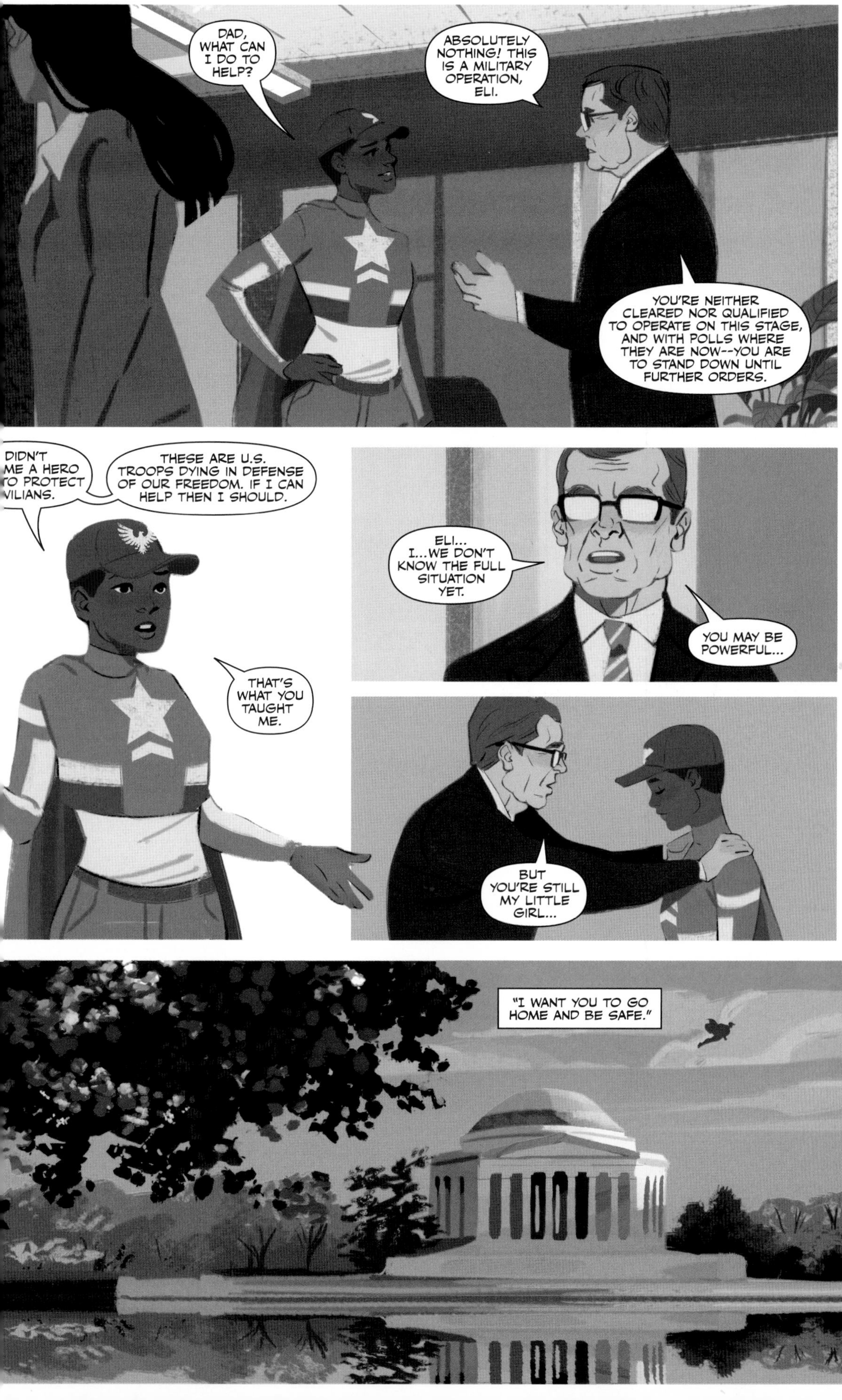
DAD, WHAT CAN I DO TO HELP?
ABSOLUTELY NOTHING! THIS IS A MILITARY OPERATION, ELI.
YOU'RE NEITHER CLEARED NOR QUALIFIED TO OPERATE ON THIS STAGE, AND WITH POLLS WHERE THEY ARE NOW--YOU ARE TO STAND DOWN UNTIL FURTHER ORDERS.
DIDN'T ME A HERO TO PROTECT VILIANS.
THESE ARE U.S. TROOPS DYING IN DEFENSE OF OUR FREEDOM. IF I CAN HELP THEN I SHOULD.
THAT'S WHAT YOU TAUGHT ME.
ELI... I...WE DON'T KNOW THE FULL SITUATION YET.
YOU MAY BE POWERFUL...
BUT YOU'RE STILL MY LITTLE GIRL...
"I WANT YOU TO GO HOME AND BE SAFE."

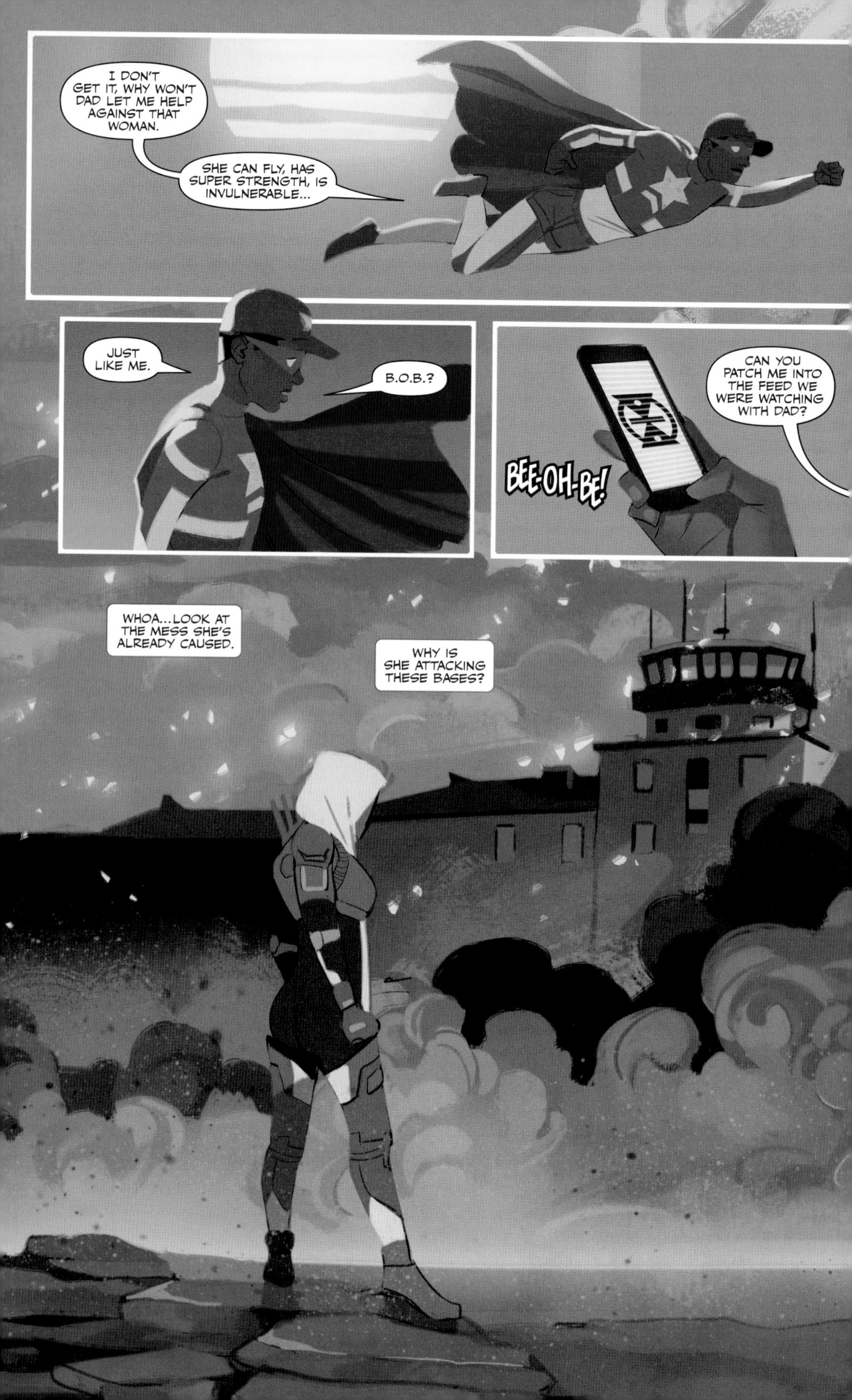
I DON'T GET IT, WHY WON'T DAD LET ME HELP AGAINST THAT WOMAN.
SHE CAN FLY, HAS SUPER STRENGTH, IS INVULNERABLE...
JUST LIKE ME.
B.O.B.?
BEE-OH-BE!
CAN YOU PATCH ME INTO THE FEED WE WERE WATCHING WITH DAD?
WHOA...LOOK AT THE MESS SHE'S ALREADY CAUSED.
WHY IS SHE ATTACKING THESE BASES?

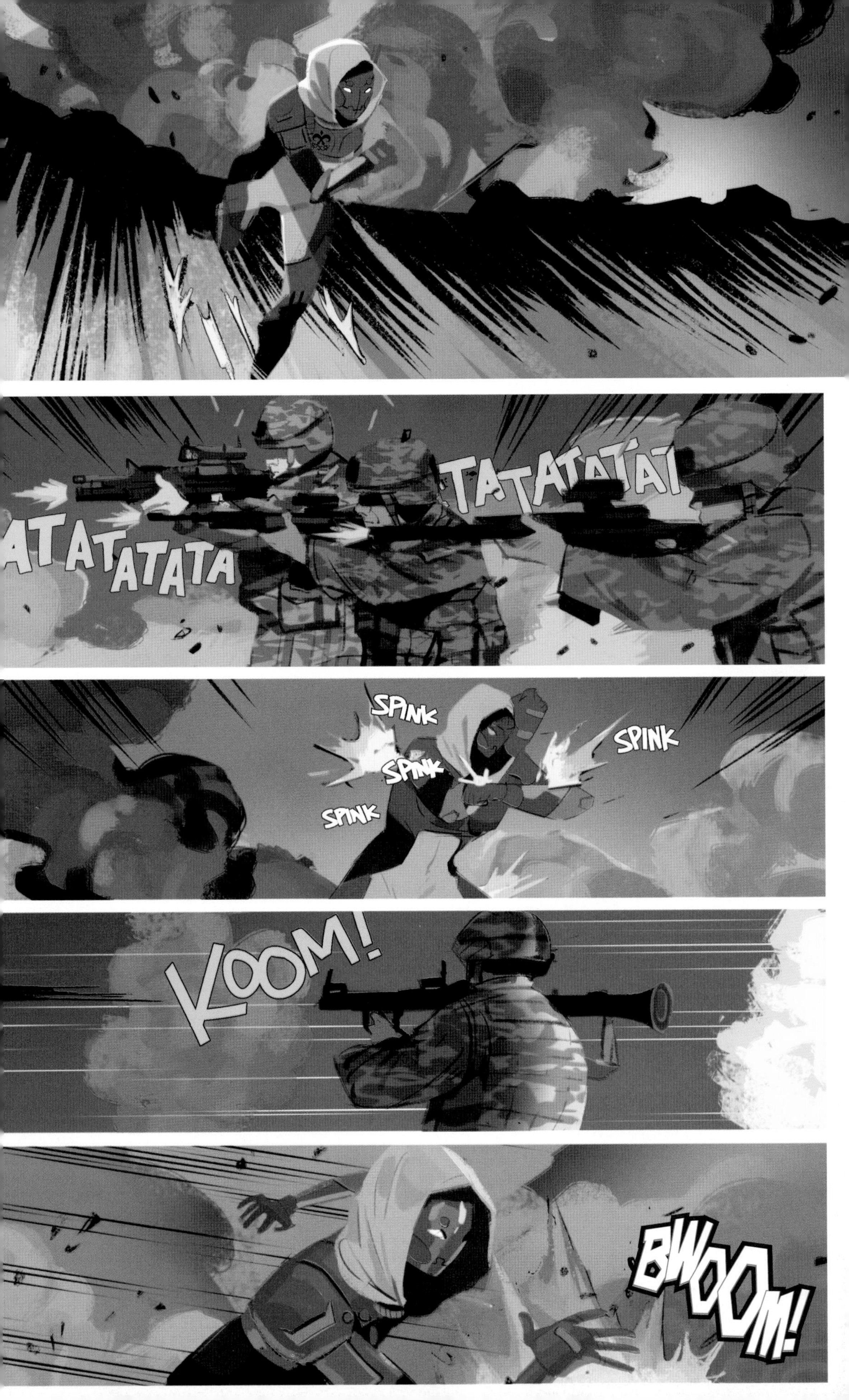
ATATATATA
TATATATAT
SPINK
SPINK
SPINK
SPINK
KOOM!
BWOOM!

KRAKKKOOOM!!

HOLY MOLEY! THEY SHOT A MISSILE AT HER!

LET'S SEE HOW SHE LIKED THAT!

SWEET BABY JESUS...

SHE AIN'T GOT A SCRATCH ON'ER.

VMMMM!

ZOOM IN, B.O.B.

OH MY GOD!

THAT'S YOUR...IT'S THE SAME SYMBOL!

BEE-OH-

I HAVE TO TALK TO HER!

BOOOOO   **OOM!**

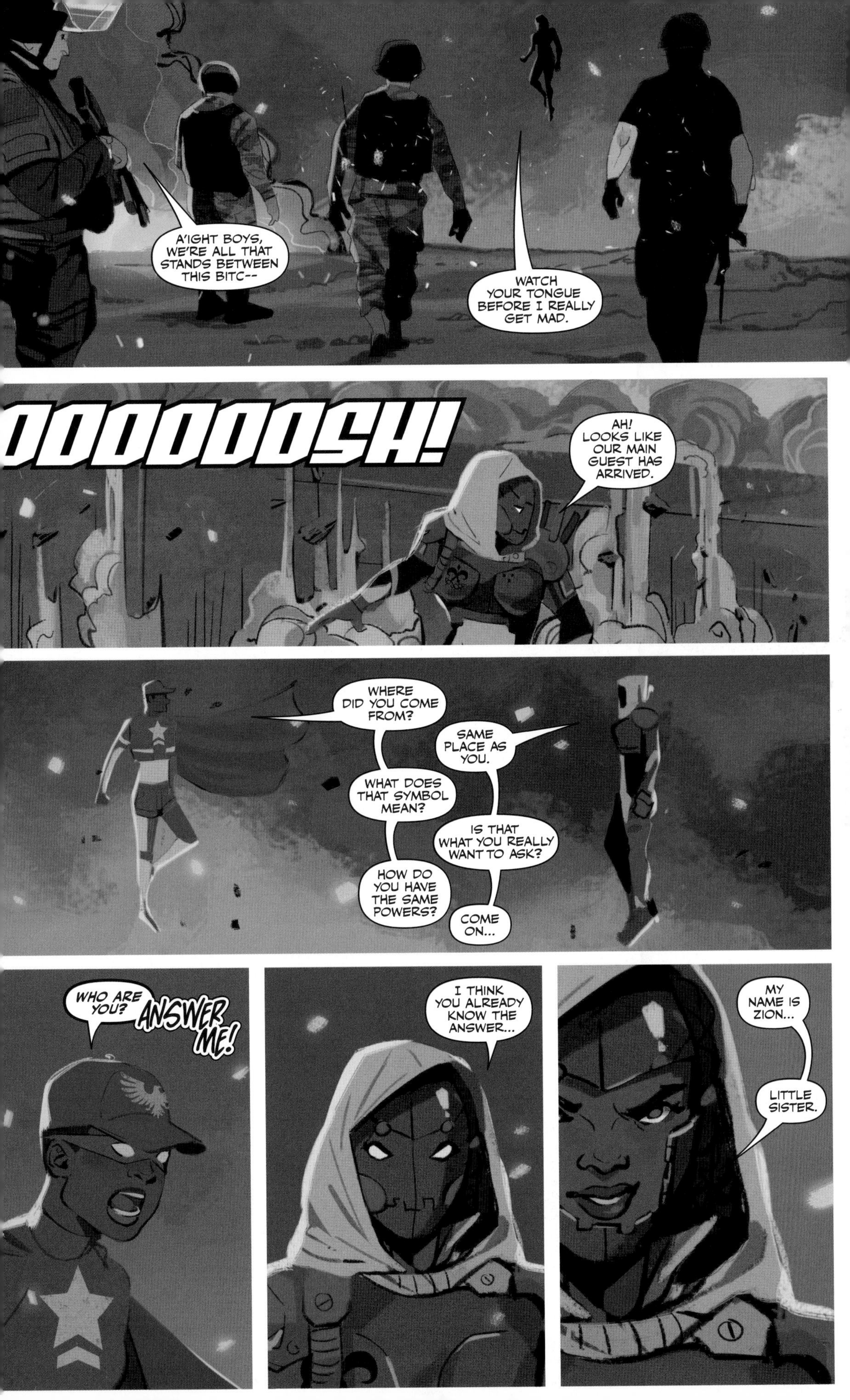
A'IGHT BOYS, WE'RE ALL THAT STANDS BETWEEN THIS BITC--
WATCH YOUR TONGUE BEFORE I REALLY GET MAD.
OOOOOOSH!
AH! LOOKS LIKE OUR MAIN GUEST HAS ARRIVED.
WHERE DID YOU COME FROM?
SAME PLACE AS YOU.
WHAT DOES THAT SYMBOL MEAN?
IS THAT WHAT YOU REALLY WANT TO ASK?
HOW DO YOU HAVE THE SAME POWERS?
COME ON...
WHO ARE YOU?
ANSWER ME!
I THINK YOU ALREADY KNOW THE ANSWER...
MY NAME IS ZION...
LITTLE SISTER.

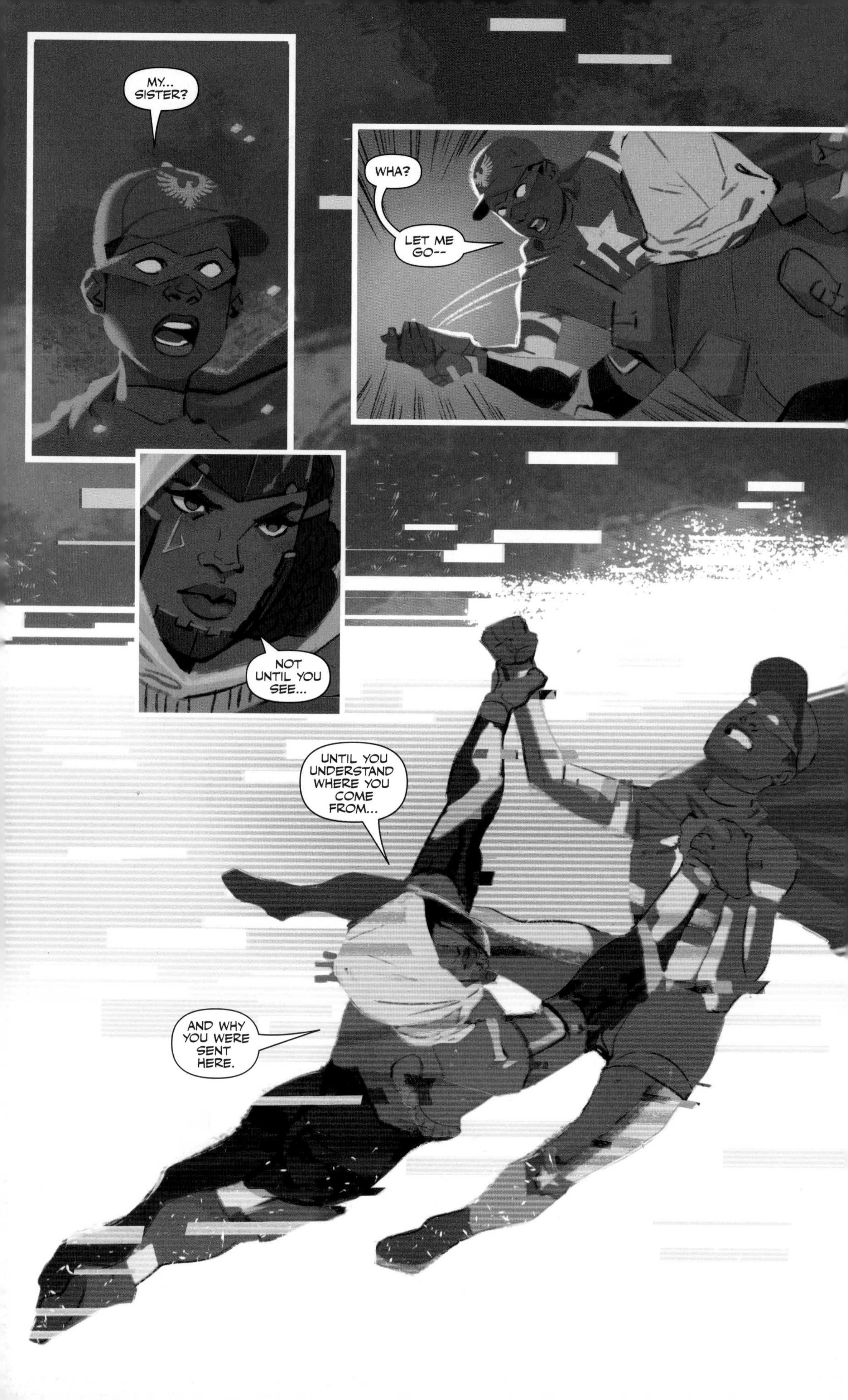
MY... SISTER?
WHA?
LET ME GO--
NOT UNTIL YOU SEE...
UNTIL YOU UNDERSTAND WHERE YOU COME FROM...
AND WHY YOU WERE SENT HERE.

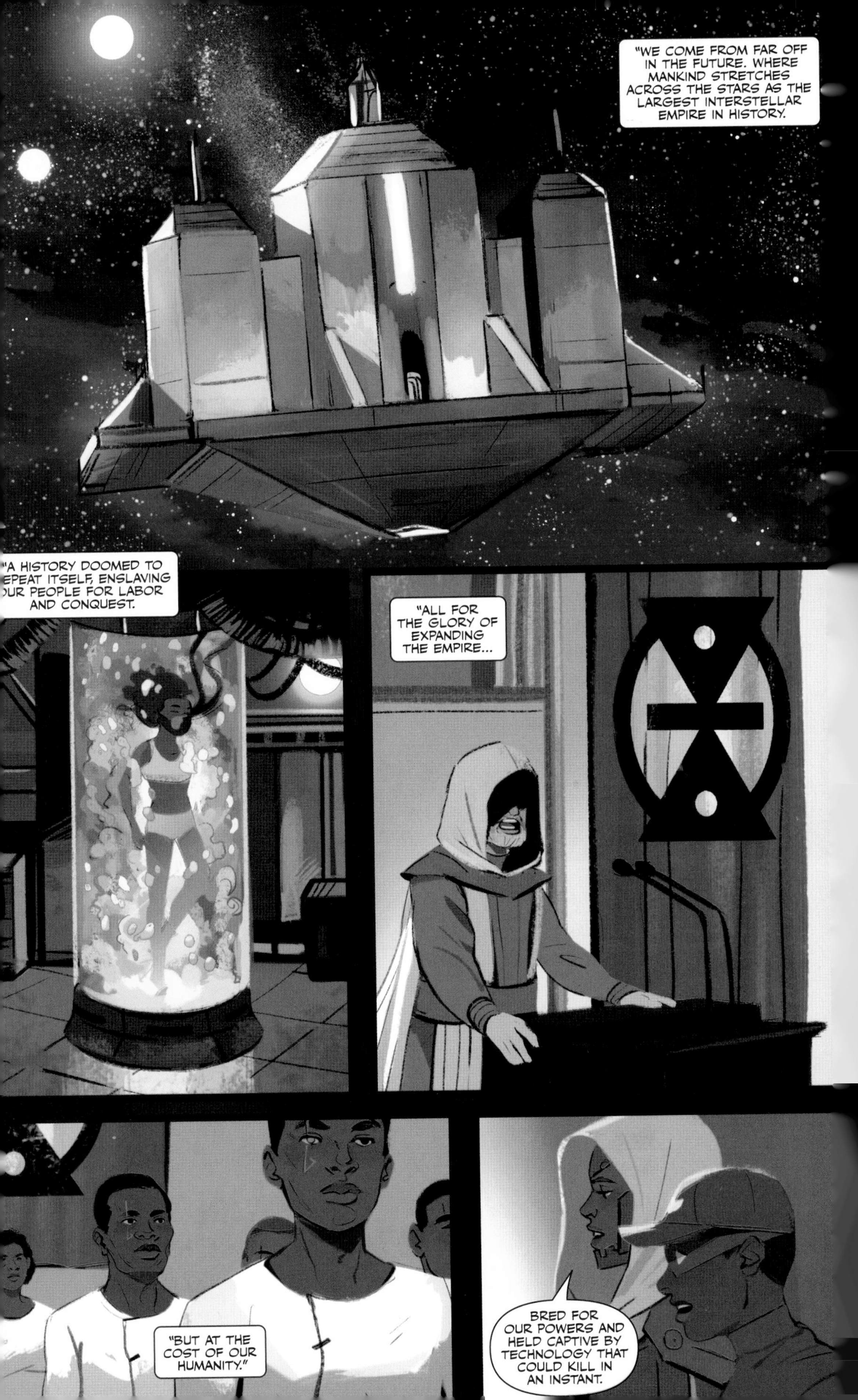
"WE COME FROM FAR OFF IN THE FUTURE. WHERE MANKIND STRETCHES ACROSS THE STARS AS THE LARGEST INTERSTELLAR EMPIRE IN HISTORY.
"A HISTORY DOOMED TO EPEAT ITSELF, ENSLAVING UR PEOPLE FOR LABOR AND CONQUEST.
"ALL FOR THE GLORY OF EXPANDING THE EMPIRE...
"BUT AT THE COST OF OUR HUMANITY."
BRED FOR OUR POWERS AND HELD CAPTIVE BY TECHNOLOGY THAT COULD KILL IN AN INSTANT.

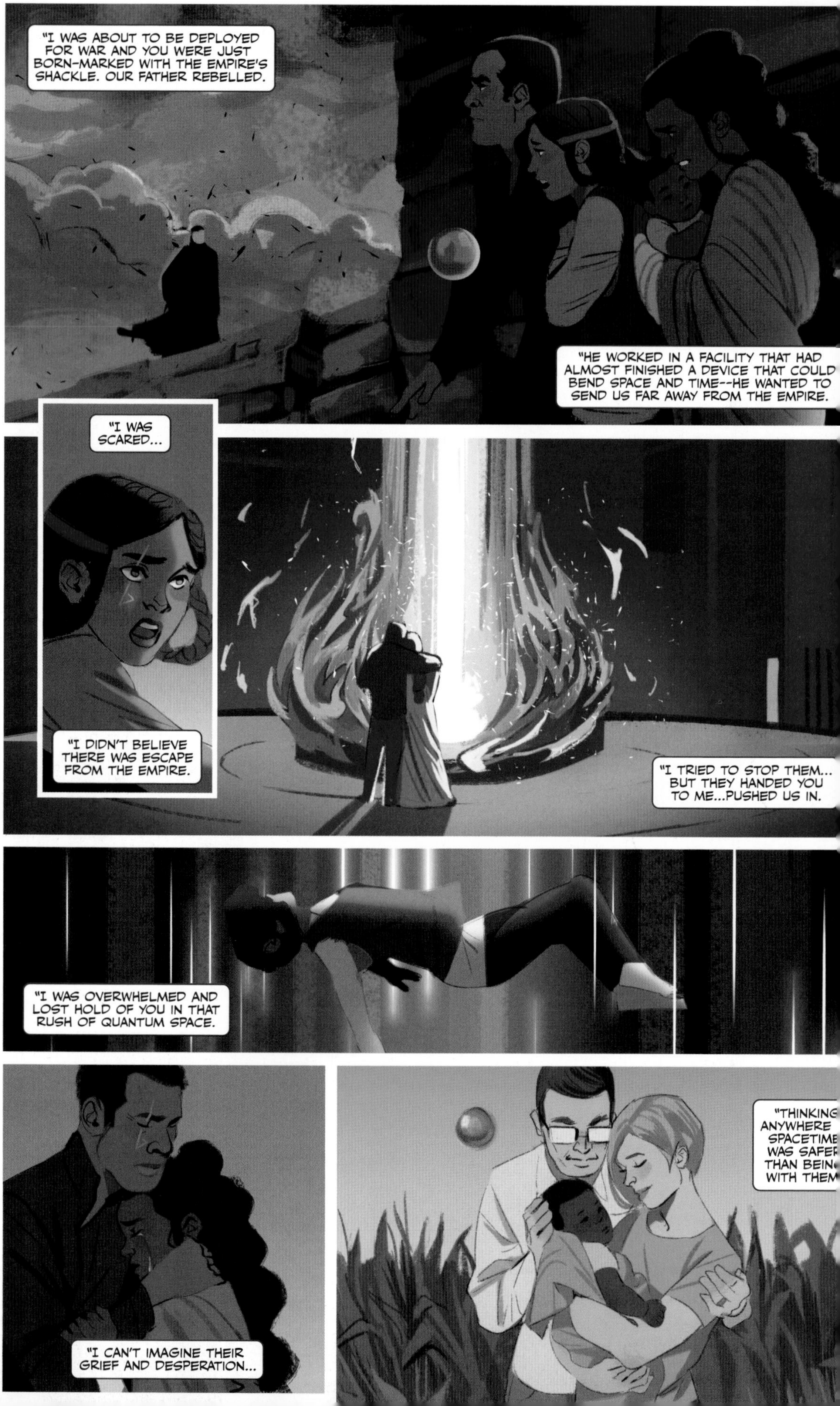
"I WAS ABOUT TO BE DEPLOYED FOR WAR AND YOU WERE JUST BORN-MARKED WITH THE EMPIRE'S SHACKLE. OUR FATHER REBELLED.
"HE WORKED IN A FACILITY THAT HAD ALMOST FINISHED A DEVICE THAT COULD BEND SPACE AND TIME--HE WANTED TO SEND US FAR AWAY FROM THE EMPIRE.
"I WAS SCARED...
"I DIDN'T BELIEVE THERE WAS ESCAPE FROM THE EMPIRE.
"I TRIED TO STOP THEM... BUT THEY HANDED YOU TO ME...PUSHED US IN.
"I WAS OVERWHELMED AND LOST HOLD OF YOU IN THAT RUSH OF QUANTUM SPACE.
"I CAN'T IMAGINE THEIR GRIEF AND DESPERATION...
"THINKING ANYWHERE SPACETIME WAS SAFER THAN BEIN WITH THEM

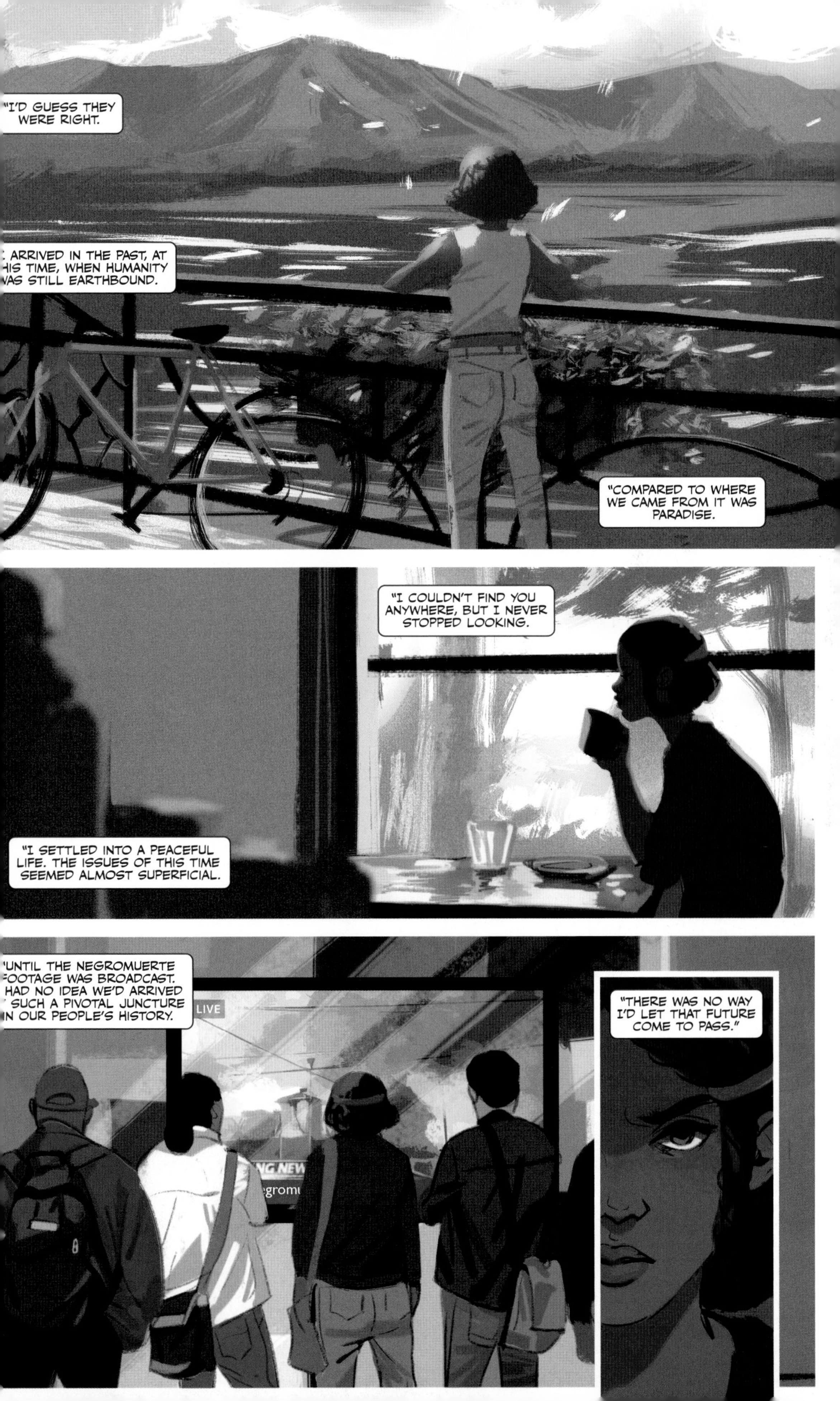
"I'D GUESS THEY WERE RIGHT.
I ARRIVED IN THE PAST, AT THIS TIME, WHEN HUMANITY WAS STILL EARTHBOUND.
"COMPARED TO WHERE WE CAME FROM IT WAS PARADISE.
"I COULDN'T FIND YOU ANYWHERE, BUT I NEVER STOPPED LOOKING.
"I SETTLED INTO A PEACEFUL LIFE. THE ISSUES OF THIS TIME SEEMED ALMOST SUPERFICIAL.
"UNTIL THE NEGROMUERTE FOOTAGE WAS BROADCAST. I HAD NO IDEA WE'D ARRIVED AT SUCH A PIVOTAL JUNCTURE IN OUR PEOPLE'S HISTORY.
LIVE
"THERE WAS NO WAY I'D LET THAT FUTURE COME TO PASS."

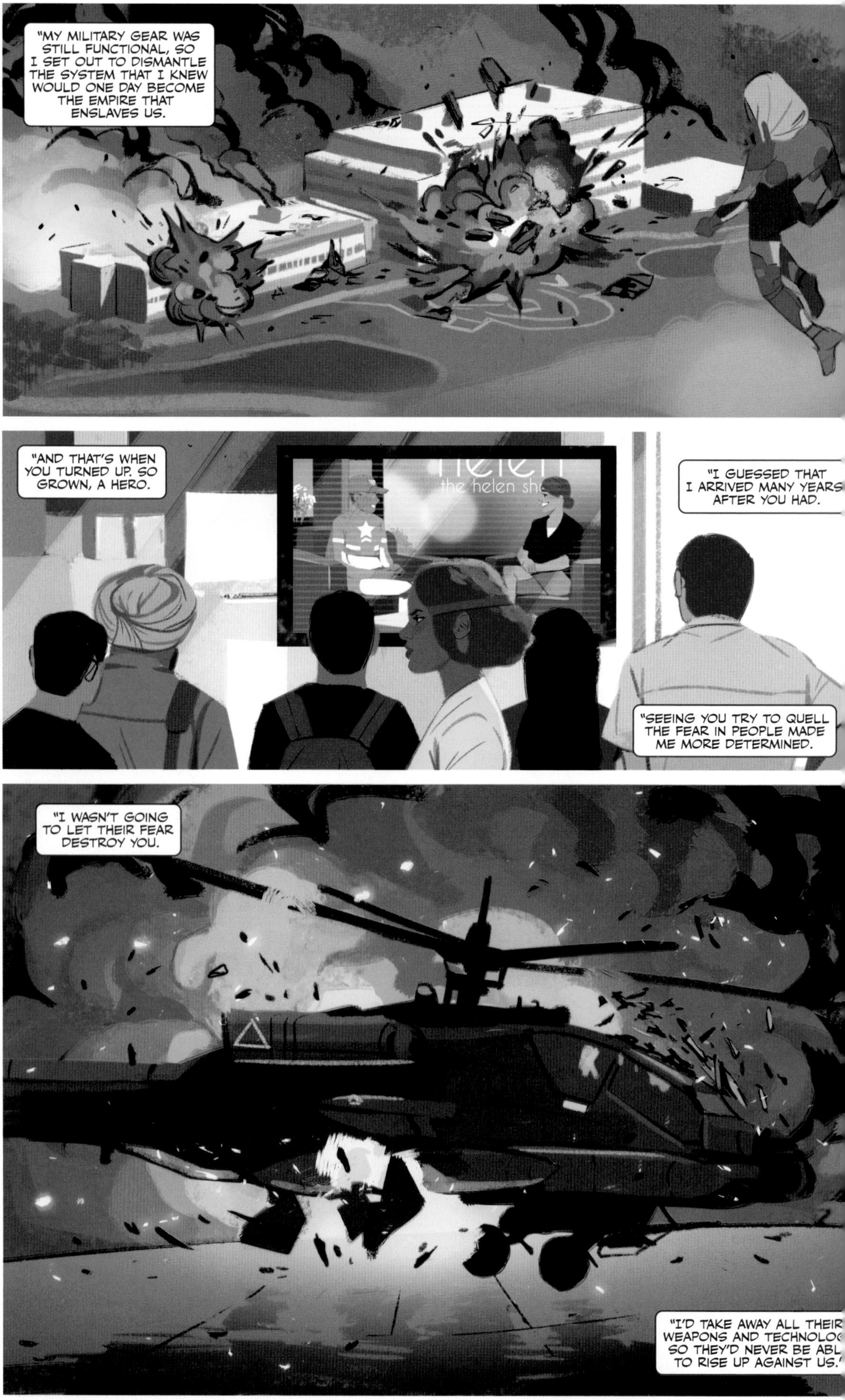
"MY MILITARY GEAR WAS STILL FUNCTIONAL, SO I SET OUT TO DISMANTLE THE SYSTEM THAT I KNEW WOULD ONE DAY BECOME THE EMPIRE THAT ENSLAVES US.
"AND THAT'S WHEN YOU TURNED UP. SO GROWN, A HERO.
the helen sh
"I GUESSED THAT I ARRIVED MANY YEARS AFTER YOU HAD.
"SEEING YOU TRY TO QUELL THE FEAR IN PEOPLE MADE ME MORE DETERMINED.
"I WASN'T GOING TO LET THEIR FEAR DESTROY YOU.
"I'D TAKE AWAY ALL THEIR WEAPONS AND TECHNOLOG SO THEY'D NEVER BE ABL TO RISE UP AGAINST US."

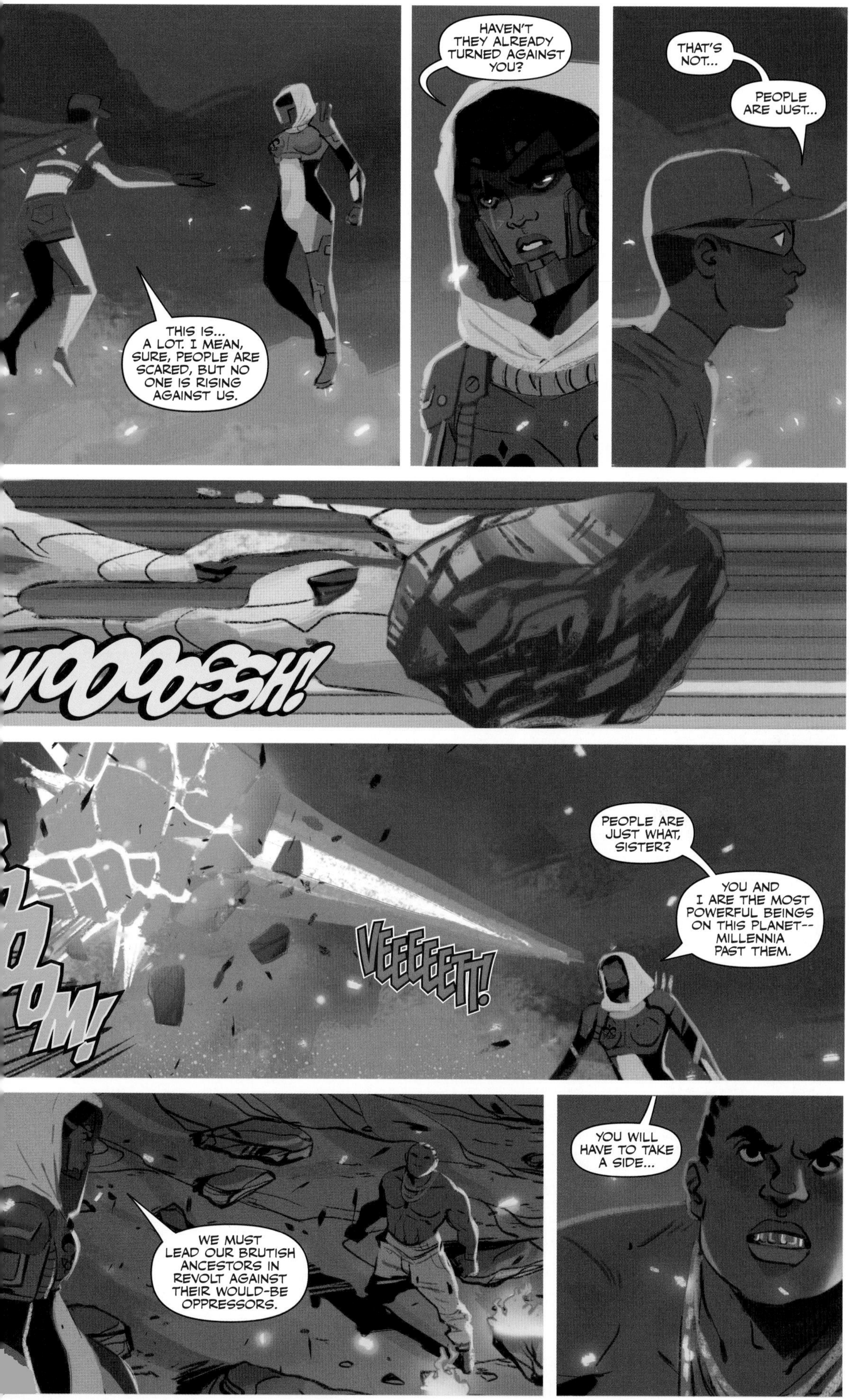
THIS IS... A LOT. I MEAN, SURE, PEOPLE ARE SCARED, BUT NO ONE IS RISING AGAINST US.
HAVEN'T THEY ALREADY TURNED AGAINST YOU?
THAT'S NOT...
PEOPLE ARE JUST...
WOOOOSSH!
VEEEEETT!
PEOPLE ARE JUST WHAT, SISTER?
YOU AND I ARE THE MOST POWERFUL BEINGS ON THIS PLANET-- MILLENNIA PAST THEM.
WE MUST LEAD OUR BRUTISH ANCESTORS IN REVOLT AGAINST THEIR WOULD-BE OPPRESSORS.
YOU WILL HAVE TO TAKE A SIDE...

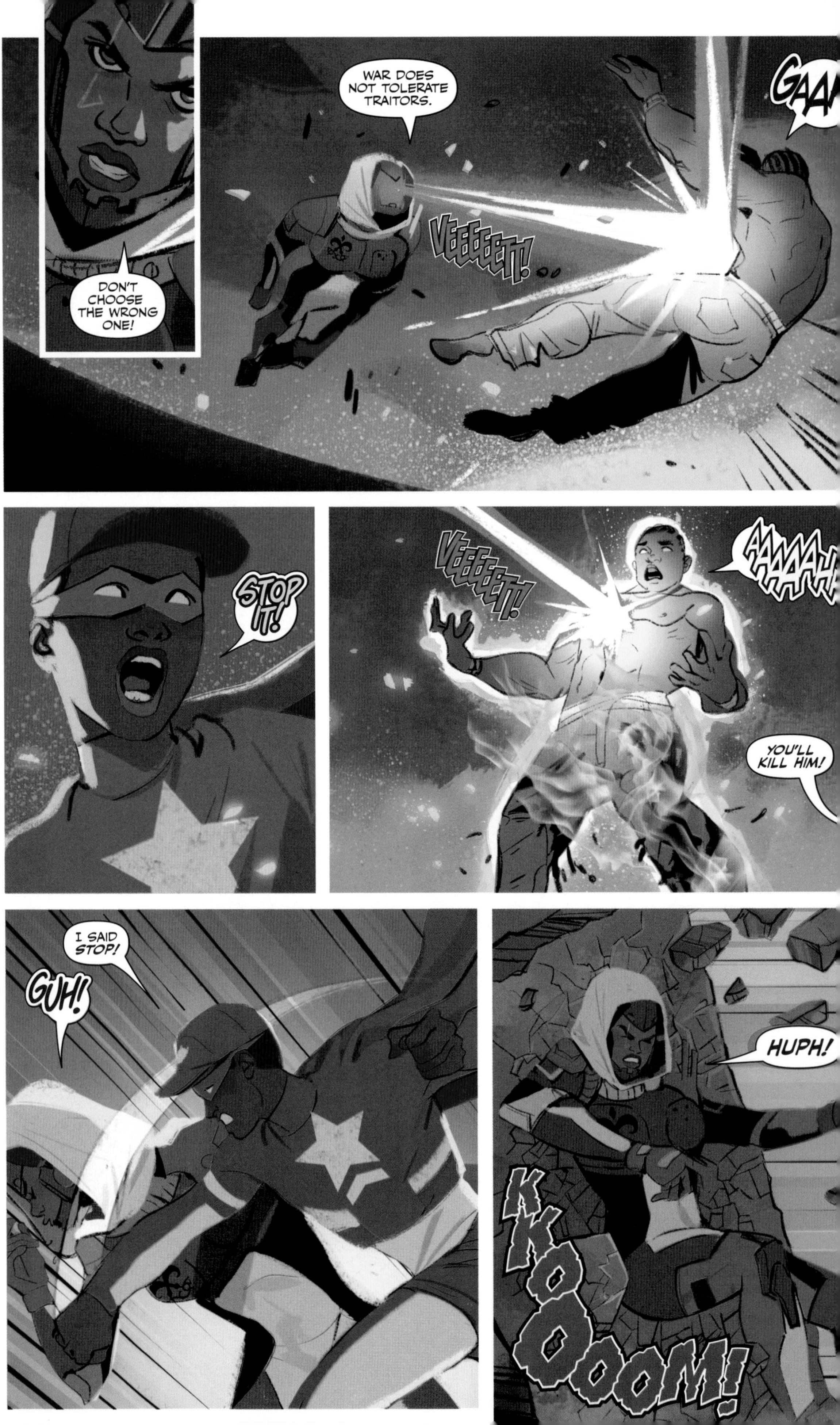
DON'T CHOOSE THE WRONG ONE!
WAR DOES NOT TOLERATE TRAITORS.
VEEEEEETT!
GAA
STOP IT!
VEEEEEETT!
AAAAAH!
YOU'LL KILL HIM!
I SAID STOP!
GUH!
HUPH!
KKOOOOM!

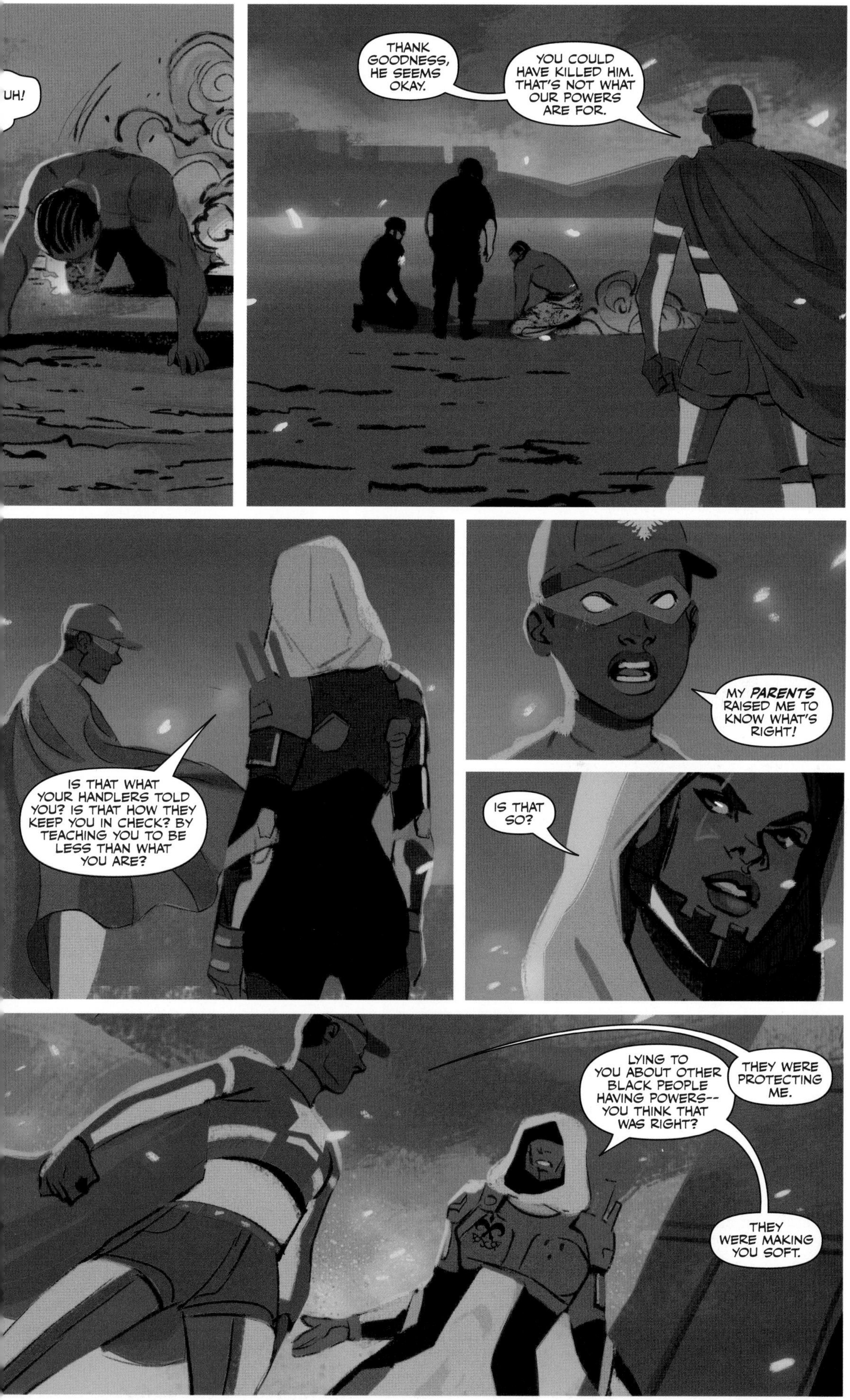

UH!
THANK GOODNESS, HE SEEMS OKAY.
YOU COULD HAVE KILLED HIM. THAT'S NOT WHAT OUR POWERS ARE FOR.
IS THAT WHAT YOUR HANDLERS TOLD YOU? IS THAT HOW THEY KEEP YOU IN CHECK? BY TEACHING YOU TO BE LESS THAN WHAT YOU ARE?
MY ***PARENTS*** RAISED ME TO KNOW WHAT'S RIGHT!
IS THAT SO?
LYING TO YOU ABOUT OTHER BLACK PEOPLE HAVING POWERS--YOU THINK THAT WAS RIGHT?
THEY WERE PROTECTING ME.
THEY WERE MAKING YOU SOFT.

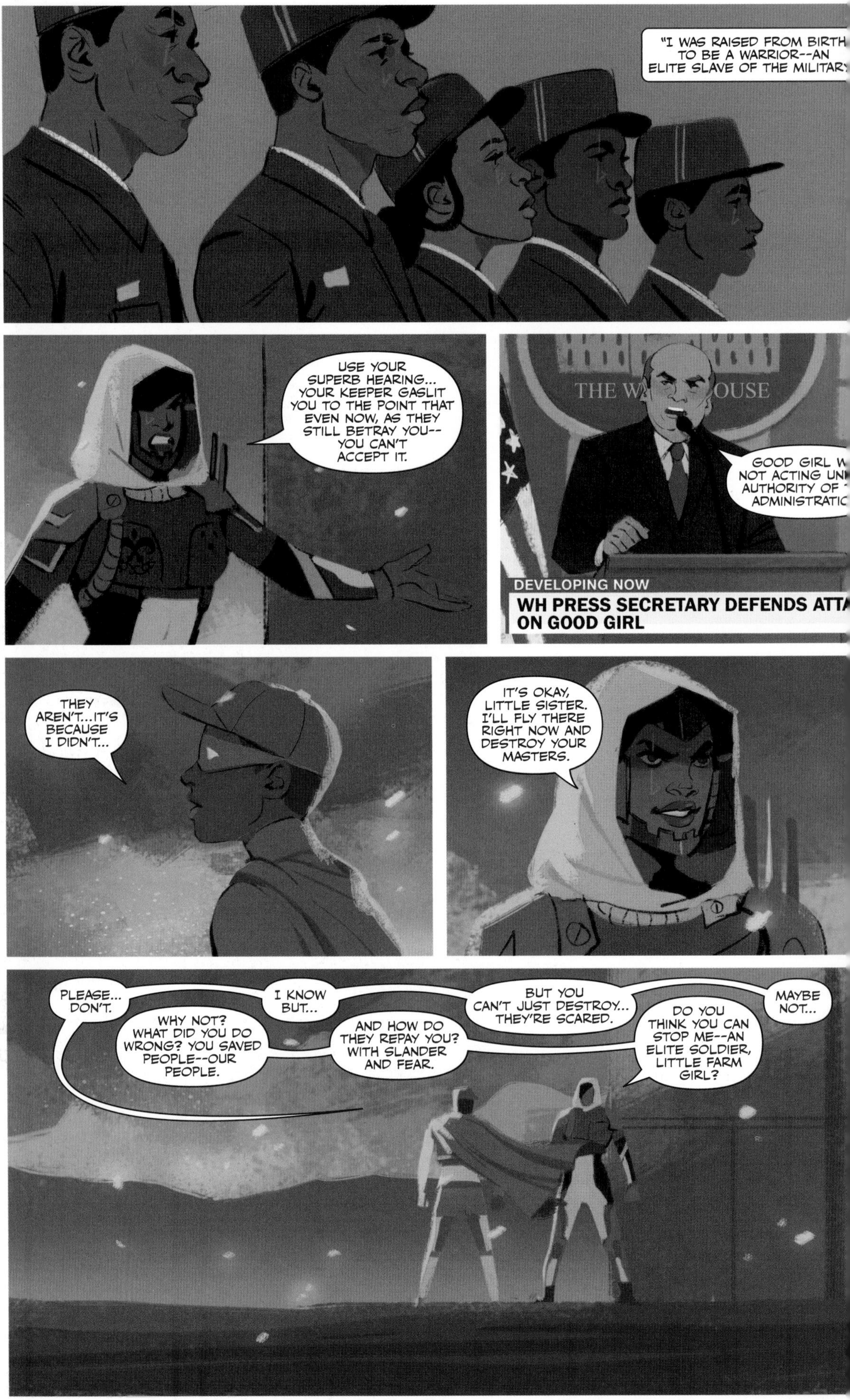
"I WAS RAISED FROM BIRTH TO BE A WARRIOR--AN ELITE SLAVE OF THE MILITARY
USE YOUR SUPERB HEARING... YOUR KEEPER GASLIT YOU TO THE POINT THAT EVEN NOW, AS THEY STILL BETRAY YOU--YOU CAN'T ACCEPT IT.
THE WHITE HOUSE
GOOD GIRL W NOT ACTING UN AUTHORITY OF ADMINISTRATIO
DEVELOPING NOW
WH PRESS SECRETARY DEFENDS ATTA ON GOOD GIRL
THEY AREN'T...IT'S BECAUSE I DIDN'T...
IT'S OKAY, LITTLE SISTER. I'LL FLY THERE RIGHT NOW AND DESTROY YOUR MASTERS.
PLEASE... DON'T.
WHY NOT? WHAT DID YOU DO WRONG? YOU SAVED PEOPLE--OUR PEOPLE.
I KNOW BUT...
AND HOW DO THEY REPAY YOU? WITH SLANDER AND FEAR.
BUT YOU CAN'T JUST DESTROY... THEY'RE SCARED.
DO YOU THINK YOU CAN STOP ME--AN ELITE SOLDIER, LITTLE FARM GIRL?
MAYBE NOT...

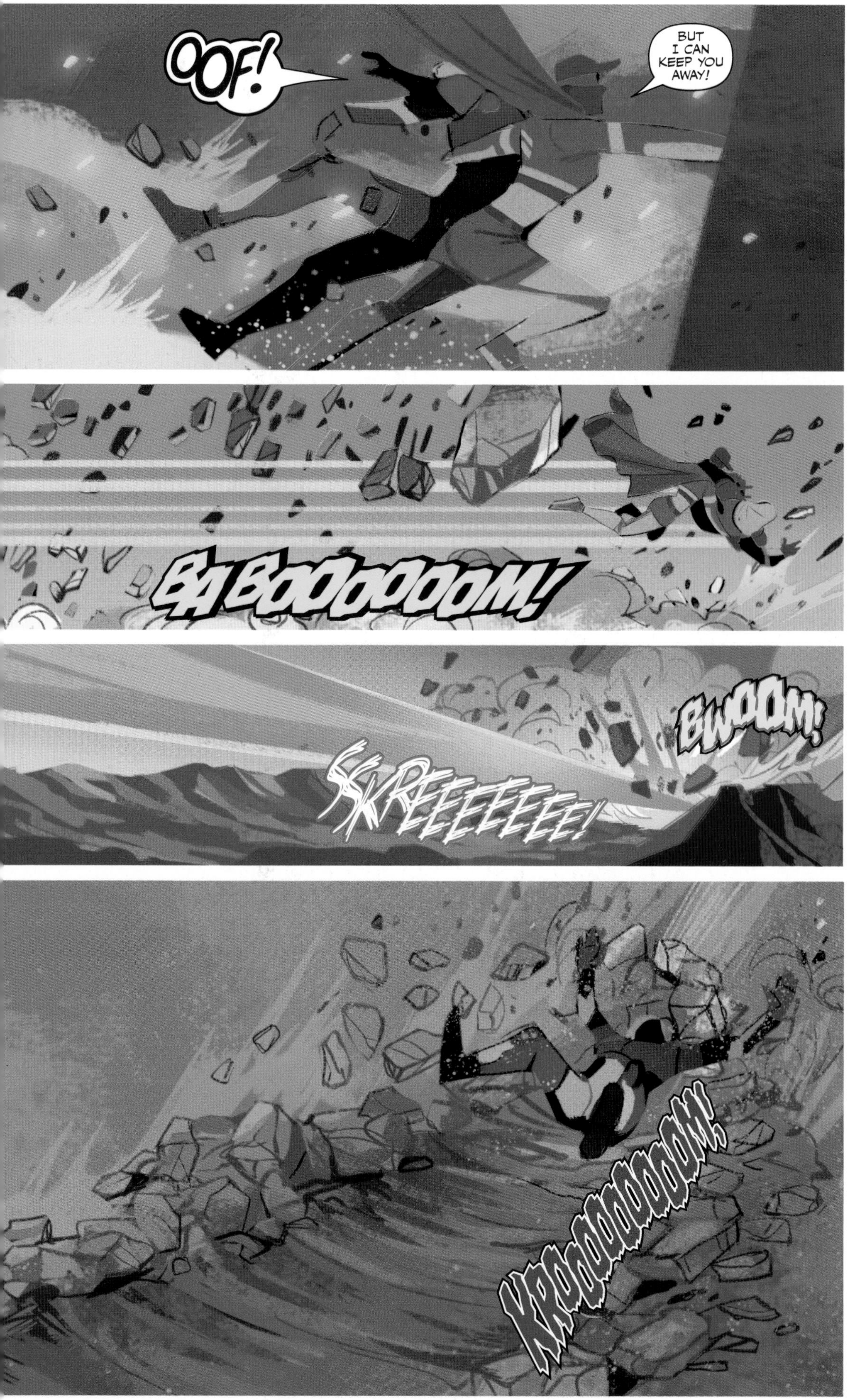
OOF!
BUT I CAN KEEP YOU AWAY!
BA BOOOOOOM!
BWOOM!
SKREEEEEEEEE!
KROOOOOOOOOM!

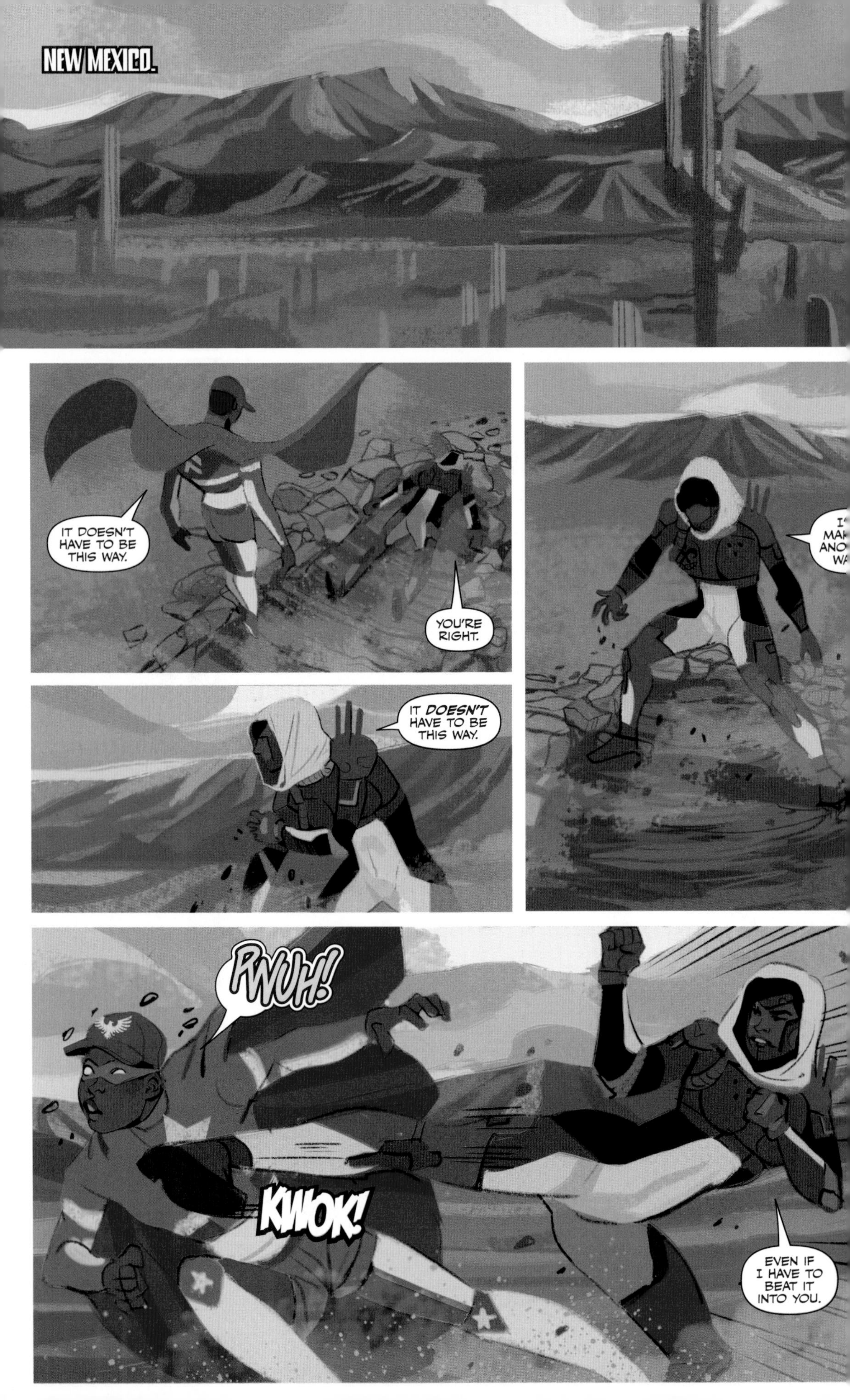
NEW MEXICO.
IT DOESN'T HAVE TO BE THIS WAY.
YOU'RE RIGHT.
IT *DOESN'T* HAVE TO BE THIS WAY.
RWUH!
KWOK!
EVEN IF I HAVE TO BEAT IT INTO YOU.

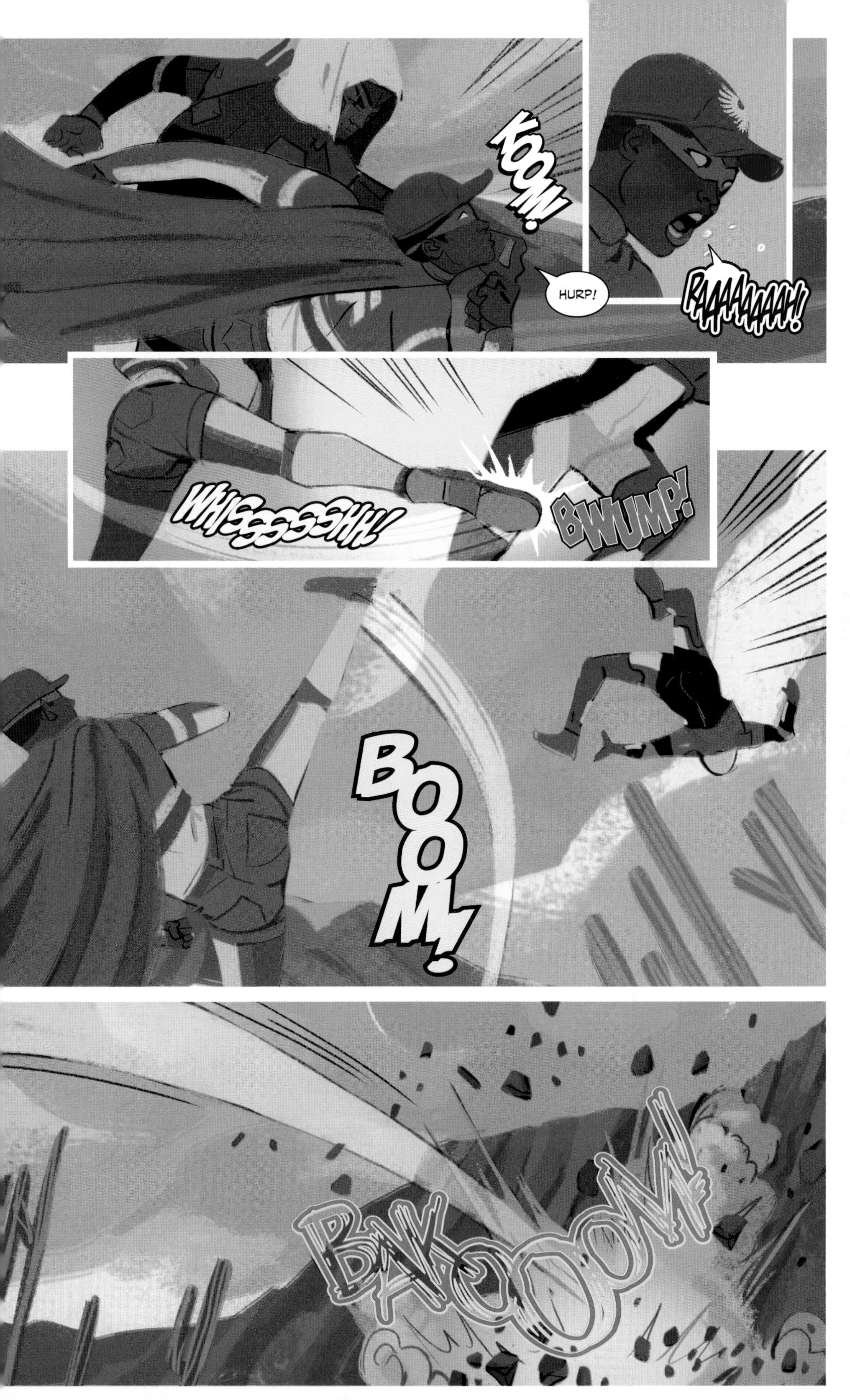
KOOM!
HURP!
RAAAAAAAAH!
WHISSSSSSHH!
BWUMP!
BOOOM!
BAKOOOM!

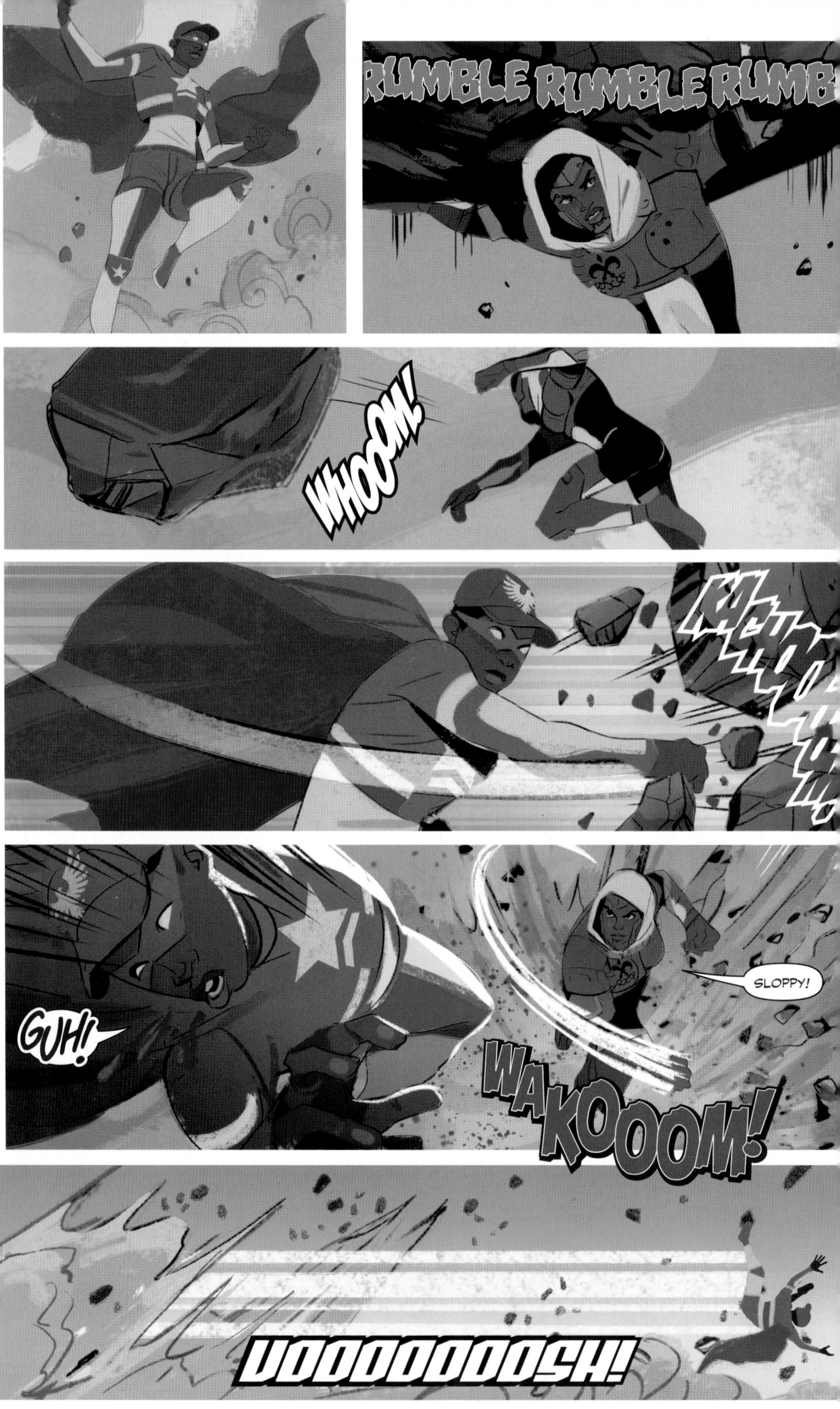
RUMBLE RUMBLE RUMB
WHOOOM!
SLOPPY!
GUH!
WAKOOOM!
VOOOOOOOSH!

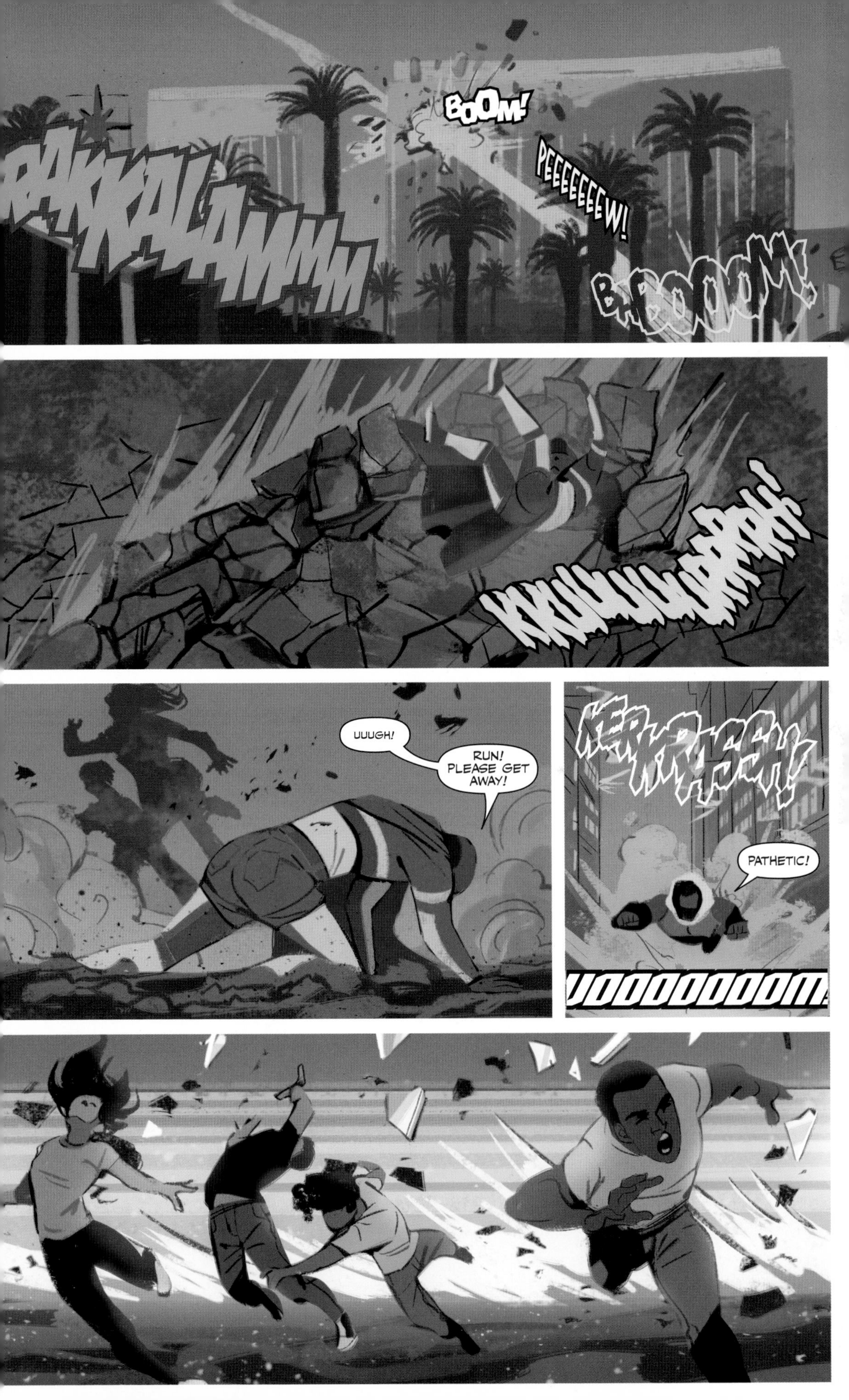
BOOM!
PEEEEEEEEW!
UUUGH!
RUN! PLEASE GET AWAY!
PATHETIC!

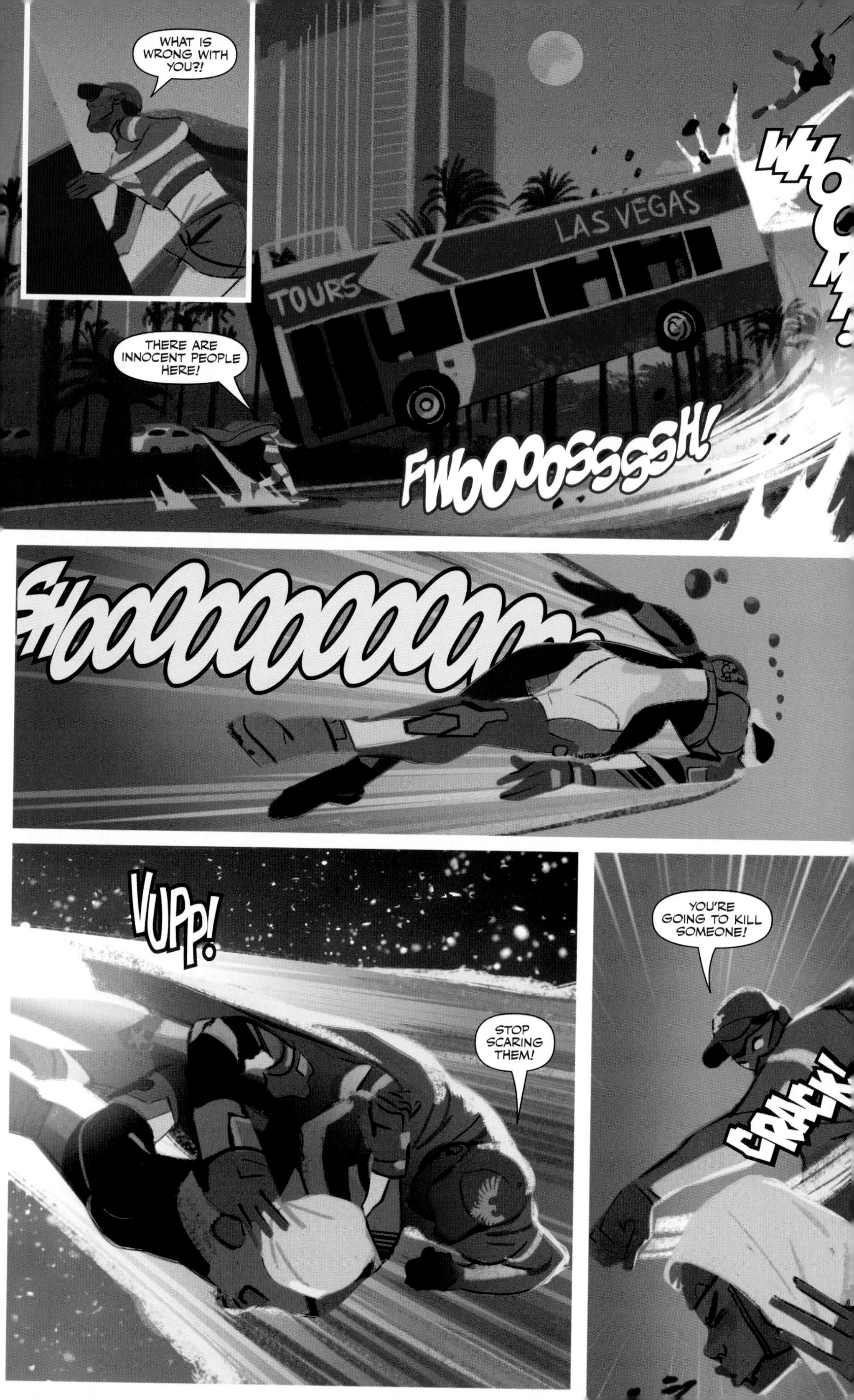
WHAT IS WRONG WITH YOU?!
LAS VEGAS
TOURS
THERE ARE INNOCENT PEOPLE HERE!
WHOOM!
FWOOOOSSSSSH!
SHOOOOOOOOOM
VUPP!
STOP SCARING THEM!
YOU'RE GOING TO KILL SOMEONE!
CRACK!

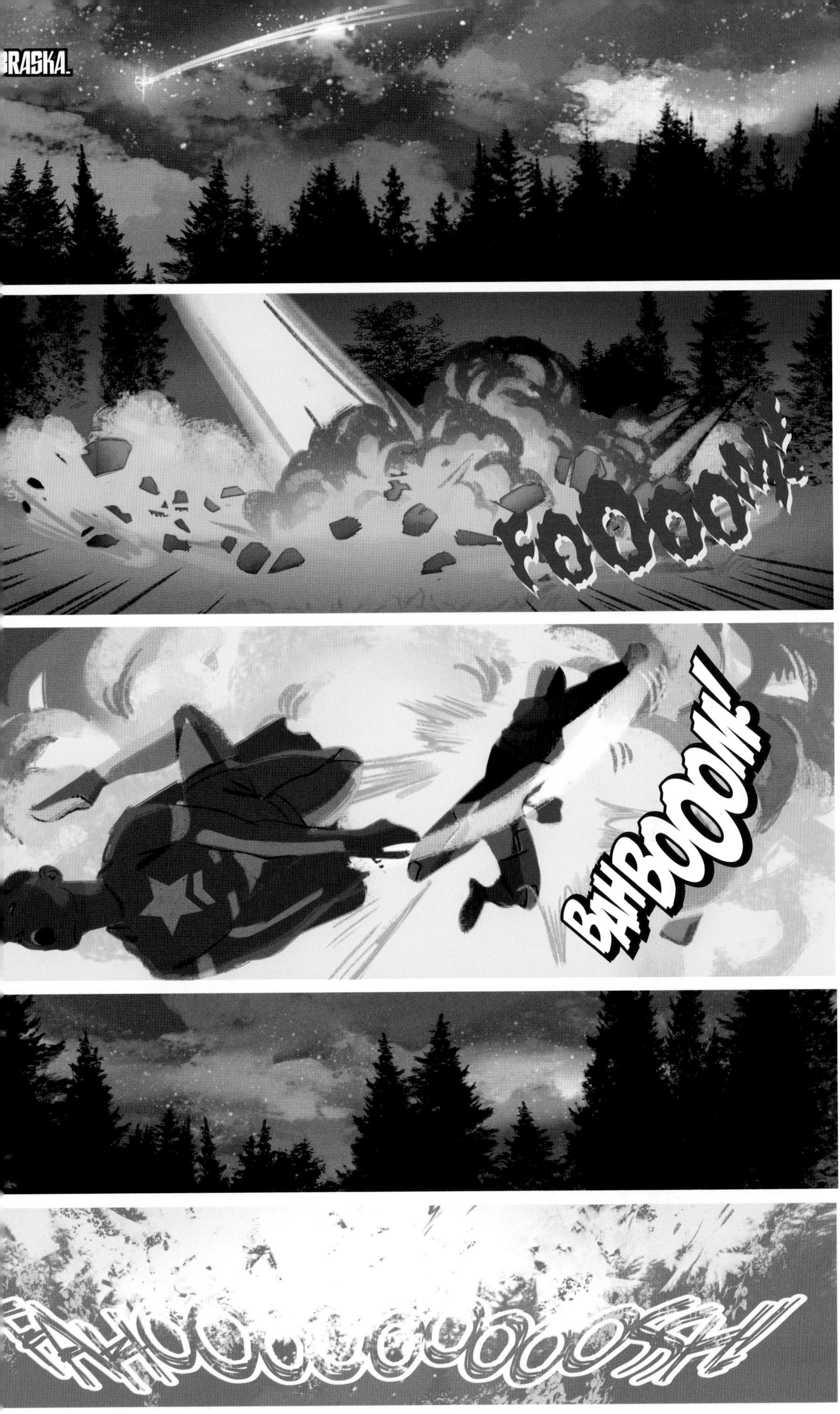
RASKA.
FOOOOOM!
BAHBOOOM!

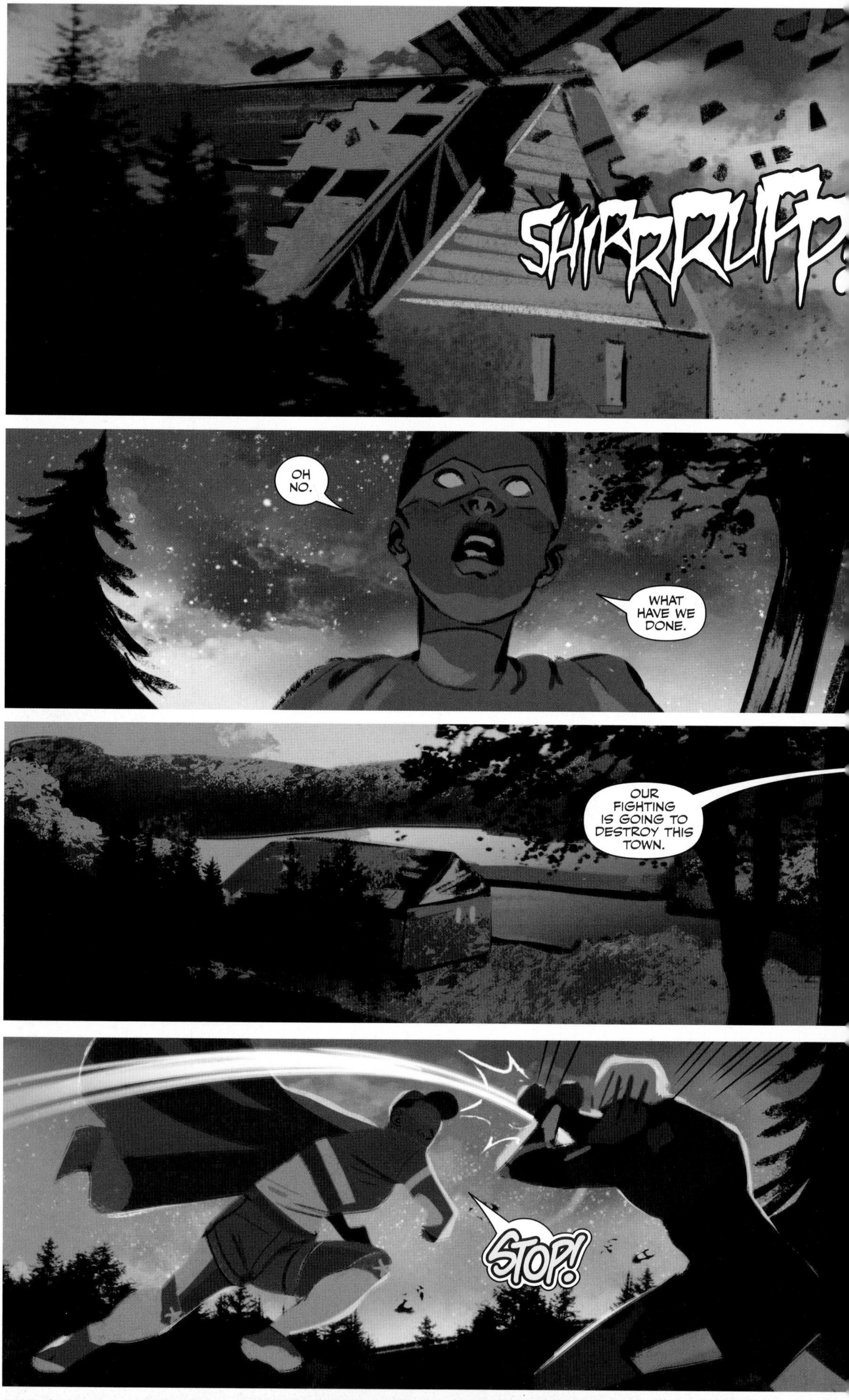
SHIRRRUFF
OH NO.
WHAT HAVE WE DONE.
OUR FIGHTING IS GOING TO DESTROY THIS TOWN.
STOP!

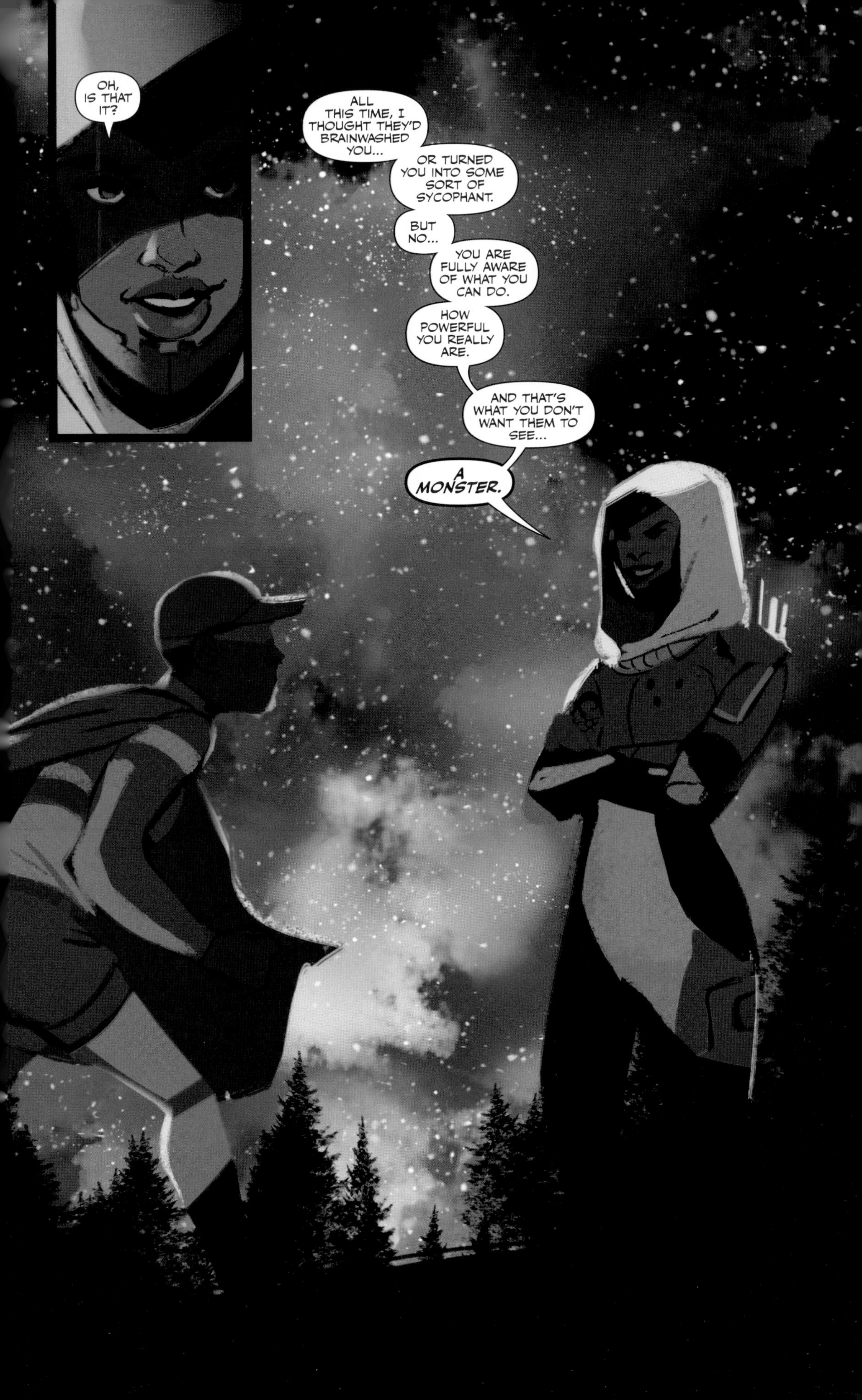
OH, IS THAT IT?
ALL THIS TIME, I THOUGHT THEY'D BRAINWASHED YOU...
OR TURNED YOU INTO SOME SORT OF SYCOPHANT.
BUT NO...
YOU ARE FULLY AWARE OF WHAT YOU CAN DO.
HOW POWERFUL YOU REALLY ARE.
AND THAT'S WHAT YOU DON'T WANT THEM TO SEE...
A MONSTER.

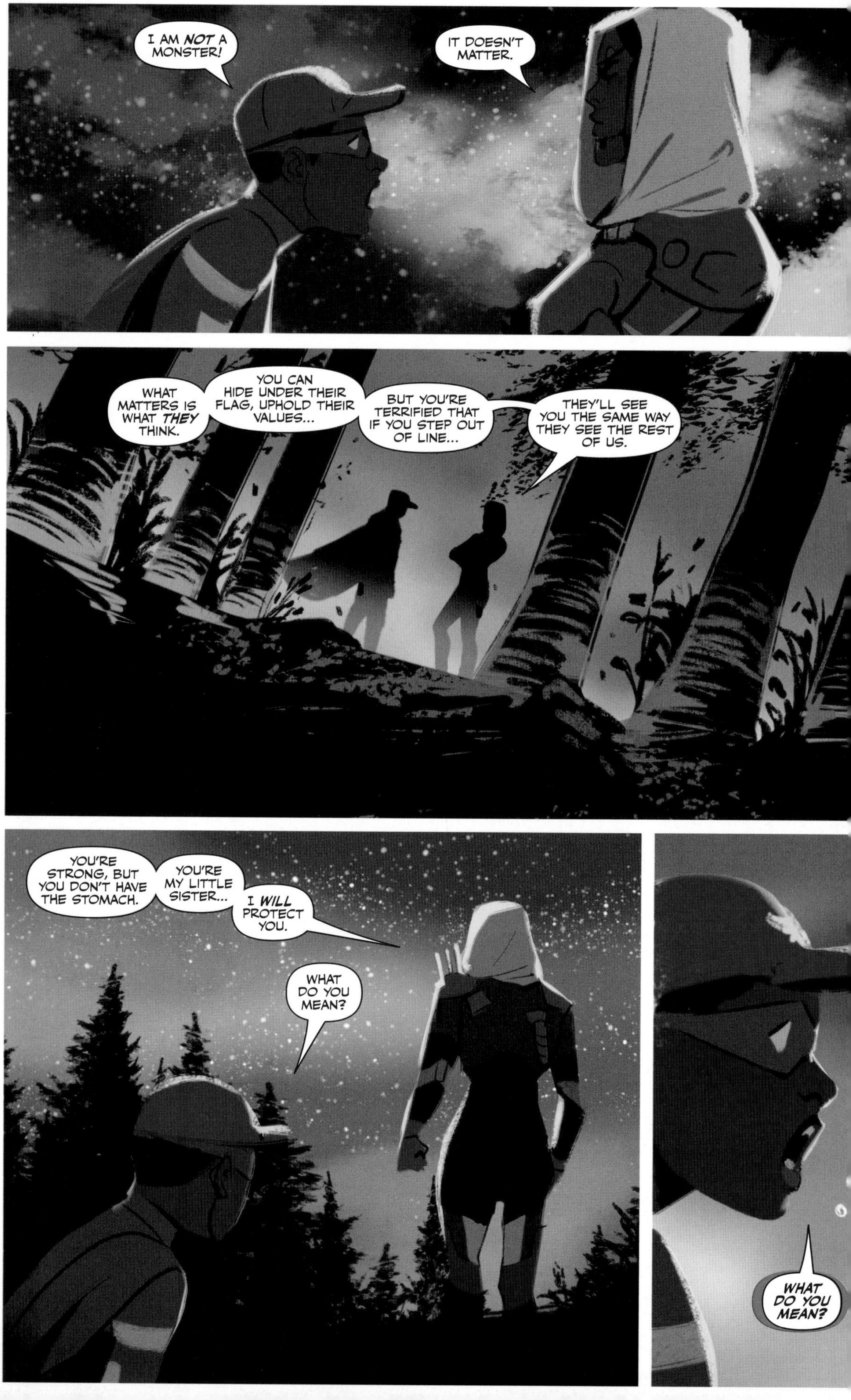
I AM *NOT* A MONSTER!
IT DOESN'T MATTER.
WHAT MATTERS IS WHAT *THEY* THINK.
YOU CAN HIDE UNDER THEIR FLAG, UPHOLD THEIR VALUES...
BUT YOU'RE TERRIFIED THAT IF YOU STEP OUT OF LINE...
THEY'LL SEE YOU THE SAME WAY THEY SEE THE REST OF US.
YOU'RE STRONG, BUT YOU DON'T HAVE THE STOMACH.
YOU'RE MY LITTLE SISTER...
I *WILL* PROTECT YOU.
WHAT DO YOU MEAN?
WHAT DO YOU MEAN?

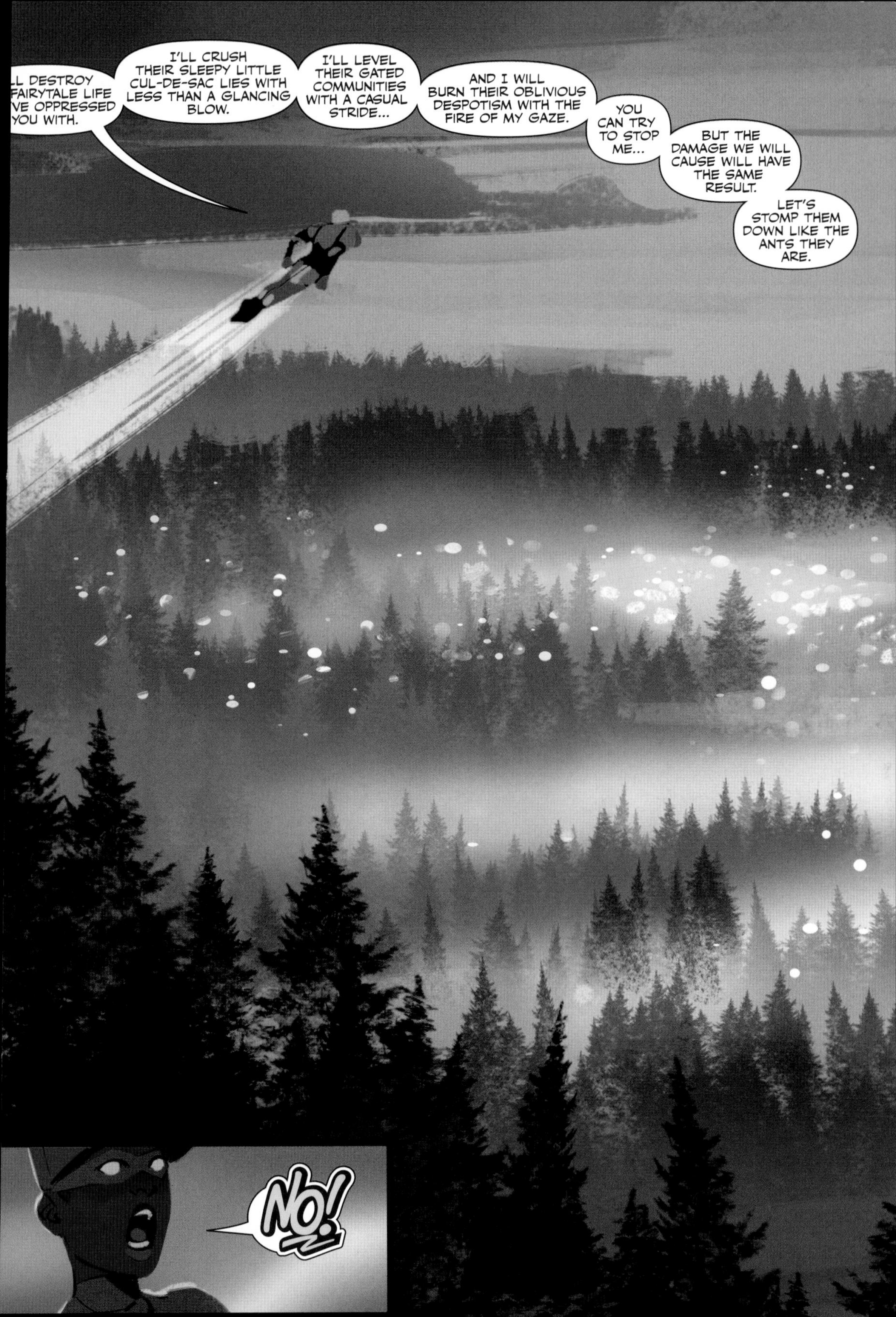
LL DESTROY FAIRYTALE LIFE VE OPPRESSED YOU WITH.
I'LL CRUSH THEIR SLEEPY LITTLE CUL-DE-SAC LIES WITH LESS THAN A GLANCING BLOW.
I'LL LEVEL THEIR GATED COMMUNITIES WITH A CASUAL STRIDE...
AND I WILL BURN THEIR OBLIVIOUS DESPOTISM WITH THE FIRE OF MY GAZE.
YOU CAN TRY TO STOP ME...
BUT THE DAMAGE WE WILL CAUSE WILL HAVE THE SAME RESULT.
LET'S STOMP THEM DOWN LIKE THE ANTS THEY ARE.
NO!

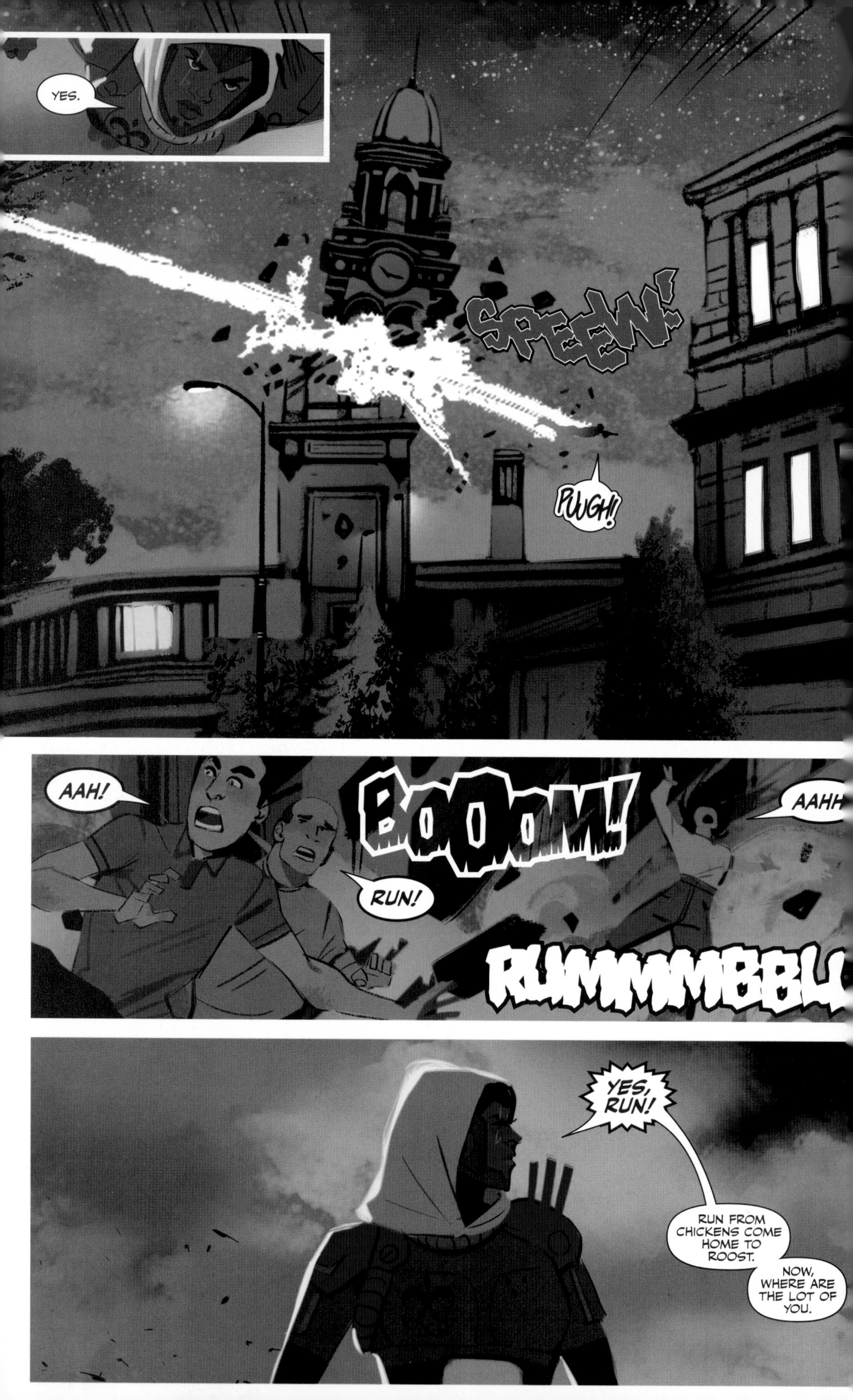
YES.
SPEEW!
PUUGH!
AAH!
BOOOM!
RUN!
AAHH
RUMMMBBL
YES, RUN!
RUN FROM CHICKENS COME HOME TO ROOST.
NOW, WHERE ARE THE LOT OF YOU.

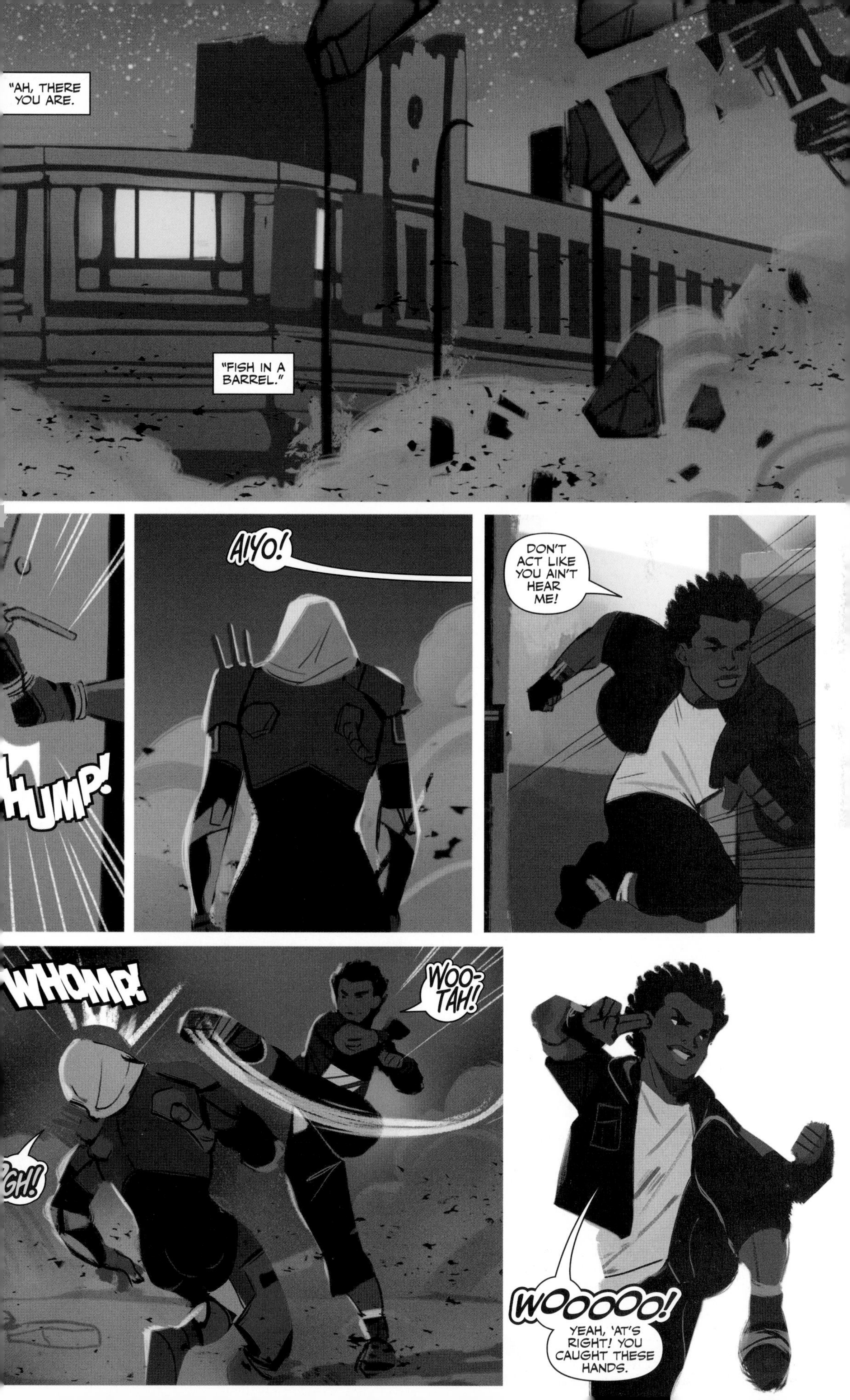
"AH, THERE YOU ARE.
"FISH IN A BARREL."
HUMP!
AIYO!
DON'T ACT LIKE YOU AIN'T HEAR ME!
WHOMP!
WOO-TAH!
GH!
WOOOOO!
YEAH, 'AT'S RIGHT! YOU CAUGHT THESE HANDS.

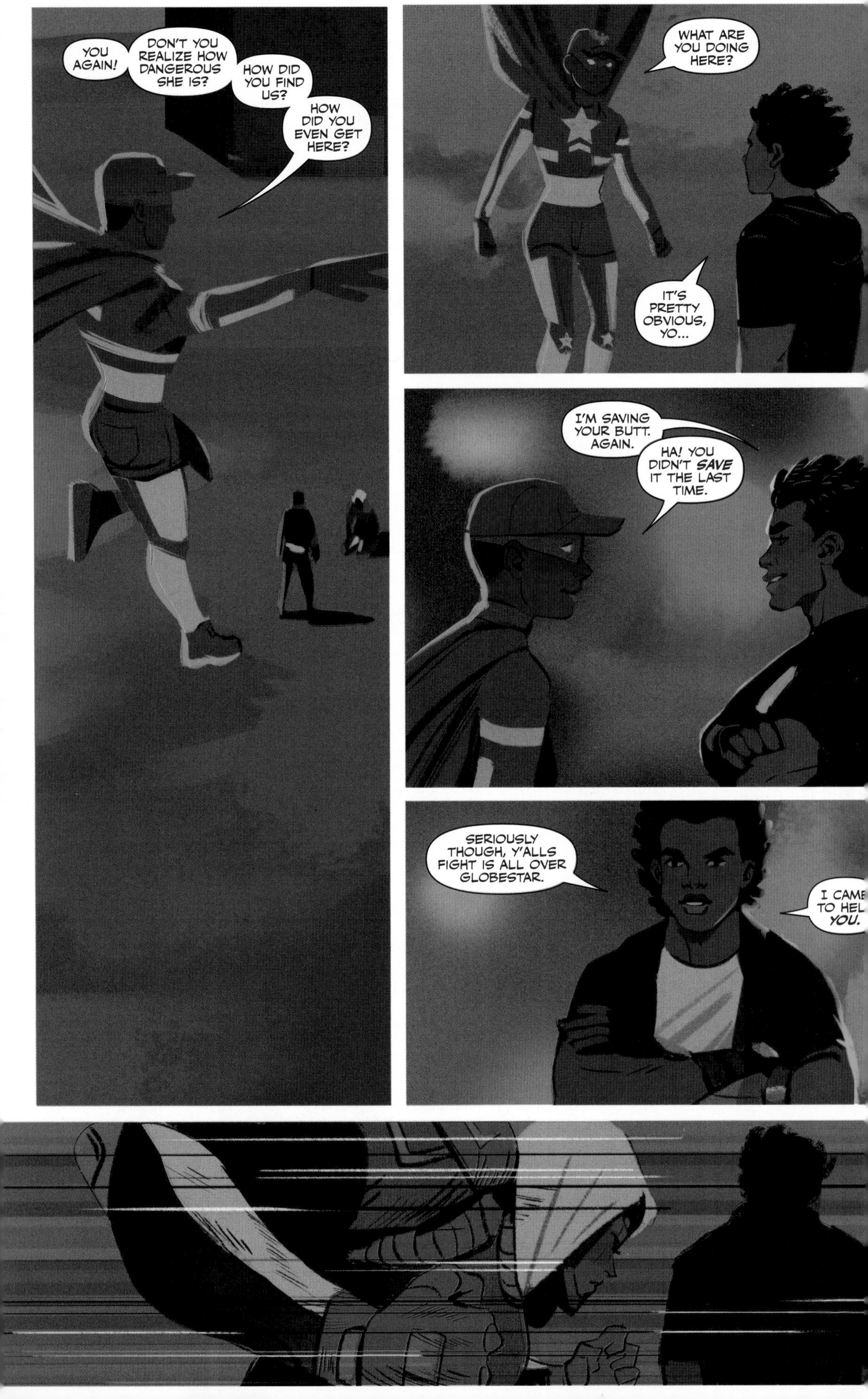

YOU AGAIN!
DON'T YOU REALIZE HOW DANGEROUS SHE IS?
HOW DID YOU FIND US?
HOW DID YOU EVEN GET HERE?
WHAT ARE YOU DOING HERE?
IT'S PRETTY OBVIOUS, YO...
I'M SAVING YOUR BUTT. AGAIN.
HA! YOU DIDN'T ***SAVE*** IT THE LAST TIME.
SERIOUSLY THOUGH, Y'ALLS FIGHT IS ALL OVER GLOBESTAR.
I CAME TO HEL ***YOU.***

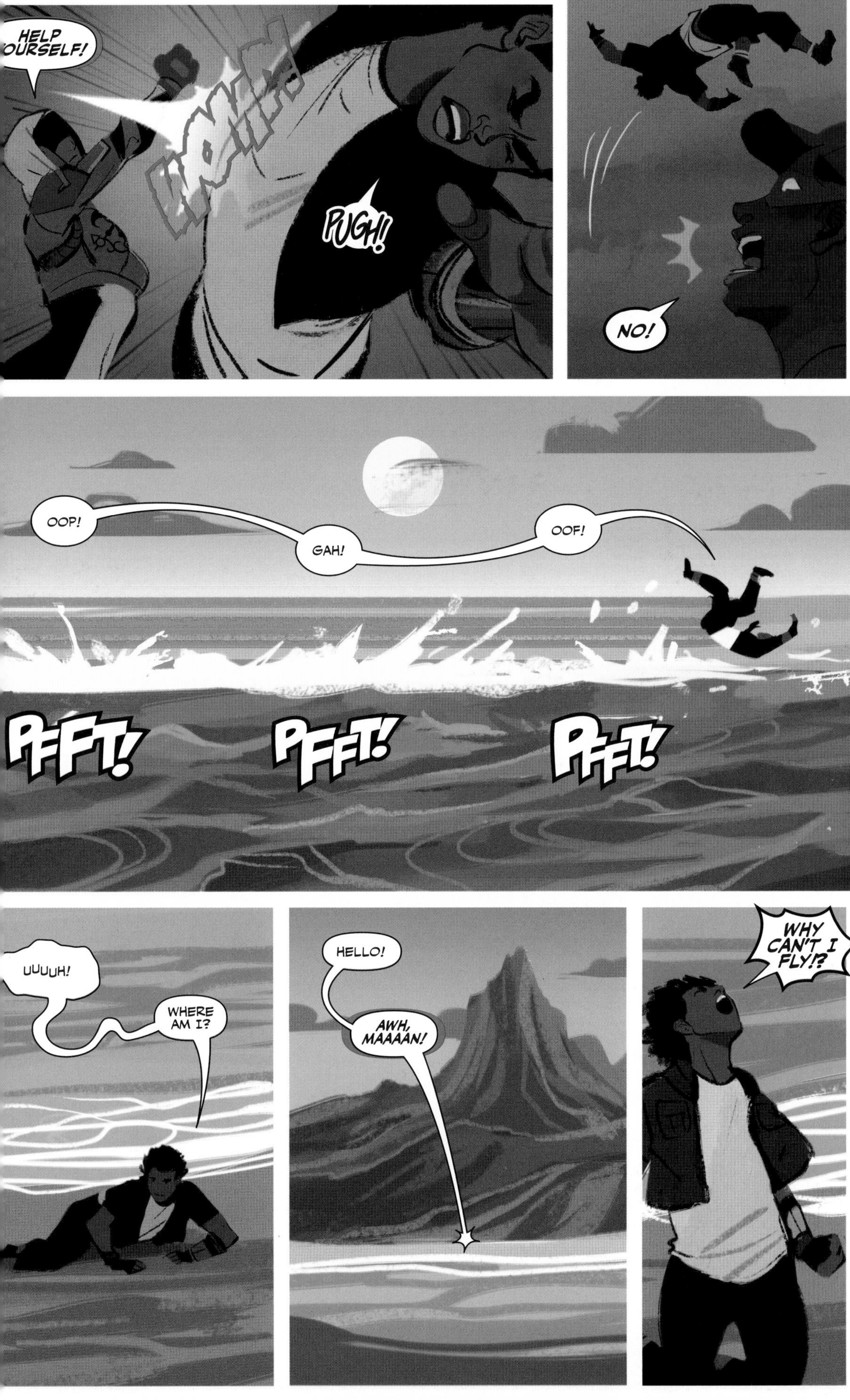

HELP YOURSELF!
PUGH!
NO!
OOP!
GAH!
OOF!
PFFT!
PFFT!
PFFT!
UUUUH!
WHERE AM I?
HELLO!
AWH, MAAAAN!
WHY CAN'T I FLY!?

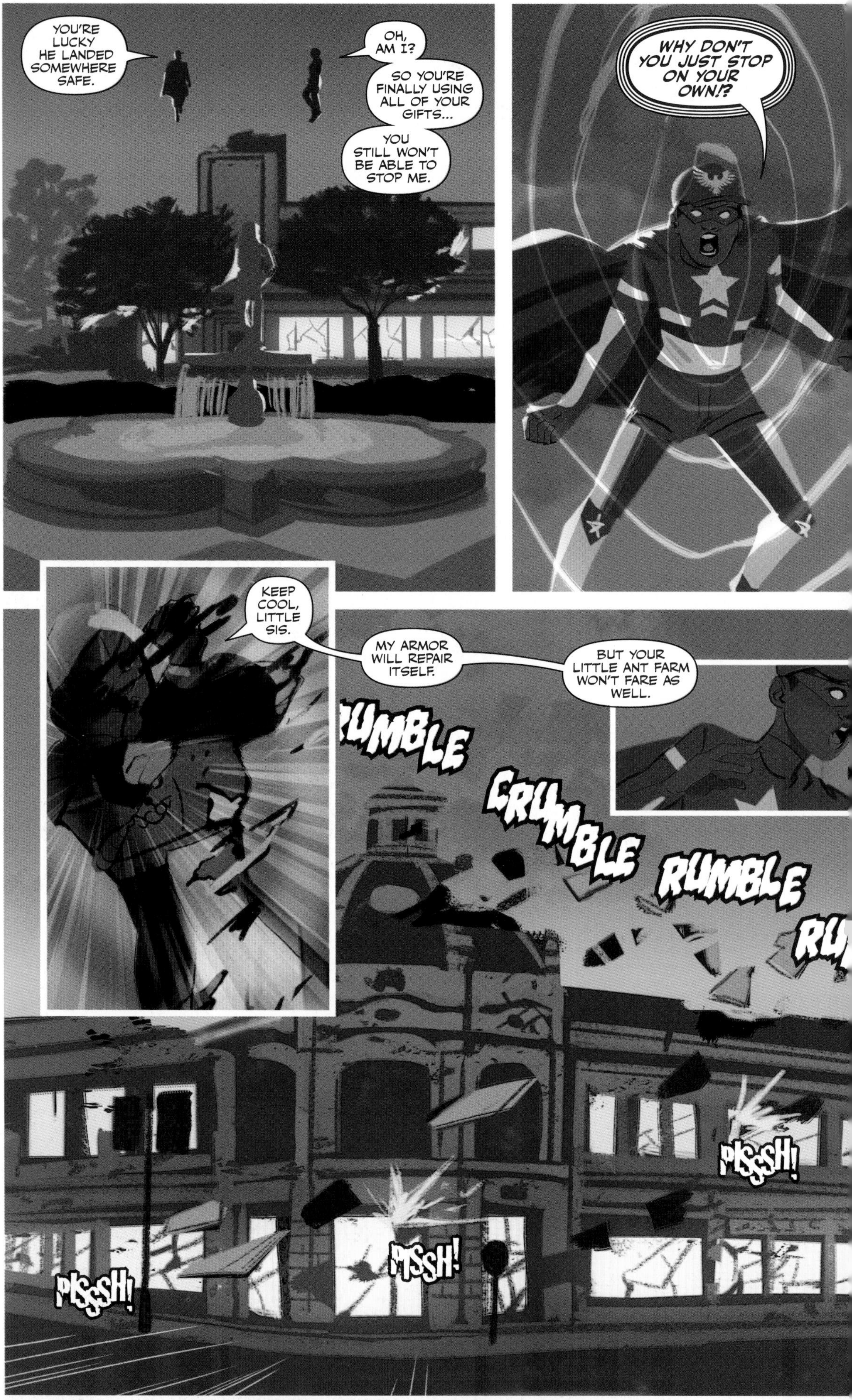
YOU'RE LUCKY HE LANDED SOMEWHERE SAFE.
OH, AM I?
SO YOU'RE FINALLY USING ALL OF YOUR GIFTS...
YOU STILL WON'T BE ABLE TO STOP ME.
WHY DON'T YOU JUST STOP ON YOUR OWN!?
KEEP COOL, LITTLE SIS.
MY ARMOR WILL REPAIR ITSELF.
BUT YOUR LITTLE ANT FARM WON'T FARE AS WELL.
RUMBLE
CRUMBLE
RUMBLE
PISSSH!
PISSH!
PISSSH!

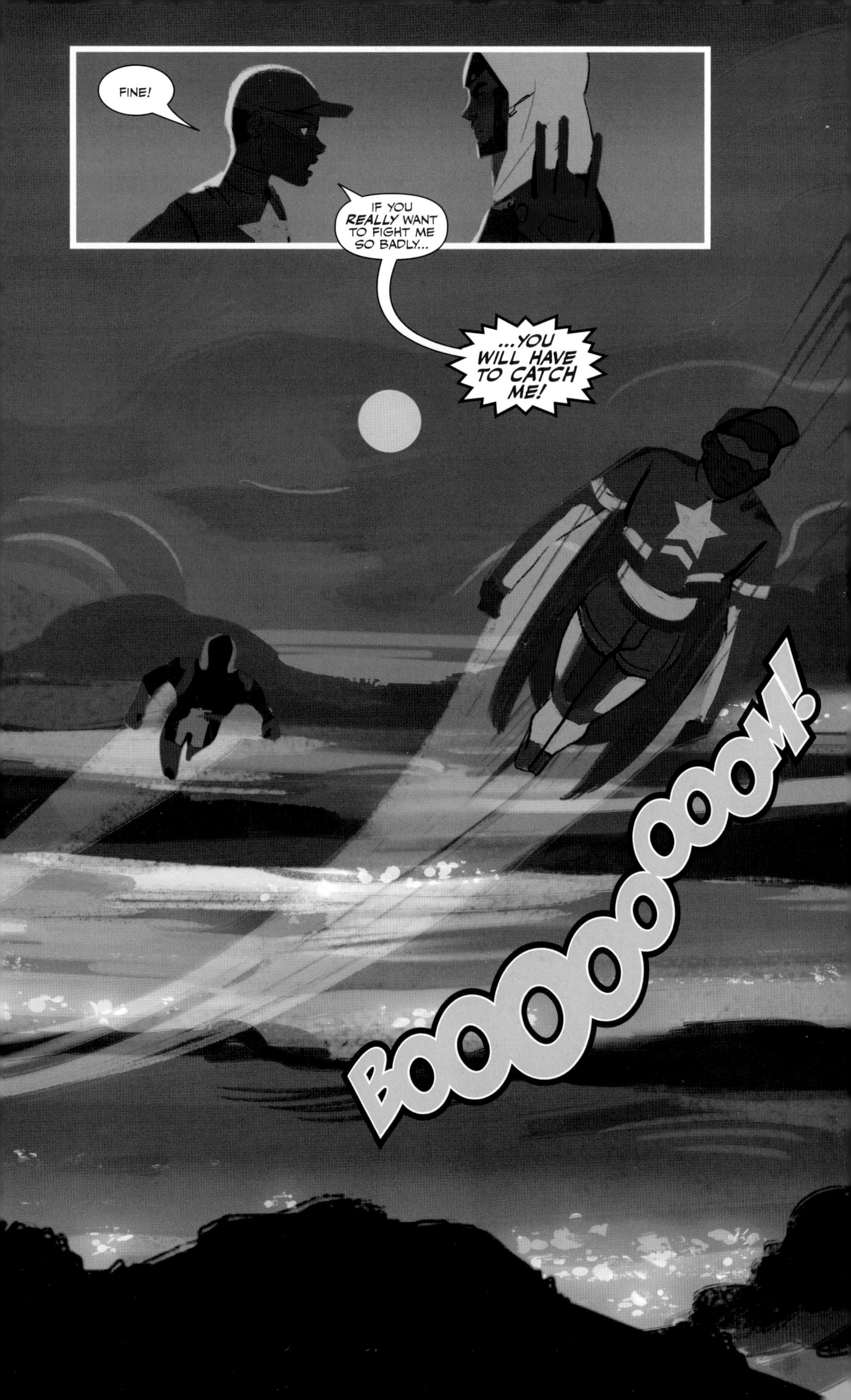
FINE!
IF YOU REALLY WANT TO FIGHT ME SO BADLY...
...YOU WILL HAVE TO CATCH ME!
BOOOOOOOOM!

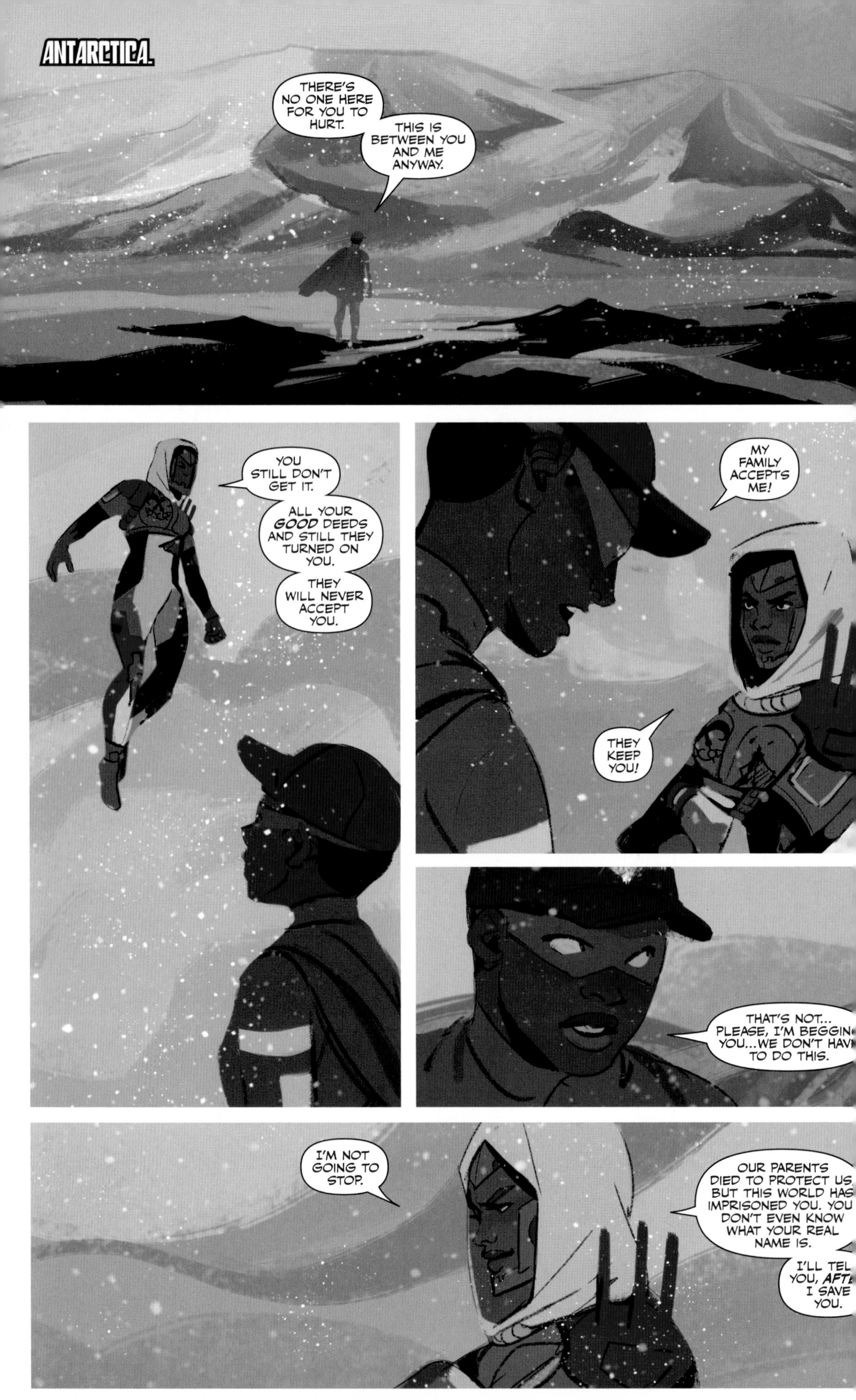
ANTARCTICA.
THERE'S NO ONE HERE FOR YOU TO HURT.
THIS IS BETWEEN YOU AND ME ANYWAY.
YOU STILL DON'T GET IT.
ALL YOUR GOOD DEEDS AND STILL THEY TURNED ON YOU.
THEY WILL NEVER ACCEPT YOU.
MY FAMILY ACCEPTS ME!
THEY KEEP YOU!
THAT'S NOT... PLEASE, I'M BEGGIN YOU...WE DON'T HAV TO DO THIS.
I'M NOT GOING TO STOP.
OUR PARENTS DIED TO PROTECT US BUT THIS WORLD HAS IMPRISONED YOU. YOU DON'T EVEN KNOW WHAT YOUR REAL NAME IS.
I'LL TEL YOU, AFT I SAVE YOU.

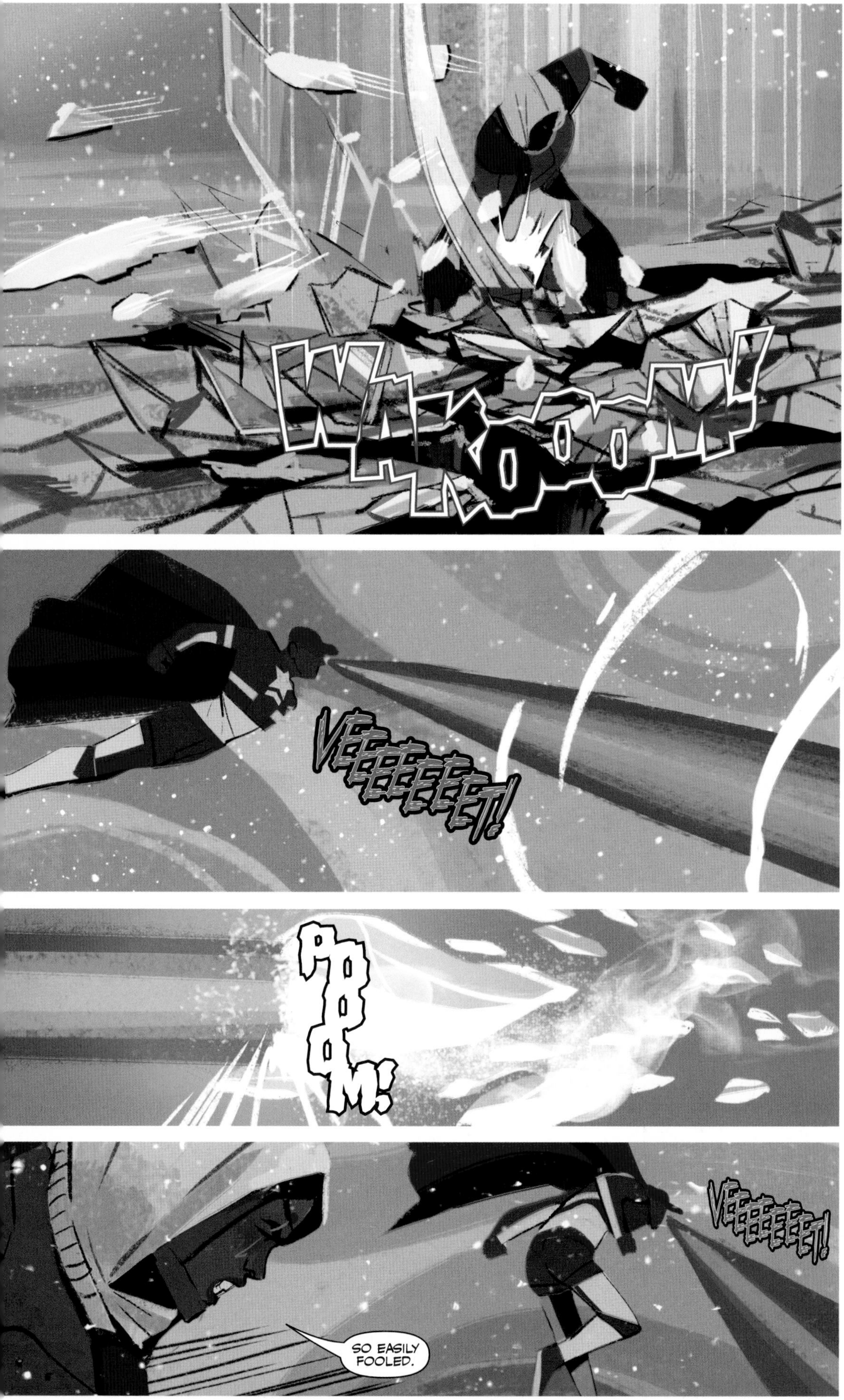
WAKOOOM!
VEEEEEEEEEET!
POOOM!
VEEEEEEEEET!
SO EASILY FOOLED.

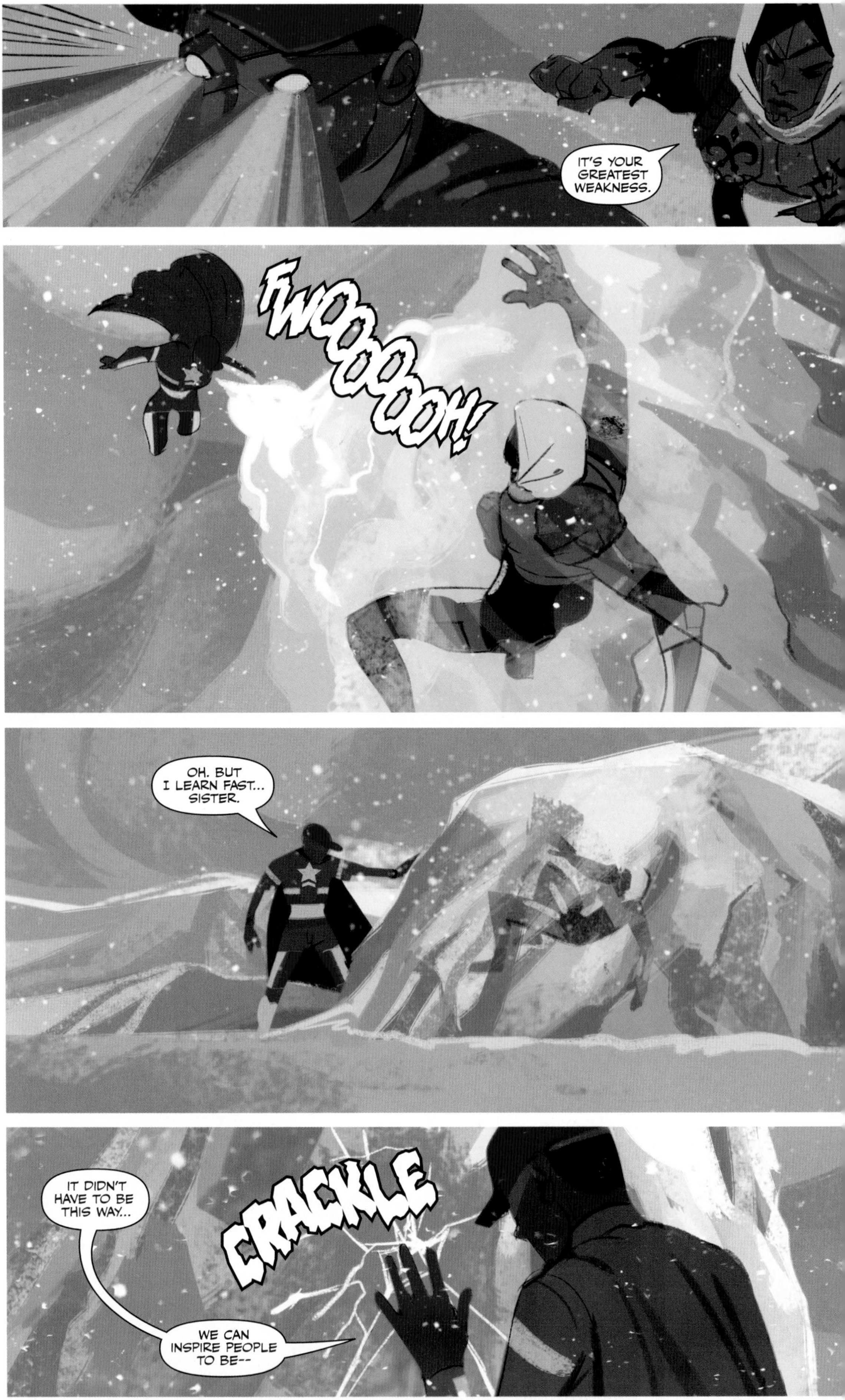
IT'S YOUR GREATEST WEAKNESS.
FWOOOOOOH!
OH. BUT I LEARN FAST... SISTER.
IT DIDN'T HAVE TO BE THIS WAY...
CRACKLE
WE CAN INSPIRE PEOPLE TO BE--

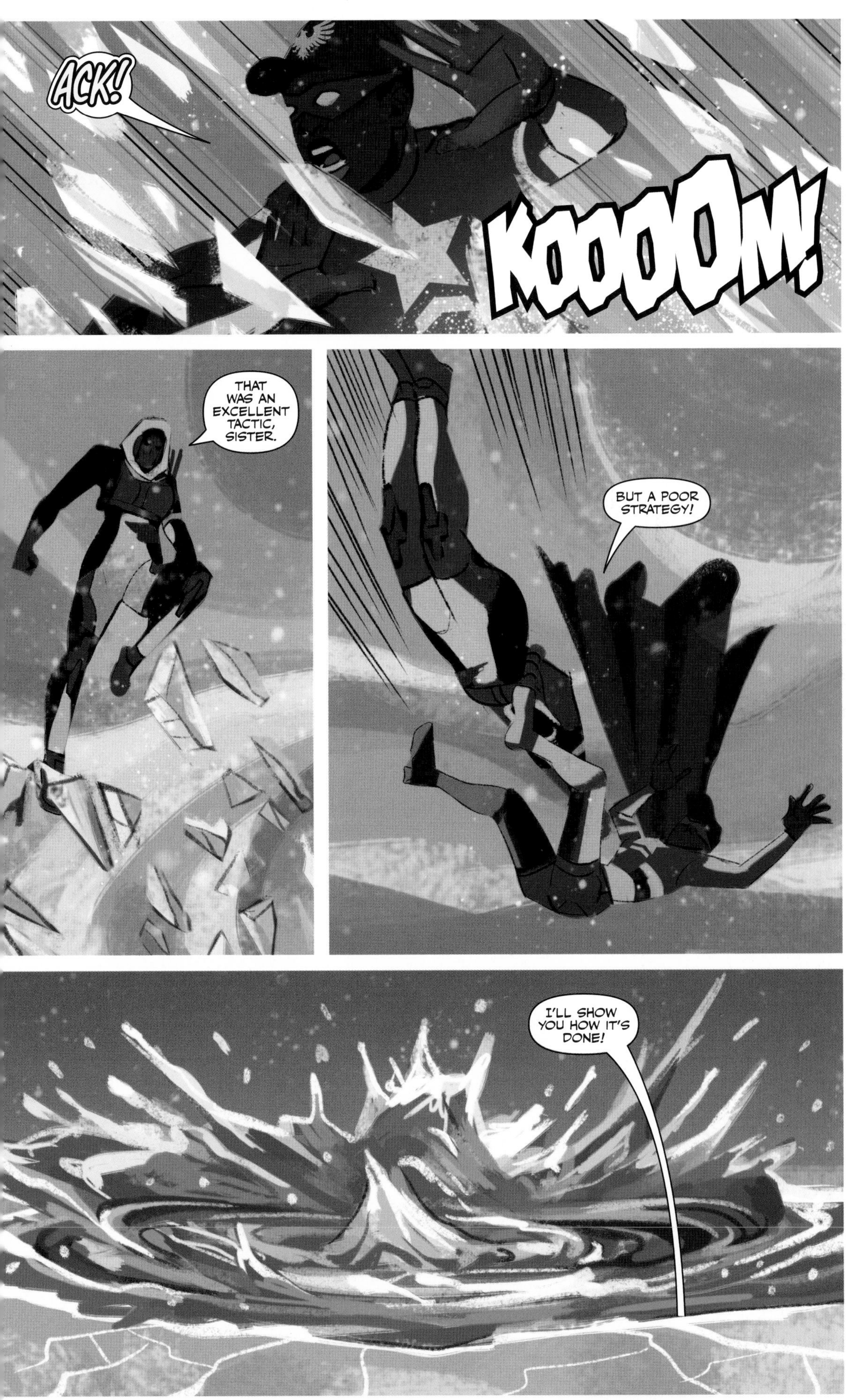
ACK!
KOOOOOM!
THAT WAS AN EXCELLENT TACTIC, SISTER.
BUT A POOR STRATEGY!
I'LL SHOW YOU HOW IT'S DONE!

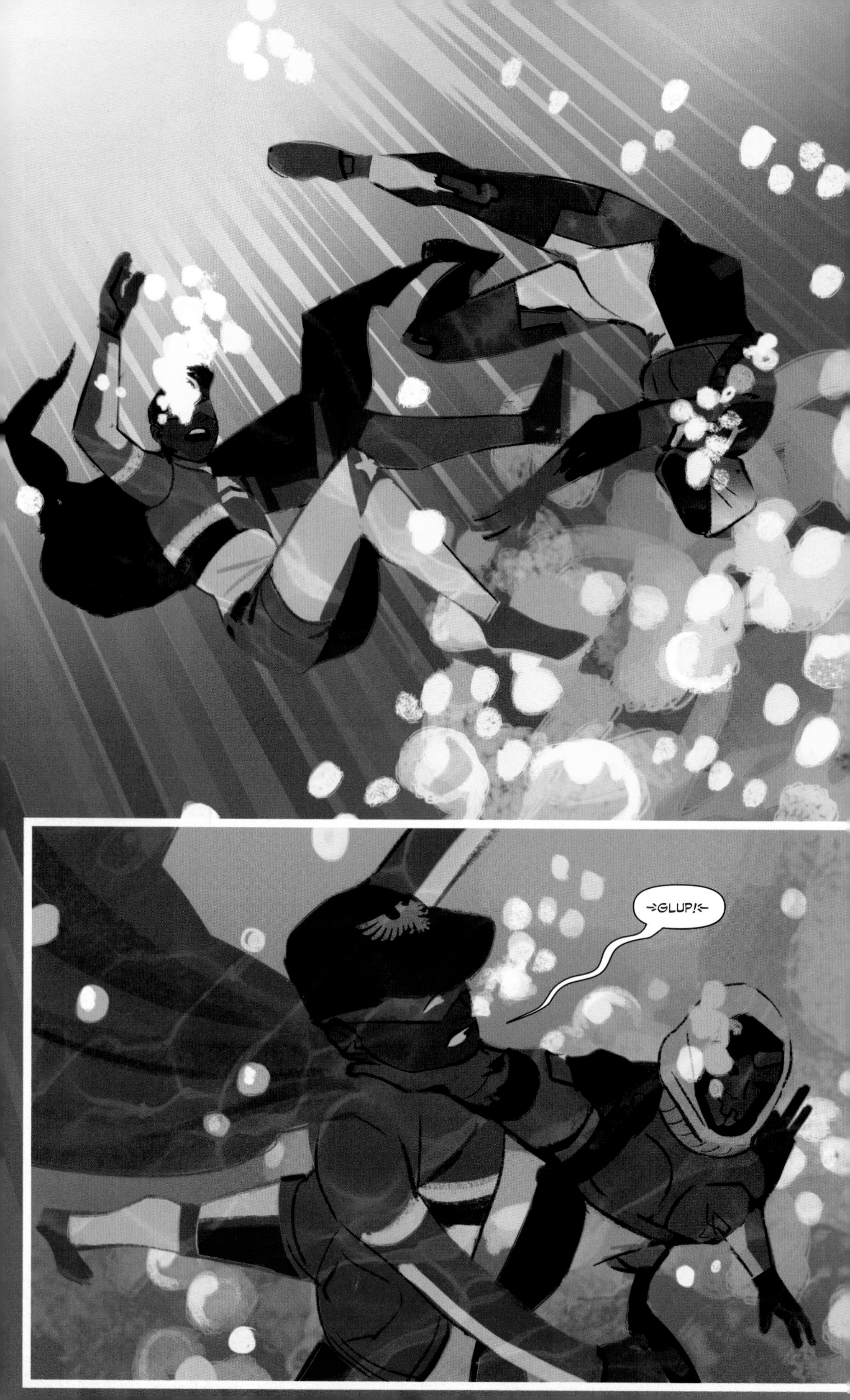
GLUP!

≥GURGLE!≤

WEEEEEET!.

VEEEEEEET!!

KOOOM!

WHUMP!

WHUMP!

WHUMP!

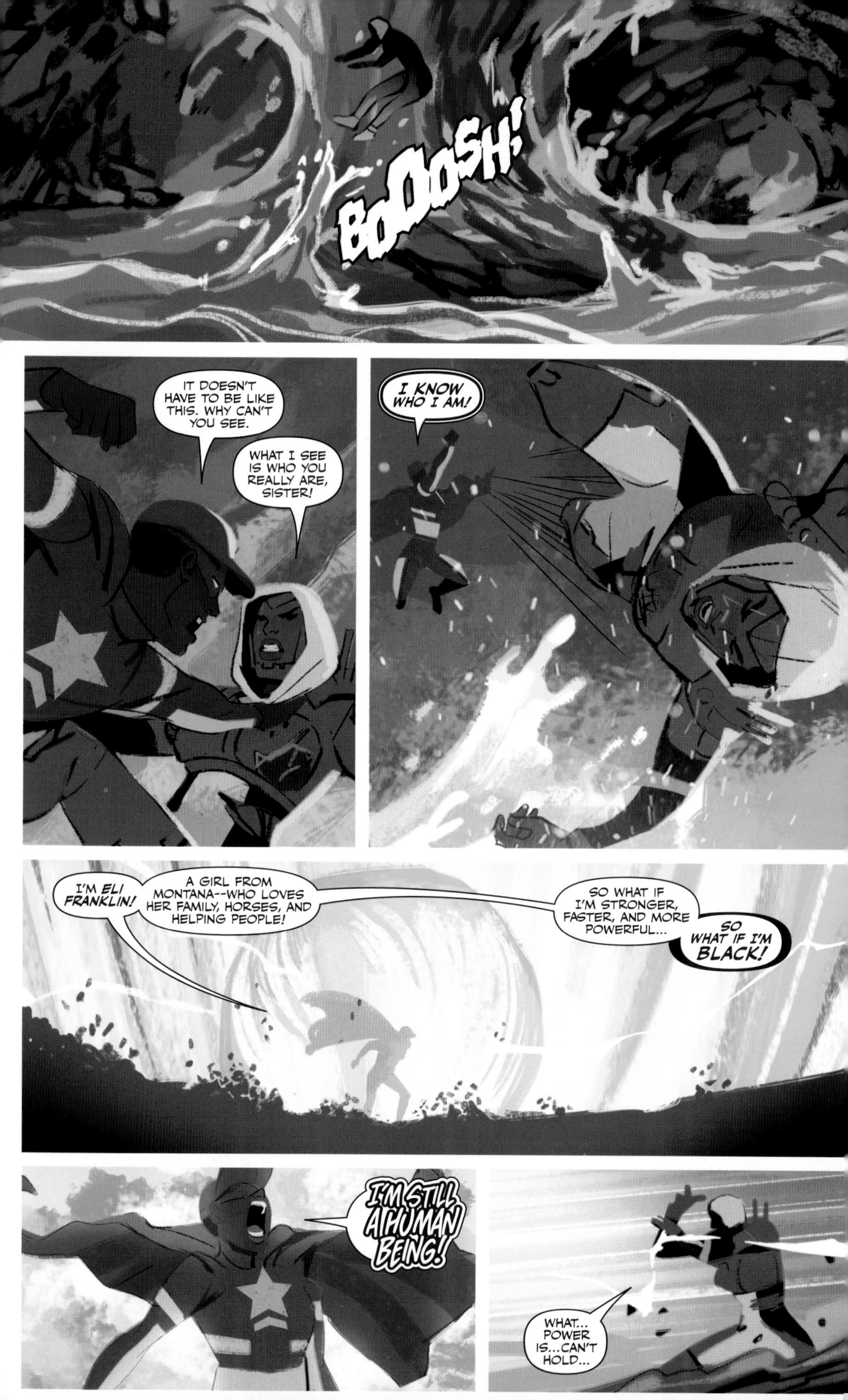
BOOOSH!
IT DOESN'T HAVE TO BE LIKE THIS. WHY CAN'T YOU SEE.
WHAT I SEE IS WHO YOU REALLY ARE, SISTER!
I KNOW WHO I AM!
I'M ELI FRANKLIN!
A GIRL FROM MONTANA--WHO LOVES HER FAMILY, HORSES, AND HELPING PEOPLE!
SO WHAT IF I'M STRONGER, FASTER, AND MORE POWERFUL...
SO WHAT IF I'M BLACK!
I'M STILL A HUMAN BEING!
WHAT... POWER IS...CAN'T HOLD...

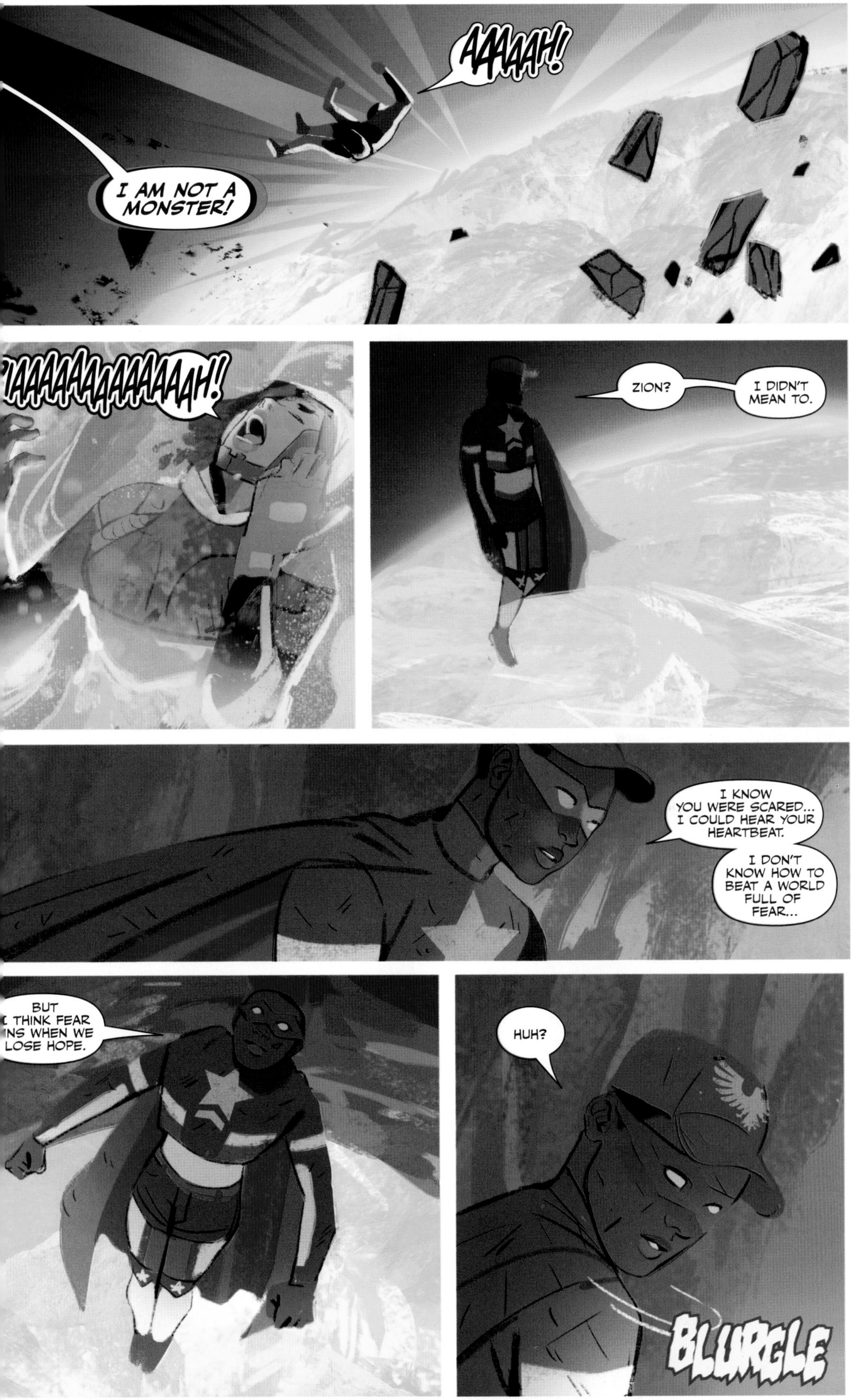
I AM NOT A MONSTER!
AAAAAH!
AAAAAAAAAAAAAAH!
ZION?
I DIDN'T MEAN TO.
I KNOW YOU WERE SCARED... I COULD HEAR YOUR HEARTBEAT.
I DON'T KNOW HOW TO BEAT A WORLD FULL OF FEAR...
BUT I THINK FEAR WINS WHEN WE LOSE HOPE.
HUH?
BLURGLE

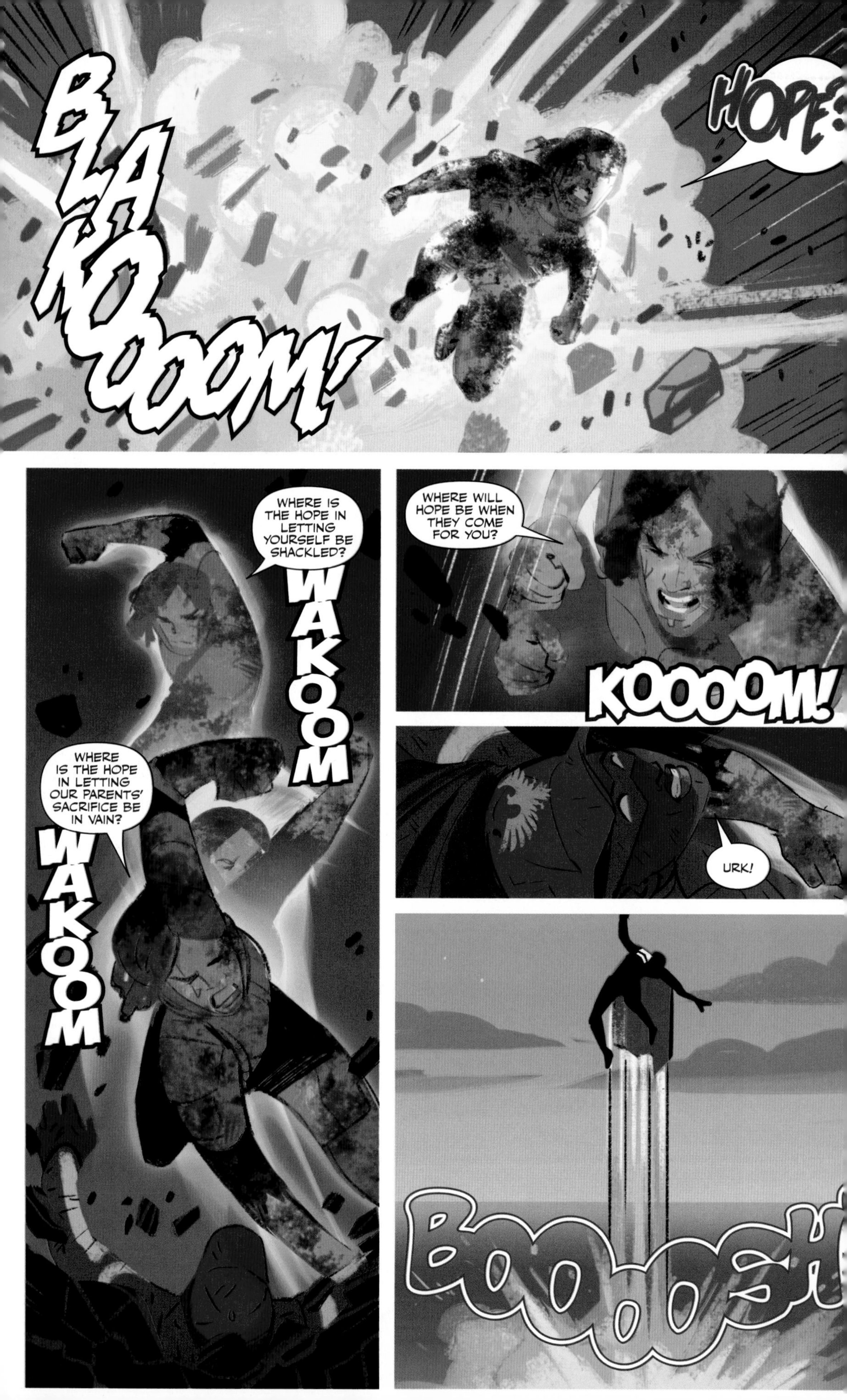
BLAKOOOOM!
HOPE?
WHERE IS THE HOPE IN LETTING YOURSELF BE SHACKLED?
WAKOOM
WHERE IS THE HOPE IN LETTING OUR PARENTS' SACRIFICE BE IN VAIN?
WAKOOM
WHERE WILL HOPE BE WHEN THEY COME FOR YOU?
KOOOOM!
URK!
BOOOOSH

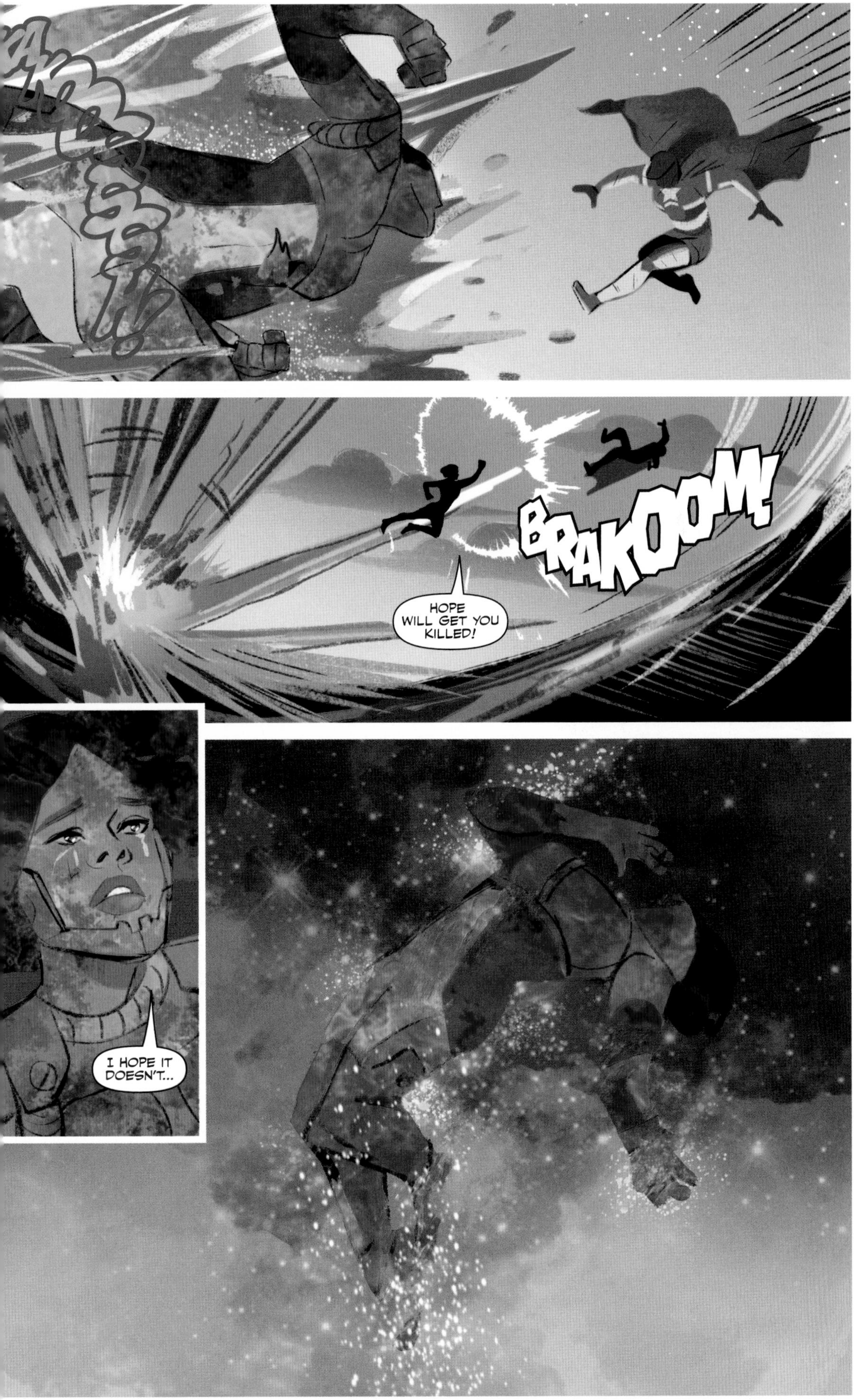
BRAKOOM!
HOPE WILL GET YOU KILLED!
I HOPE IT DOESN'T...

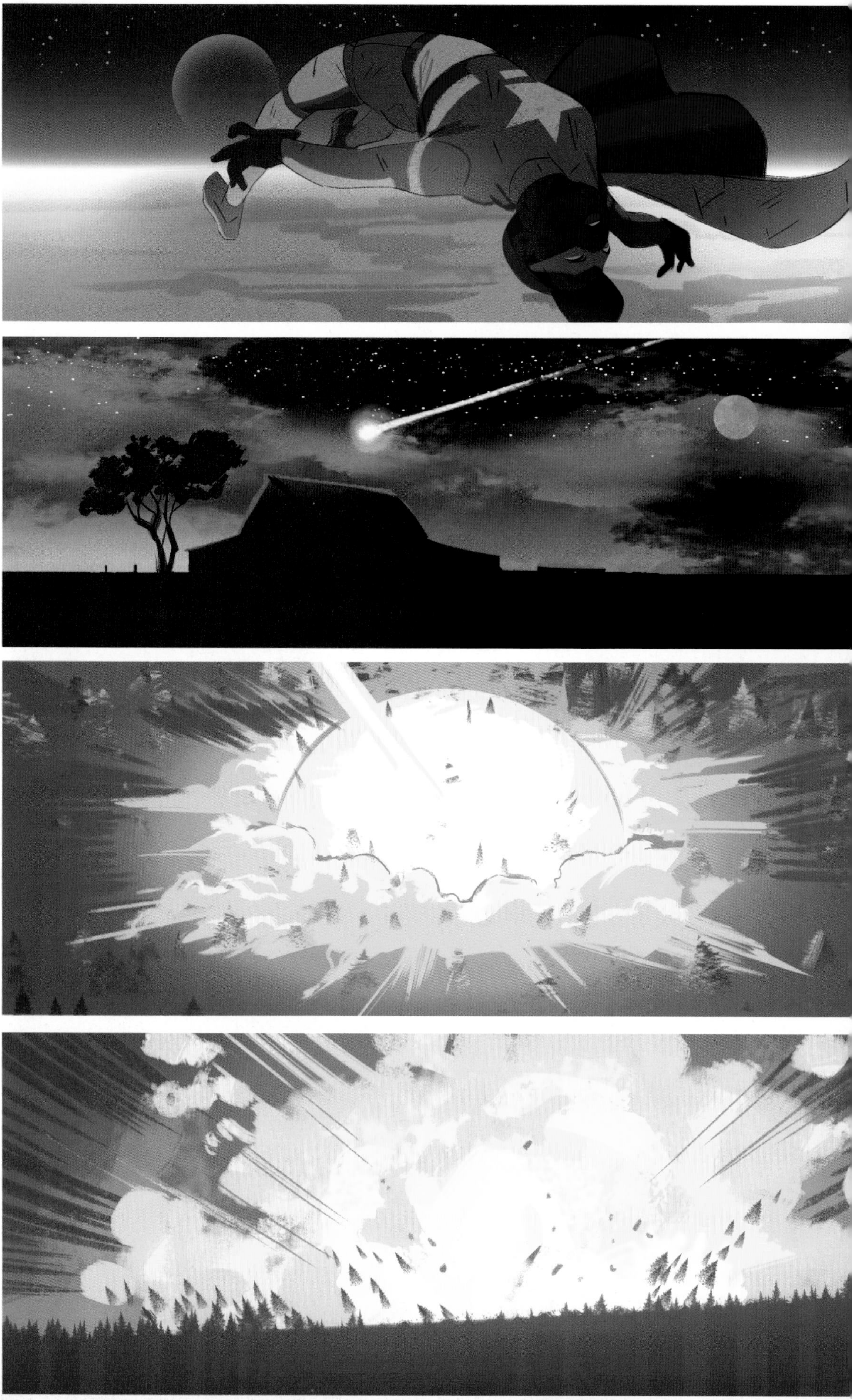

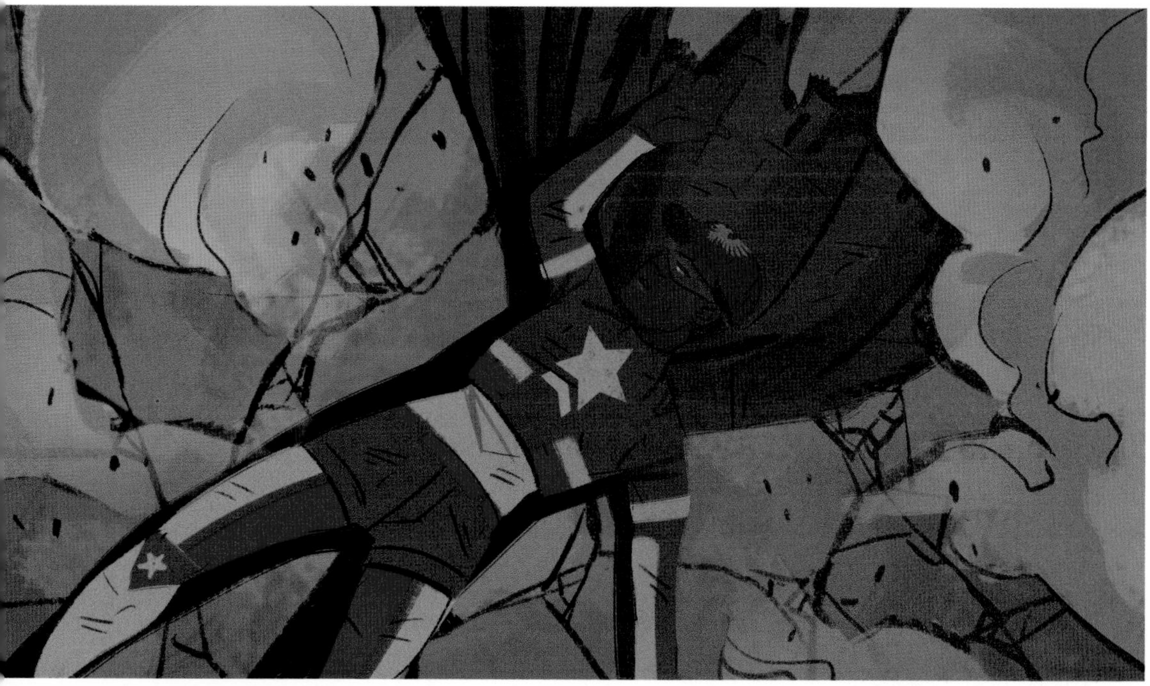
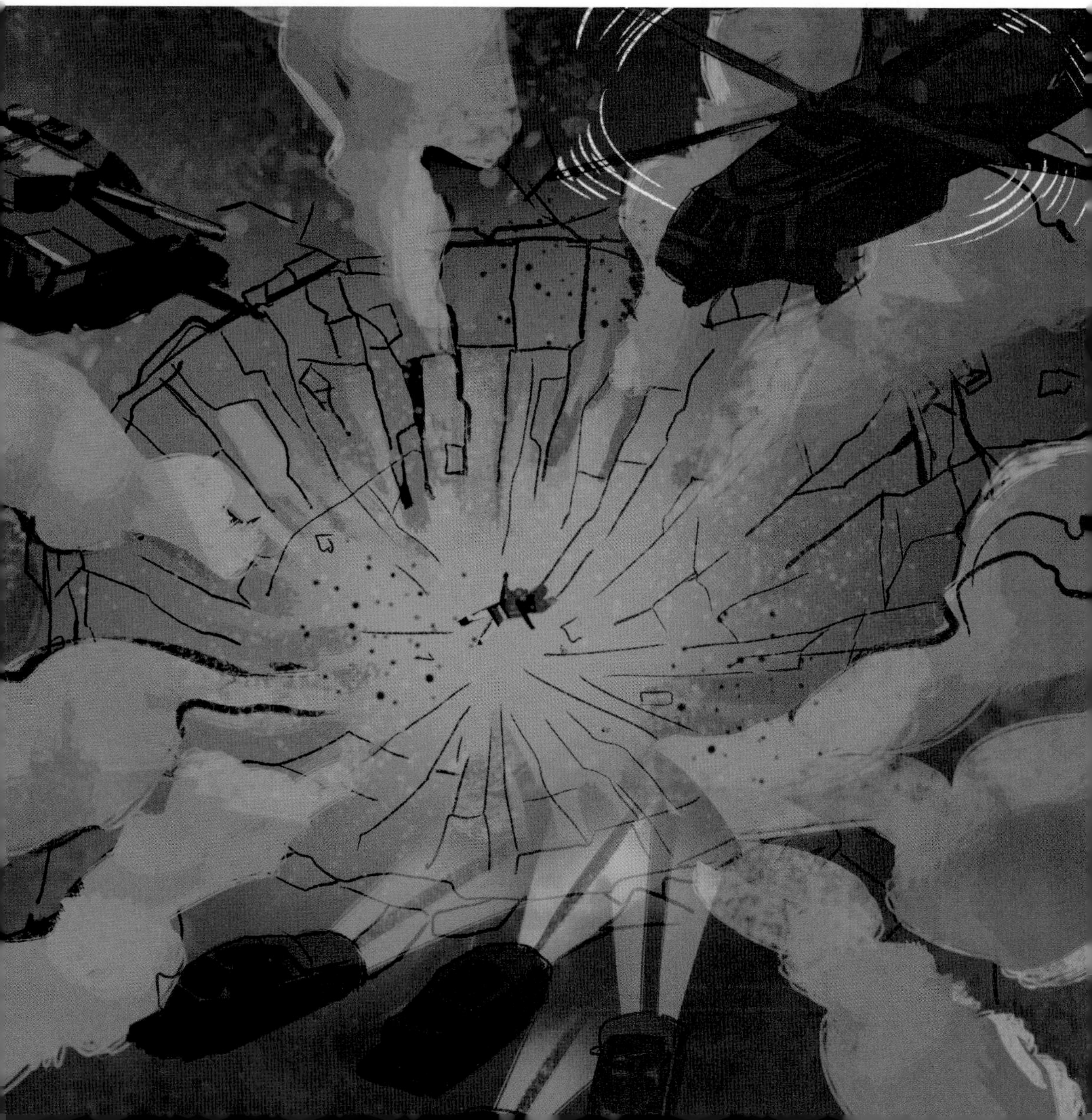

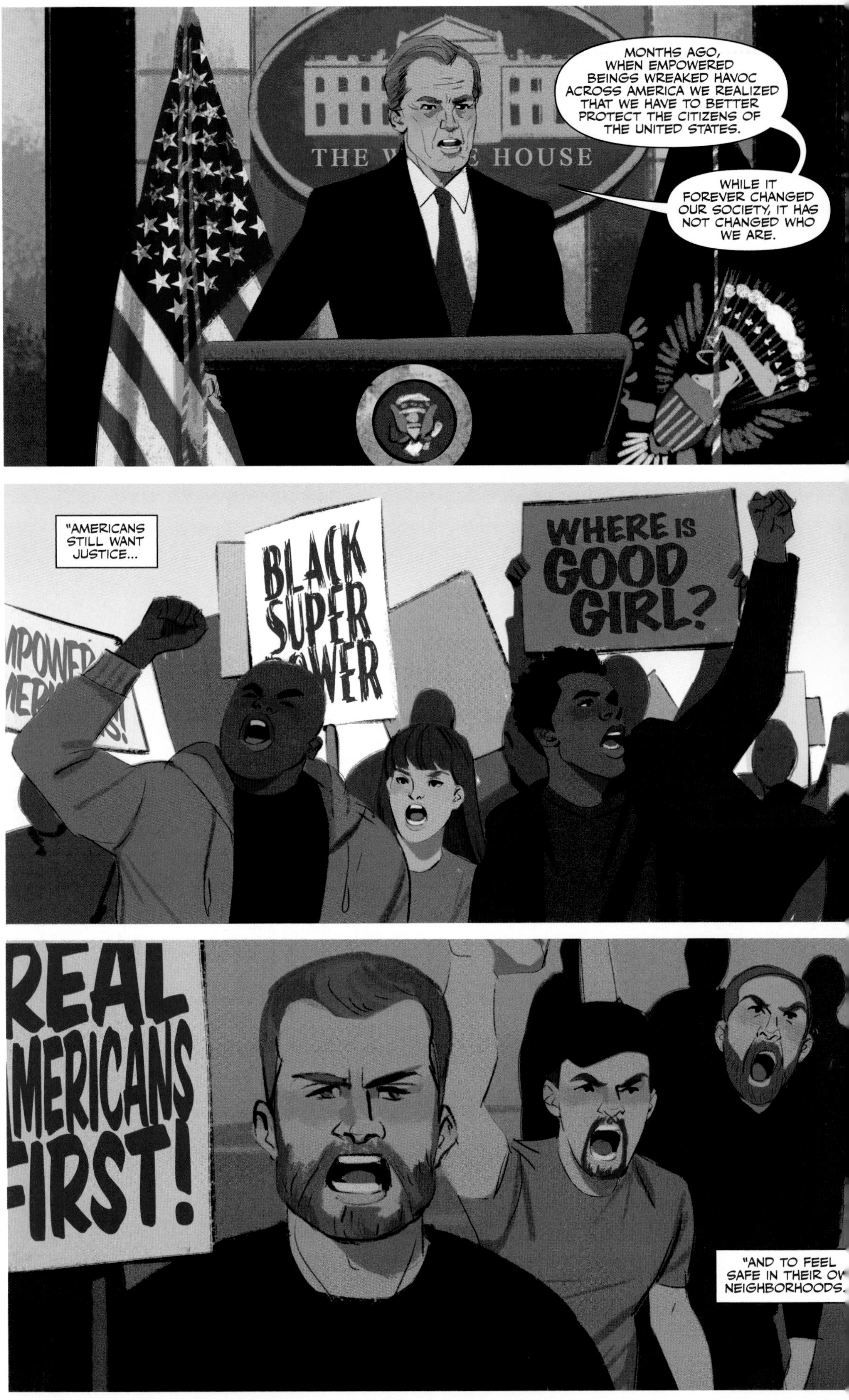
THE W HOUSE
MONTHS AGO, WHEN EMPOWERED BEINGS WREAKED HAVOC ACROSS AMERICA WE REALIZED THAT WE HAVE TO BETTER PROTECT THE CITIZENS OF THE UNITED STATES.
WHILE IT FOREVER CHANGED OUR SOCIETY, IT HAS NOT CHANGED WHO WE ARE.
"AMERICANS STILL WANT JUSTICE...
BLACK SUPER
WHERE IS GOOD GIRL?
REAL
MERICANS
IRST!
"AND TO FEEL SAFE IN THEIR O
NEIGHBORHOODS.

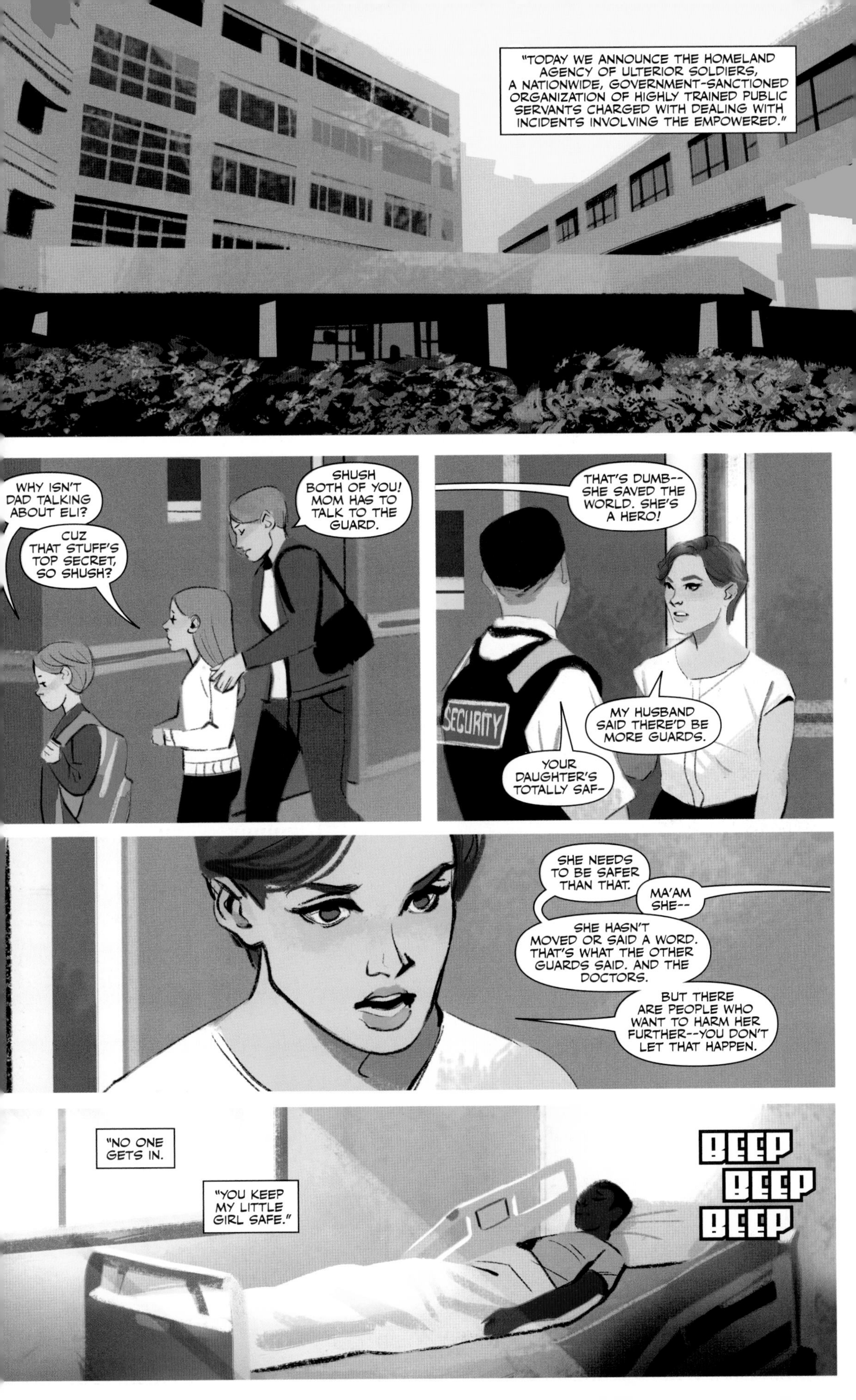
"TODAY WE ANNOUNCE THE HOMELAND AGENCY OF ULTERIOR SOLDIERS, A NATIONWIDE, GOVERNMENT-SANCTIONED ORGANIZATION OF HIGHLY TRAINED PUBLIC SERVANTS CHARGED WITH DEALING WITH INCIDENTS INVOLVING THE EMPOWERED."
WHY ISN'T DAD TALKING ABOUT ELI?
CUZ THAT STUFF'S TOP SECRET, SO SHUSH?
SHUSH BOTH OF YOU! MOM HAS TO TALK TO THE GUARD.
THAT'S DUMB--SHE SAVED THE WORLD. SHE'S A HERO!
SECURITY
MY HUSBAND SAID THERE'D BE MORE GUARDS.
YOUR DAUGHTER'S TOTALLY SAF-
SHE NEEDS TO BE SAFER THAN THAT.
MA'AM SHE--
SHE HASN'T MOVED OR SAID A WORD. THAT'S WHAT THE OTHER GUARDS SAID. AND THE DOCTORS.
BUT THERE ARE PEOPLE WHO WANT TO HARM HER FURTHER--YOU DON'T LET THAT HAPPEN.
"NO ONE GETS IN.
"YOU KEEP MY LITTLE GIRL SAFE."
BEEP
BEEP
BEEP

BEEP
BEEP
BEEP

BEEP
BEEP
BEEP

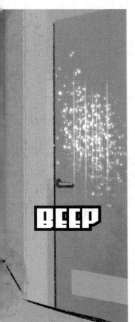

BEEP

DANG! IT TOOK A MINUTE BUT...

BEEP

FINALLY FOUND YOU.

BEEP

YOU SAVED EVERYBODY. SO NOW I'MA SAVE YOU.

BEEP

BEEP

BEEP

IT'S TO W U

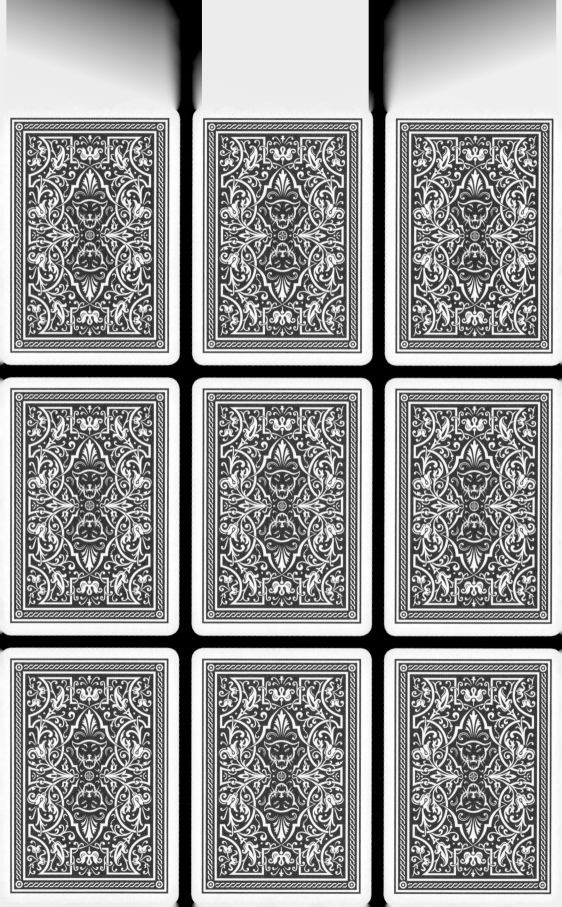

Remove flap A and B and cut out cards to create a full deck of menstruation cards.
[See Chapter 4.]

PERIOD

Play this card to block an opponent's **PERIOD**.

category	*flow*
PERIOD	**6**

PERIOD

Play this card to block an opponent's **PERIOD**.

category	*flow*
PERIOD	**1**

PERIOD

Play this card to block an opponent's **PERIOD**.

category	*flow*
PERIOD	**4**

PERIOD

Play this card to block an opponent's **PERIOD**.

category	*flow*
PERIOD	**7**

PERIOD

Play this card to block an opponent's **PERIOD**.

category	*flow*
PERIOD	**3**

PERIOD

Play this card to block an opponent's **PERIOD**.

category	*flow*
PERIOD	**2**

TAMPON

Play this card on an opponent's **PERIOD** card to block menstruation.

category	*absorption*
TAMPON	**2**

TAMPON

Play this card on an opponent's **PERIOD** card to block menstruation.

category	*absorption*
TAMPON	**4**

TAMPON

Play this card on an opponent's **PERIOD** card to block menstruation.

category	*absorption*
TAMPON	**5**

TAMPON

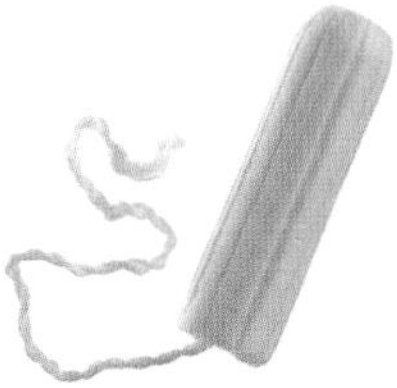

Play this card on an opponent's **PERIOD** card to block menstruation.

category	*absorption*
TAMPON	**3**

TAMPON

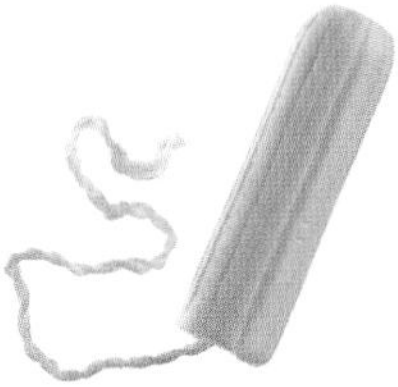

Play this card on an opponent's **PERIOD** card to block menstruation.

category	*absorption*
TAMPON	**1**

PANTHER

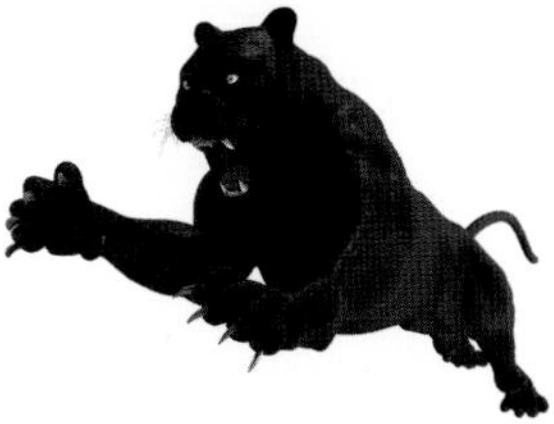

Play this card on an open **PERIOD** card in front of you.

category	*kills*
PANTHER	

PANTHER

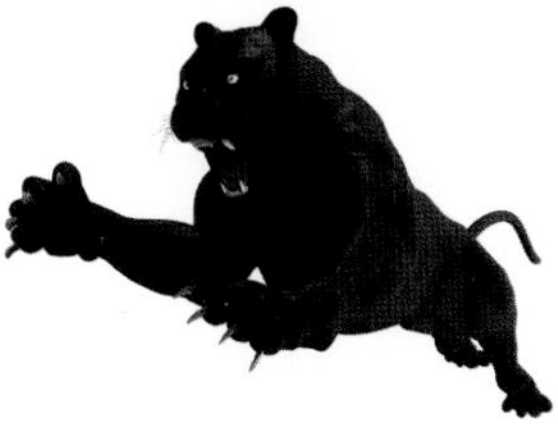

Play this card on an open **PERIOD** card in front of you.

category	*kills*
PANTHER	

TAMPON EATER

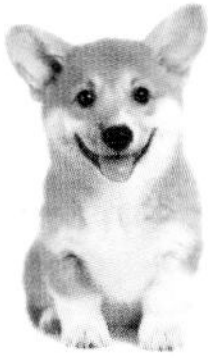

Use this card to remove a **TAMPON** from the field of play. Discard it, along with the corgi.

category	*points*
CORGI	

PANTHER

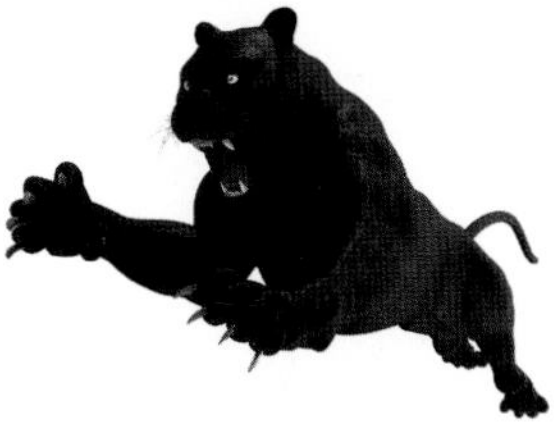

Play this card on an open **PERIOD** card in front of you.

category	*kills*
PANTHER	

PANTHER

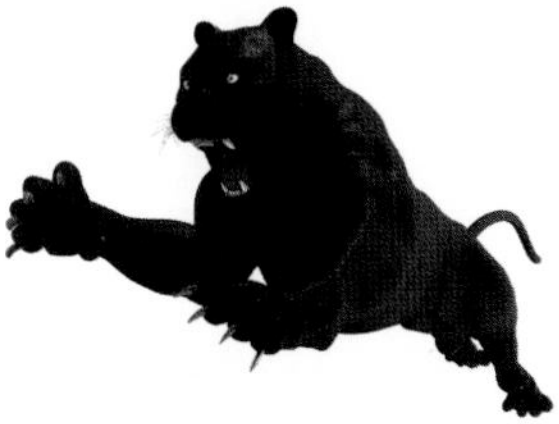

Play this card on an open **PERIOD** card in front of you.

category	*kills*
PANTHER	

PANTHER

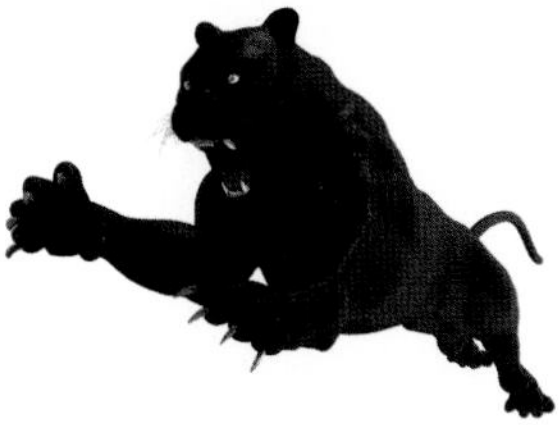

Play this card on an open **PERIOD** card in front of you.

category	*kills*
PANTHER	

PANTHER

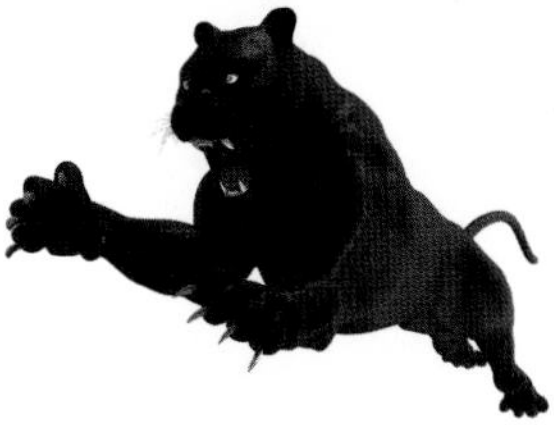

Play this card on an open **PERIOD** card in front of you.

category	*kills*
PANTHER	

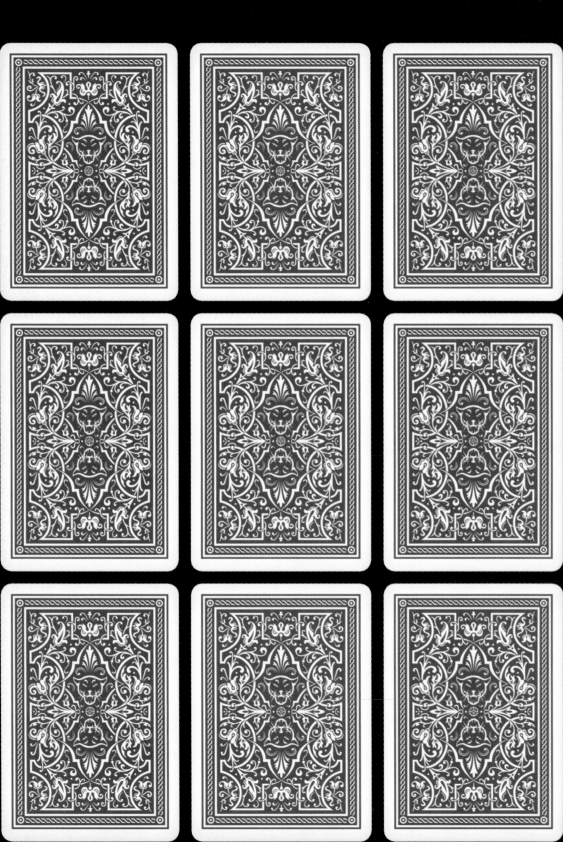

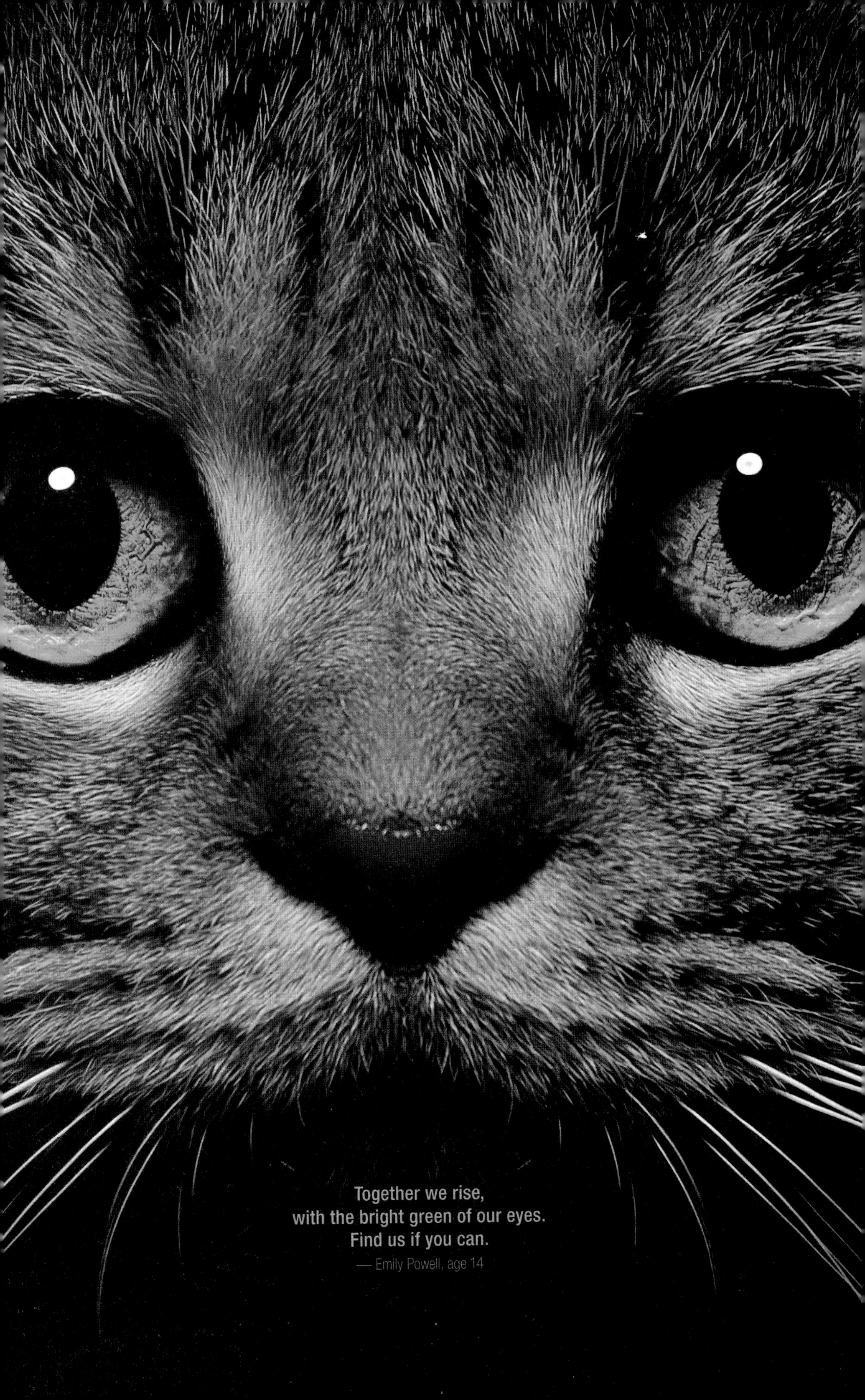
Together we rise,
with the bright green of our eyes.
Find us if you can.
— Emily Powell, age 14

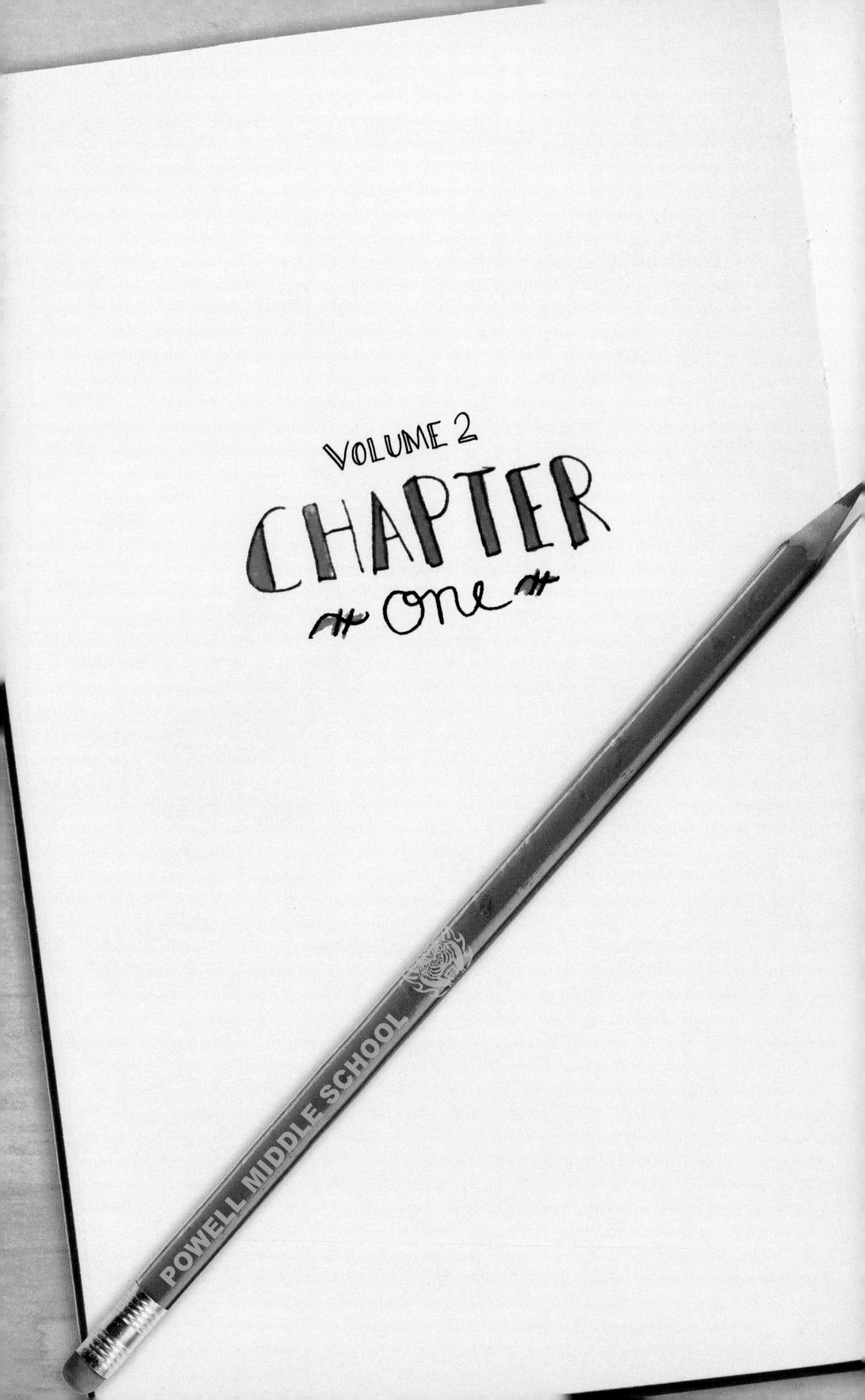
VOLUME 2
CHAPTER
one
POWELL MIDDLE SCHOOL

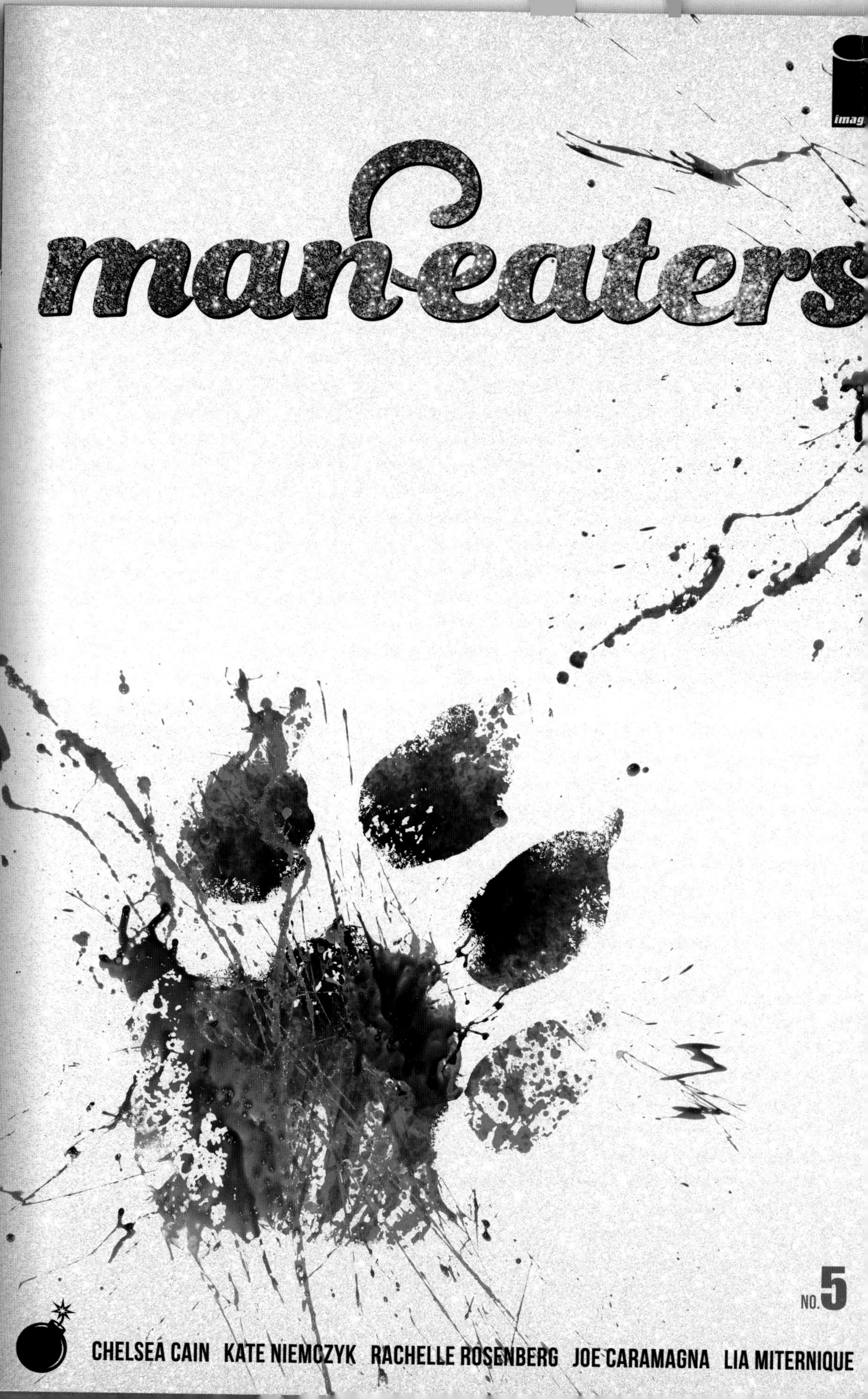
man-eaters
NO. 5
CHELSEA CAIN KATE NIEMCZYK RACHELLE ROSENBERG JOE CARAMAGNA LIA MITERNIQUE

A soft and cute cat,
unless you pet the wrong way.
Then I will kill you.

Emily Powell, Age 13

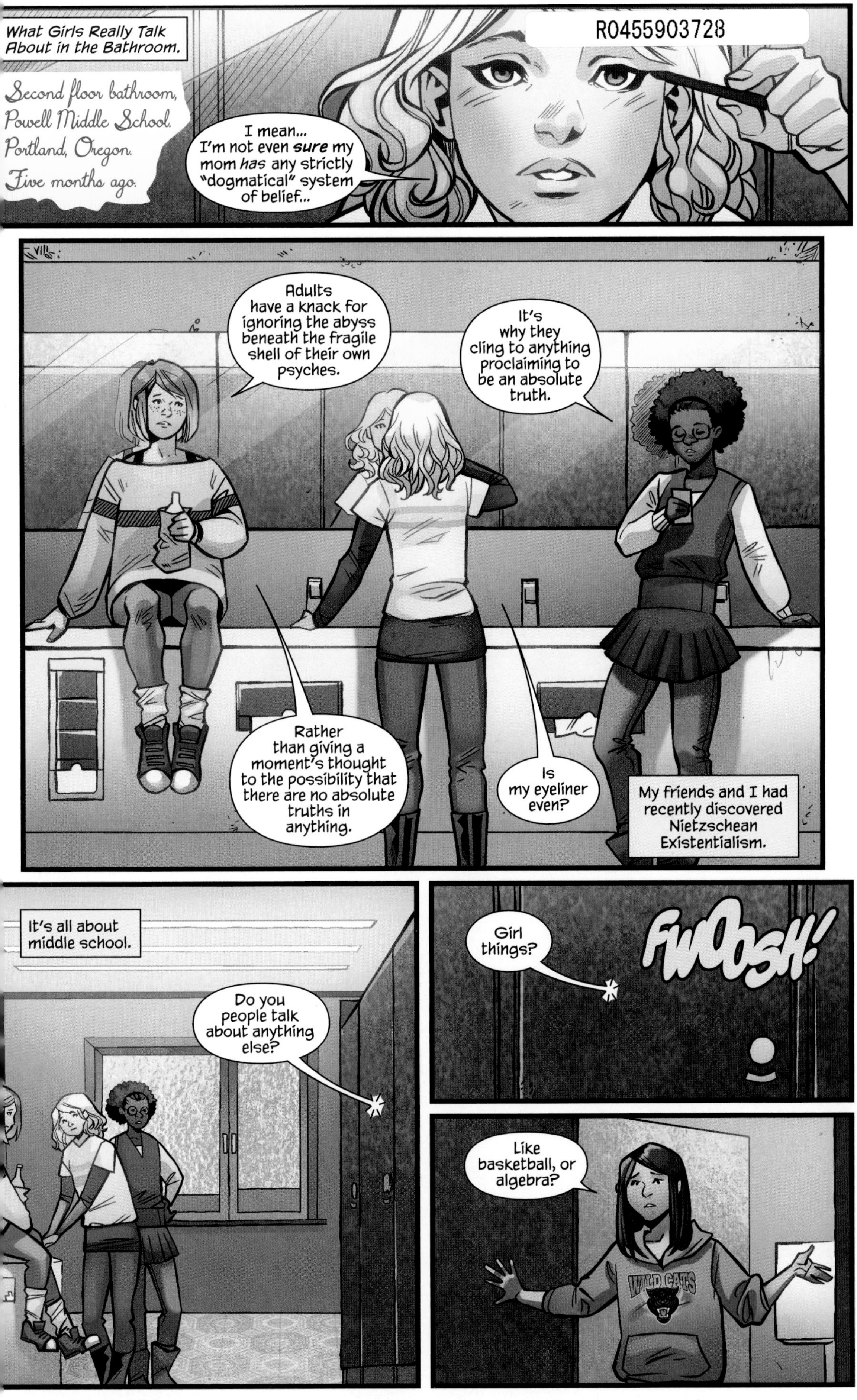
What Girls Really Talk About in the Bathroom.
Second floor bathroom, Powell Middle School. Portland, Oregon. Five months ago.
I mean... I'm not even sure my mom has any strictly "dogmatical" system of belief...
Adults have a knack for ignoring the abyss beneath the fragile shell of their own psyches.
It's why they cling to anything proclaiming to be an absolute truth.
Rather than giving a moment's thought to the possibility that there are no absolute truths in anything.
Is my eyeliner even?
My friends and I had recently discovered Nietzschean Existentialism.
It's all about middle school.
Do you people talk about anything else?
Girl things?
FWOOSH!
Like basketball, or algebra?
WILD CATS

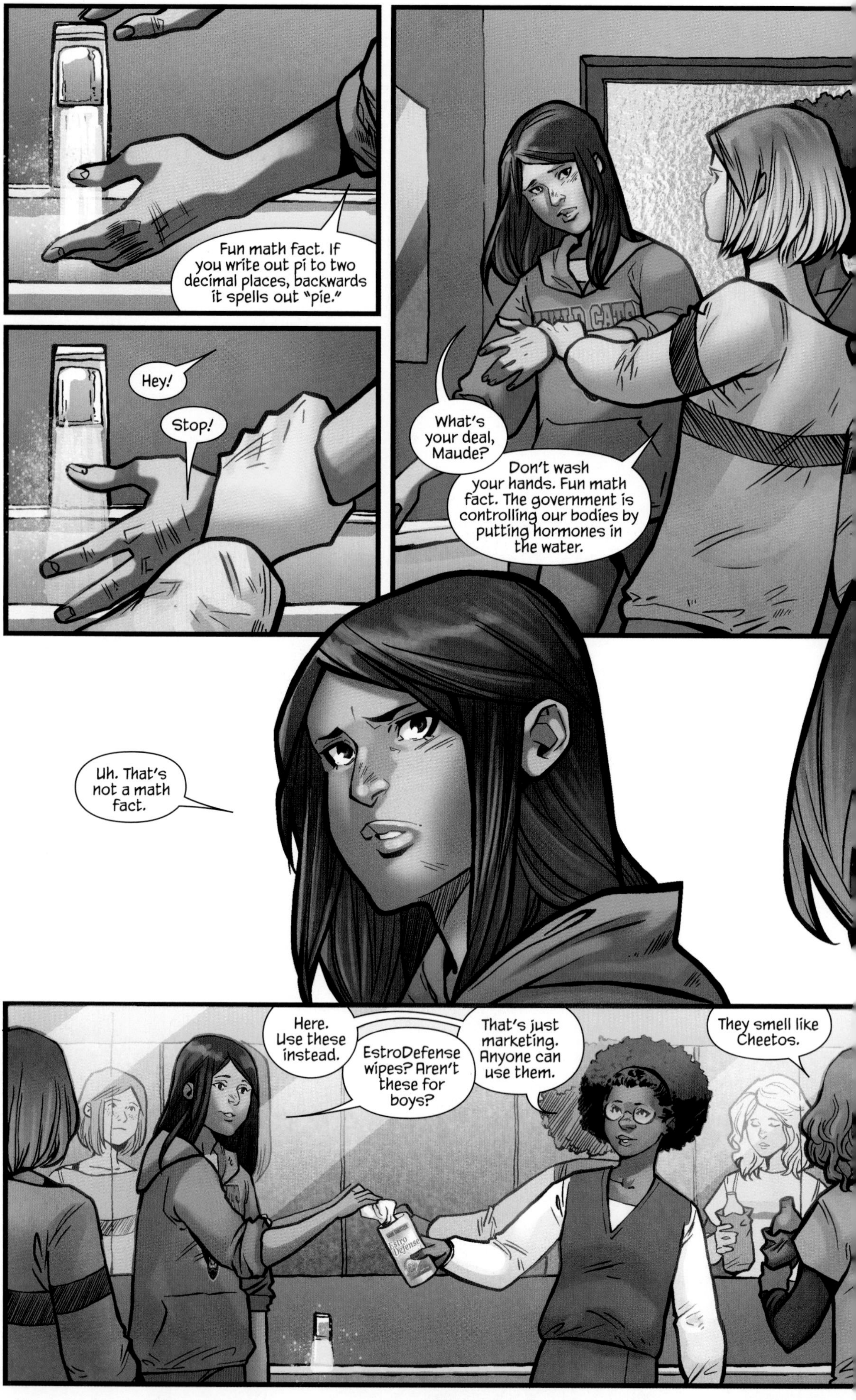
Fun math fact. If you write out pi to two decimal places, backwards it spells out "pie."
What's your deal, Maude?
Don't wash your hands. Fun math fact. The government is controlling our bodies by putting hormones in the water.
Hey!
Stop!
Uh. That's not a math fact.
Here. Use these instead.
EstroDefense wipes? Aren't these for boys?
That's just marketing. Anyone can use them.
They smell like Cheetos.
EstroDefense

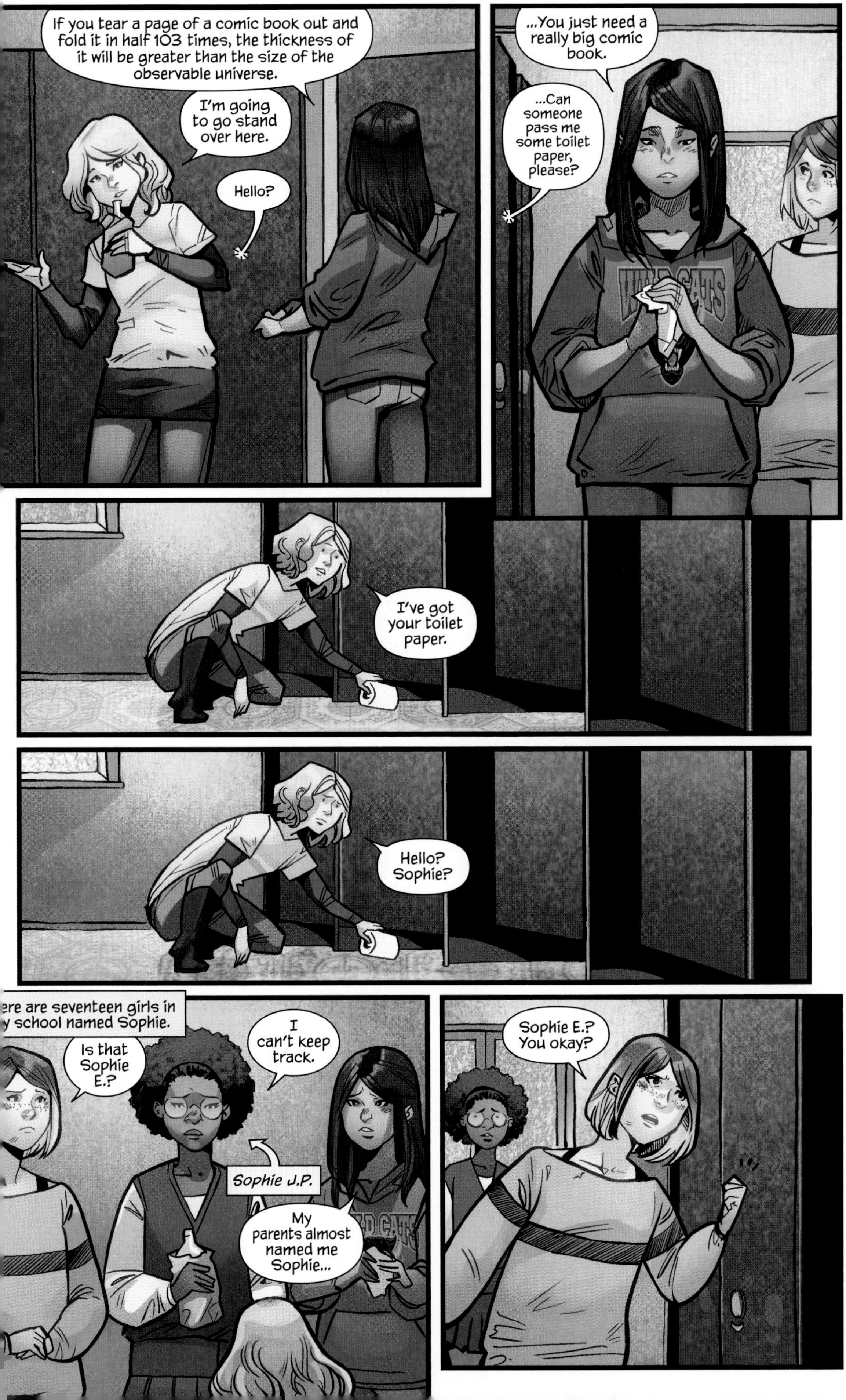
If you tear a page of a comic book out and fold it in half 103 times, the thickness of it will be greater than the size of the observable universe.
I'm going to go stand over here.
Hello?
...You just need a really big comic book.
...Can someone pass me some toilet paper, please?
I've got your toilet paper.
Hello? Sophie?
ere are seventeen girls in y school named Sophie.
Is that Sophie E.?
I can't keep track.
Sophie J.P.
My parents almost named me Sophie...
Sophie E.? You okay?

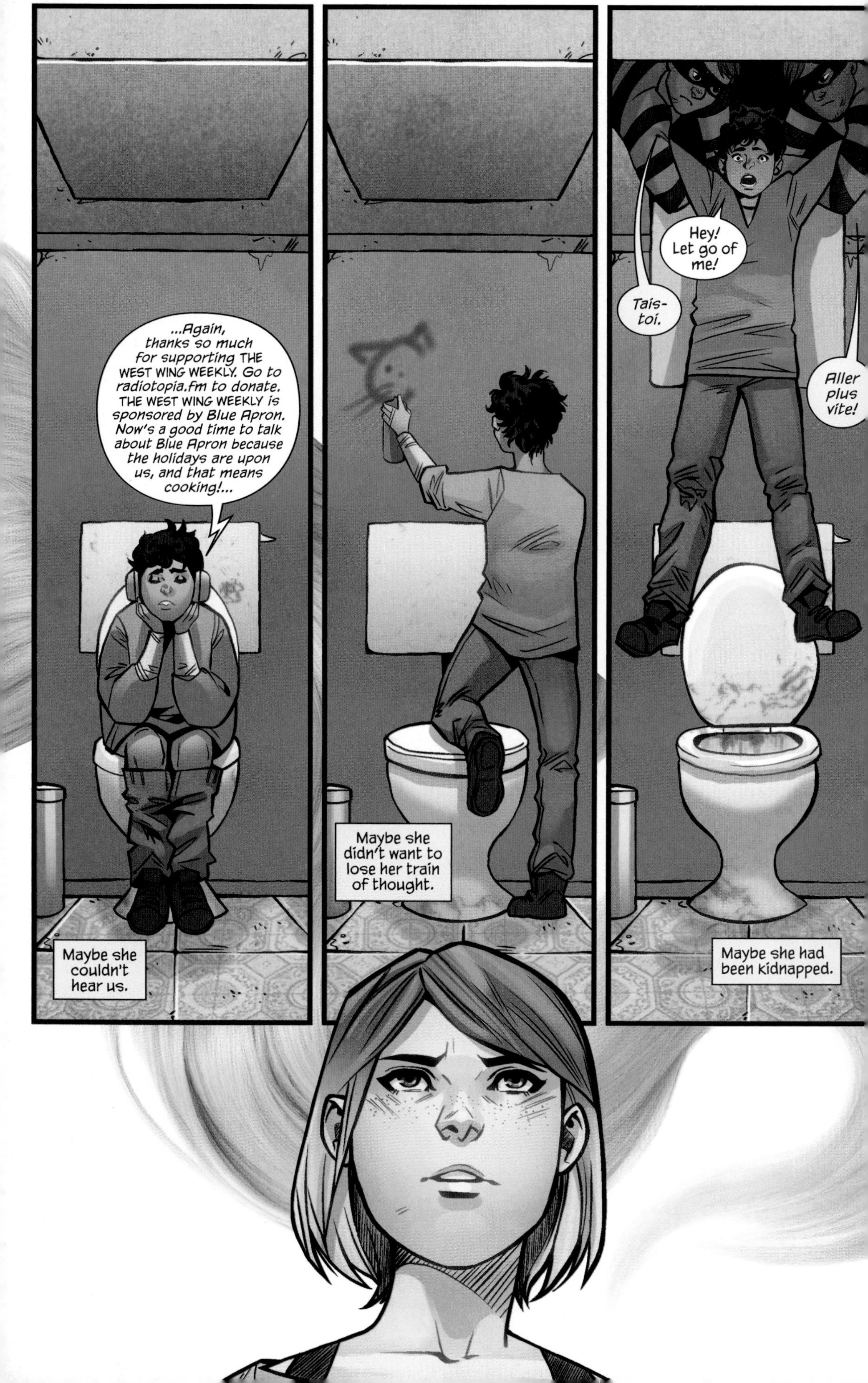

...Again, thanks so much for supporting THE WEST WING WEEKLY. Go to radiotopia.fm to donate. THE WEST WING WEEKLY is sponsored by Blue Apron. Now's a good time to talk about Blue Apron because the holidays are upon us, and that means cooking!...
Maybe she couldn't hear us.
Maybe she didn't want to lose her train of thought.
Hey! Let go of me!
Tais-toi.
Aller plus vite!
Maybe she had been kidnapped.

[Clip from HORNED GLORY]

[Middle School Capstone Project by Sophie E.]

[Used with permission.]

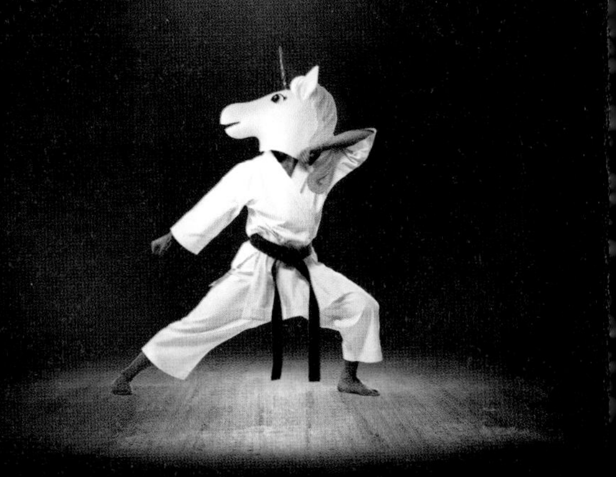

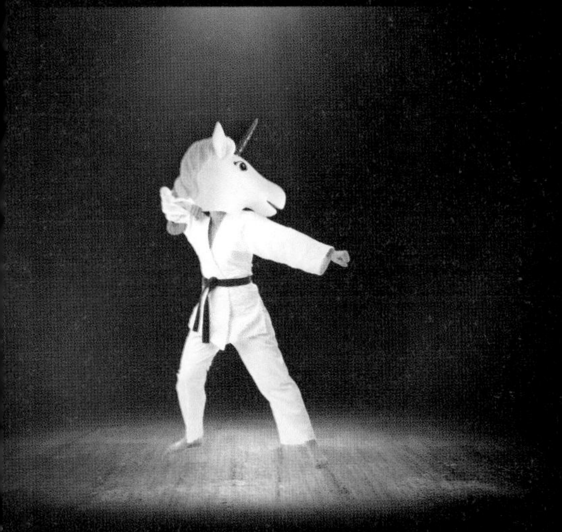

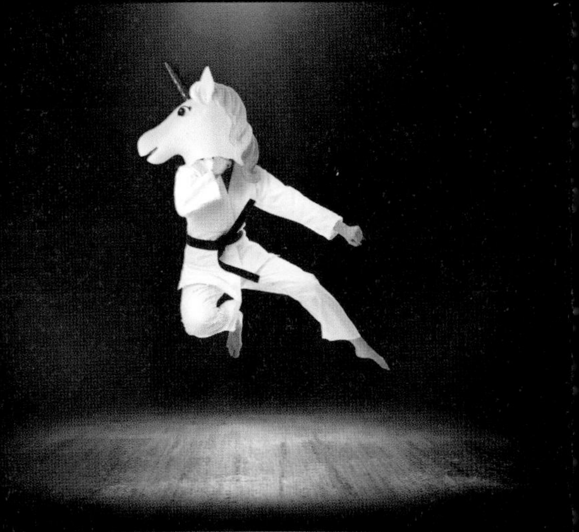

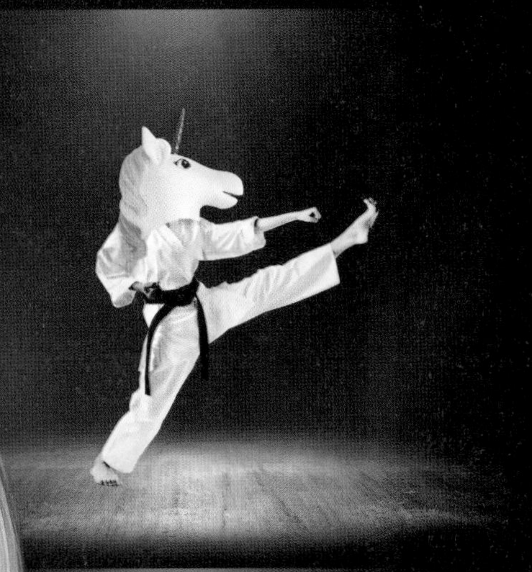

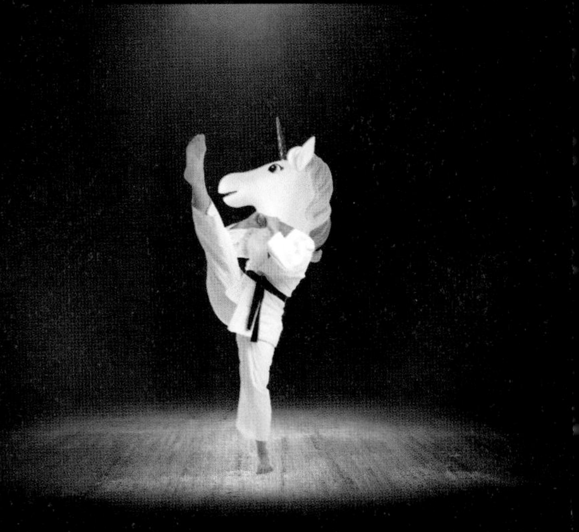

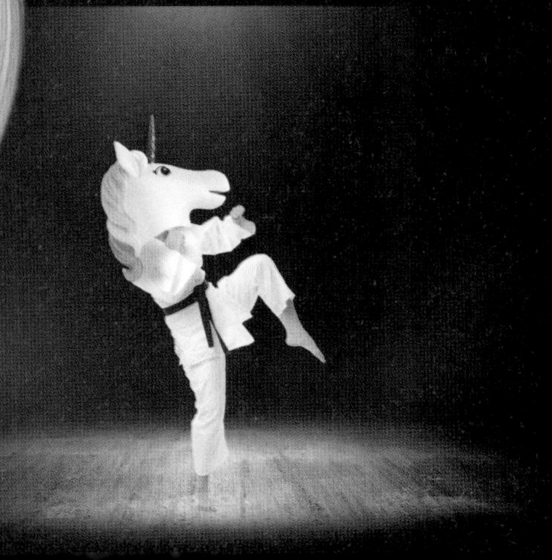

[Finis.]

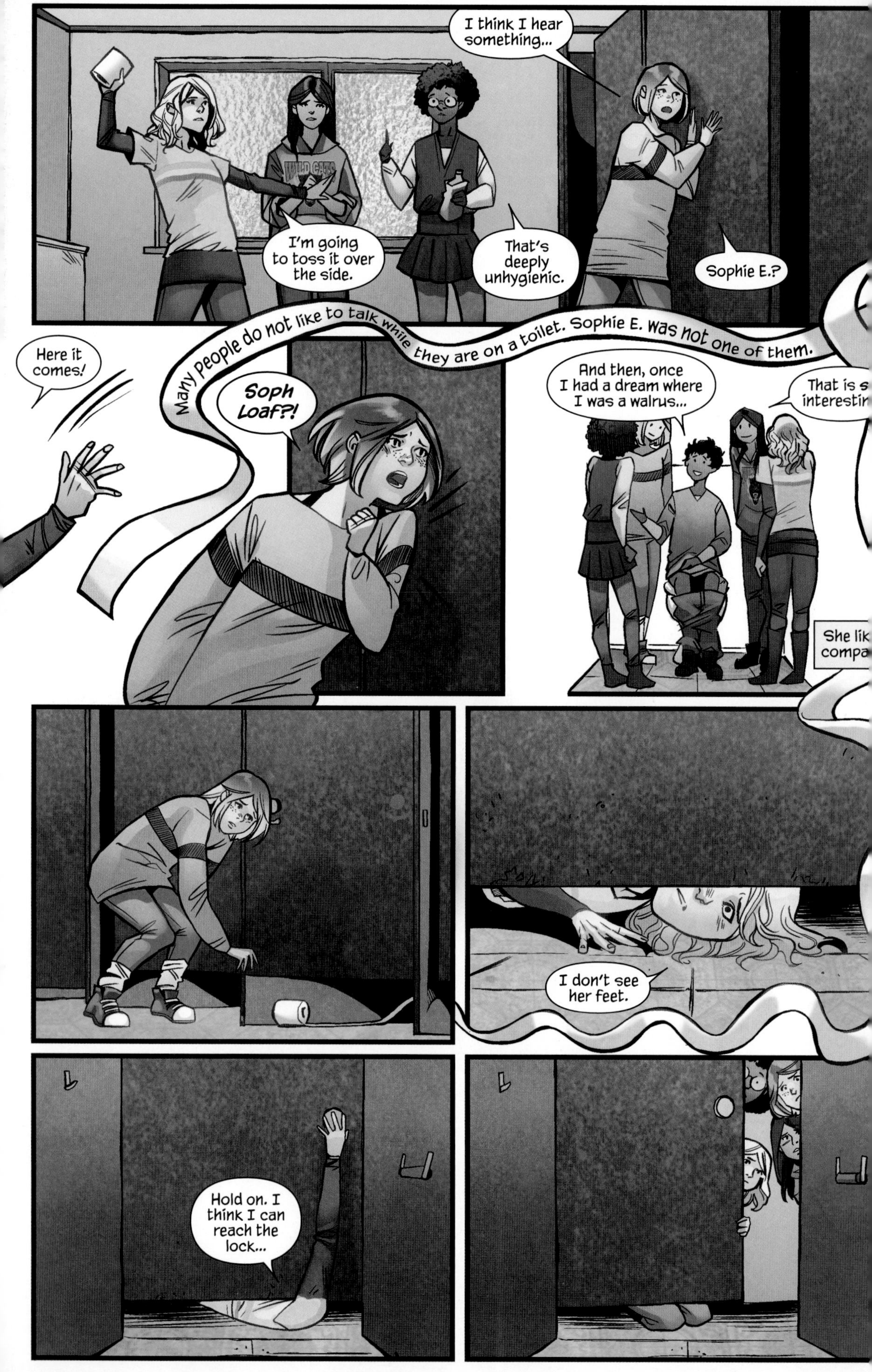
I think I hear something...
I'm going to toss it over the side.
That's deeply unhygienic.
Sophie E.?
Here it comes!
Many people do not like to talk while they are on a toilet. Sophie E. was not one of them.
Soph Loaf?!
And then, once I had a dream where I was a walrus...
I don't see her feet.
Hold on. I think I can reach the lock...

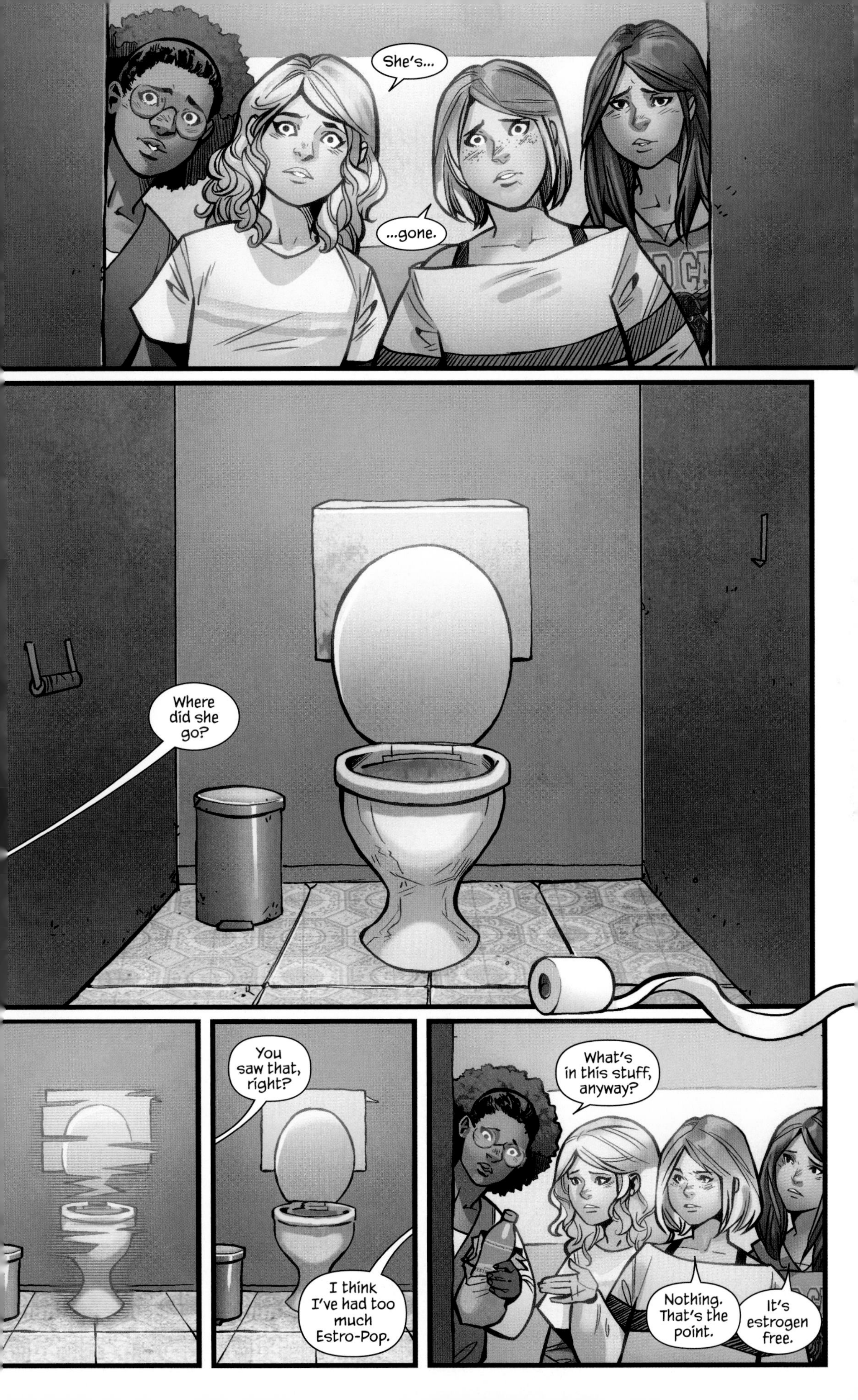
She's...
...gone.
Where did she go?
You saw that, right?
I think I've had too much Estro-Pop.
What's in this stuff, anyway?
Nothing. That's the point.
It's estrogen free.

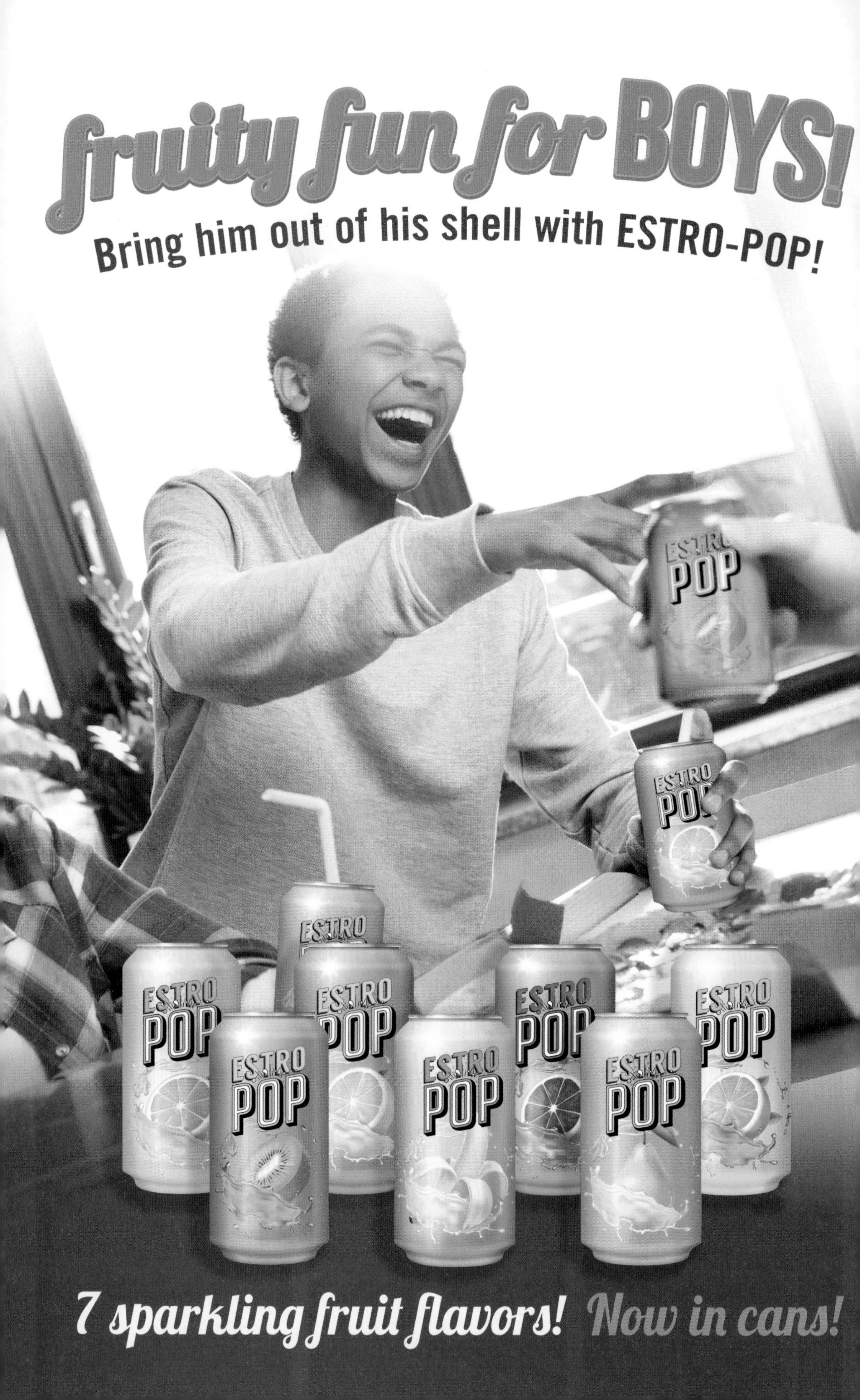
fruity fun for BOYS!
Bring him out of his shell with ESTRO-POP!
ESTRO POP
7 sparkling fruit flavors! Now in cans!

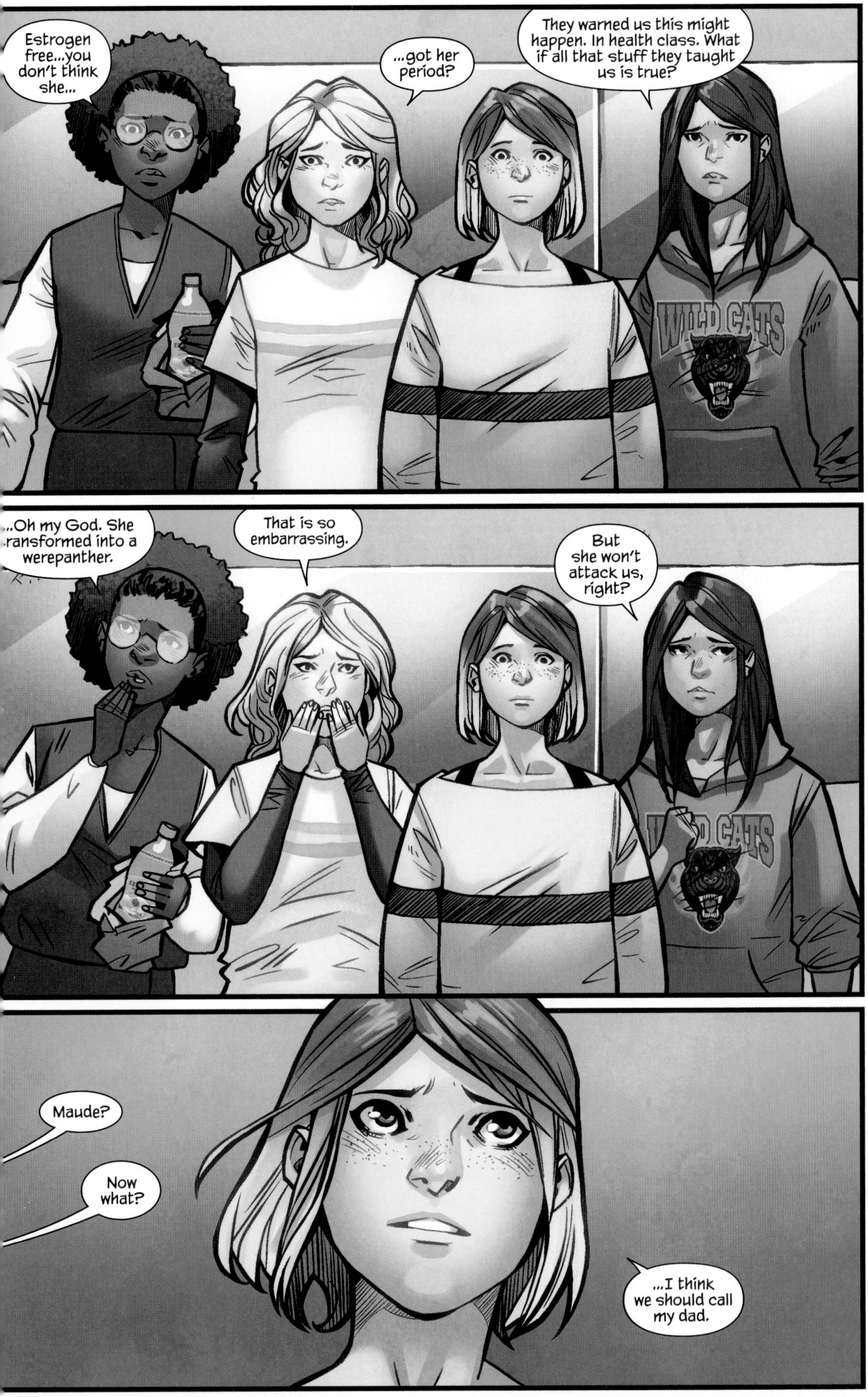
Estrogen free...you don't think she...
...got her period?
They warned us this might happen. In health class. What if all that stuff they taught us is true?
..Oh my God. She ransformed into a werepanther.
That is so embarrassing.
But she won't attack us, right?
WILD CATS
Maude?
Now what?
...I think we should call my dad.

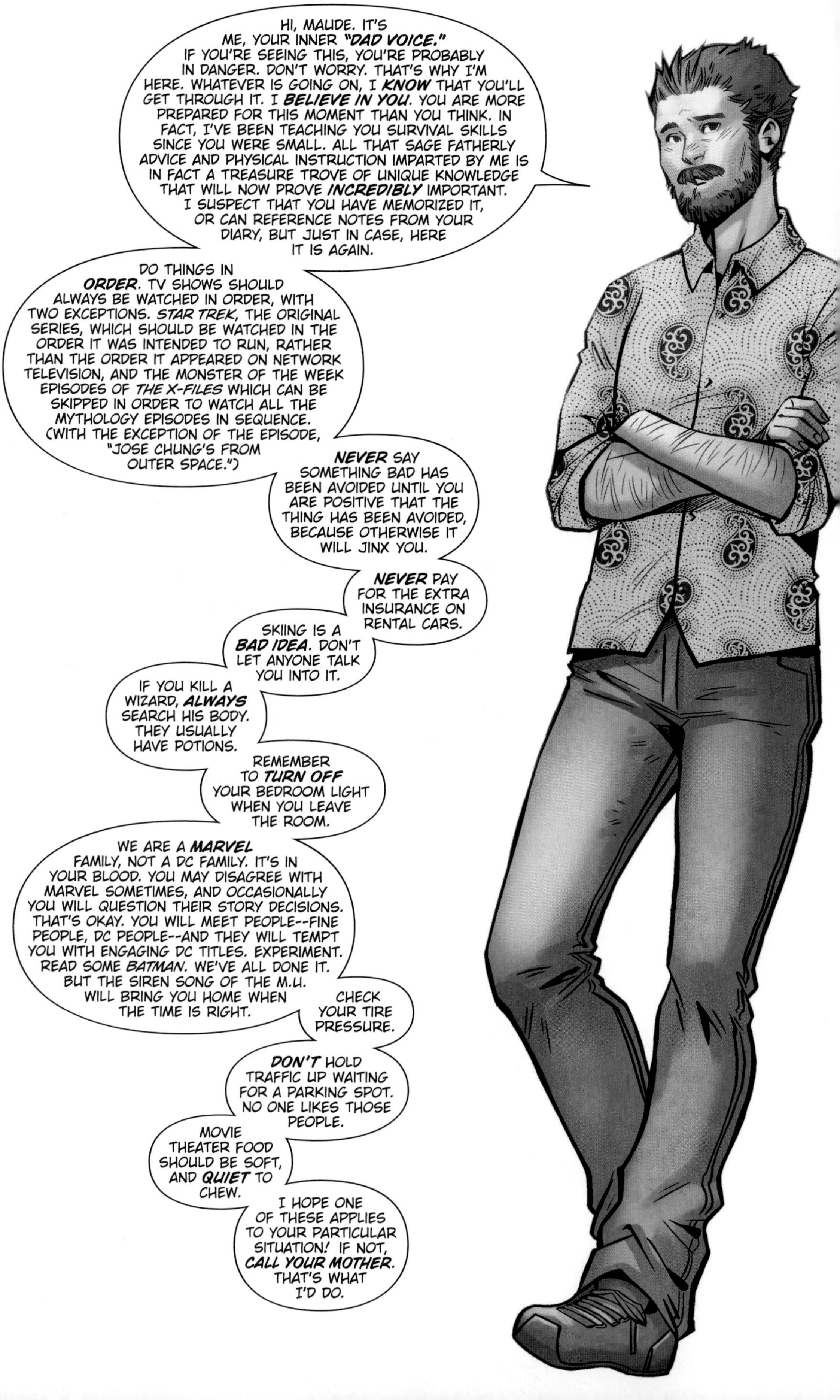
HI, MAUDE. IT'S ME, YOUR INNER "DAD VOICE." IF YOU'RE SEEING THIS, YOU'RE PROBABLY IN DANGER. DON'T WORRY. THAT'S WHY I'M HERE. WHATEVER IS GOING ON, I KNOW THAT YOU'LL GET THROUGH IT. I BELIEVE IN YOU. YOU ARE MORE PREPARED FOR THIS MOMENT THAN YOU THINK. IN FACT, I'VE BEEN TEACHING YOU SURVIVAL SKILLS SINCE YOU WERE SMALL. ALL THAT SAGE FATHERLY ADVICE AND PHYSICAL INSTRUCTION IMPARTED BY ME IS IN FACT A TREASURE TROVE OF UNIQUE KNOWLEDGE THAT WILL NOW PROVE INCREDIBLY IMPORTANT. I SUSPECT THAT YOU HAVE MEMORIZED IT, OR CAN REFERENCE NOTES FROM YOUR DIARY, BUT JUST IN CASE, HERE IT IS AGAIN.
DO THINGS IN ORDER. TV SHOWS SHOULD ALWAYS BE WATCHED IN ORDER, WITH TWO EXCEPTIONS. STAR TREK, THE ORIGINAL SERIES, WHICH SHOULD BE WATCHED IN THE ORDER IT WAS INTENDED TO RUN, RATHER THAN THE ORDER IT APPEARED ON NETWORK TELEVISION, AND THE MONSTER OF THE WEEK EPISODES OF THE X-FILES WHICH CAN BE SKIPPED IN ORDER TO WATCH ALL THE MYTHOLOGY EPISODES IN SEQUENCE. (WITH THE EXCEPTION OF THE EPISODE, "JOSE CHUNG'S FROM OUTER SPACE.")
NEVER SAY SOMETHING BAD HAS BEEN AVOIDED UNTIL YOU ARE POSITIVE THAT THE THING HAS BEEN AVOIDED, BECAUSE OTHERWISE IT WILL JINX YOU.
NEVER PAY FOR THE EXTRA INSURANCE ON RENTAL CARS.
SKIING IS A BAD IDEA. DON'T LET ANYONE TALK YOU INTO IT.
IF YOU KILL A WIZARD, ALWAYS SEARCH HIS BODY. THEY USUALLY HAVE POTIONS.
REMEMBER TO TURN OFF YOUR BEDROOM LIGHT WHEN YOU LEAVE THE ROOM.
WE ARE A MARVEL FAMILY, NOT A DC FAMILY. IT'S IN YOUR BLOOD. YOU MAY DISAGREE WITH MARVEL SOMETIMES, AND OCCASIONALLY YOU WILL QUESTION THEIR STORY DECISIONS. THAT'S OKAY. YOU WILL MEET PEOPLE--FINE PEOPLE, DC PEOPLE--AND THEY WILL TEMPT YOU WITH ENGAGING DC TITLES. EXPERIMENT. READ SOME BATMAN. WE'VE ALL DONE IT. BUT THE SIREN SONG OF THE M.U. WILL BRING YOU HOME WHEN THE TIME IS RIGHT.
CHECK YOUR TIRE PRESSURE.
DON'T HOLD TRAFFIC UP WAITING FOR A PARKING SPOT. NO ONE LIKES THOSE PEOPLE.
MOVIE THEATER FOOD SHOULD BE SOFT, AND QUIET TO CHEW.
I HOPE ONE OF THESE APPLIES TO YOUR PARTICULAR SITUATION! IF NOT, CALL YOUR MOTHER. THAT'S WHAT I'D DO.

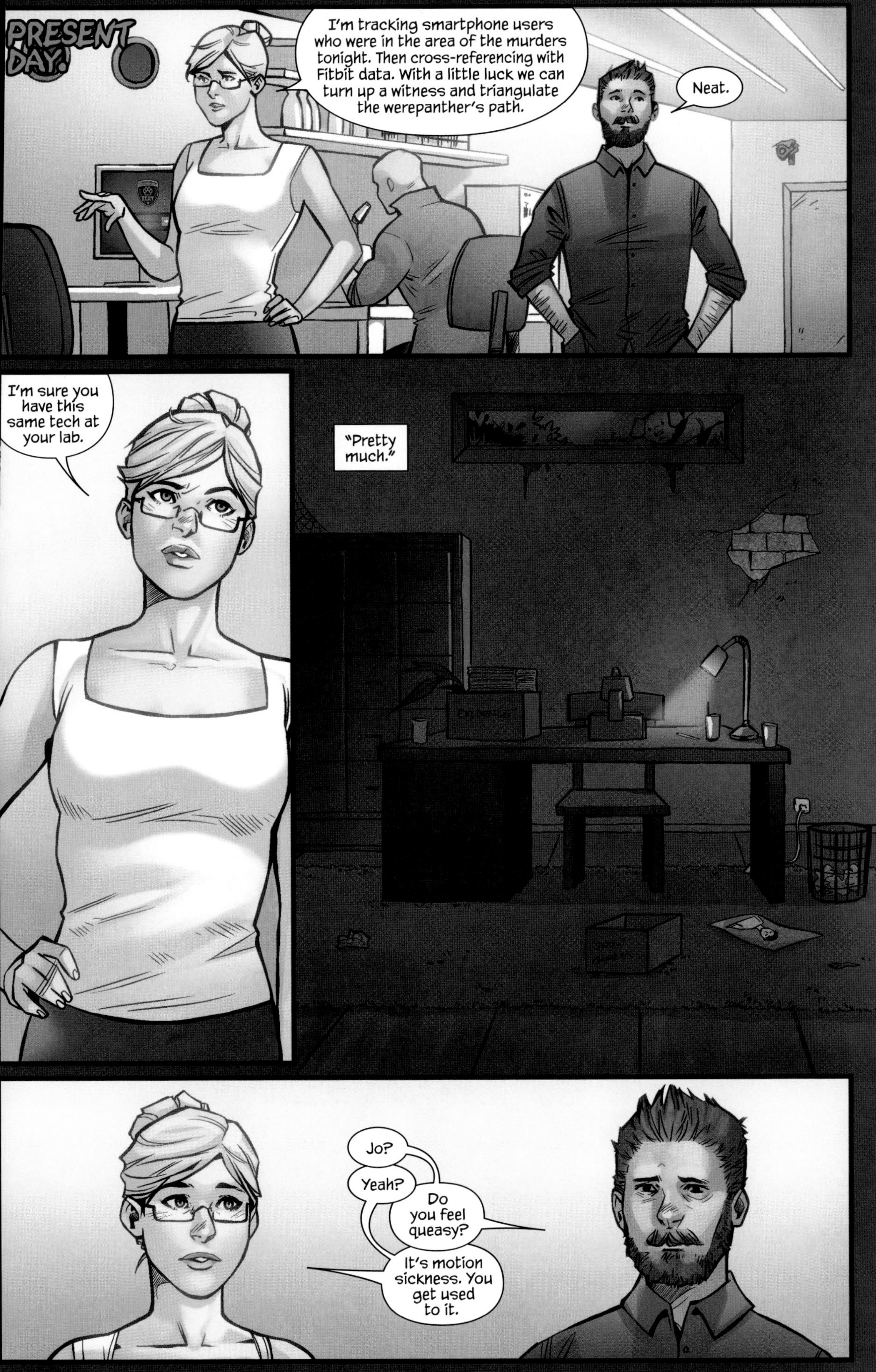

PRESENT DAY.
I'm tracking smartphone users who were in the area of the murders tonight. Then cross-referencing with Fitbit data. With a little luck we can turn up a witness and triangulate the werepanther's path.
Neat.
I'm sure you have this same tech at your lab.
"Pretty much."
Jo?
Yeah?
Do you feel queasy?
It's motion sickness. You get used to it.

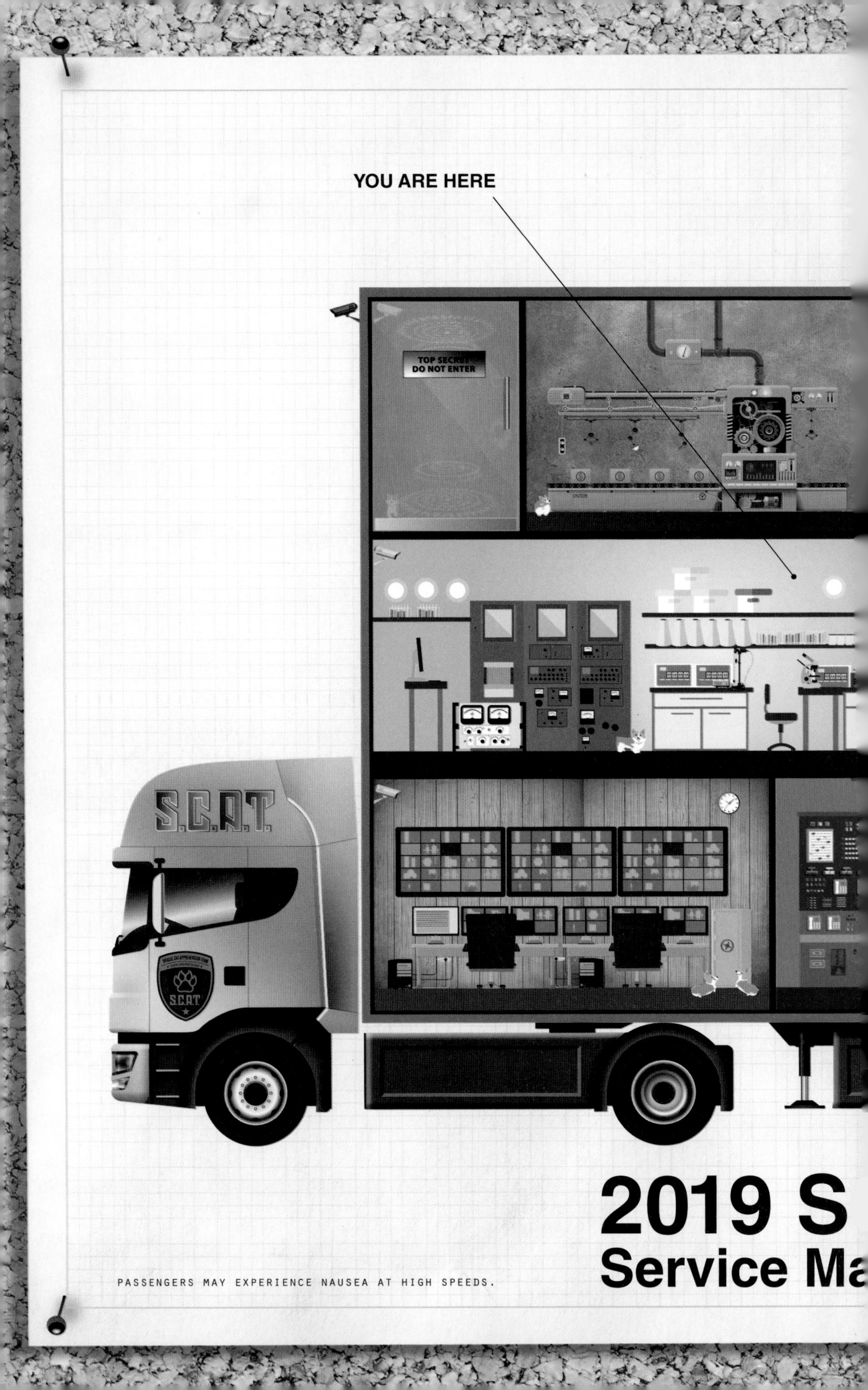
YOU ARE HERE
TOP SECRET
DO NOT ENTER
S.C.A.T.
S.C.A.T.
2019 S
Service Ma
PASSENGERS MAY EXPERIENCE NAUSEA AT HIGH SPEEDS.

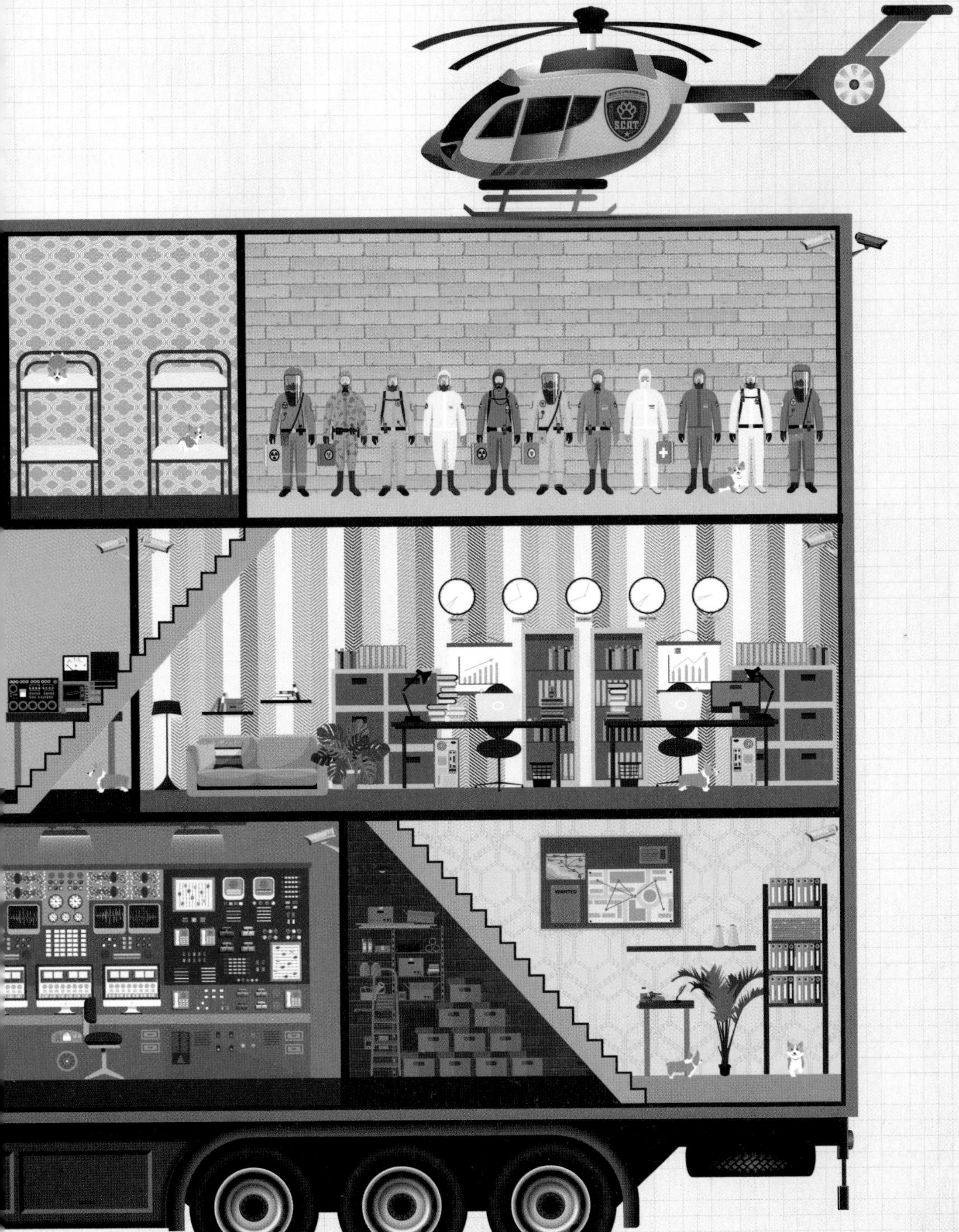
S.C.A.T.
WANTED

AT Mobile Crime Lab

al Pull-out Poster

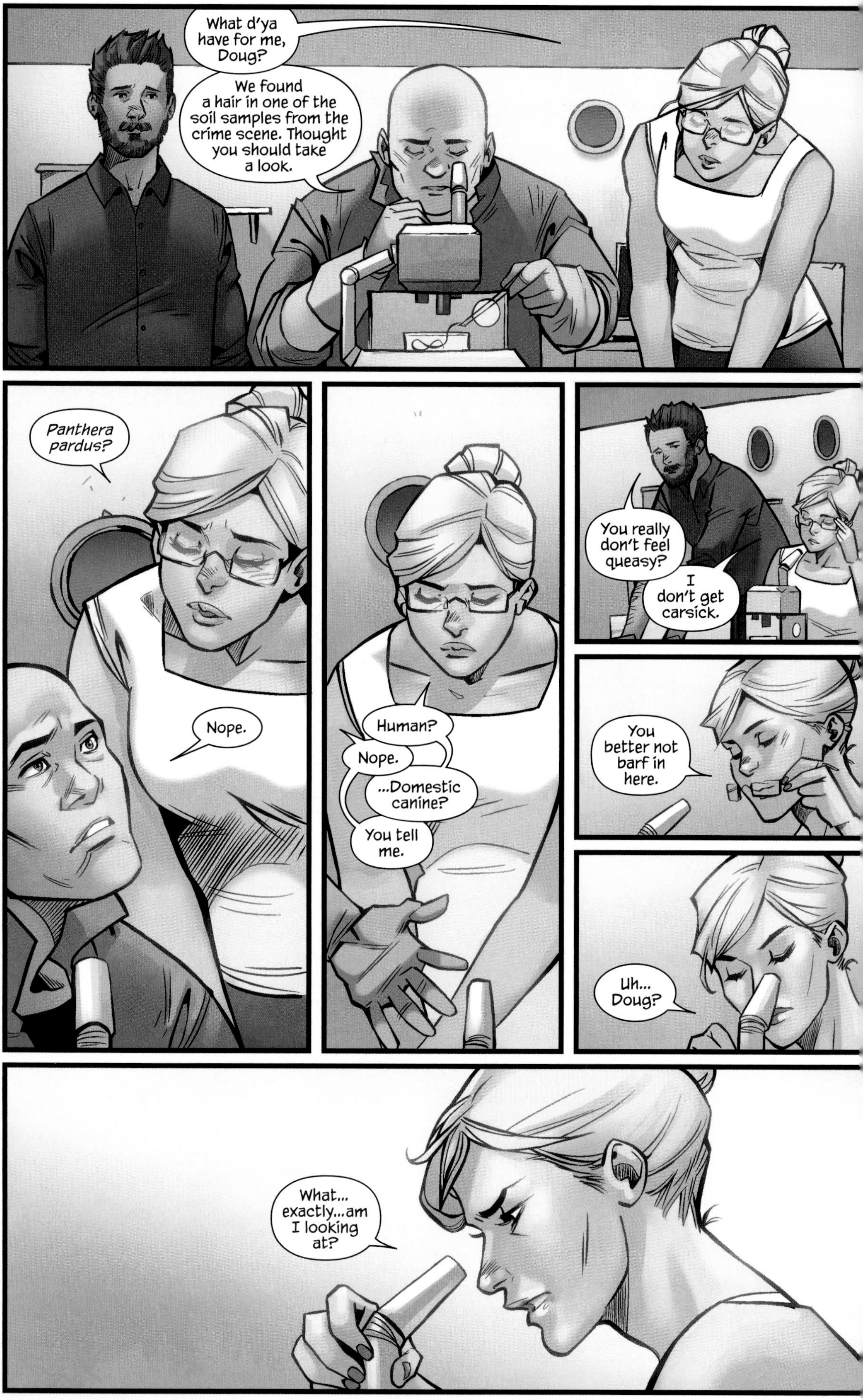
What d'ya have for me, Doug?
We found a hair in one of the soil samples from the crime scene. Thought you should take a look.
Panthera pardus?
Nope.
Human?
Nope.
...Domestic canine?
You tell me.
You really don't feel queasy?
I don't get carsick.
You better not barf in here.
Uh... Doug?
What... exactly...am I looking at?

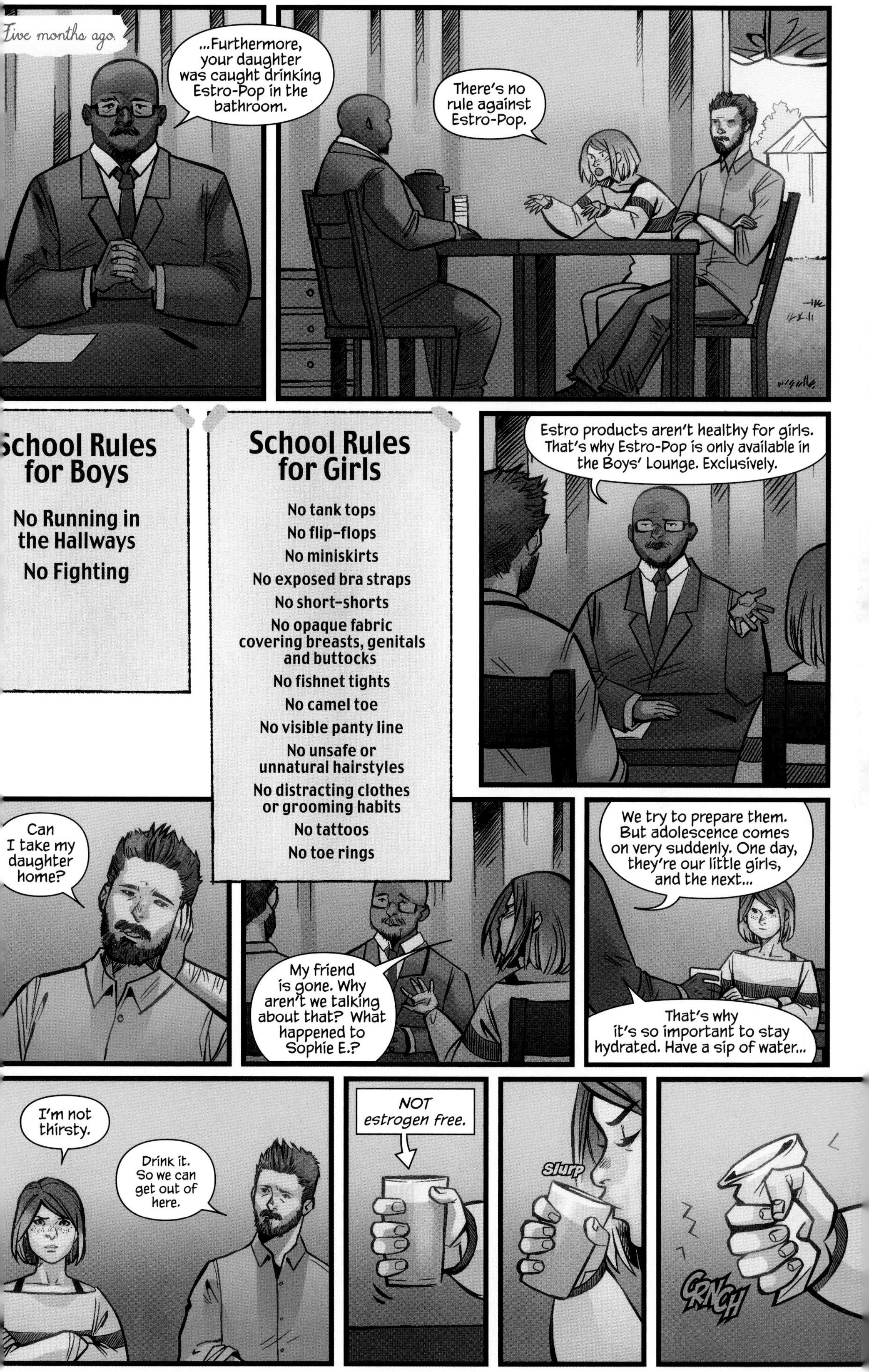
Five months ago.
...Furthermore, your daughter was caught drinking Estro-Pop in the bathroom.
There's no rule against Estro-Pop.
School Rules for Boys
No Running in the Hallways
No Fighting
School Rules for Girls
No tank tops
No flip-flops
No miniskirts
No exposed bra straps
No short-shorts
No opaque fabric covering breasts, genitals and buttocks
No fishnet tights
No camel toe
No visible panty line
No unsafe or unnatural hairstyles
No distracting clothes or grooming habits
No tattoos
No toe rings
Estro products aren't healthy for girls. That's why Estro-Pop is only available in the Boys' Lounge. Exclusively.
Can I take my daughter home?
My friend is gone. Why aren't we talking about that? What happened to Sophie E.?
We try to prepare them. But adolescence comes on very suddenly. One day, they're our little girls, and the next...
That's why it's so important to stay hydrated. Have a sip of water...
I'm not thirsty.
Drink it. So we can get out of here.
NOT estrogen free.
SLURP
CRNCH

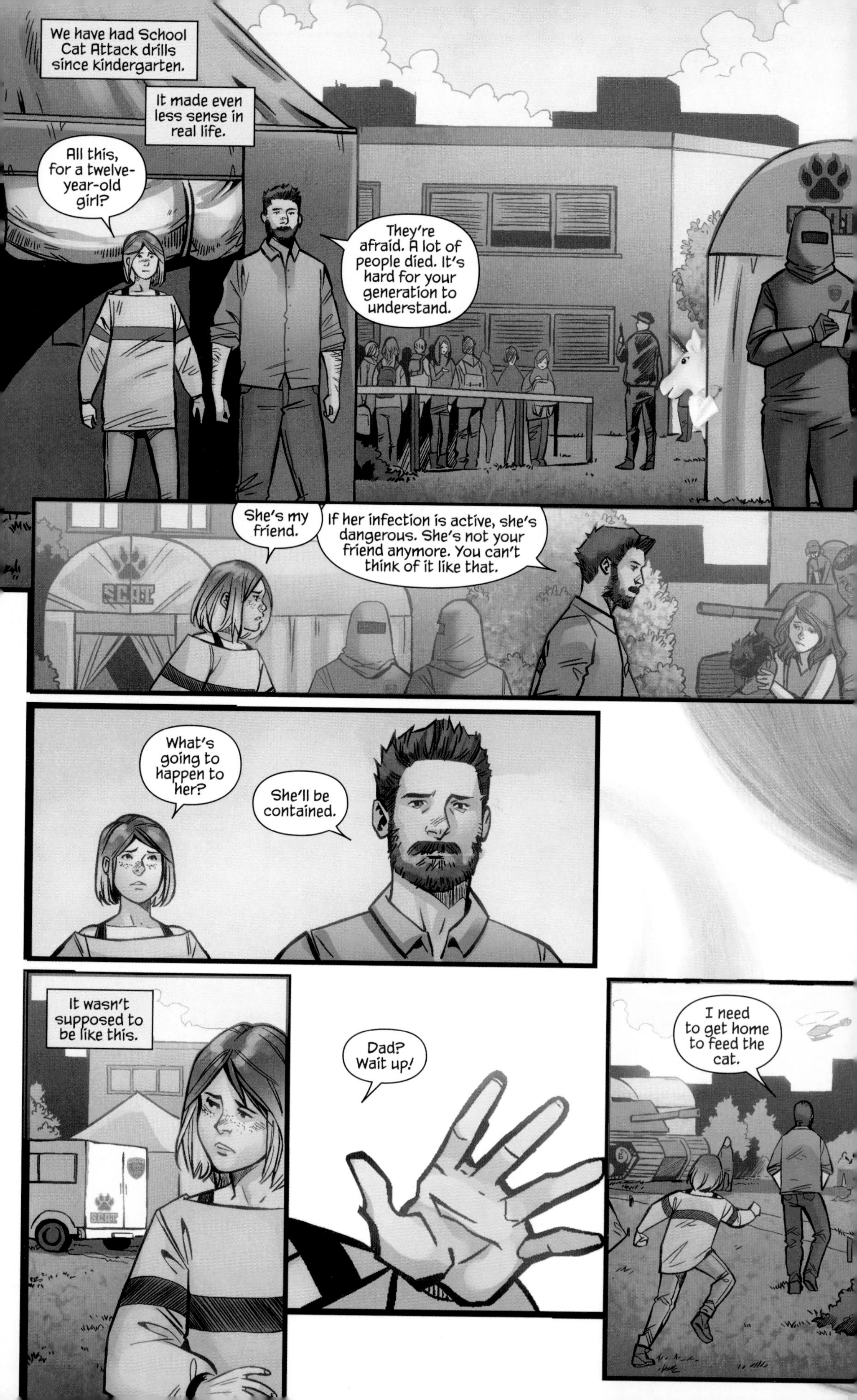
We have had School Cat Attack drills since kindergarten.
It made even less sense in real life.
All this, for a twelve-year-old girl?
They're afraid. A lot of people died. It's hard for your generation to understand.
She's my friend.
If her infection is active, she's dangerous. She's not your friend anymore. You can't think of it like that.
What's going to happen to her?
She'll be contained.
It wasn't supposed to be like this.
Dad? Wait up!
I need to get home to feed the cat.

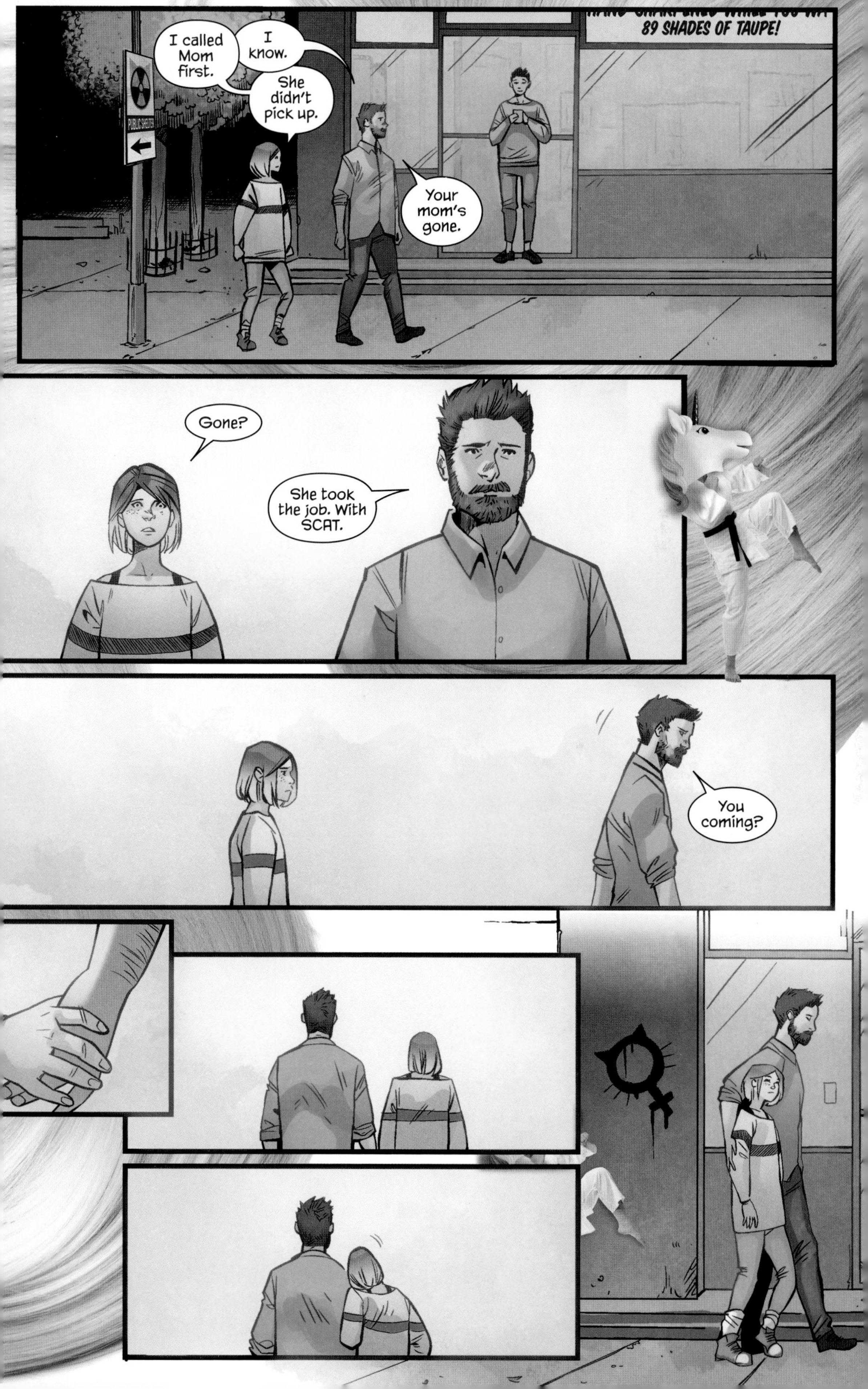
89 SHADES OF TAUPE!
PUBLIC SHELTER
I called Mom first.
I know.
She didn't pick up.
Your mom's gone.
Gone?
She took the job. With SCAT.
You coming?

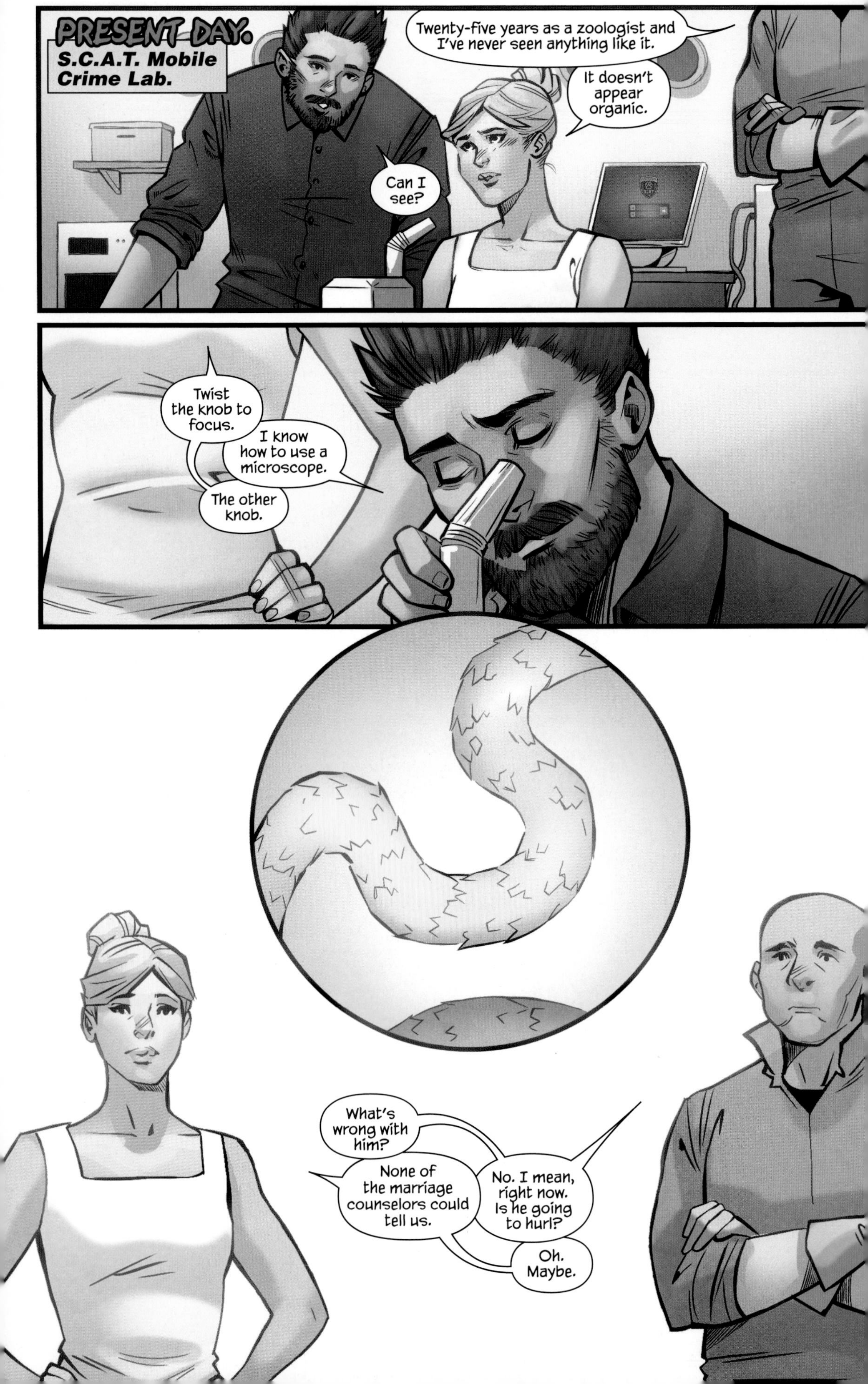
PRESENT DAY.
S.C.A.T. Mobile Crime Lab.
Twenty-five years as a zoologist and I've never seen anything like it.
It doesn't appear organic.
Can I see?
Twist the knob to focus.
I know how to use a microscope.
The other knob.
What's wrong with him?
None of the marriage counselors could tell us.
No. I mean, right now. Is he going to hurl?
Oh. Maybe.

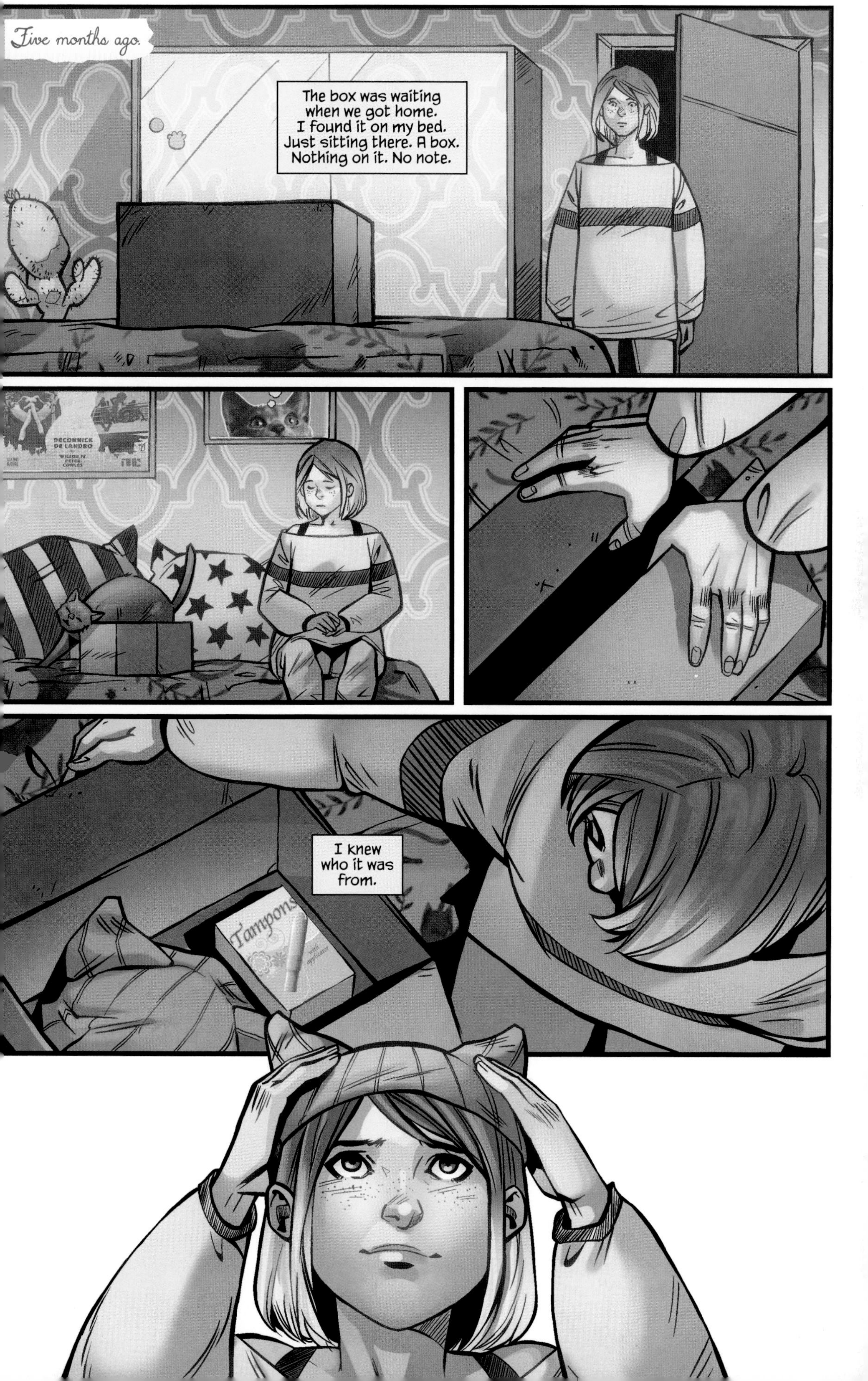
Five months ago.
The box was waiting when we got home. I found it on my bed. Just sitting there. A box. Nothing on it. No note.
I knew who it was from.
Tampons
with applicator

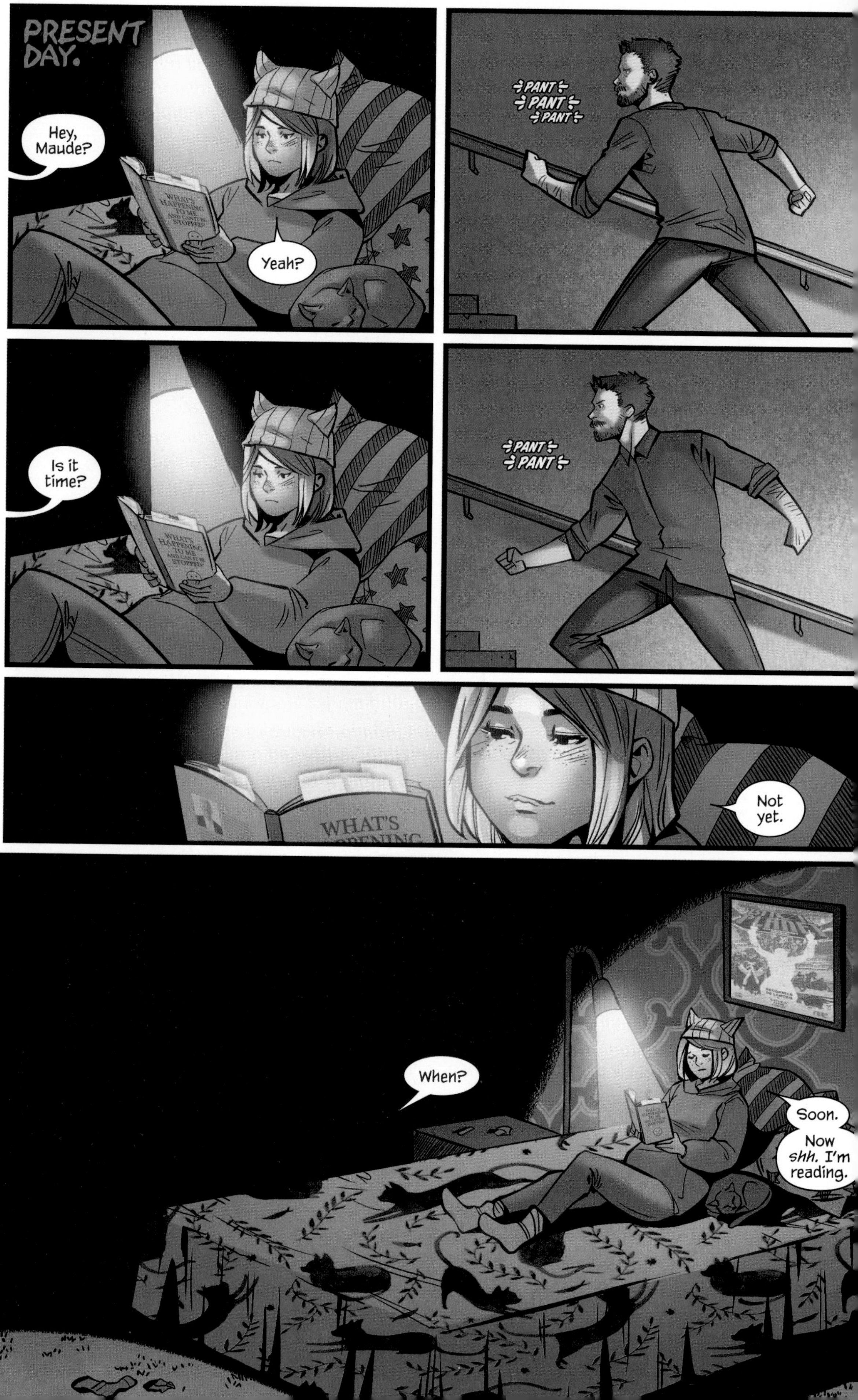
PRESENT DAY.
Hey, Maude?
WHAT'S HAPPENING TO ME AND CAN IT BE STOPPED?
Yeah?
PANT
PANT
PANT
Is it time?
WHAT'S HAPPENING TO ME AND CAN IT BE STOPPED?
PANT
PANT
Not yet.
When?
Soon.
Now *shh.* I'm reading.

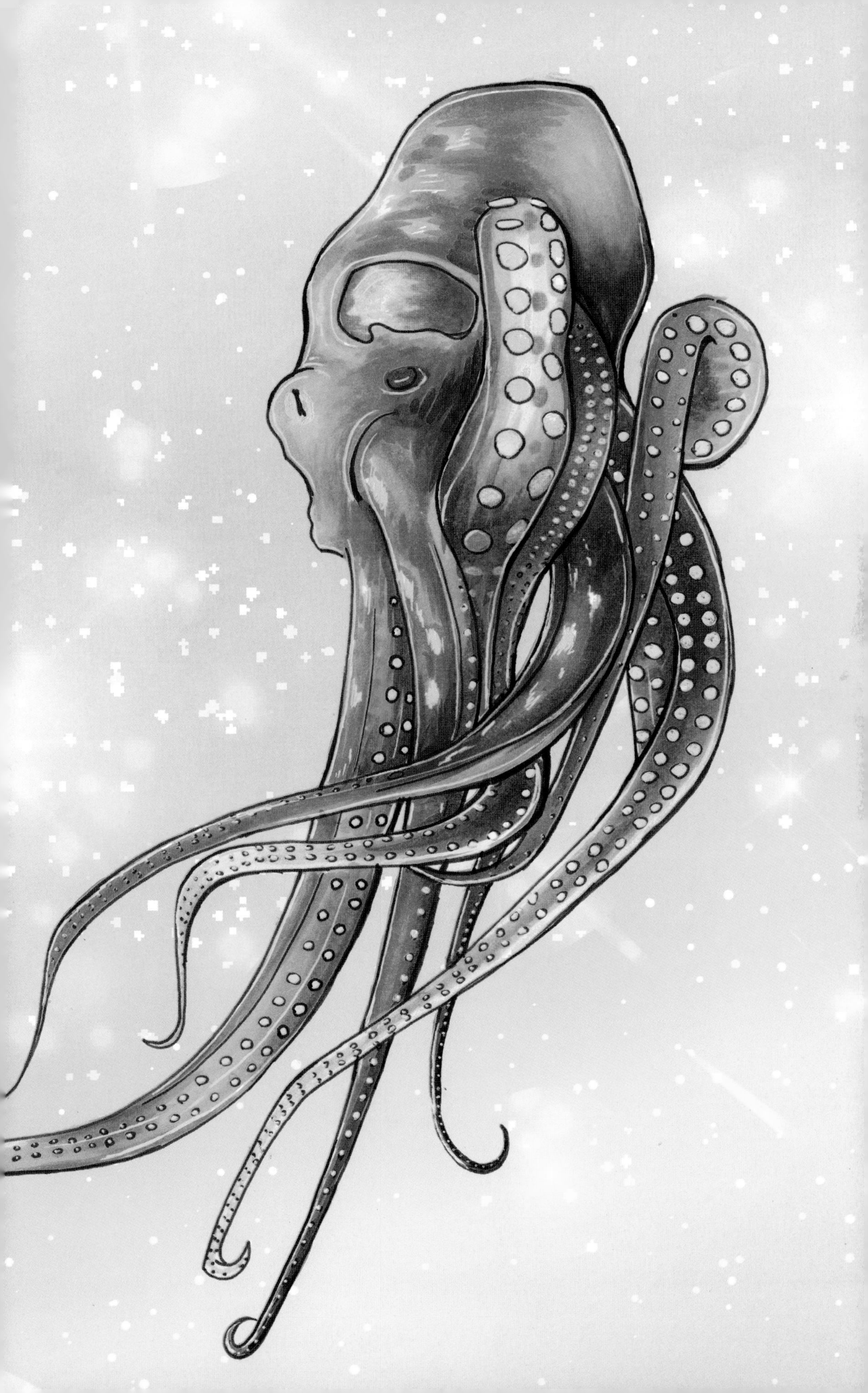

HERE I AM

ELIZA FANTASTIC MOHAN, AGE 13

You said we were forever
two souls entwined
happy together
you said a lot of things
and guess what stuck?
"Goodbye you little _____"
Sure made an impression
Here we were
Here I am
Clinging to the hope
That I'll find you again
And when I do
I'll come back to you
On my knees, begging,
"Please"
Words have been spoken
Tears have been shed
You made me into something
I never would have been
Here we were
Here I am
You used to confine me
But now I'm thriving
Here we were
Here I am
I thought I needed you
I was wrong again
You broke my heart
Shattered it in two
But now I know
I can do so much without you
You locked me in a cage
Threw away the key
But I took that time to ponder
Wonder
Question
Chant
Now
Finally
I'm
Free

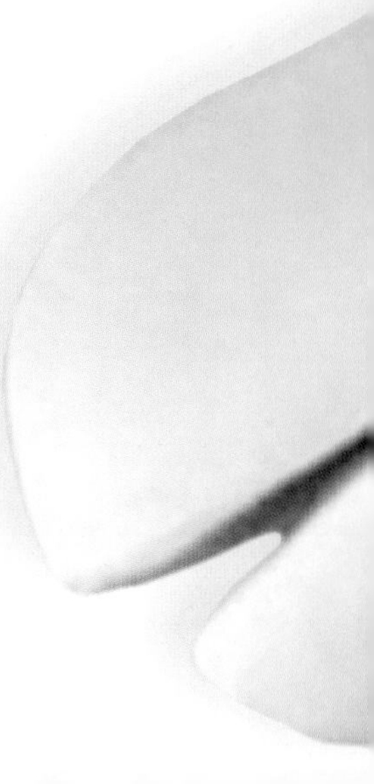

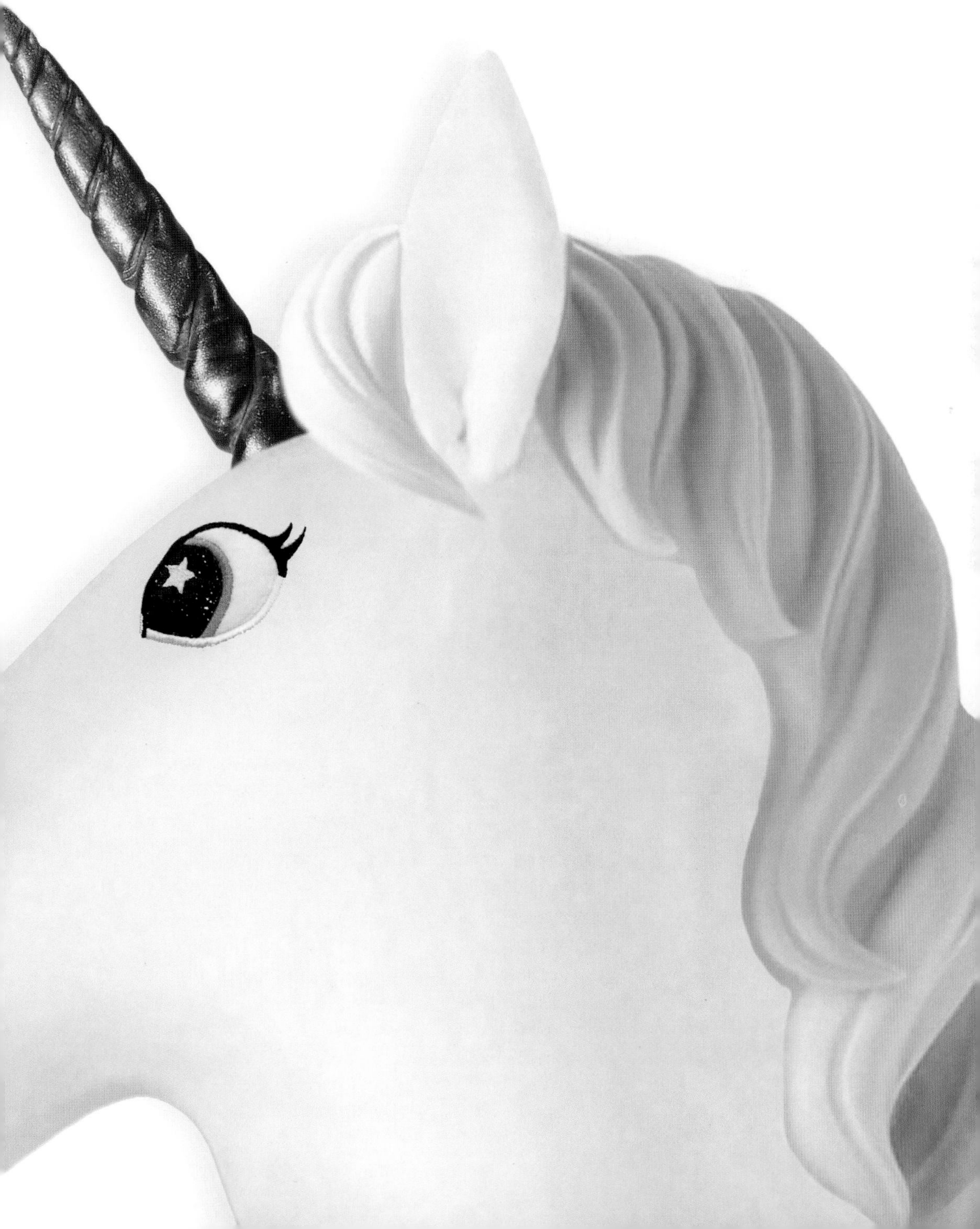

MISSING

HAVE YOU SEEN THIS GIRL?

Sophie E.

Age: 13   Height: 5'4"   Weight: 120

LAST SEEN AT SCHOOL IN THE SECOND FLOOR RESTROOM
IF YOU HAVE ANY INFORMATION OR HAVE SEEN SOPHIE PLEASE CONTACT
THE PACIFIC NORTHWEST S.C.A.T. OFFICE OR CALL 911

DO NOT APPROACH

MINISTRY OF
TROUBLE
INCORPORATED

 WRITER/CREATOR
CHELSEA CAIN

 PENCILS
KATE NIEMCZYK

 INKS
ELISE MCCALL

 COLORIST
RACHELLE ROSENBERG

 LETTERER
JOE CARAMAGNA

 COVER/CO-CREATOR
LIA MITERNIQUE

 **ADDITIONAL
INTERIOR ART**
LIA MITERNIQUE
STELLA GREENVOSS

 HAIKU
EMILY POWELL

 POEM
ELIZA FANTASTIC MOHAN

 SWAGGER
KATIE LANE

YOU HAVE BEEN CONTACTED BY THE MINISTRY OF TROUBLE. AWAIT FURTHER INSTRUCTIONS. ☿

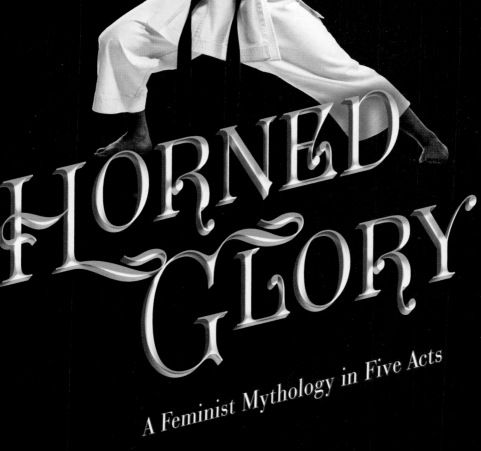

a Sophie E. production

HORNED GLORY

A Feminist Mythology in Five Acts

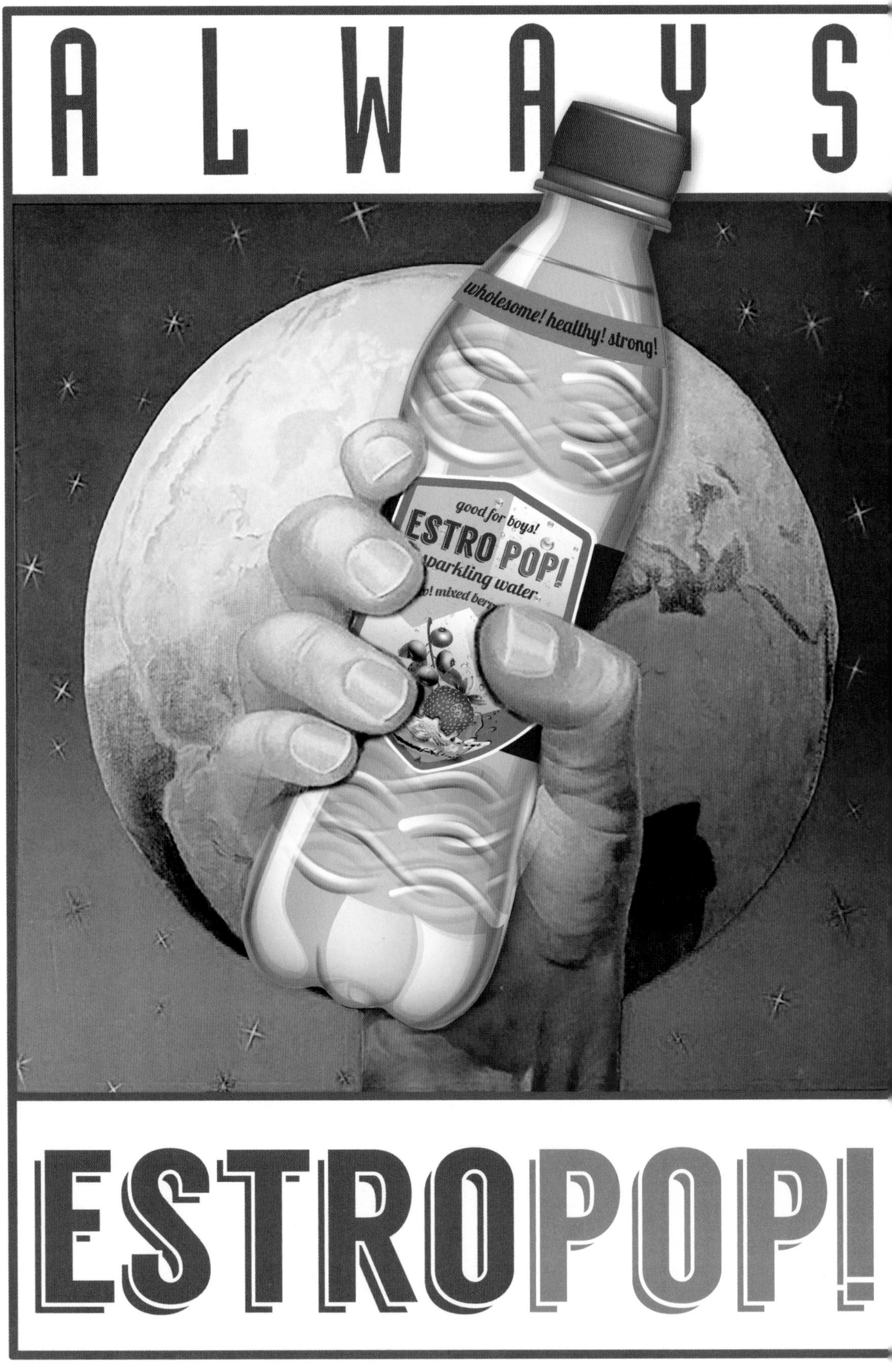
ALWAYS
wholesome! healthy! strong!
good for boys!
ESTRO POP!
sparkling water
ESTROPOP!

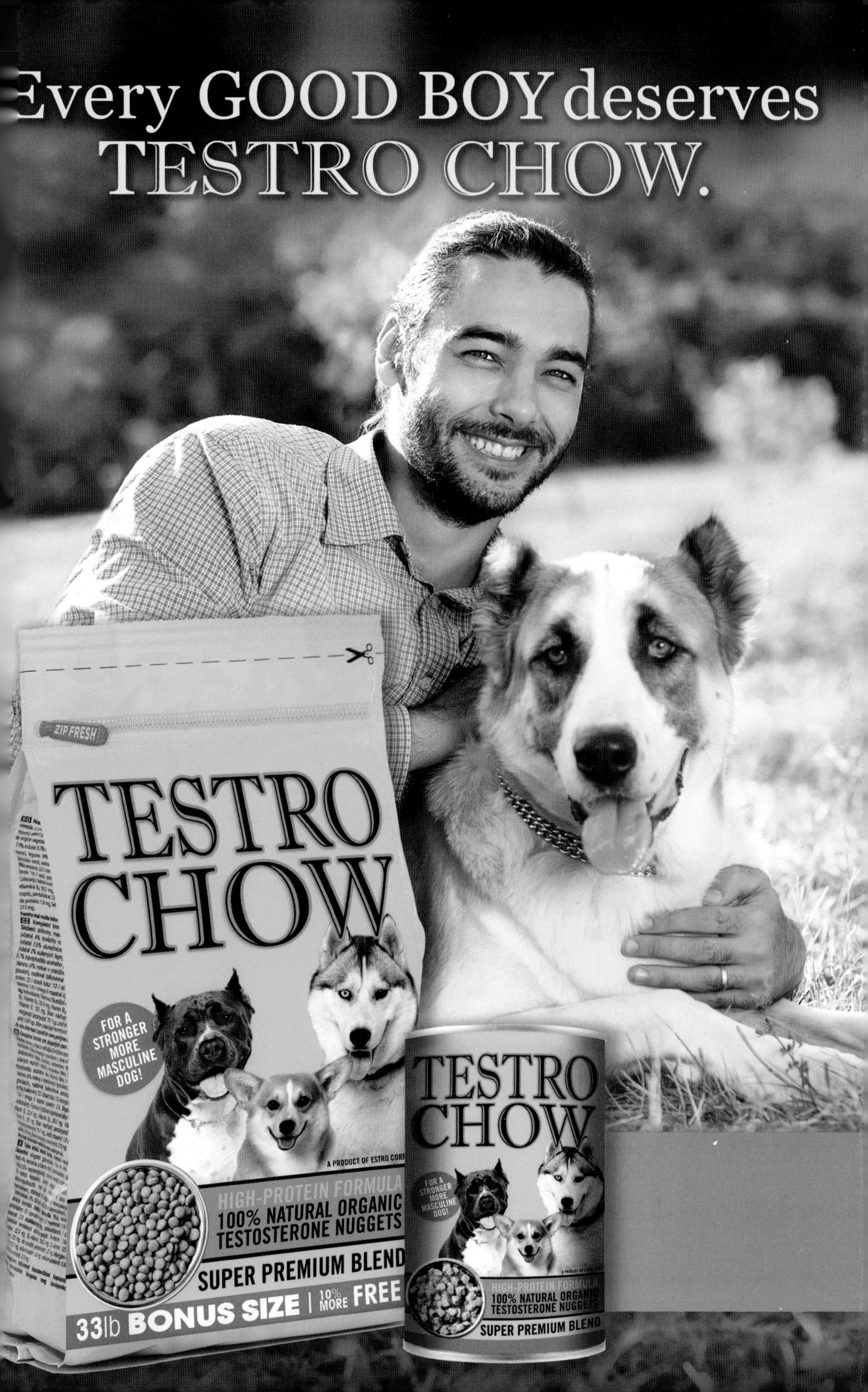
Every GOOD BOY deserves
TESTRO CHOW.
ZIP FRESH
TESTRO
CHOW
FOR A STRONGER MORE MASCULINE DOG!
HIGH-PROTEIN FORMULA
100% NATURAL ORGANIC
TESTOSTERONE NUGGETS
SUPER PREMIUM BLEND
33lb BONUS SIZE | 10% MORE FREE
TESTRO
CHOW
FOR A STRONGER MORE MASCULINE DOG!
HIGH-PROTEIN FORMULA
100% NATURAL ORGANIC
TESTOSTERONE NUGGETS
SUPER PREMIUM BLEND

VOLUME 2

CHAPTER
two

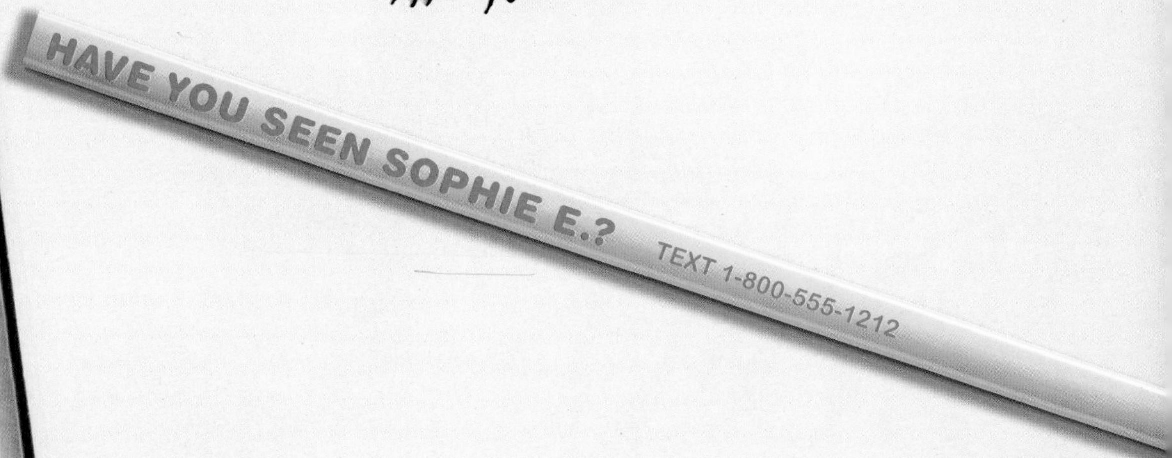
HAVE YOU SEEN SOPHIE E.?
TEXT 1-800-555-1212

man-eaters™

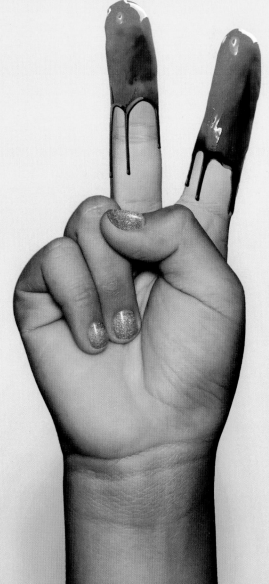

NO. 6

CHELSEA CAIN KATE NIEMCZYK RACHELLE ROSENBERG JOE CARAMAGNA LIA MITERNIQUE

POWELL MIDDLE SCHOOL

October 17

Dear Parent or Guardian,

There has been a case of menstruation at your child's school. On Tuesday, October 4, at approximately 1:05 PM, a seventh grade student at Powell Middle School experienced a menstrual event in the second floor girls' bathroom.

Your child may have been exposed.

For the safety of our community, female students - and any males with female sex organs - must report to the school nurse's office for a puberty check before being permitted to attend school.

With your help, we can contain this outbreak.

Sincerely,

SIAN McARTHUR
School Nurse

Portland Public Schools are partially funded by Estro Corp and the Estro Corp Foundation

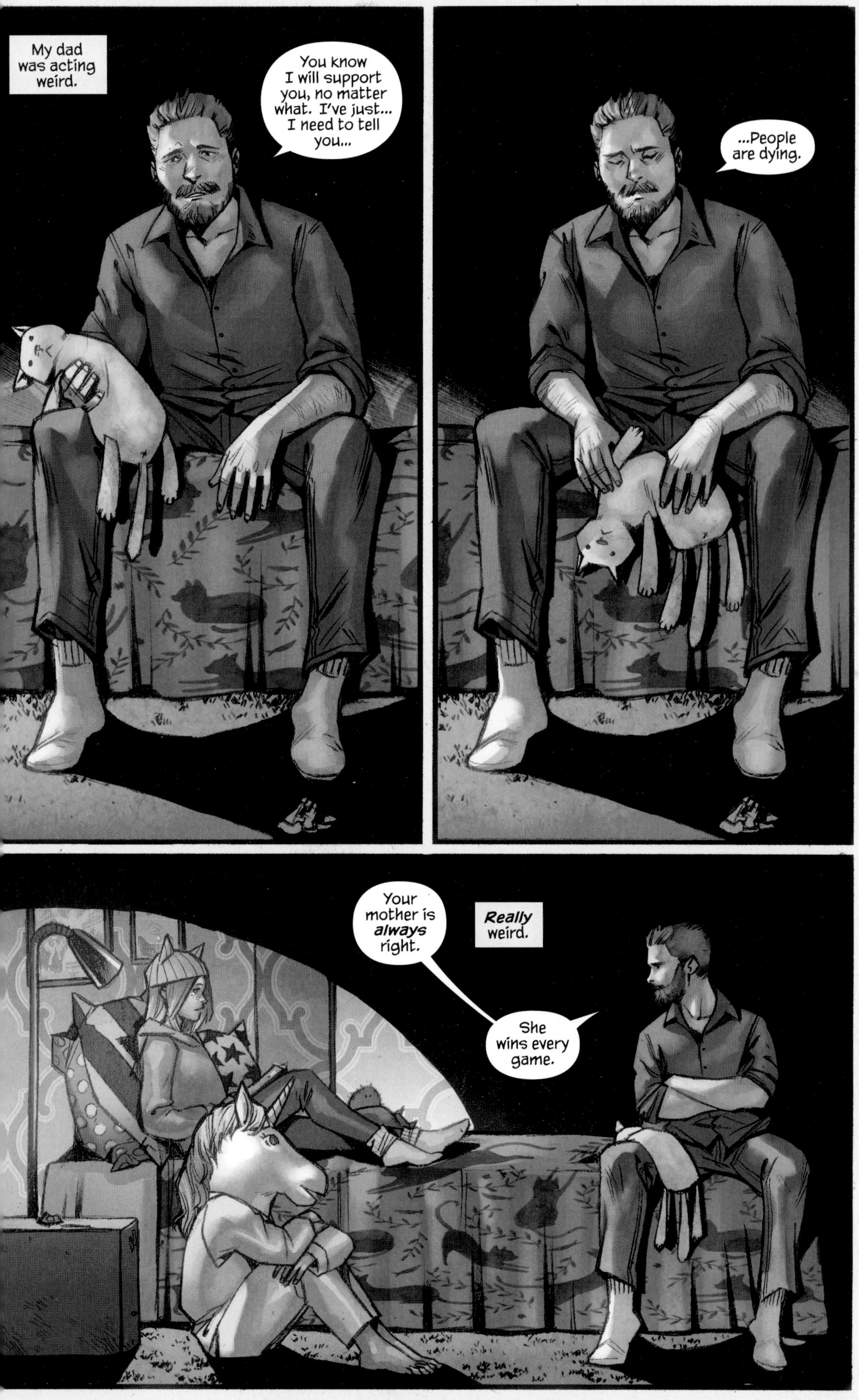
My dad was acting weird.
You know I will support you, no matter what. I've just... I need to tell you...
...People are dying.
Your mother is *always* right.
Really weird.
She wins every game.

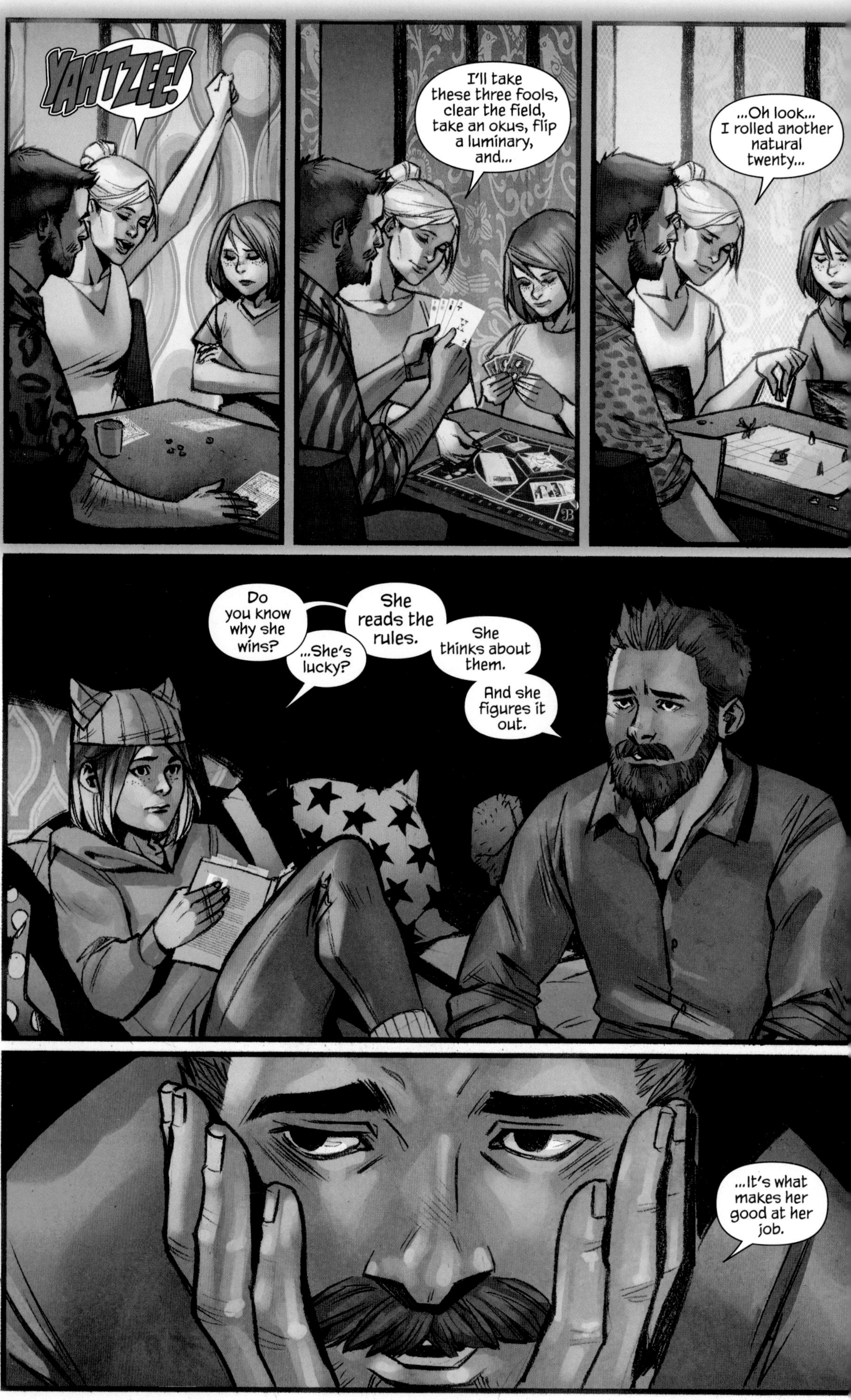
YAHTZEE!
I'll take these three fools, clear the field, take an okus, flip a luminary, and...
...Oh look... I rolled another natural twenty...
Do you know why she wins?
...She's lucky?
She reads the rules.
She thinks about them.
And she figures it out.
...It's what makes her good at her job.

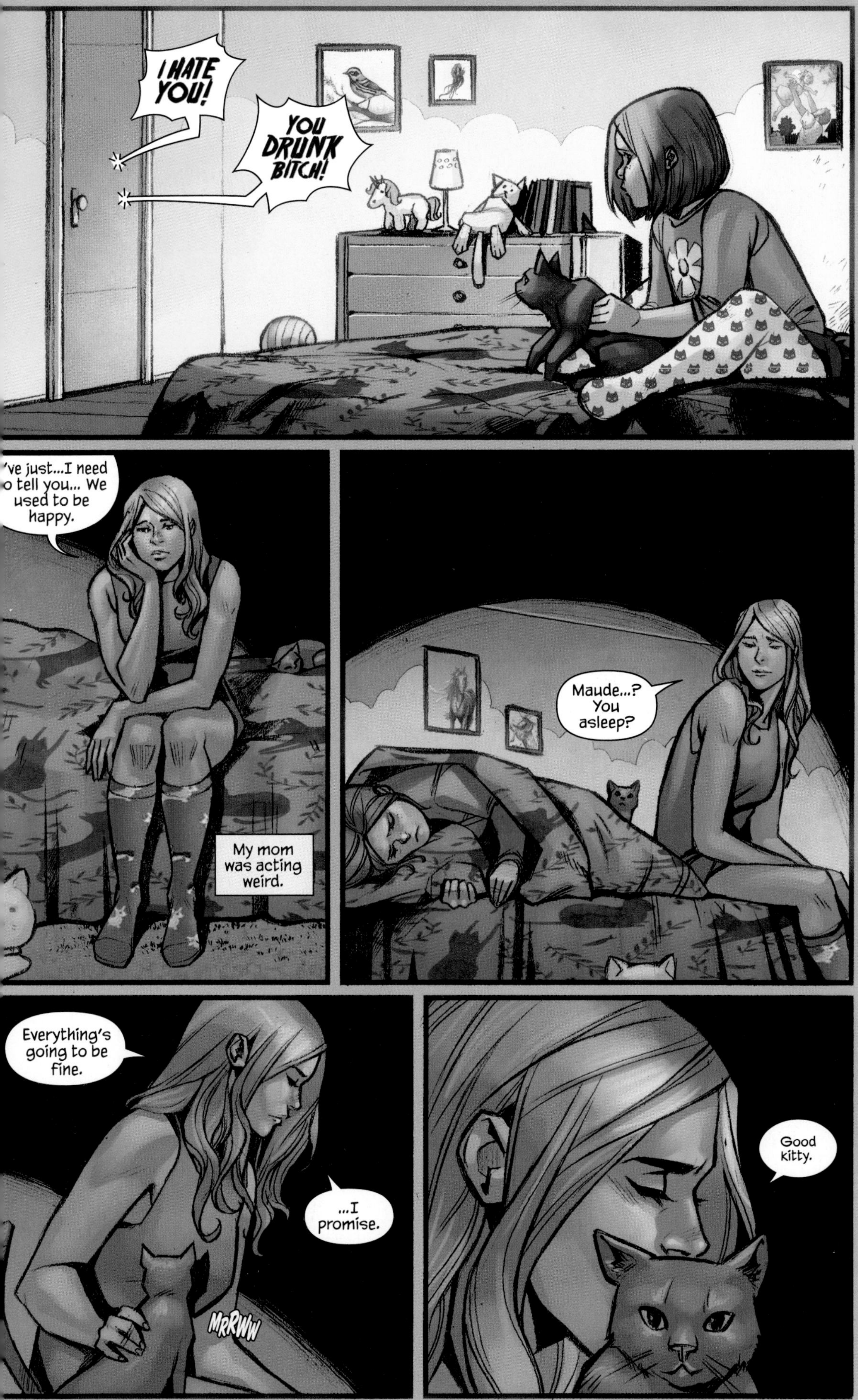

I HATE YOU!
YOU DRUNK BITCH!
've just...I need
o tell you... We used to be happy.
My mom was acting weird.
Maude...? You asleep?
Everything's going to be fine.
...I promise.
MRRWW
Good kitty.

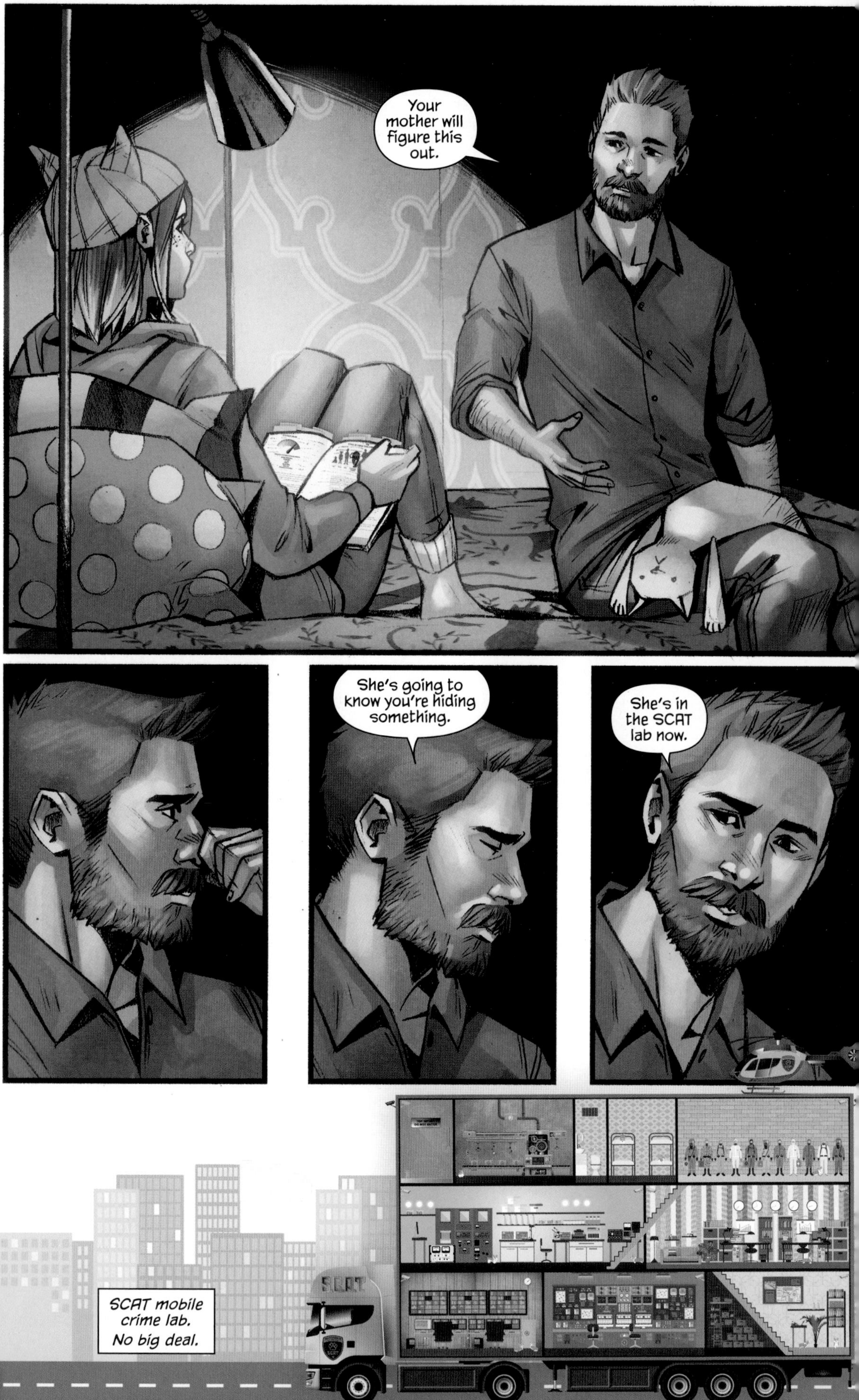
Your mother will figure this out.
She's going to know you're hiding something.
She's in the SCAT lab now.
SCAT mobile crime lab. No big deal.

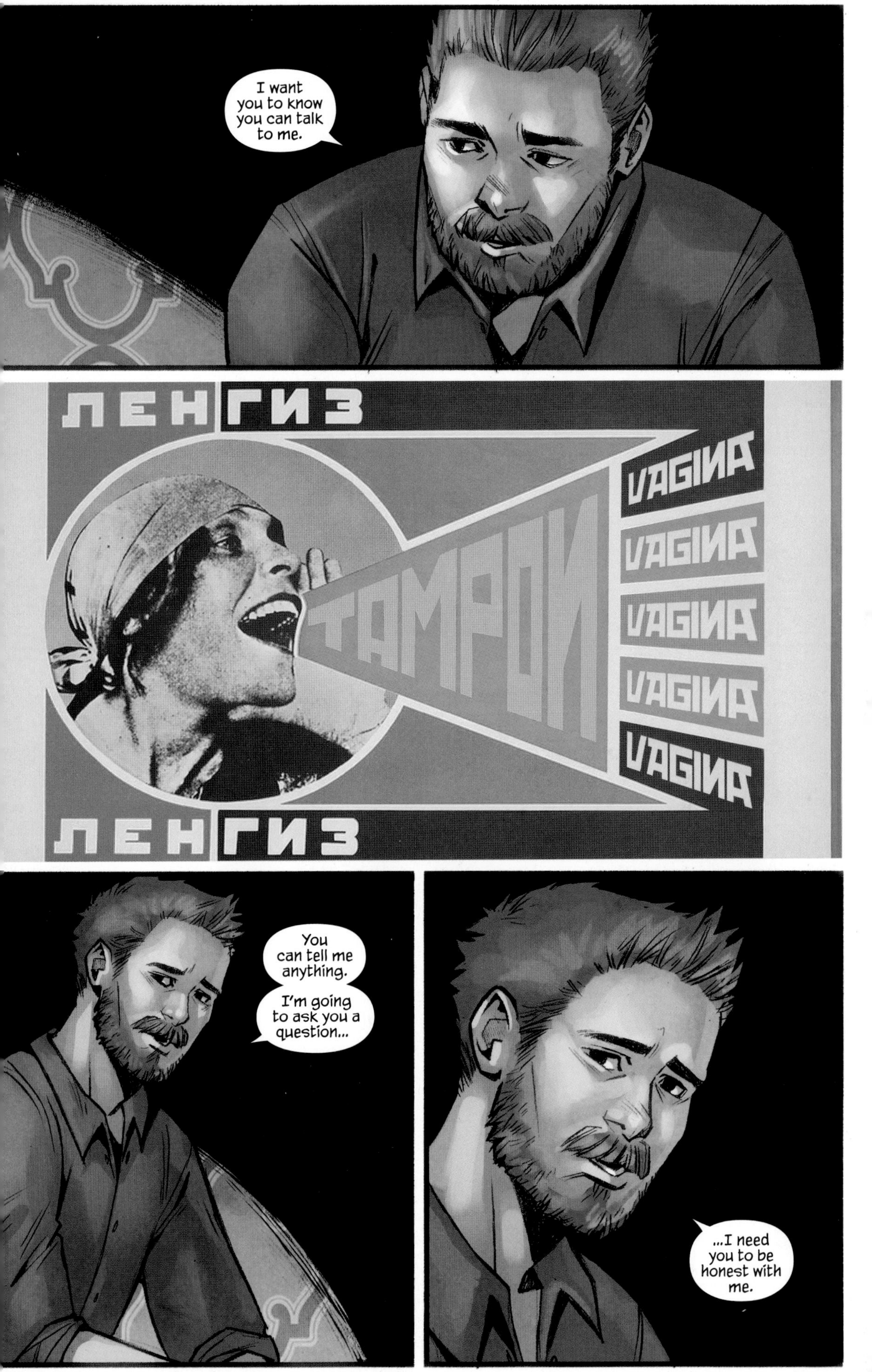
I want you to know you can talk to me.
ЛЕНГИЗ
TAMPON
VAGINA
VAGINA
VAGINA
VAGINA
VAGINA
ЛЕНГИЗ
You can tell me anything.
I'm going to ask you a question...
...I need you to be honest with me.

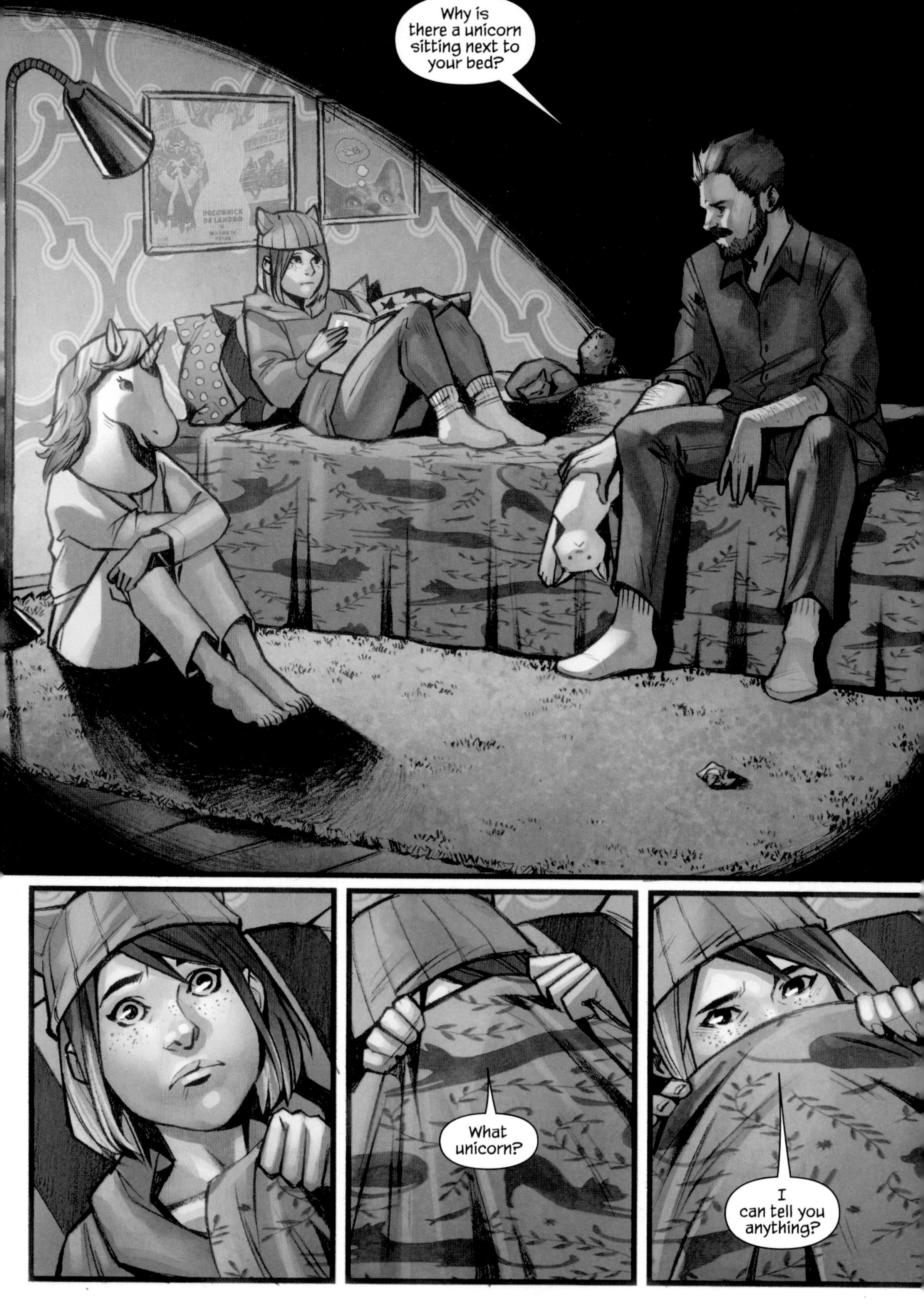
Why is there a unicorn sitting next to your bed?
What unicorn?
I can tell you anything?

Angry Unicorn

FILTER

HORNED GLORY - A Feminist Mythology in Five Acts
SophieE • 1.2m views • 5 months ago

I wrote a play. It's about a girl who discovers she's a unicorn and a taekwondo master who discovers she's a girl. I hope you enjoy it! (Hi, Grandma and Grandpa!)
My theme was: "instantiation."
I only got a B because my teacher said the assignment was to write a paragraph not produce a 17 minutes live stage production.
But it fulfilled my PE requirement.

REPOST OF STRANGE UNICORN KID
Casey • 987k views • 5 months ago

OMG I FOUND THIS WEIRD VIDEO ON THE INTERNET AND HAVE TO REPOST HERE. THIS IS THE BEST THING I'VE EVER SEEN LOLOLLLOLLLLOL

I Have A Horn - Top Female Songs 2019
Amanda Dennis • 35k views • 3 months ago

Hi, everyone. This is a song I wrote about identity and gender politics and unicorns and cats and the sound of rain. It's really special to me. And I hope you like it, too.

Unicorn EN COLÈRE
Sabine • 11k views • 3 months ago

Bonjour! J'avais l'habitude de se sentir seul et triste. Puis j'ai vu la vidéo de licorne en colère. Maintenant, j'ai beaucoup d'amis. Nous avons tous regarder l'unicorn en colère ensemble. Vive la Licorne en Colère!

Gniewnego jednorożec
Kate Niemczyk • 9.2k views • 2 months ago

Witam, wszystkich! Uwielbiam gniewnego jednorożcowych wyzwól mię. Czy masz?

READY FOR HER CLOSE-UP - Grant Elementary School
Marcia • 8.2k views • 2 months ago

Samantha, getting ready for her school production of Horned Glory.
(Some play she found on the Internet?) Samantha plays the lead!

HAS ANYONE SEEN THIS UNICORN? - SE PORTLAND
Jerry • 8.1k views • 1 day ago

Um…Has anyone else seen this creepy kid in a unicorn mask in the Portland area? I was able to video it at a distance…

Act I

"If I don't like something that's going on in my life, I change it. And I don't sit and complain about it for a year."

– Kim Kardashian

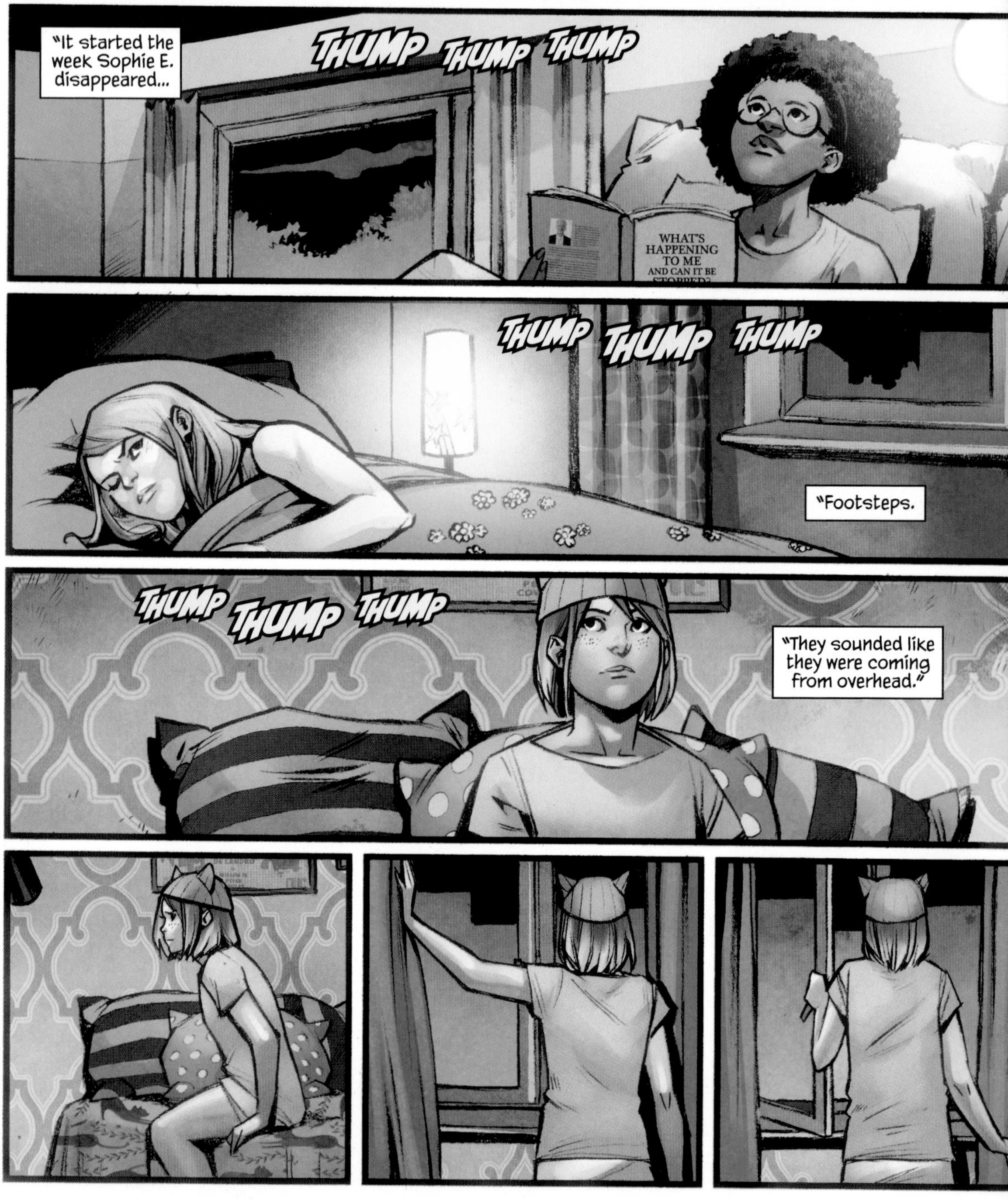

"It started the week Sophie E. disappeared...
THUMP THUMP THUMP
WHAT'S HAPPENING TO ME AND CAN IT BE
THUMP THUMP THUMP
"Footsteps.
THUMP THUMP THUMP
"They sounded like they were coming from overhead."

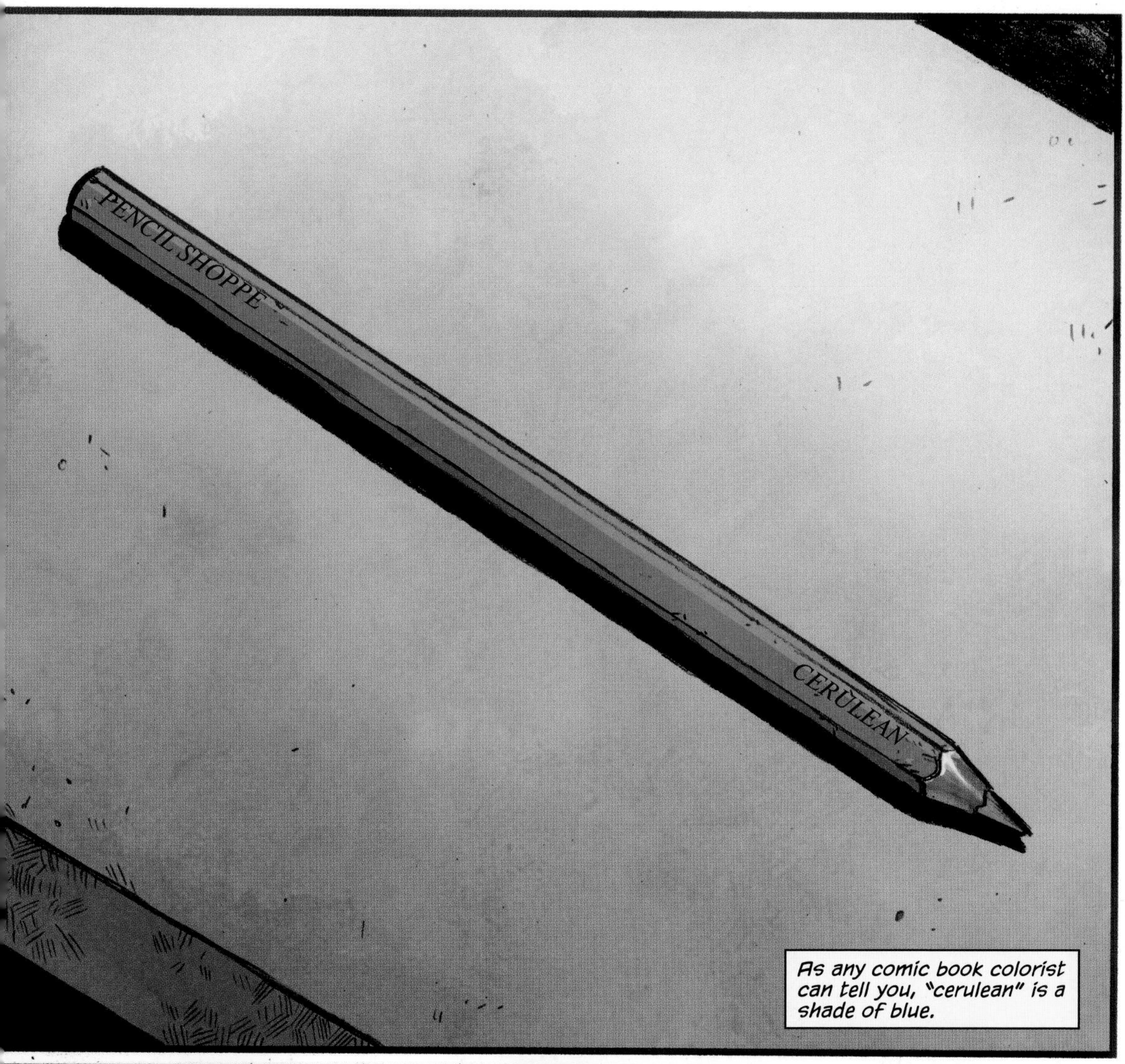
PENCIL SHOPPE
CERULEAN
As any comic book colorist can tell you, "cerulean" is a shade of blue.

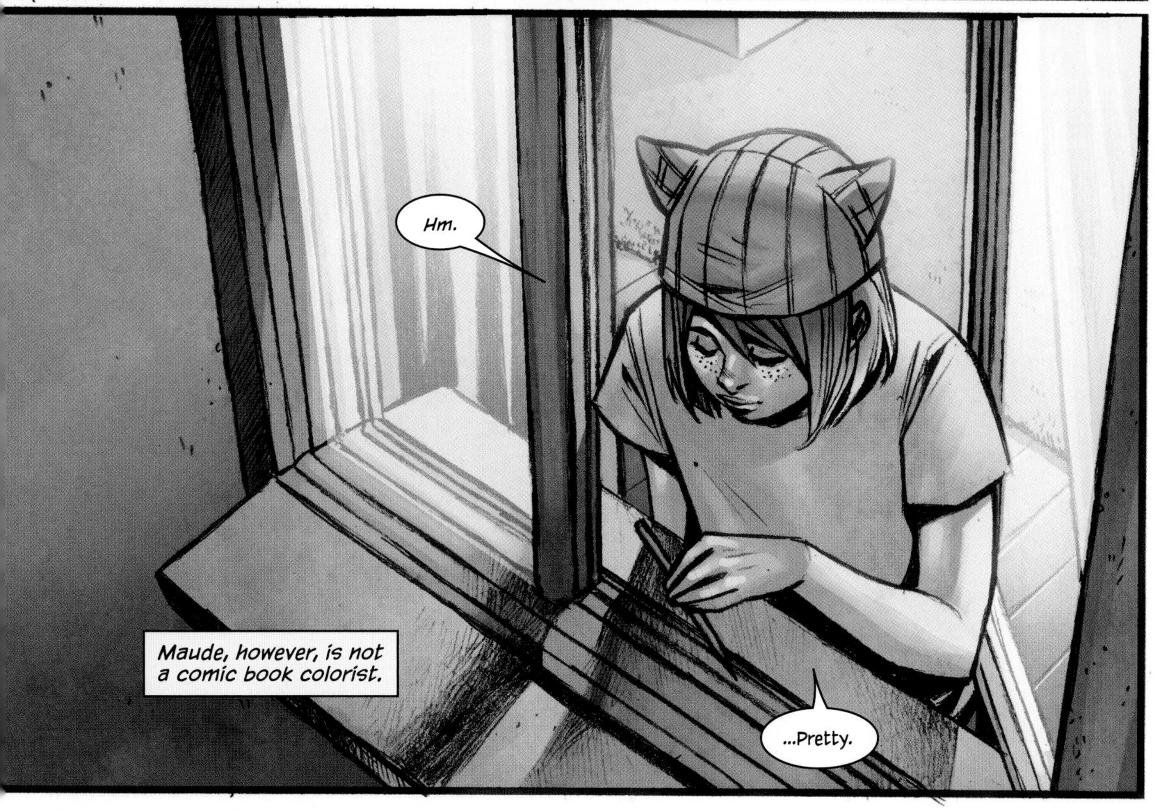
Hm.
Maude, however, is not a comic book colorist.
...Pretty.

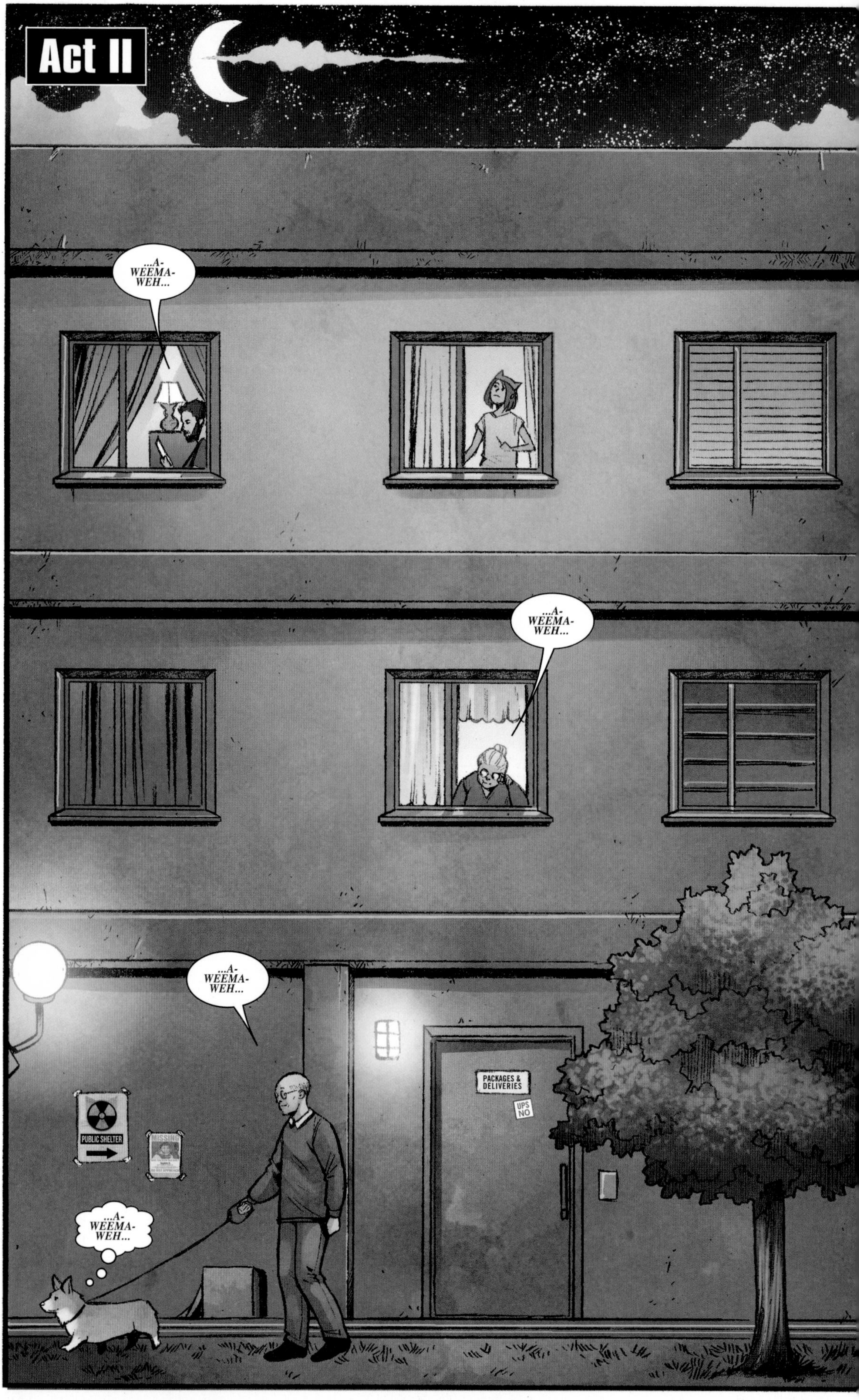
Act II
...A-WEEMA-WEH...
...A-WEEMA-WEH...
...A-WEEMA-WEH...
PUBLIC SHELTER
MISSING
PACKAGES & DELIVERIES
UPS NO
...A-WEEMA-WEH...

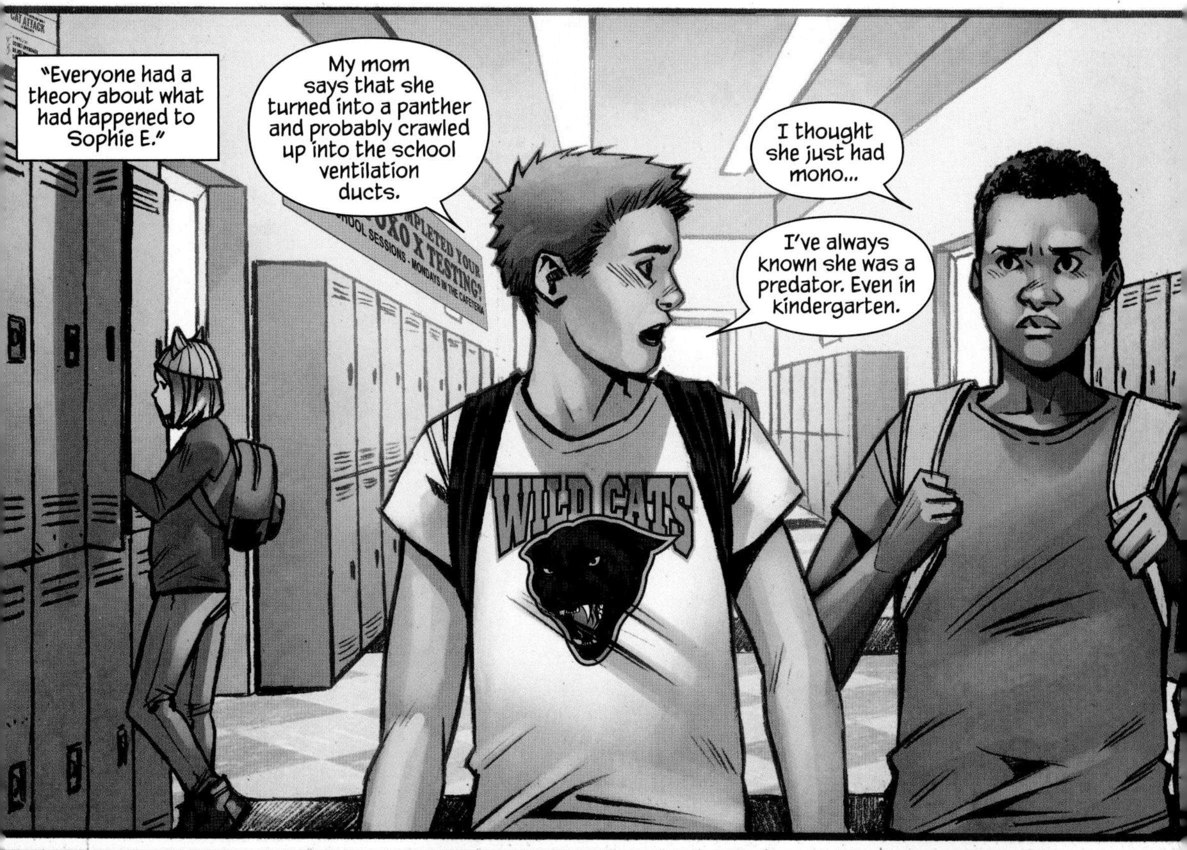
"Everyone had a theory about what had happened to Sophie E."
My mom says that she turned into a panther and probably crawled up into the school ventilation ducts.
I thought she just had mono...
I've always known she was a predator. Even in kindergarten.
WILD CATS

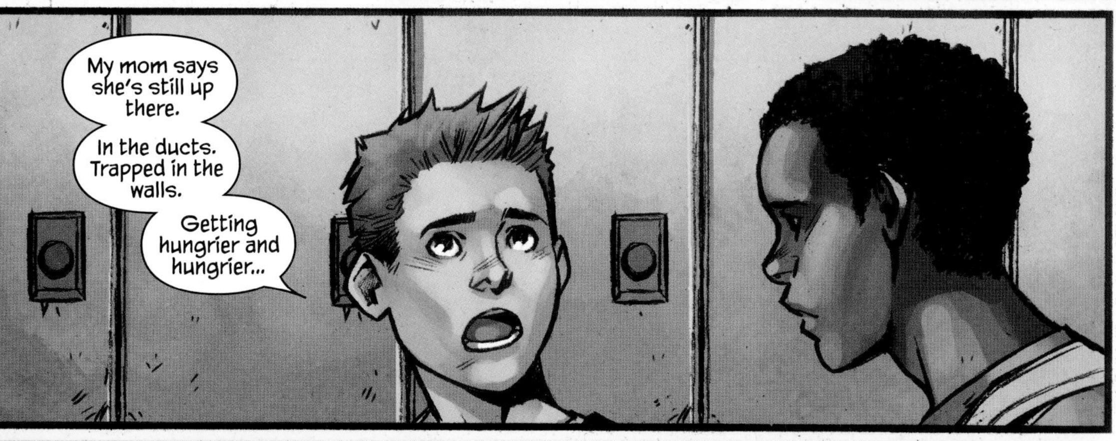
My mom says she's still up there.
In the ducts. Trapped in the walls.
Getting hungrier and hungrier...

Act III

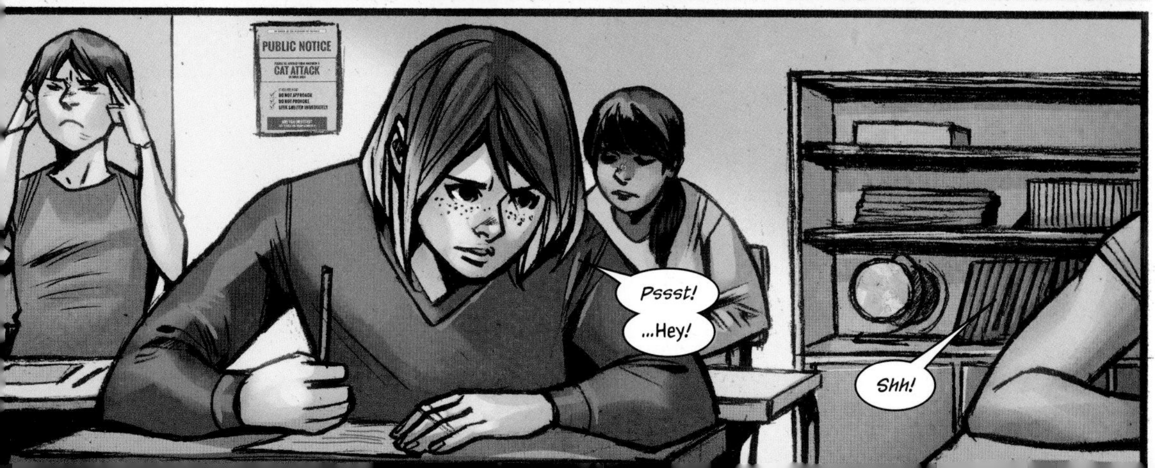
PUBLIC NOTICE
CAT ATTACK
DO NOT APPROACH
DO NOT PROVOKE
SEEK SHELTER IMMEDIATELY
Pssst!
...Hey!
Shh!

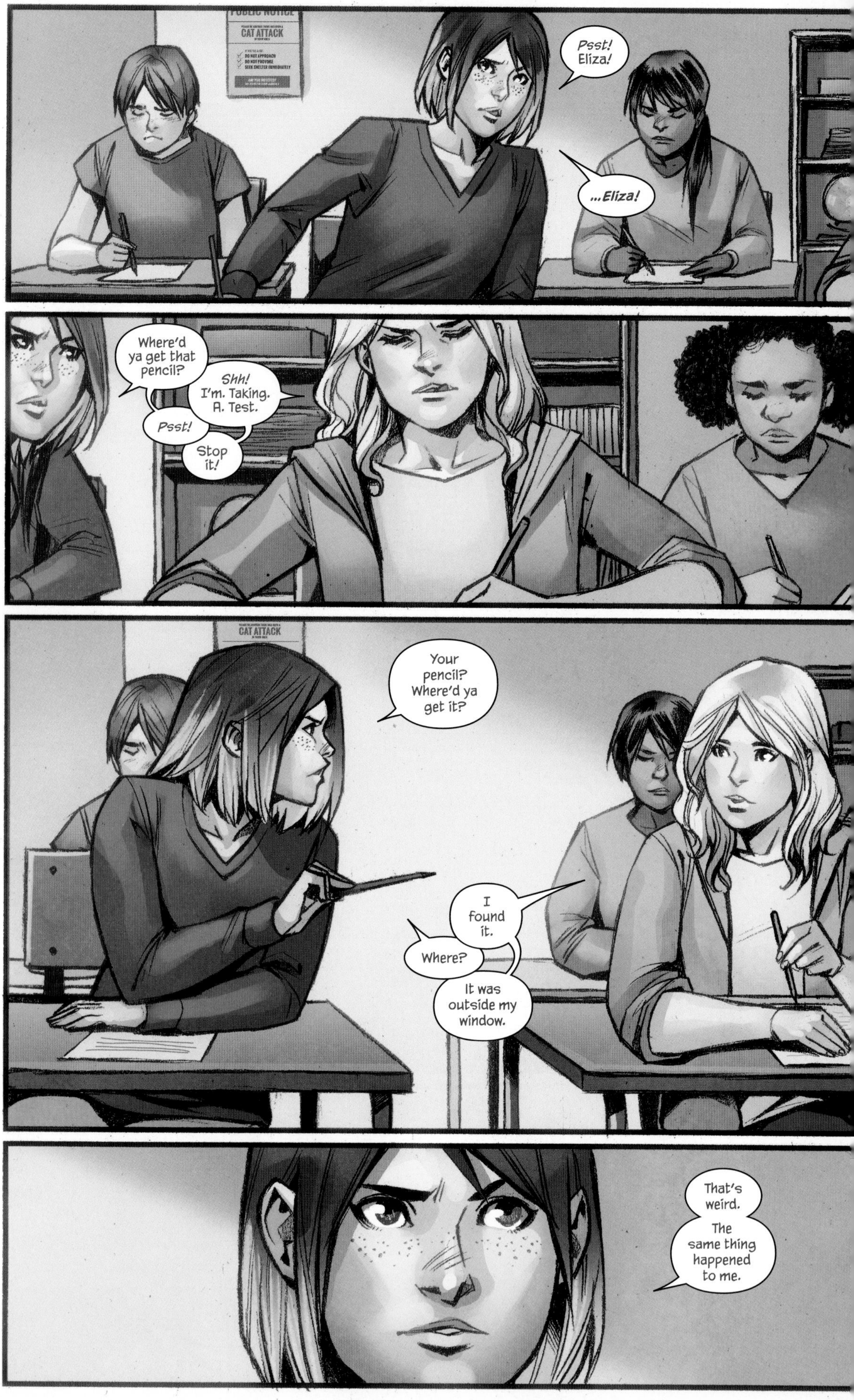
CAT ATTACK
Psst! Eliza!
...Eliza!
Where'd ya get that pencil?
Shh! I'm. Taking. A. Test.
Psst!
Stop it!
CAT ATTACK
Your pencil? Where'd ya get it?
I found it.
Where?
It was outside my window.
That's weird.
The same thing happened to me.

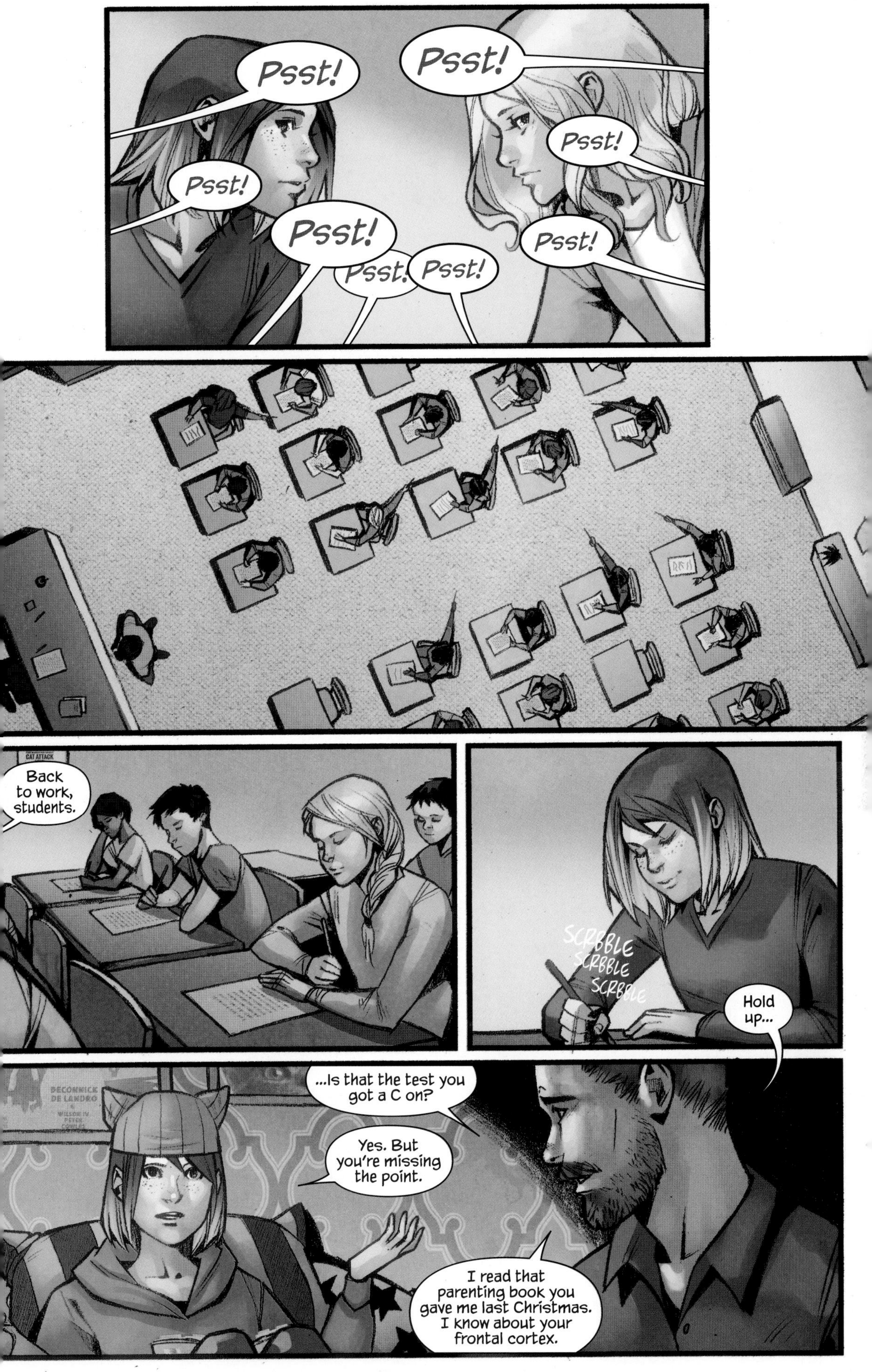
Psst!
Psst!
Psst!
Psst!
Psst!
Psst!
Psst!
Psst!
Back to work, students.
SCRBBLE
SCRBBLE
SCRBBLE
Hold up...
...Is that the test you got a C on?
Yes. But you're missing the point.
I read that parenting book you gave me last Christmas. I know about your frontal cortex.

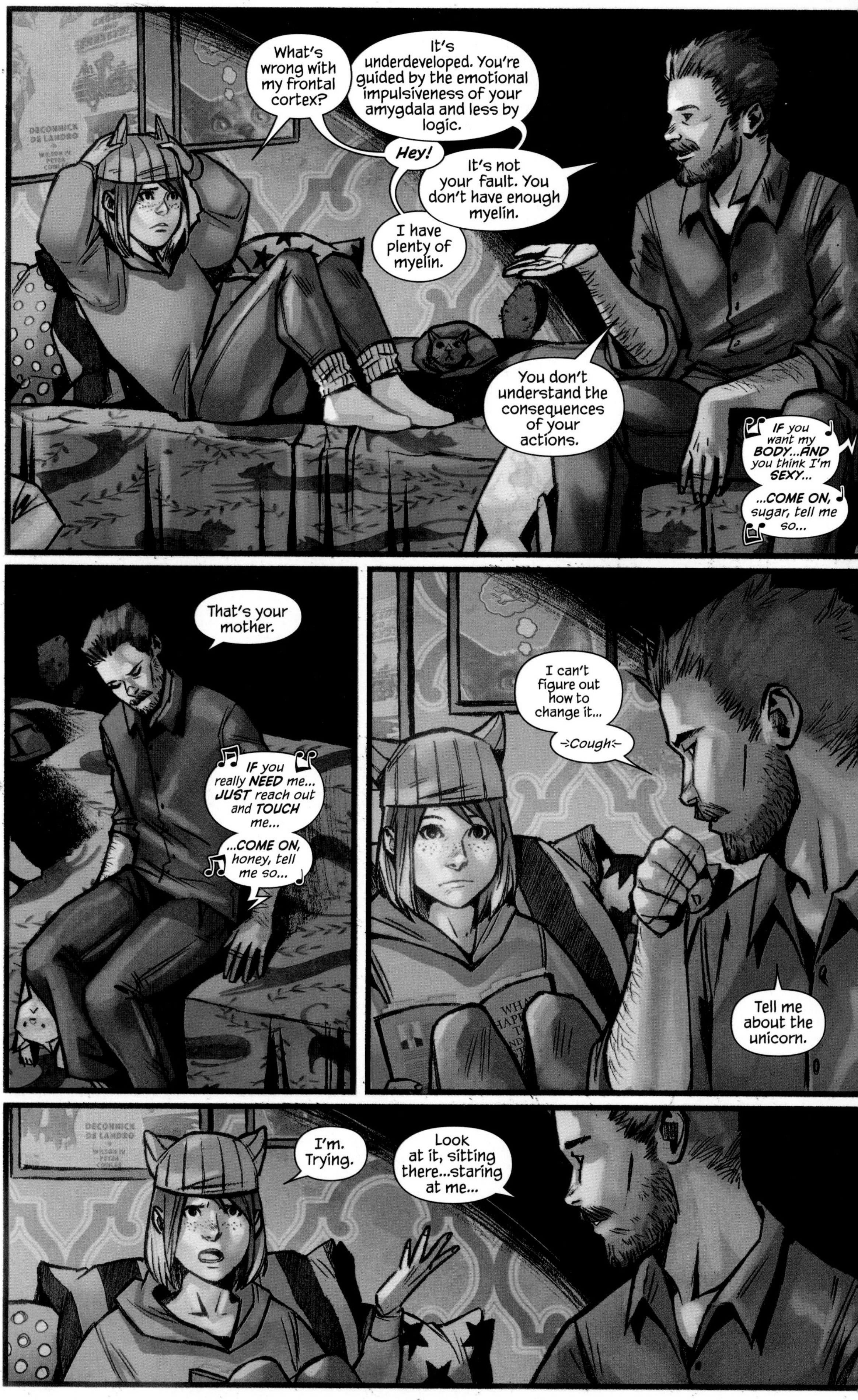
What's wrong with my frontal cortex?
It's underdeveloped. You're guided by the emotional impulsiveness of your amygdala and less by logic.
Hey!
It's not your fault. You don't have enough myelin.
I have plenty of myelin.
You don't understand the consequences of your actions.
IF you want my BODY...AND you think I'm SEXY...
...COME ON, sugar, tell me so...
That's your mother.
IF you really NEED me... JUST reach out and TOUCH me...
...COME ON, honey, tell me so...
I can't figure out how to change it...
Cough
Tell me about the unicorn.
I'm. Trying.
Look at it, sitting there...staring at me...

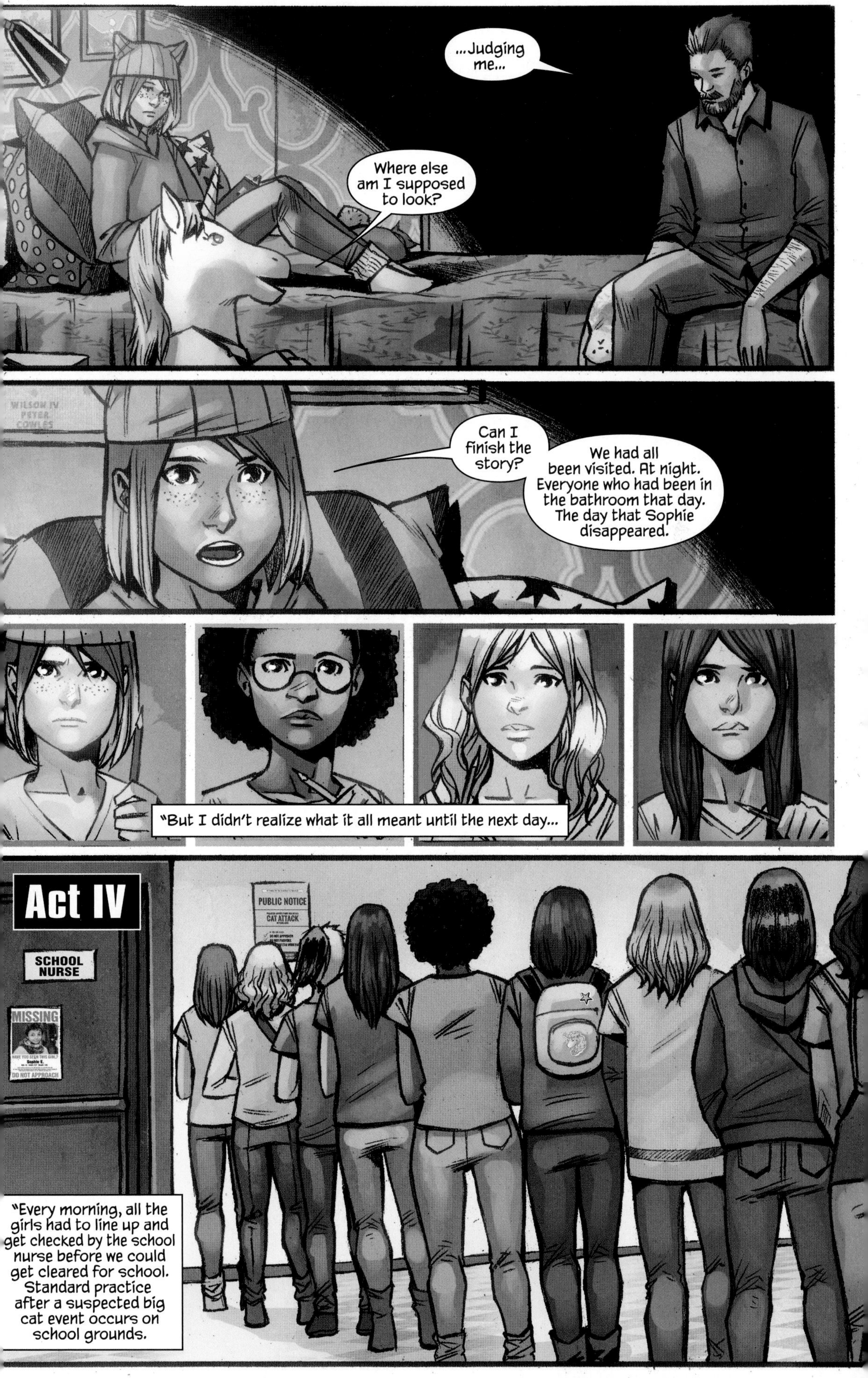

...Judging me...
Where else am I supposed to look?
WILSON IV
PETER
COWLES
Can I finish the story?
We had all been visited. At night. Everyone who had been in the bathroom that day. The day that Sophie disappeared.
"But I didn't realize what it all meant until the next day...
Act IV
SCHOOL NURSE
MISSING
Sophie E.
DO NOT APPROACH
PUBLIC NOTICE
CAT ATTACK
"Every morning, all the girls had to line up and get checked by the school nurse before we could get cleared for school. Standard practice after a suspected big cat event occurs on school grounds.

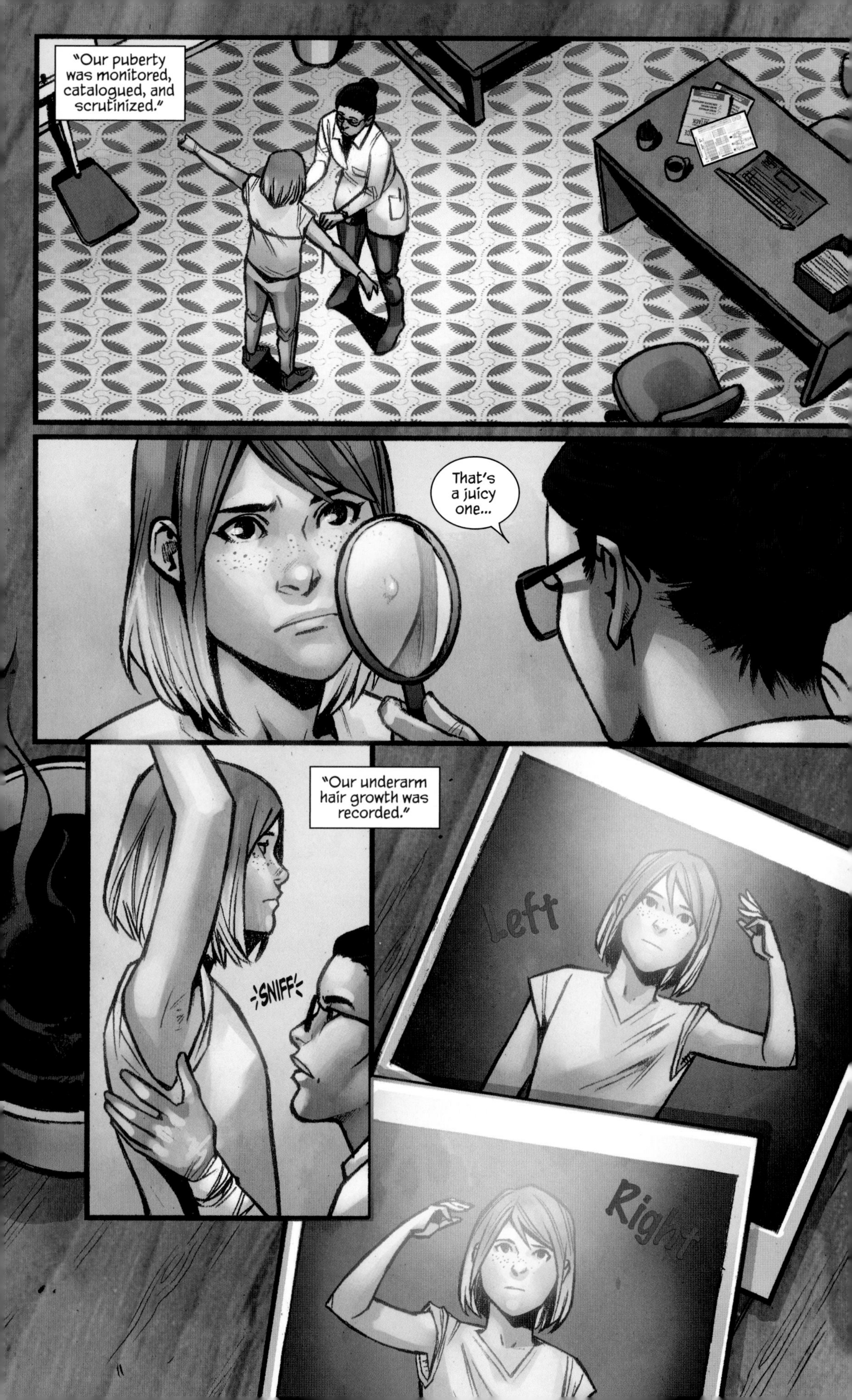
"Our puberty was monitored, catalogued, and scrutinized."
That's a juicy one...
"Our underarm hair growth was recorded."
SNIFF
Left
Right

Puberty Observation Form

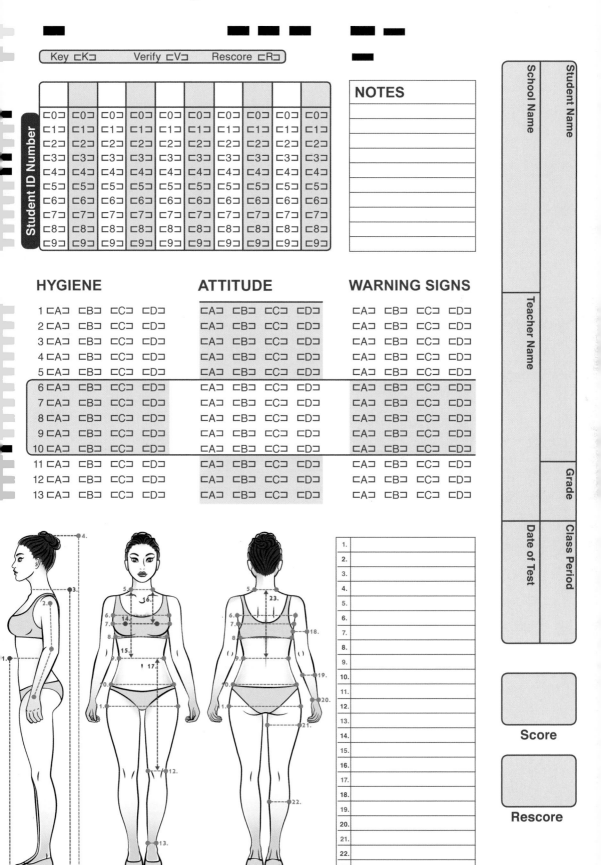

Key ⊏K⊐ Verify ⊏V⊐ Rescore ⊏R⊐

Student ID Number

⊏0⊐	⊏0⊐	⊏0⊐	⊏0⊐	⊏0⊐	⊏0⊐	⊏0⊐	⊏0⊐	⊏0⊐	⊏0⊐
⊏1⊐	⊏1⊐	⊏1⊐	⊏1⊐	⊏1⊐	⊏1⊐	⊏1⊐	⊏1⊐	⊏1⊐	⊏1⊐
⊏2⊐	⊏2⊐	⊏2⊐	⊏2⊐	⊏2⊐	⊏2⊐	⊏2⊐	⊏2⊐	⊏2⊐	⊏2⊐
⊏3⊐	⊏3⊐	⊏3⊐	⊏3⊐	⊏3⊐	⊏3⊐	⊏3⊐	⊏3⊐	⊏3⊐	⊏3⊐
⊏4⊐	⊏4⊐	⊏4⊐	⊏4⊐	⊏4⊐	⊏4⊐	⊏4⊐	⊏4⊐	⊏4⊐	⊏4⊐
⊏5⊐	⊏5⊐	⊏5⊐	⊏5⊐	⊏5⊐	⊏5⊐	⊏5⊐	⊏5⊐	⊏5⊐	⊏5⊐
⊏6⊐	⊏6⊐	⊏6⊐	⊏6⊐	⊏6⊐	⊏6⊐	⊏6⊐	⊏6⊐	⊏6⊐	⊏6⊐
⊏7⊐	⊏7⊐	⊏7⊐	⊏7⊐	⊏7⊐	⊏7⊐	⊏7⊐	⊏7⊐	⊏7⊐	⊏7⊐
⊏8⊐	⊏8⊐	⊏8⊐	⊏8⊐	⊏8⊐	⊏8⊐	⊏8⊐	⊏8⊐	⊏8⊐	⊏8⊐
⊏9⊐	⊏9⊐	⊏9⊐	⊏9⊐	⊏9⊐	⊏9⊐	⊏9⊐	⊏9⊐	⊏9⊐	⊏9⊐

NOTES

HYGIENE

1 ⊏A⊐ ⊏B⊐ ⊏C⊐ ⊏D⊐
2 ⊏A⊐ ⊏B⊐ ⊏C⊐ ⊏D⊐
3 ⊏A⊐ ⊏B⊐ ⊏C⊐ ⊏D⊐
4 ⊏A⊐ ⊏B⊐ ⊏C⊐ ⊏D⊐
5 ⊏A⊐ ⊏B⊐ ⊏C⊐ ⊏D⊐
6 ⊏A⊐ ⊏B⊐ ⊏C⊐ ⊏D⊐
7 ⊏A⊐ ⊏B⊐ ⊏C⊐ ⊏D⊐
8 ⊏A⊐ ⊏B⊐ ⊏C⊐ ⊏D⊐
9 ⊏A⊐ ⊏B⊐ ⊏C⊐ ⊏D⊐
10 ⊏A⊐ ⊏B⊐ ⊏C⊐ ⊏D⊐
11 ⊏A⊐ ⊏B⊐ ⊏C⊐ ⊏D⊐
12 ⊏A⊐ ⊏B⊐ ⊏C⊐ ⊏D⊐
13 ⊏A⊐ ⊏B⊐ ⊏C⊐ ⊏D⊐

ATTITUDE

⊏A⊐ ⊏B⊐ ⊏C⊐ ⊏D⊐
⊏A⊐ ⊏B⊐ ⊏C⊐ ⊏D⊐
⊏A⊐ ⊏B⊐ ⊏C⊐ ⊏D⊐
⊏A⊐ ⊏B⊐ ⊏C⊐ ⊏D⊐
⊏A⊐ ⊏B⊐ ⊏C⊐ ⊏D⊐
⊏A⊐ ⊏B⊐ ⊏C⊐ ⊏D⊐
⊏A⊐ ⊏B⊐ ⊏C⊐ ⊏D⊐
⊏A⊐ ⊏B⊐ ⊏C⊐ ⊏D⊐
⊏A⊐ ⊏B⊐ ⊏C⊐ ⊏D⊐
⊏A⊐ ⊏B⊐ ⊏C⊐ ⊏D⊐
⊏A⊐ ⊏B⊐ ⊏C⊐ ⊏D⊐
⊏A⊐ ⊏B⊐ ⊏C⊐ ⊏D⊐
⊏A⊐ ⊏B⊐ ⊏C⊐ ⊏D⊐

WARNING SIGNS

⊏A⊐ ⊏B⊐ ⊏C⊐ ⊏D⊐
⊏A⊐ ⊏B⊐ ⊏C⊐ ⊏D⊐
⊏A⊐ ⊏B⊐ ⊏C⊐ ⊏D⊐
⊏A⊐ ⊏B⊐ ⊏C⊐ ⊏D⊐
⊏A⊐ ⊏B⊐ ⊏C⊐ ⊏D⊐
⊏A⊐ ⊏B⊐ ⊏C⊐ ⊏D⊐
⊏A⊐ ⊏B⊐ ⊏C⊐ ⊏D⊐
⊏A⊐ ⊏B⊐ ⊏C⊐ ⊏D⊐
⊏A⊐ ⊏B⊐ ⊏C⊐ ⊏D⊐
⊏A⊐ ⊏B⊐ ⊏C⊐ ⊏D⊐
⊏A⊐ ⊏B⊐ ⊏C⊐ ⊏D⊐
⊏A⊐ ⊏B⊐ ⊏C⊐ ⊏D⊐
⊏A⊐ ⊏B⊐ ⊏C⊐ ⊏D⊐

Student Name

School Name

Teacher Name

Grade

Class Period

Date of Test

Score

Rescore

1.
2.
3.
4.
5.
6.
7.
8.
9.
10.
11.
12.
13.
14.
15.
16.
17.
18.
19.
20.
21.
22.
23.

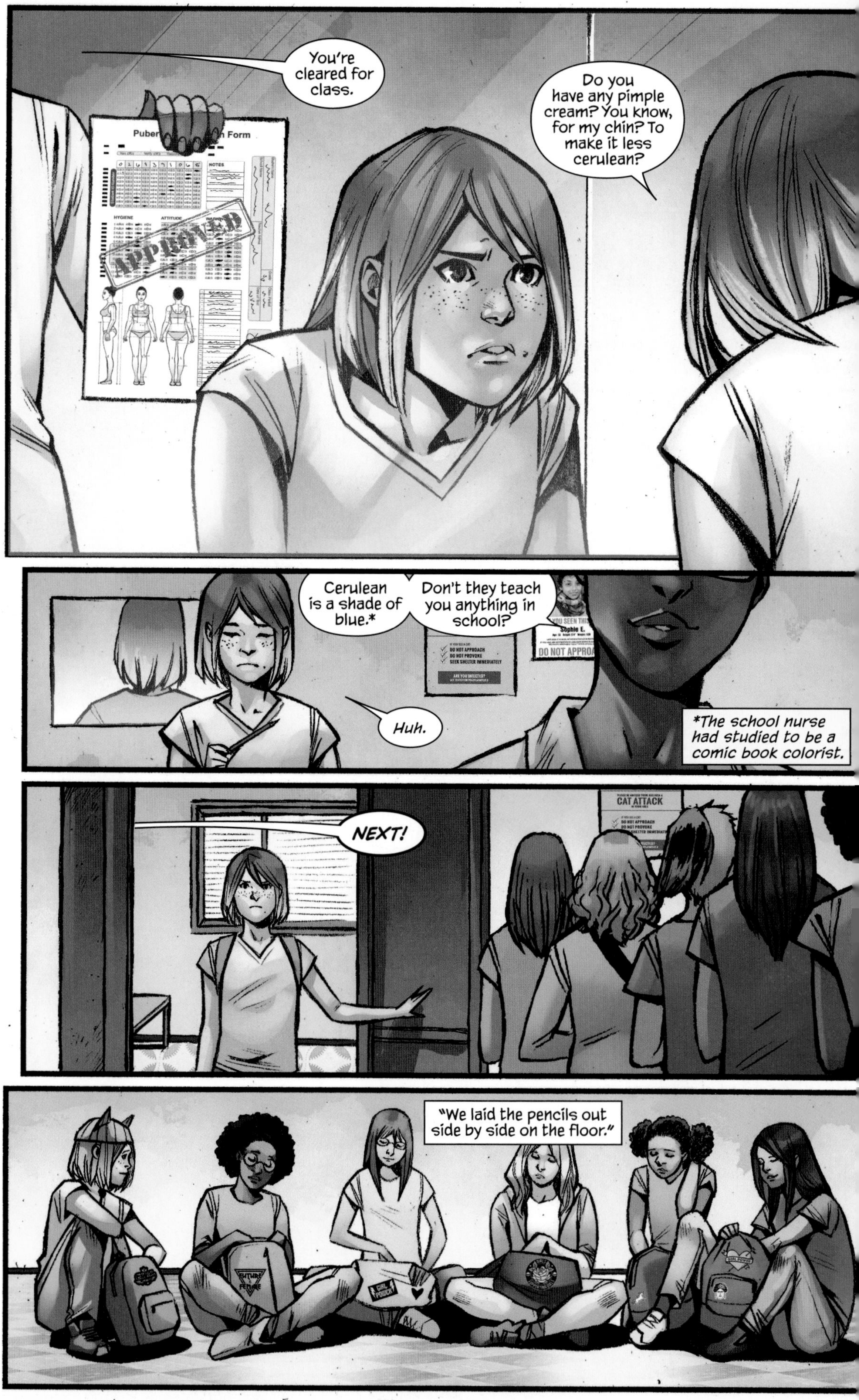

You're cleared for class.
APPROVED
Do you have any pimple cream? You know, for my chin? To make it less cerulean?
Cerulean is a shade of blue.*
Don't they teach you anything in school?
DO NOT APPROACH
Huh.
*The school nurse had studied to be a comic book colorist.
NEXT!
CAT ATTACK
"We laid the pencils out side by side on the floor."

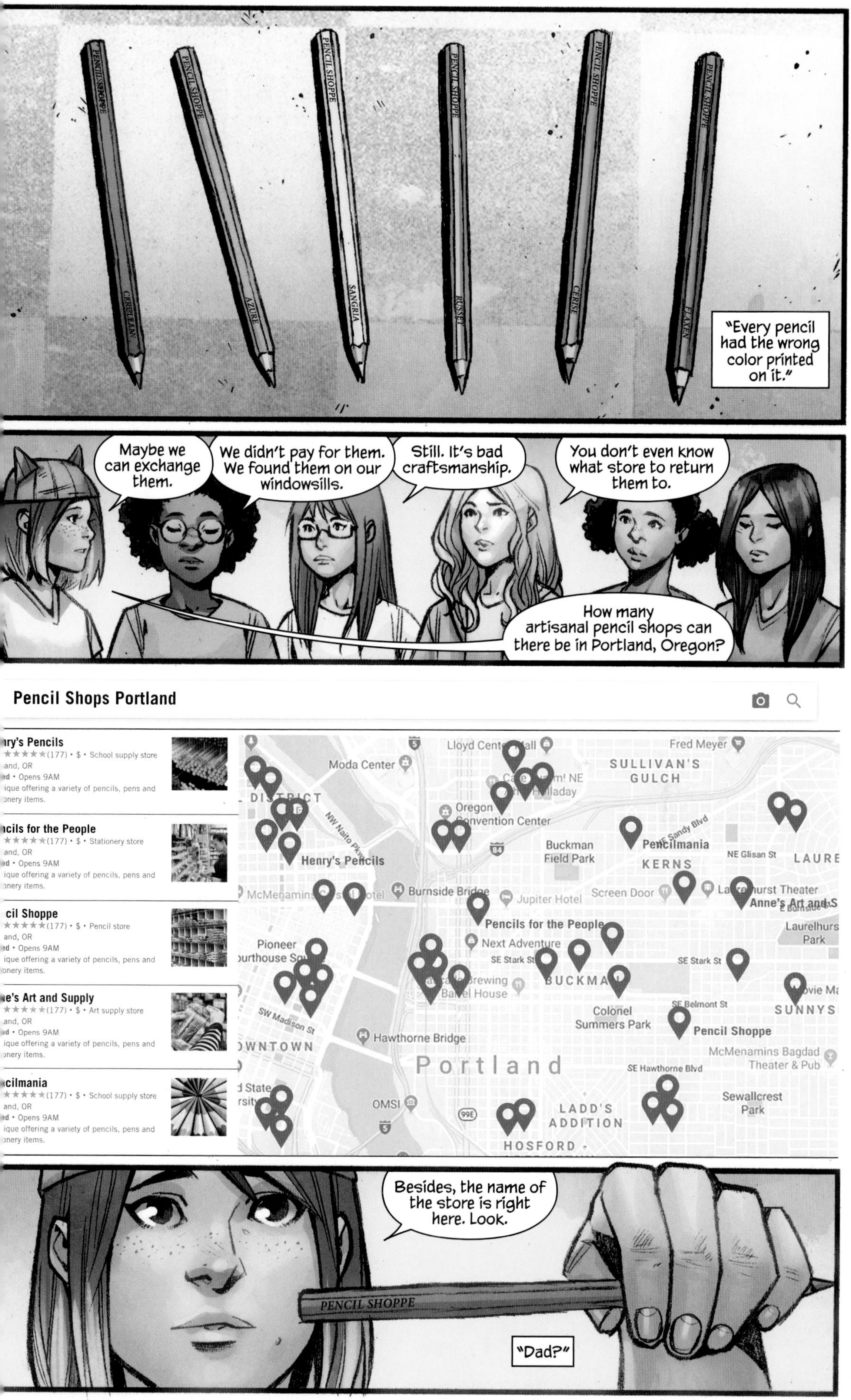
PENCIL SHOPPE
CERULEAN
PENCIL SHOPPE
AZURE
PENCIL SHOPPE
SANGRIA
PENCIL SHOPPE
RUSSET
PENCIL SHOPPE
CERISE
PENCIL SHOPPE
FLAXEN
"Every pencil had the wrong color printed on it."
Maybe we can exchange them.
We didn't pay for them. We found them on our windowsills.
Still. It's bad craftsmanship.
You don't even know what store to return them to.
How many artisanal pencil shops can there be in Portland, Oregon?
Pencil Shops Portland
ry's Pencils
★★★★★(177) • $ • School supply store
and, OR
d • Opens 9AM
ique offering a variety of pencils, pens and
onery items.
ncils for the People
★★★★★(177) • $ • Stationery store
and, OR
d • Opens 9AM
ique offering a variety of pencils, pens and
onery items.
cil Shoppe
★★★★★(177) • $ • Pencil store
and, OR
d • Opens 9AM
ique offering a variety of pencils, pens and
onery items.
e's Art and Supply
★★★★★(177) • $ • Art supply store
and, OR
d • Opens 9AM
ique offering a variety of pencils, pens and
onery items.
cilmania
★★★★★(177) • $ • School supply store
and, OR
d • Opens 9AM
ique offering a variety of pencils, pens and
onery items.
Lloyd Center Mall
Fred Meyer
Moda Center
SULLIVAN'S GULCH
Oregon Convention Center
NW Naito Pkwy
Henry's Pencils
Buckman Field Park
NE Sandy Blvd
Pencilmania
NE Glisan St
KERNS
LAURE
Burnside Bridge
Jupiter Hotel
Screen Door
Anne's Art and S
Pencils for the People
Laurelhurst Park
Pioneer
Next Adventure
SE Stark St
SE Stark St
SW Madison St
Hawthorne Bridge
BUCKMA
Colonel Summers Park
SE Belmont St
Pencil Shoppe
SUNNYS
DOWNTOWN
McMenamins Bagdad Theater & Pub
Portland
SE Hawthorne Blvd
OMSI
LADD'S ADDITION
Sewallcrest Park
HOSFORD -
Besides, the name of the store is right here. Look.
PENCIL SHOPPE
"Dad?"

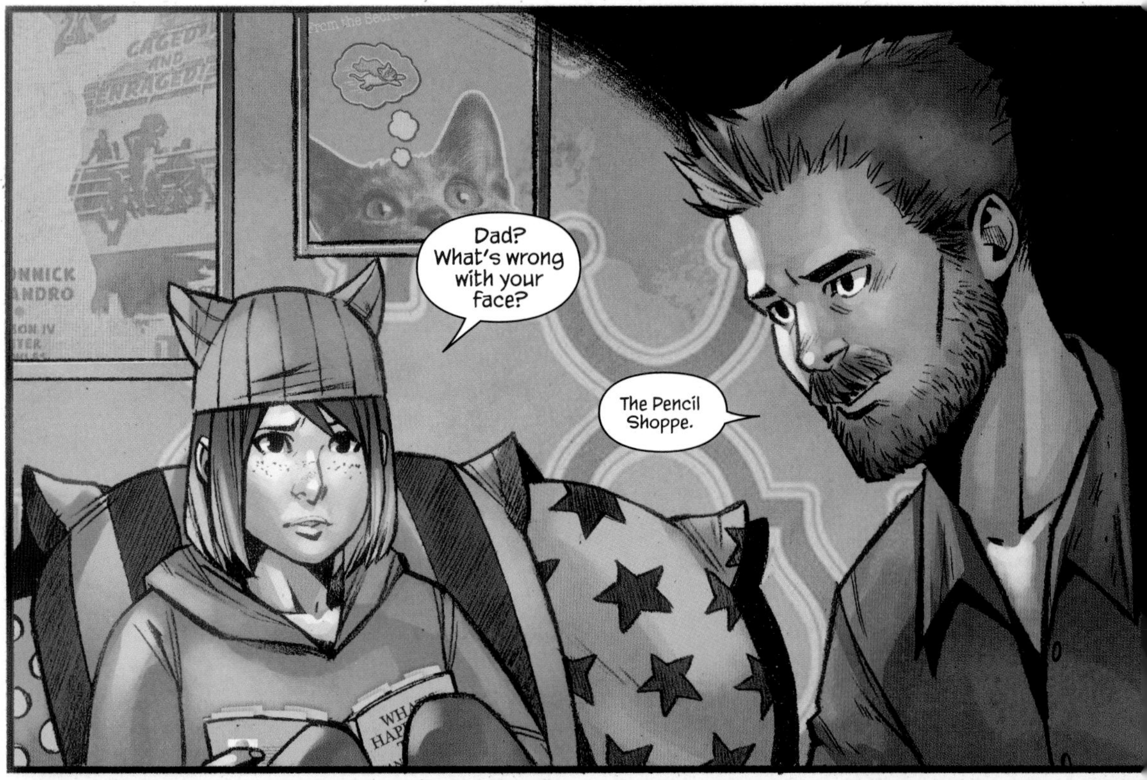
Dad? What's wrong with your face?
The Pencil Shoppe.

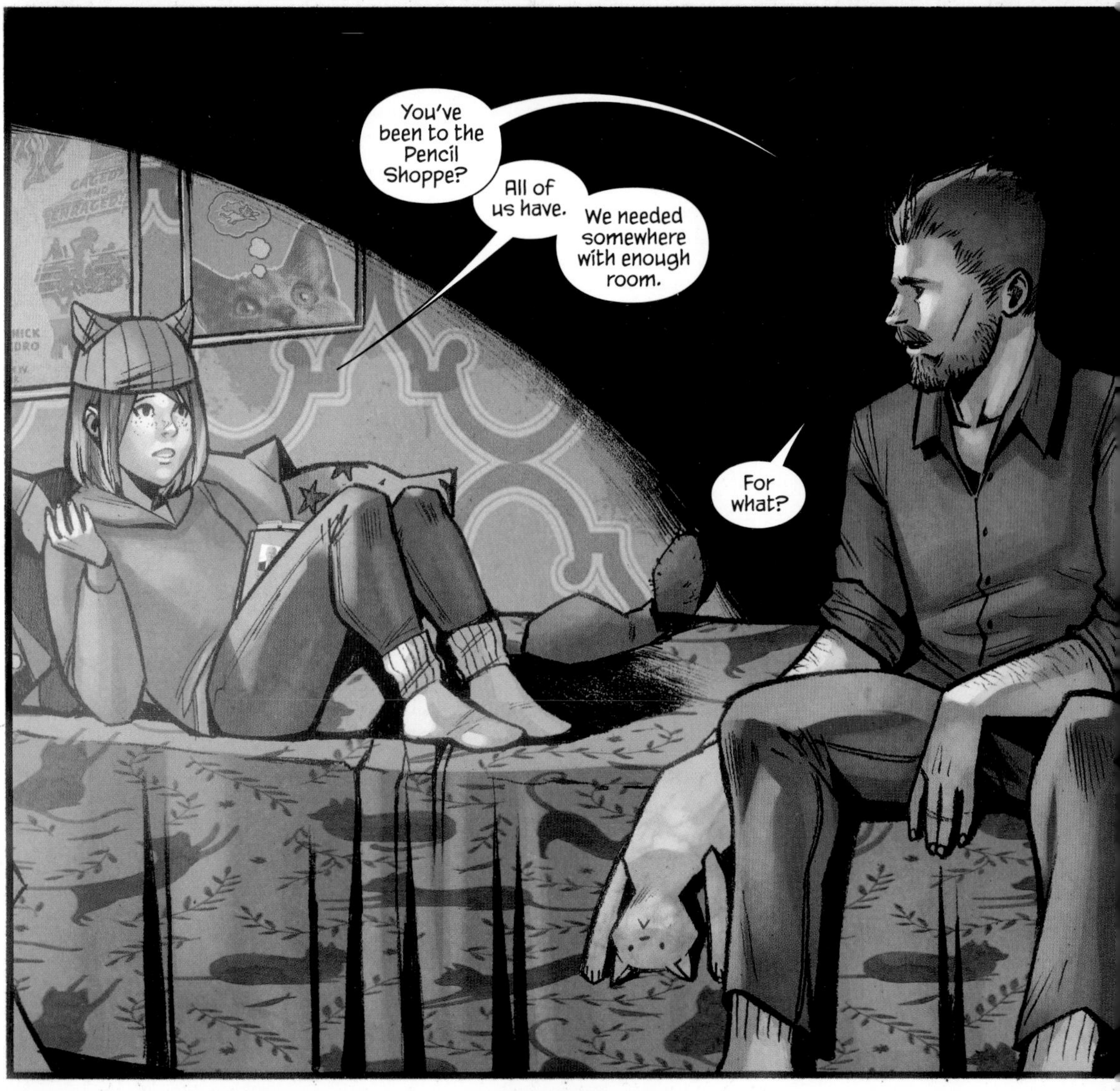
You've been to the Pencil Shoppe?
All of us have.
We needed somewhere with enough room.
For what?

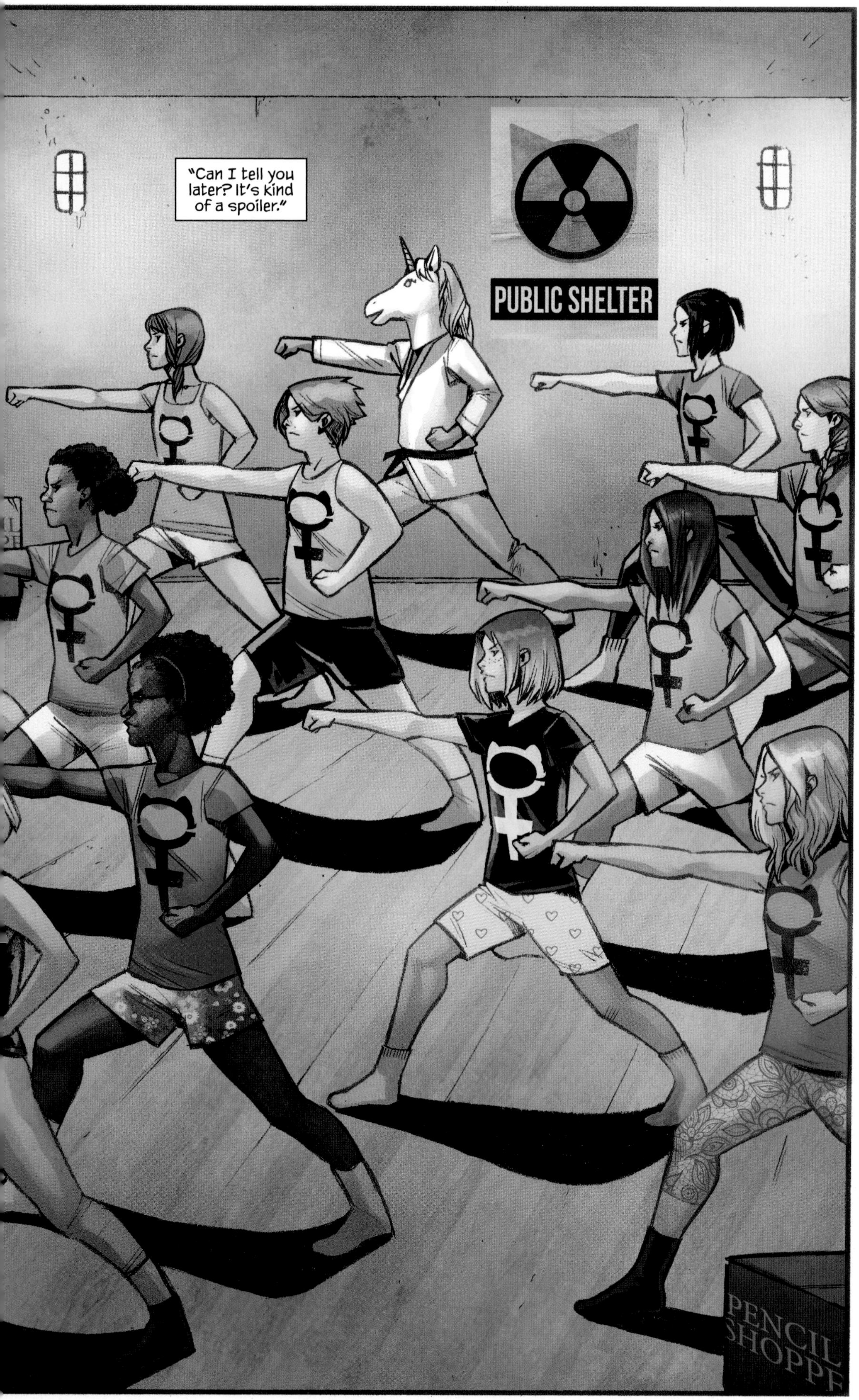
"Can I tell you later? It's kind of a spoiler."
PUBLIC SHELTER
PENCIL SHOPPE

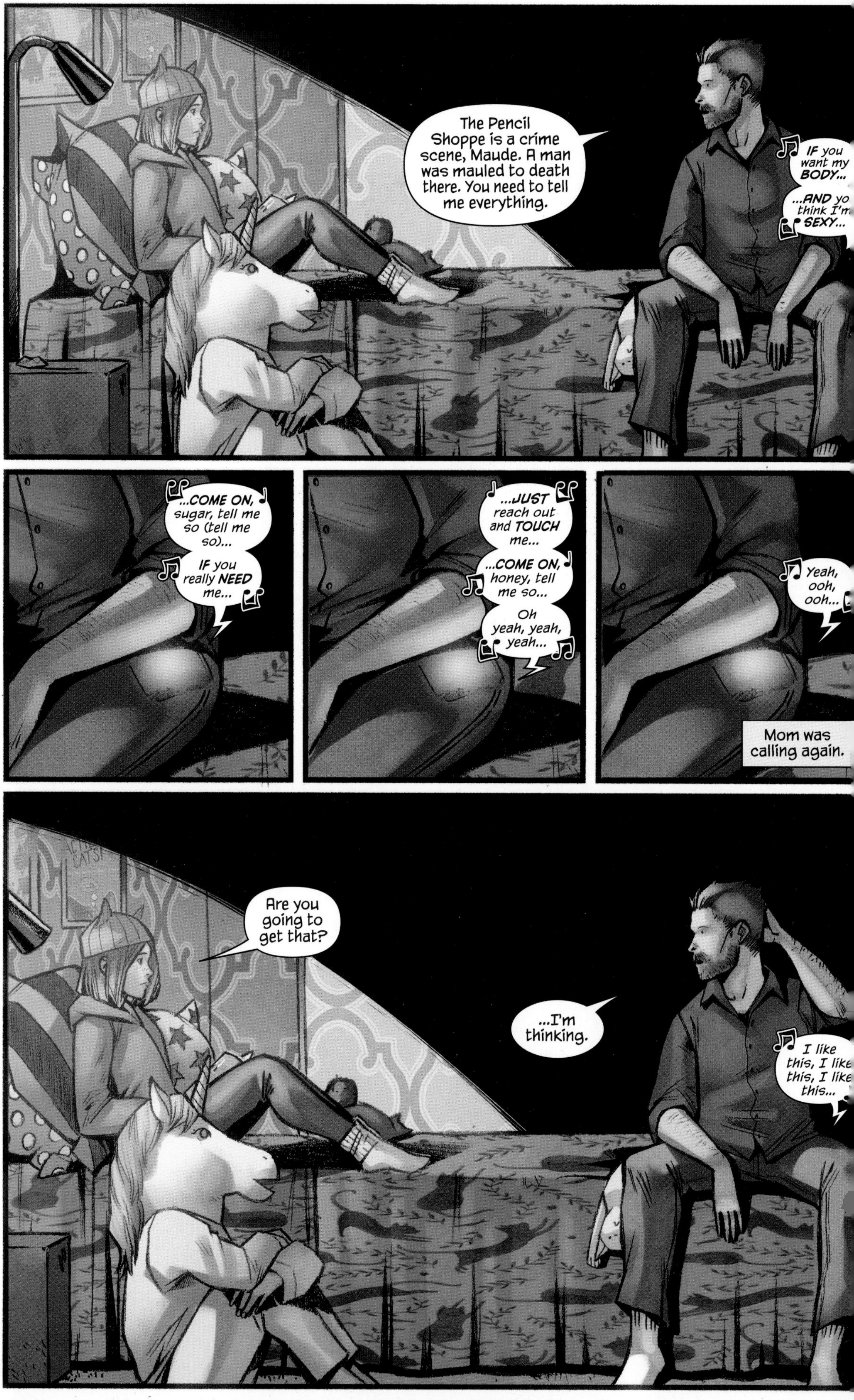
The Pencil Shoppe is a crime scene, Maude. A man was mauled to death there. You need to tell me everything.
IF you want my BODY...
...AND yo think I'm SEXY...
...COME ON, sugar, tell me so (tell me so)...
IF you really NEED me...
...JUST reach out and TOUCH me...
...COME ON, honey, tell me so...
Oh yeah, yeah, yeah...
Yeah, ooh, ooh...
Mom was calling again.
Are you going to get that?
...I'm thinking.
I like this, I like this, I like this...

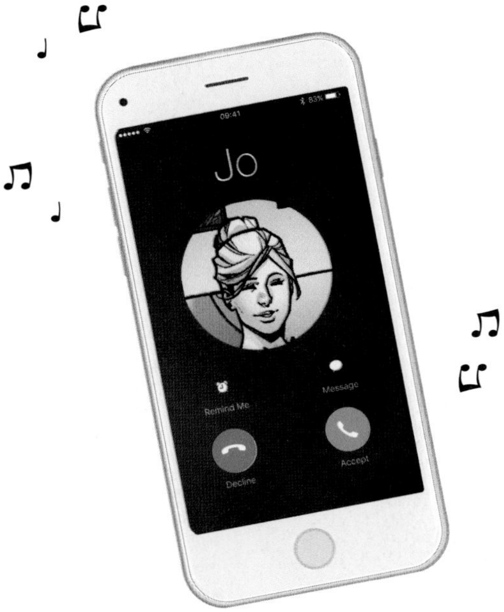

09:41
Jo
Remind Me
Message
Decline
Accept

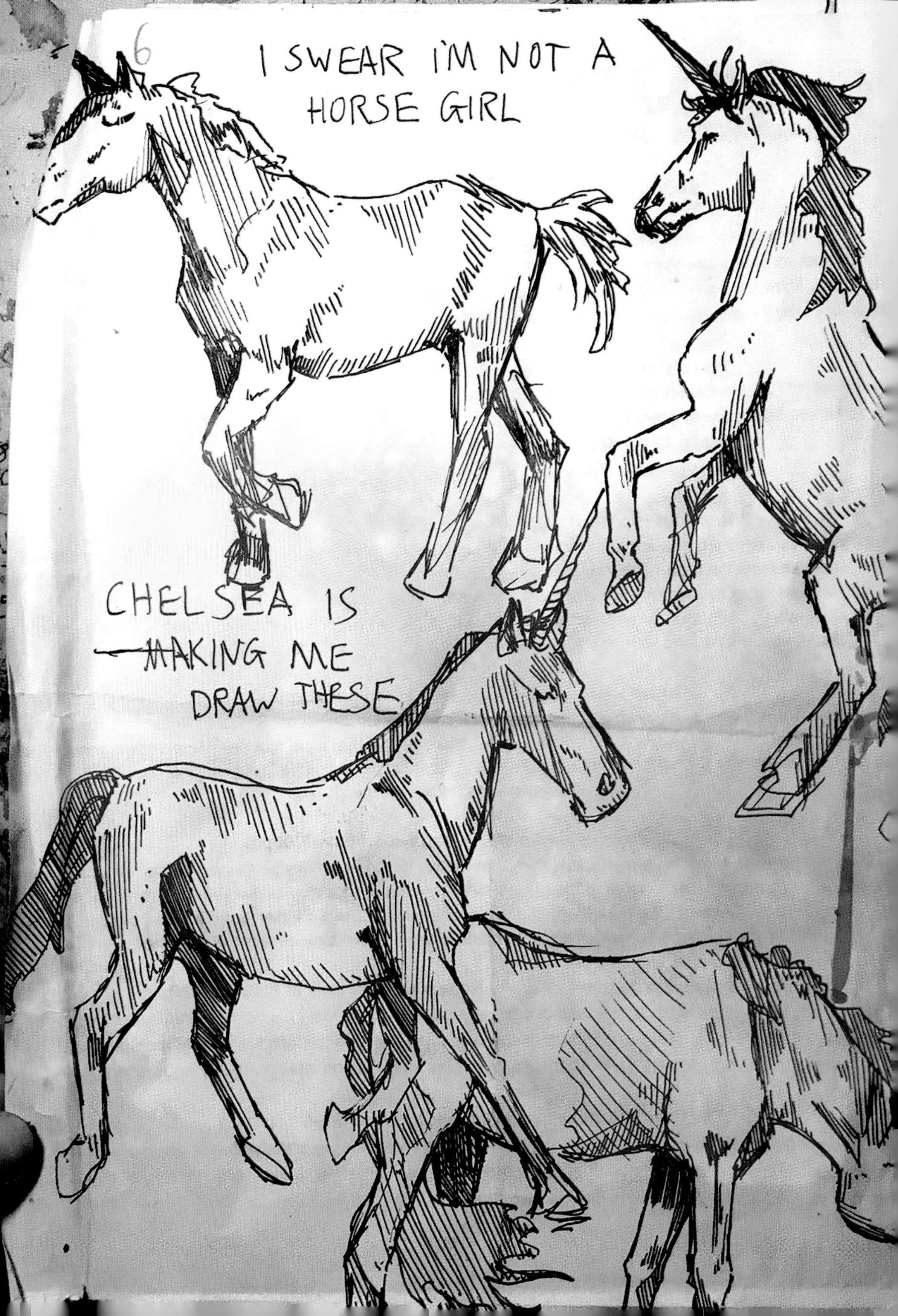
6
I SWEAR I'M NOT A HORSE GIRL
CHELSEA IS MAKING ME DRAW THESE

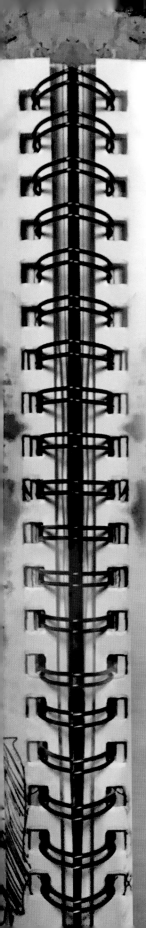

MINISTRY OF
TROUBLE
I N C O R P O R A T E D

 WRITER/CREATOR
CHELSEA CAIN

 PENCILS
KATE NIEMCZYK

 COLORIST
RACHELLE ROSENBERG

 LETTERER
JOE CARAMAGNA

 COVER/CO-CREATOR,
ADS, SUPPLEMENTAL ART
LIA MITERNIQUE

 ADDITIONAL INTERIOR ART
STELLA GREENVOSS

 COMING SOON
ELISE MCCALL

YOU HAVE BEEN CONTACTED BY THE MINISTRY OF TROUBLE. AWAIT FURTHER INSTRUCTIONS. ☿

VOLUME 2

CHAPTER three

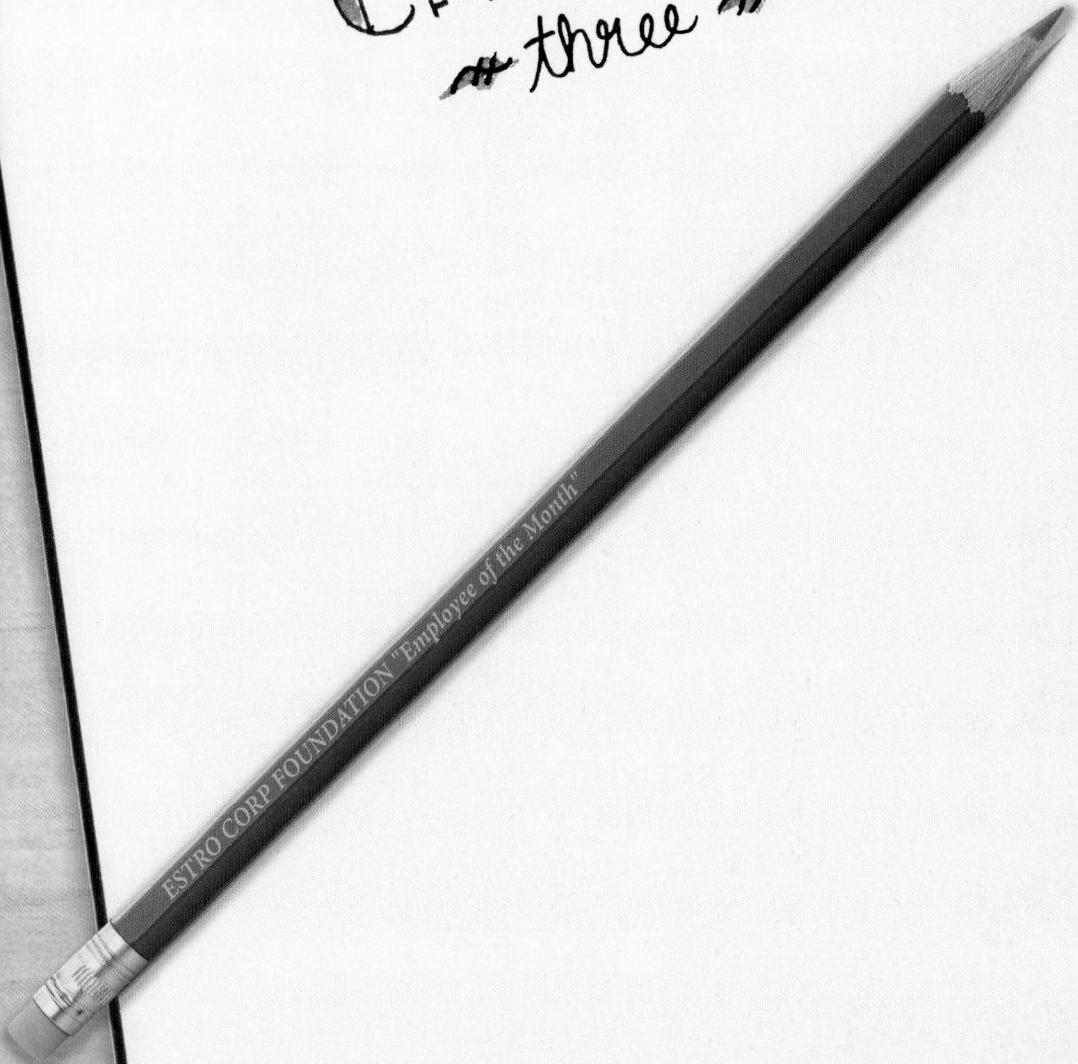
ESTRO CORP FOUNDATION "Employee of the Month"

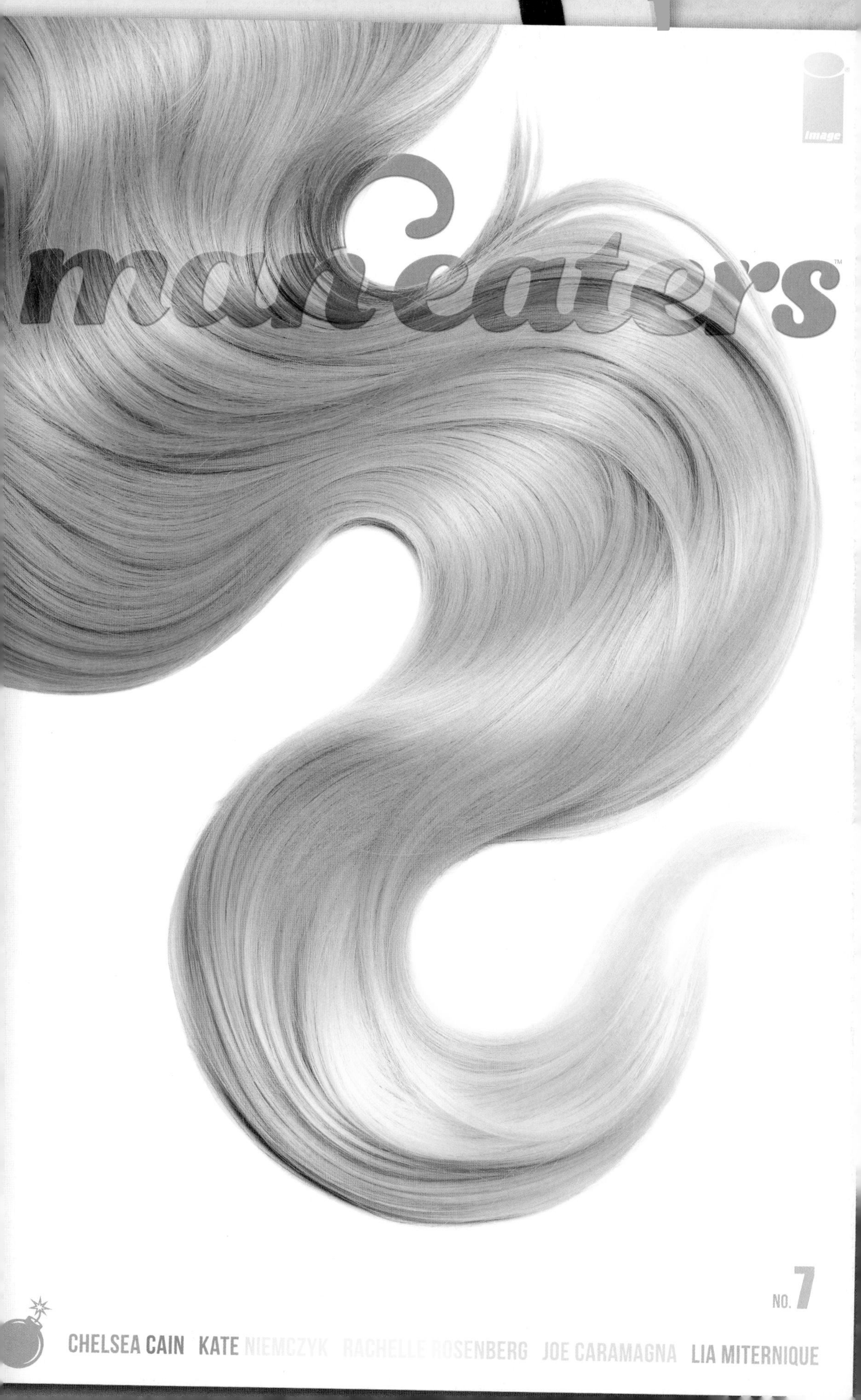
image
maneaters™
NO. 7
CHELSEA CAIN KATE NIEMCZYK RACHELLE ROSENBERG JOE CARAMAGNA LIA MITERNIQUE

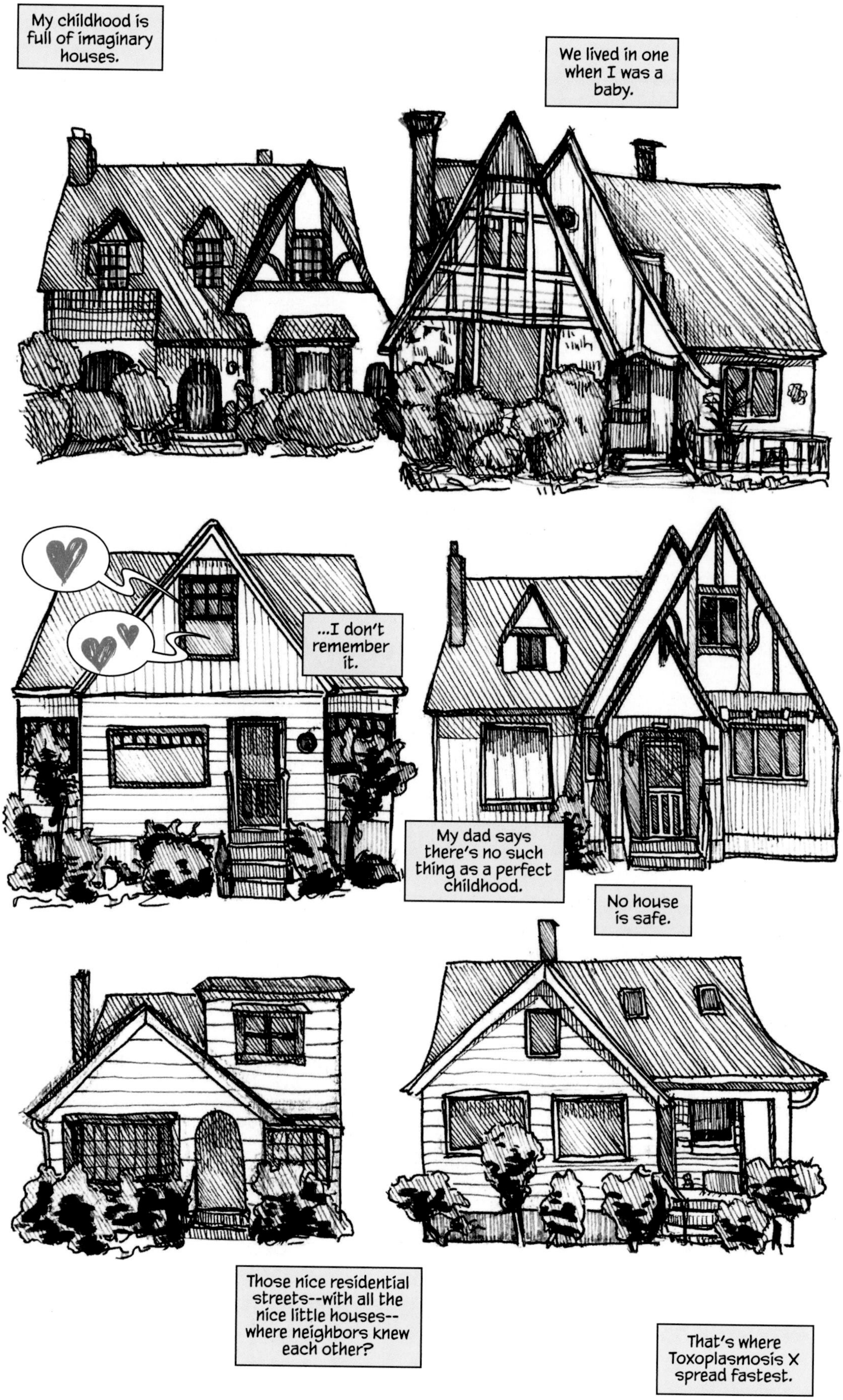
My childhood is full of imaginary houses.
We lived in one when I was a baby.
...I don't remember it.
My dad says there's no such thing as a perfect childhood.
No house is safe.
Those nice residential streets--with all the nice little houses--where neighbors knew each other?
That's where Toxoplasmosis X spread fastest.

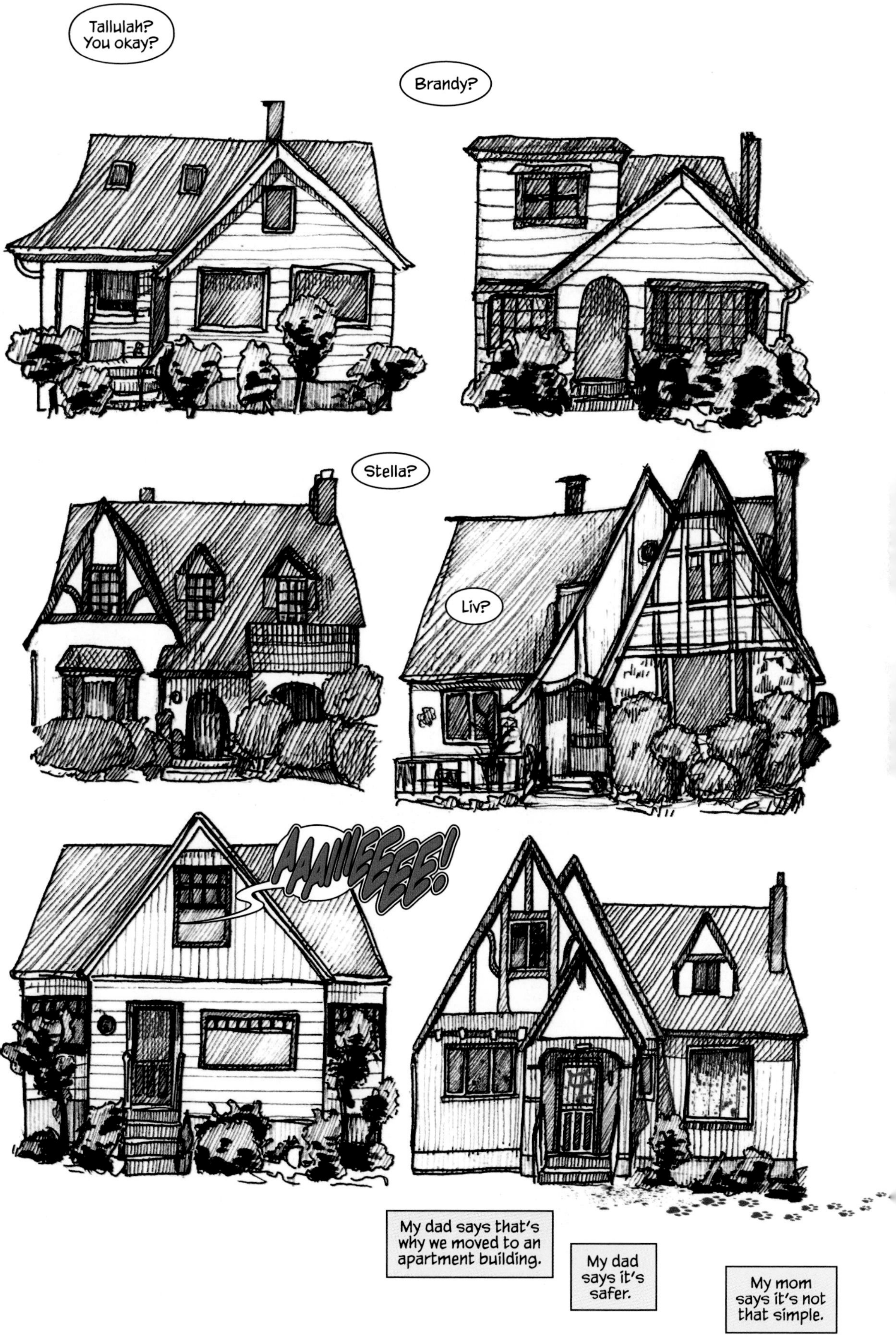
Tallulah? You okay?
Brandy?
Stella?
Liv?
AAAIIIEEEEE!
My dad says that's why we moved to an apartment building.
My dad says it's safer.
My mom says it's not that simple.

MOTHER BLUEPRINT

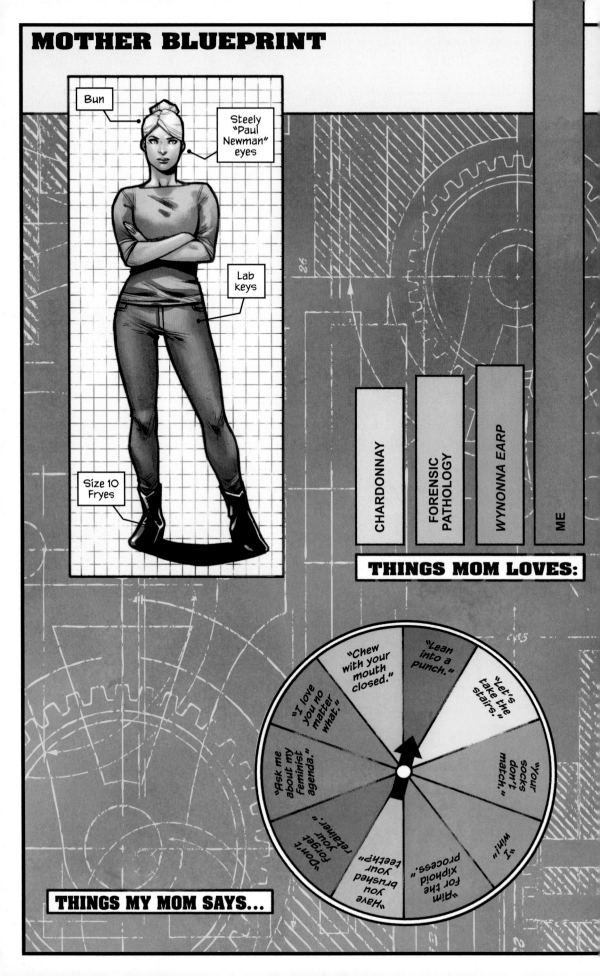

Bun

Steely "Paul Newman" eyes

Lab keys

Size 10 Fryes

THINGS MOM LOVES:

CHARDONNAY

FORENSIC PATHOLOGY

WYNONNA EARP

ME

THINGS MY MOM SAYS...

"Chew with your mouth closed."

"Lean into a punch."

"I love you no matter what."

"Let's take the stairs."

"Ask me about my feminist agenda."

"Your socks don't match."

"Don't forget your retainer."

"Have you brushed your teeth?"

"Aim for the xiphoid process."

"I win!"

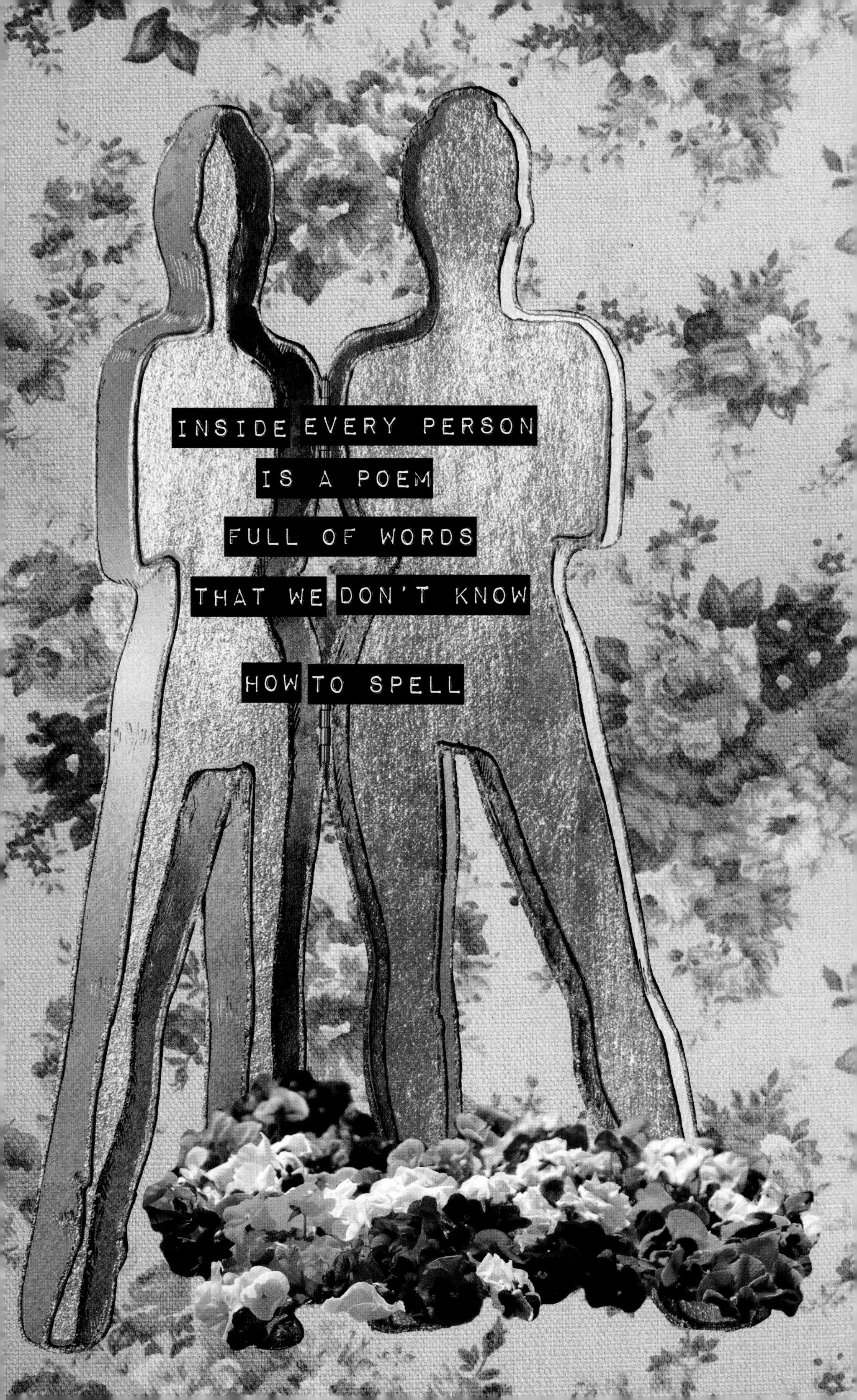
INSIDE EVERY PERSON
IS A POEM
FULL OF WORDS
THAT WE DON'T KNOW
HOW TO SPELL

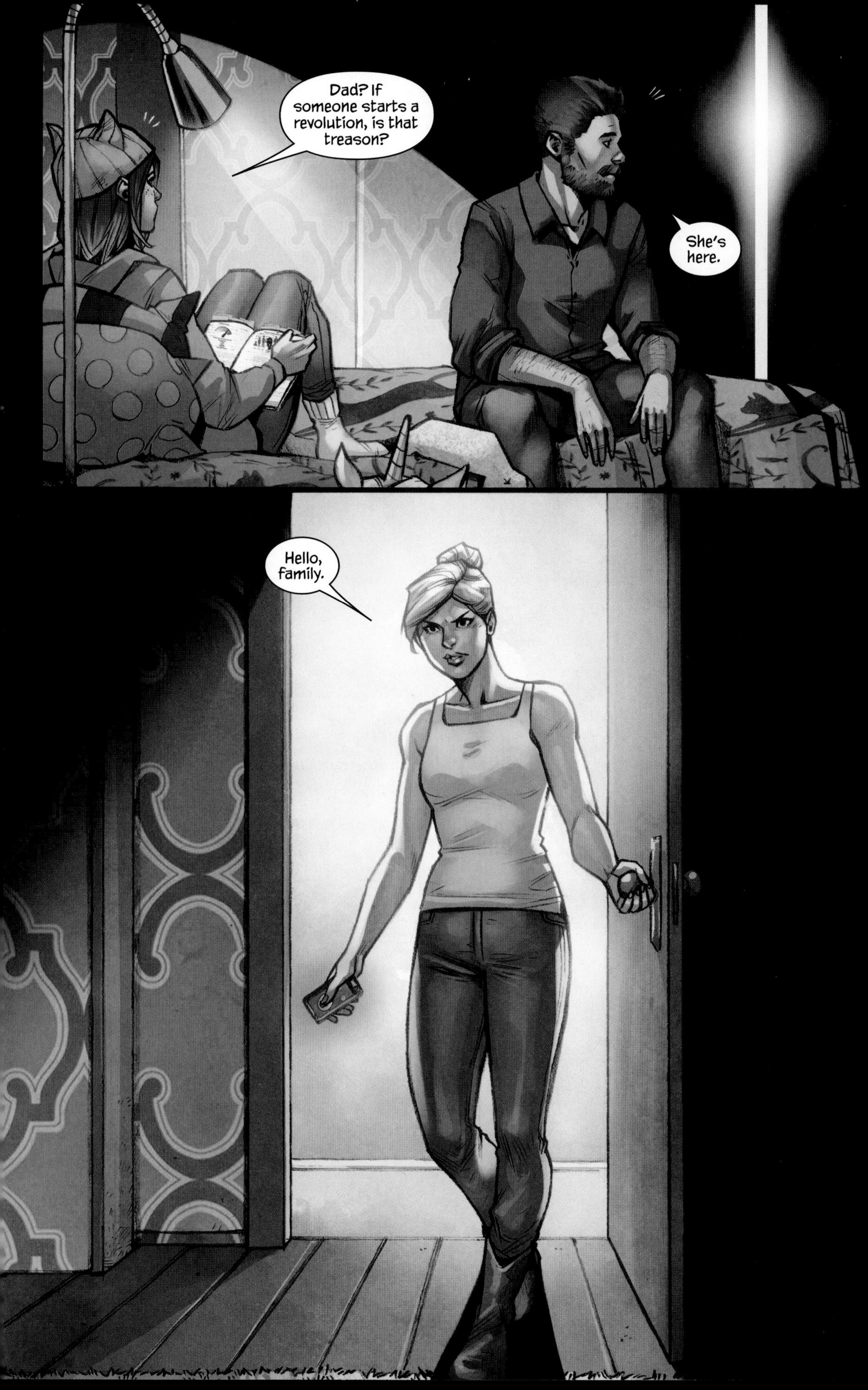
Dad? If someone starts a revolution, is that treason?
She's here.
Hello, family.

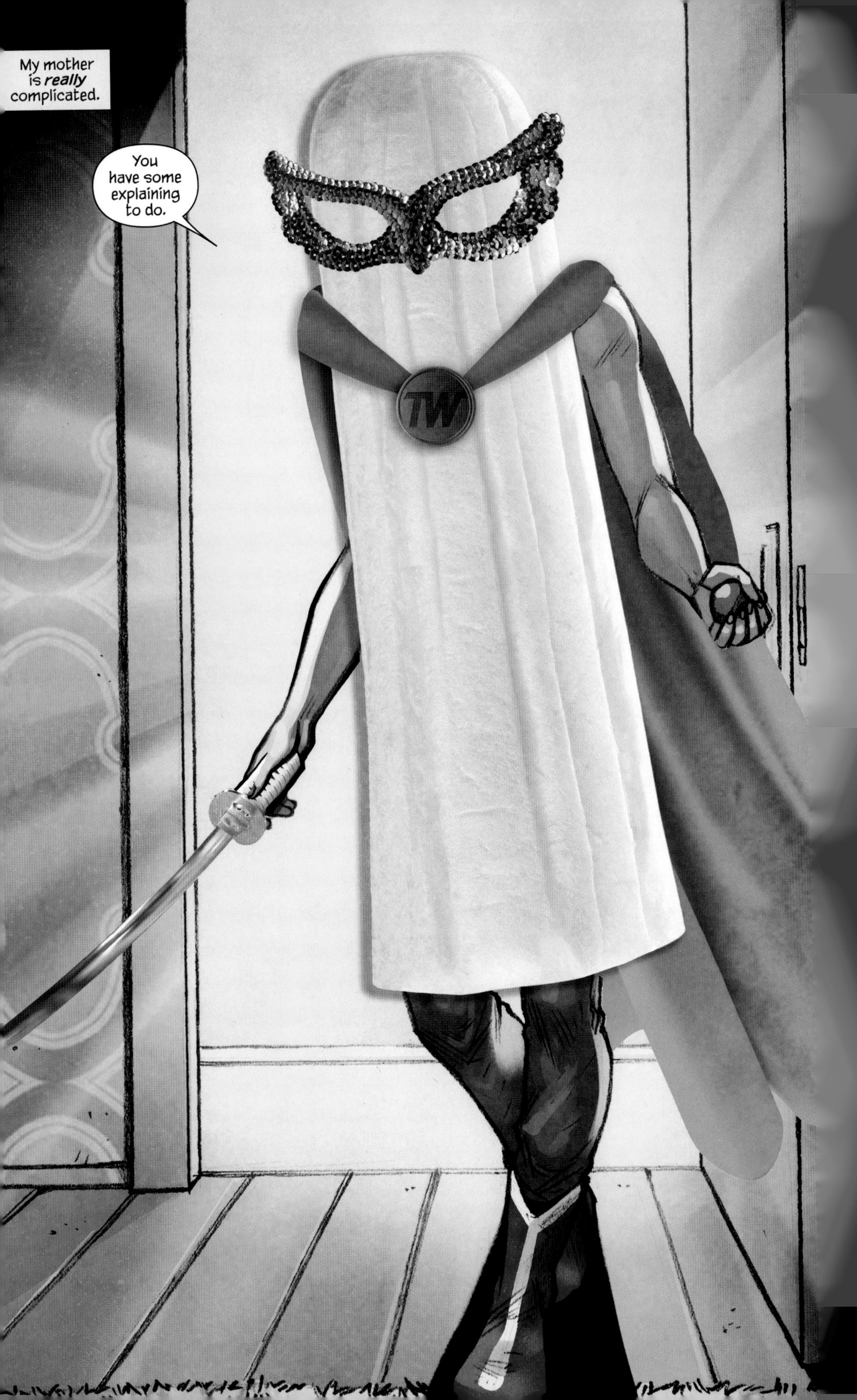
My mother is *really* complicated.
You have some explaining to do.
TW

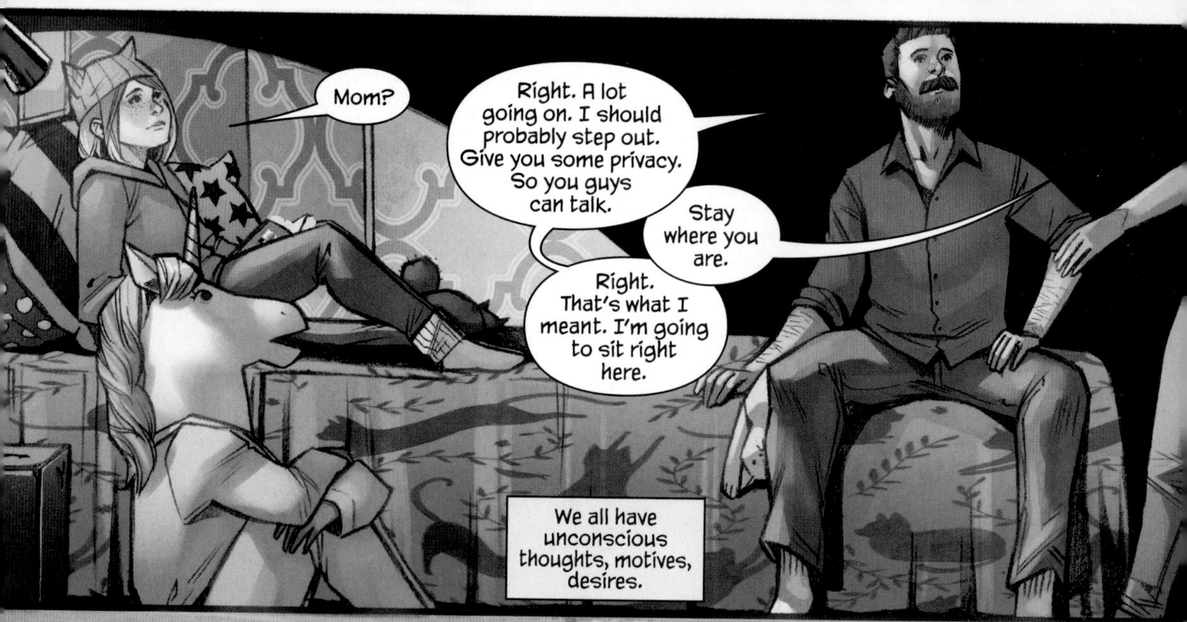

Mom?
Right. A lot going on. I should probably step out. Give you some privacy. So you guys can talk.
Stay where you are.
Right. That's what I meant. I'm going to sit right here.
We all have unconscious thoughts, motives, desires.

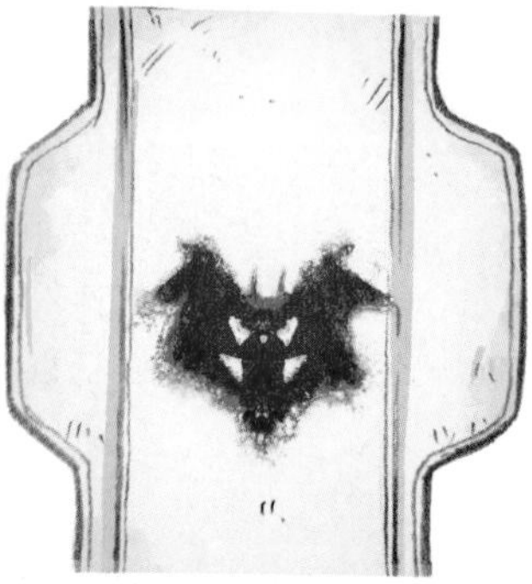

Card 1

What do you see? See side B for psychological interpretation

[SIDE A]

[SIDE B]

a. **If you see an X-ray**. You are prone to bottling up your emotions.

b. **If you see a professor, or other benevolent paternal figure**. You are kind and free-thinking.

c. **If you see a stingray**. Stop apologizing.

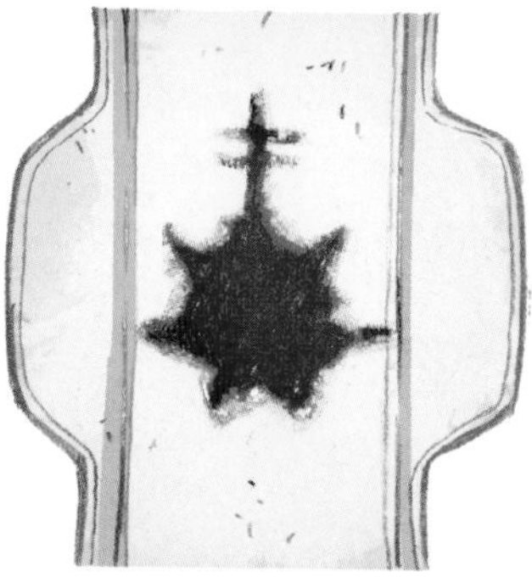

Card 6

What do you see? See side B for psychological interpretation

[SIDE A]

[SIDE B]

a. **If you see an animal hide**. Obviously you have a fetish. But you know this.

b. **If you see a boat or submarine or a person with big nose**. You are sexually dominant. And most people think you're a jackass.

c. **If you see a rug or anything rug-adjacent**. You find it hard to be alone, and maybe shouldn't be so needy.

d. **If you see a mushroom, or mushroom cloud**. You're high right now.

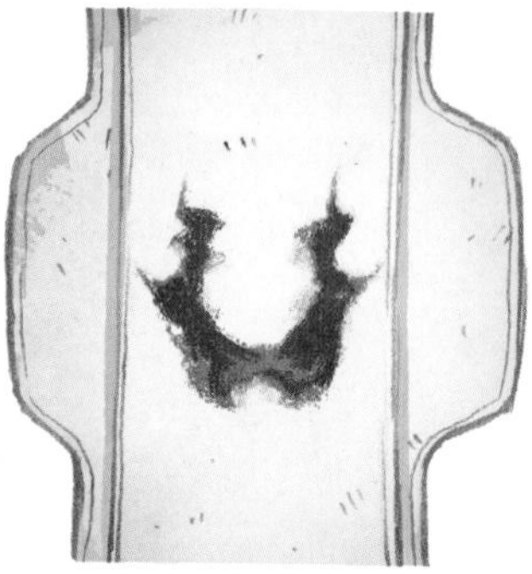

Card 7

What do you see? See side B for psychological interpretation

[SIDE A]

[SIDE B]

a. **If you have no fucking idea what this is**. You may have difficulty relating to females.

b. **If you see a female figure, children, or faces**. Good news! You probably don't have significant mother issues.

c. **If you see anything related to girls, fighting or gossiping or engaging in any sort of negative behavior**. You have serious relationship issues with women, and it's your mother's fault.

d. **If you see an oil lamp**. You're schizophrenic.

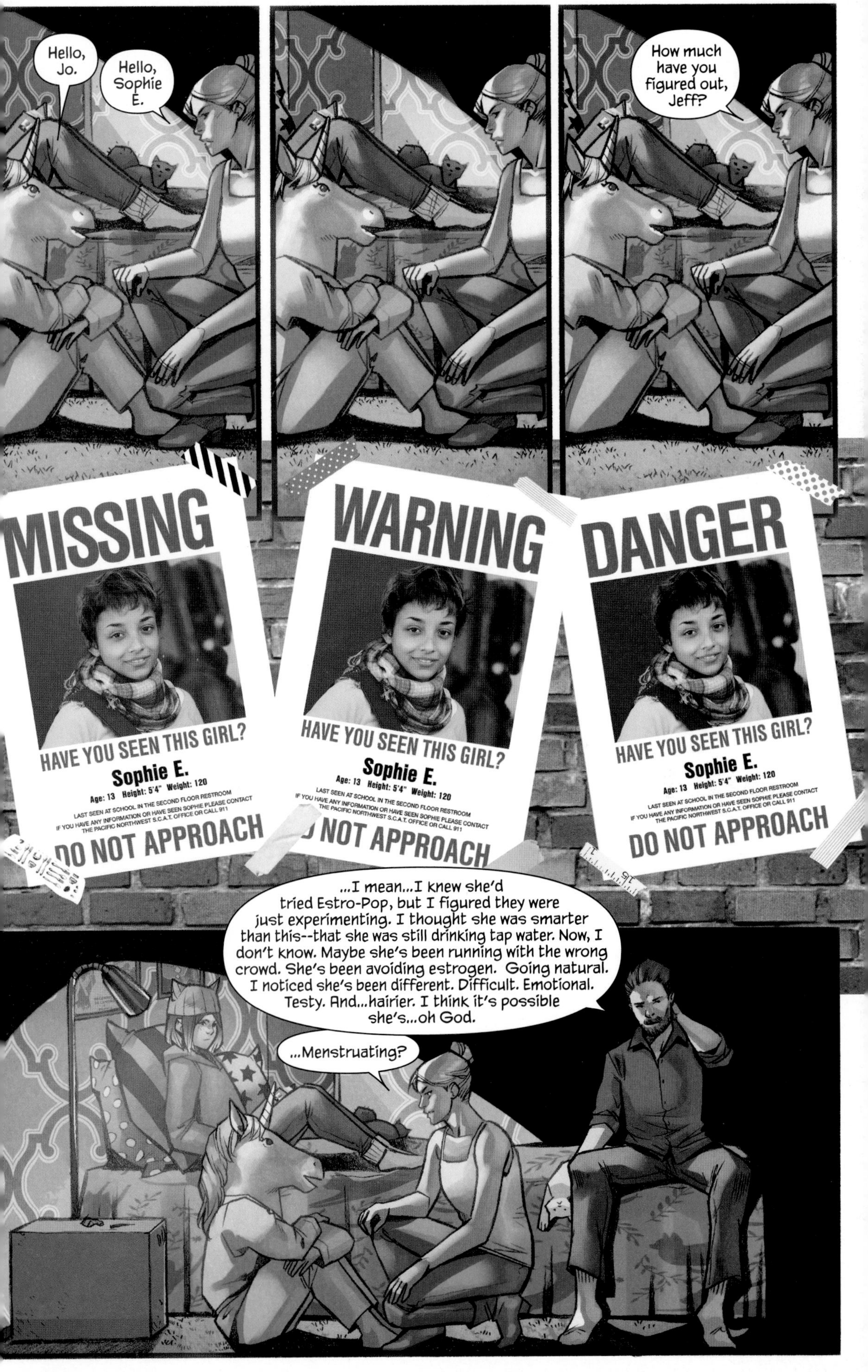
Hello, Jo.
Hello, Sophie E.
How much have you figured out, Jeff?
MISSING
HAVE YOU SEEN THIS GIRL?
Sophie E.
Age: 13 Height: 5'4" Weight: 120
LAST SEEN AT SCHOOL IN THE SECOND FLOOR RESTROOM
IF YOU HAVE ANY INFORMATION OR HAVE SEEN SOPHIE PLEASE CONTACT
THE PACIFIC NORTHWEST S.C.A.T. OFFICE OR CALL 911
DO NOT APPROACH
WARNING
HAVE YOU SEEN THIS GIRL?
Sophie E.
Age: 13 Height: 5'4" Weight: 120
LAST SEEN AT SCHOOL IN THE SECOND FLOOR RESTROOM
IF YOU HAVE ANY INFORMATION OR HAVE SEEN SOPHIE PLEASE CONTACT
THE PACIFIC NORTHWEST S.C.A.T. OFFICE OR CALL 911
O NOT APPROACH
DANGER
HAVE YOU SEEN THIS GIRL?
Sophie E.
Age: 13 Height: 5'4" Weight: 120
LAST SEEN AT SCHOOL IN THE SECOND FLOOR RESTROOM
IF YOU HAVE ANY INFORMATION OR HAVE SEEN SOPHIE PLEASE CONTACT
THE PACIFIC NORTHWEST S.C.A.T. OFFICE OR CALL 911
DO NOT APPROACH
...I mean...I knew she'd tried Estro-Pop, but I figured they were just experimenting. I thought she was smarter than this--that she was still drinking tap water. Now, I don't know. Maybe she's been running with the wrong crowd. She's been avoiding estrogen. Going natural. I noticed she's been different. Difficult. Emotional. Testy. And...hairier. I think it's possible she's...oh God.
...Menstruating?

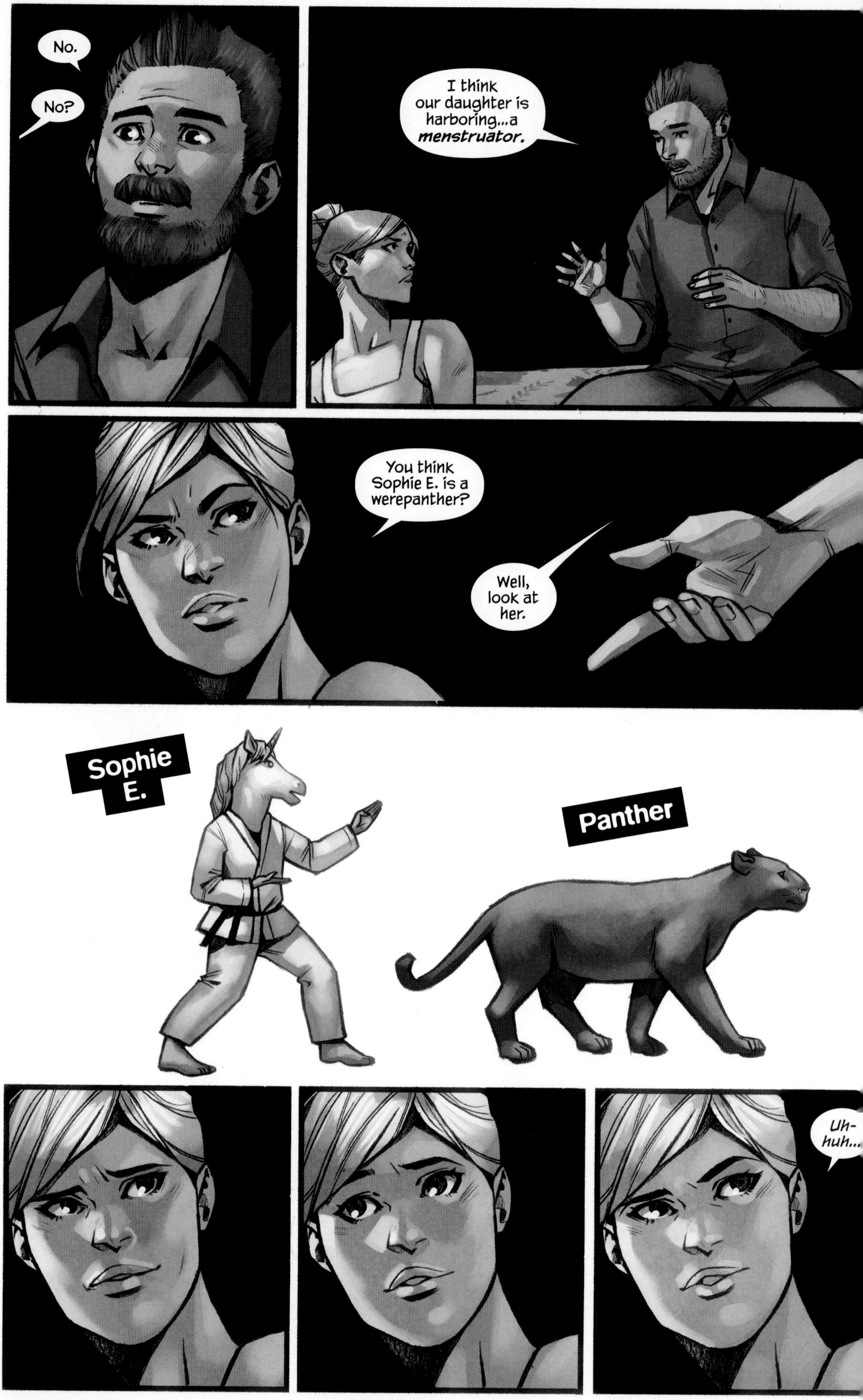
No.
No?
I think our daughter is harboring...a *menstruator.*
You think Sophie E. is a werepanther?
Well, look at her.
Sophie E.
Panther
Uh-huh...

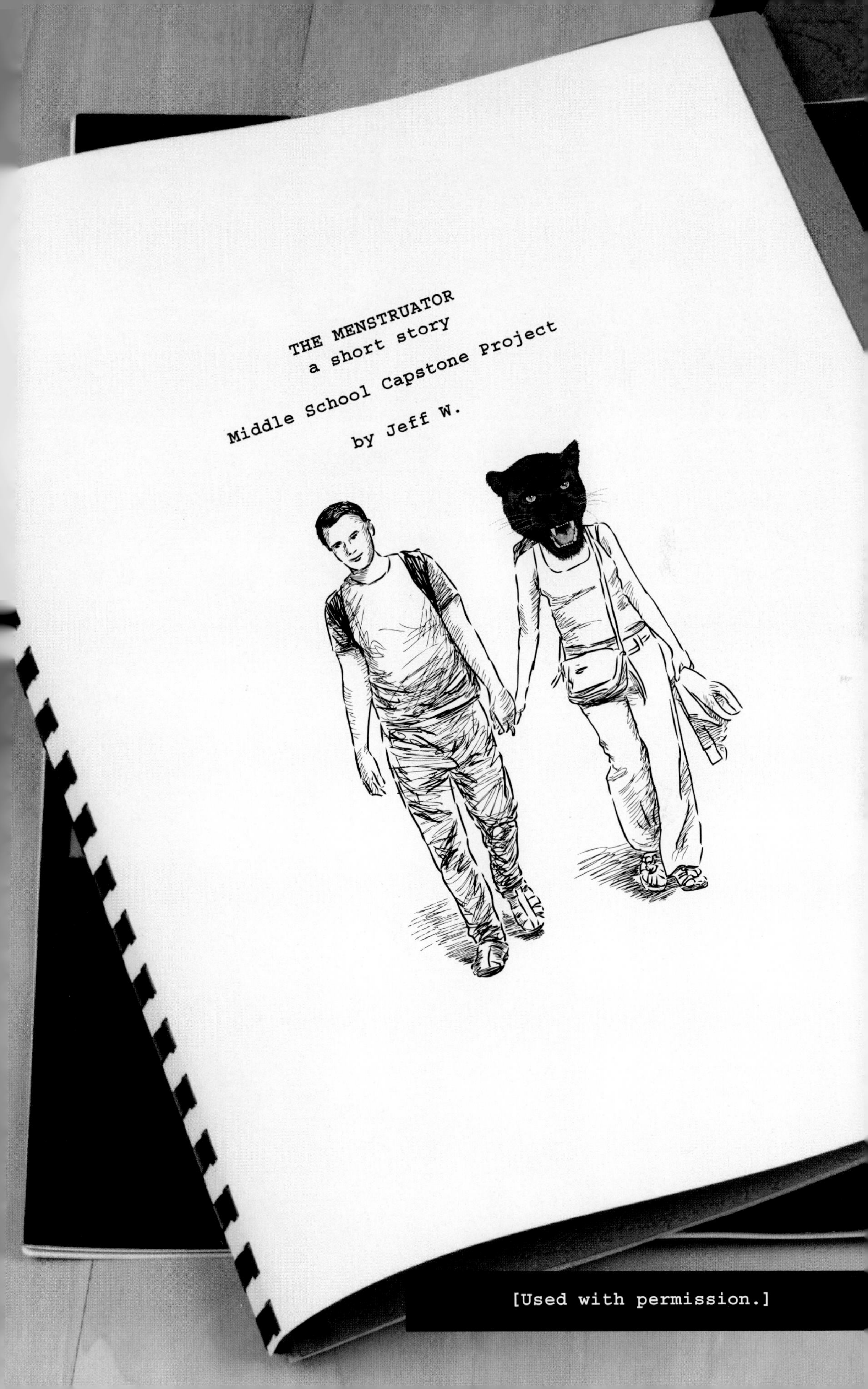
THE MENSTRUATOR
a short story
Middle School Capstone Project
by Jeff W.

[Used with permission.]

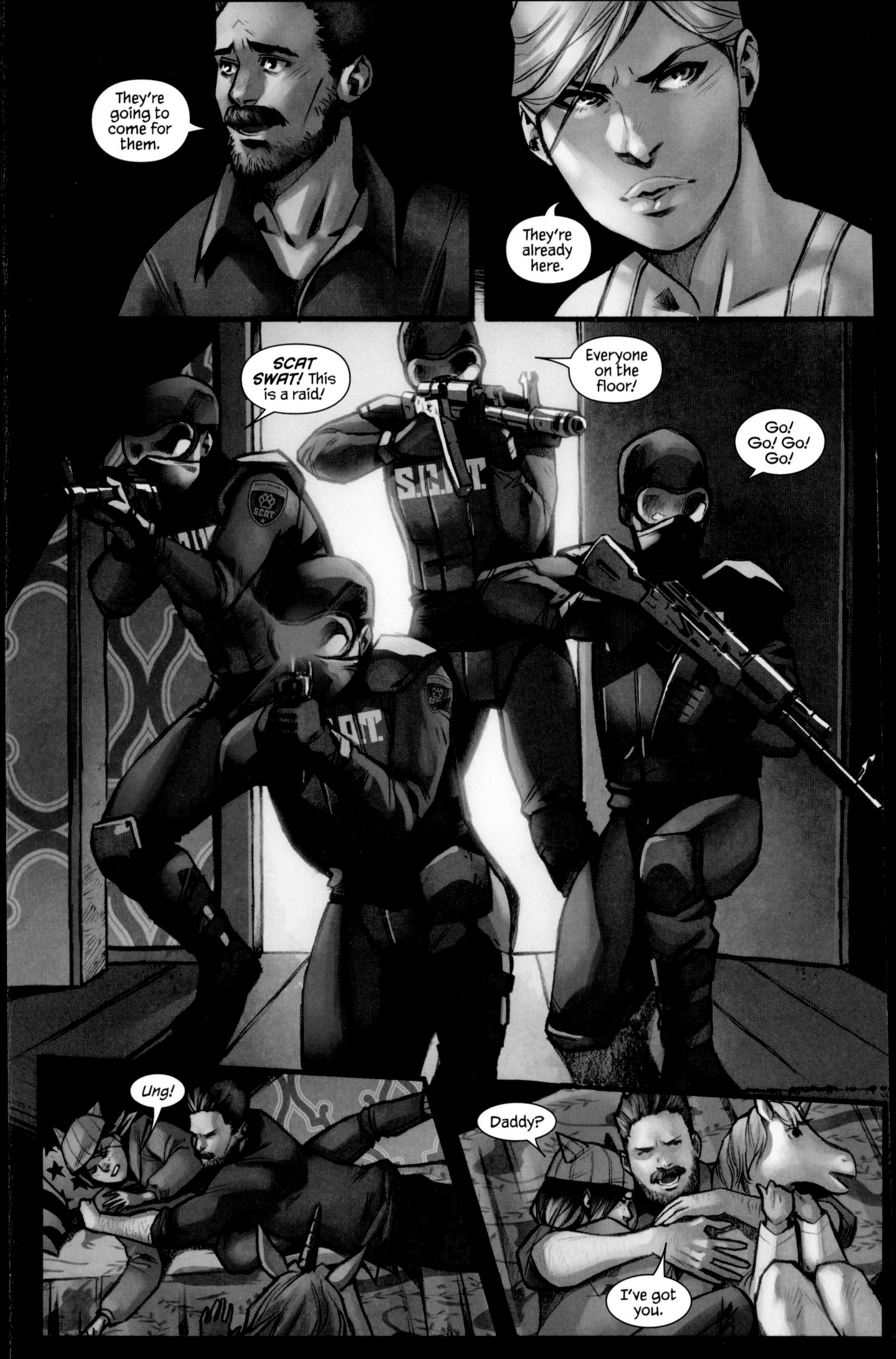

They're going to come for them.
They're already here.
SCAT SWAT! This is a raid!
Everyone on the floor!
Go! Go! Go! Go!
S.C.A.T.
Ung!
Daddy?
I've got you.

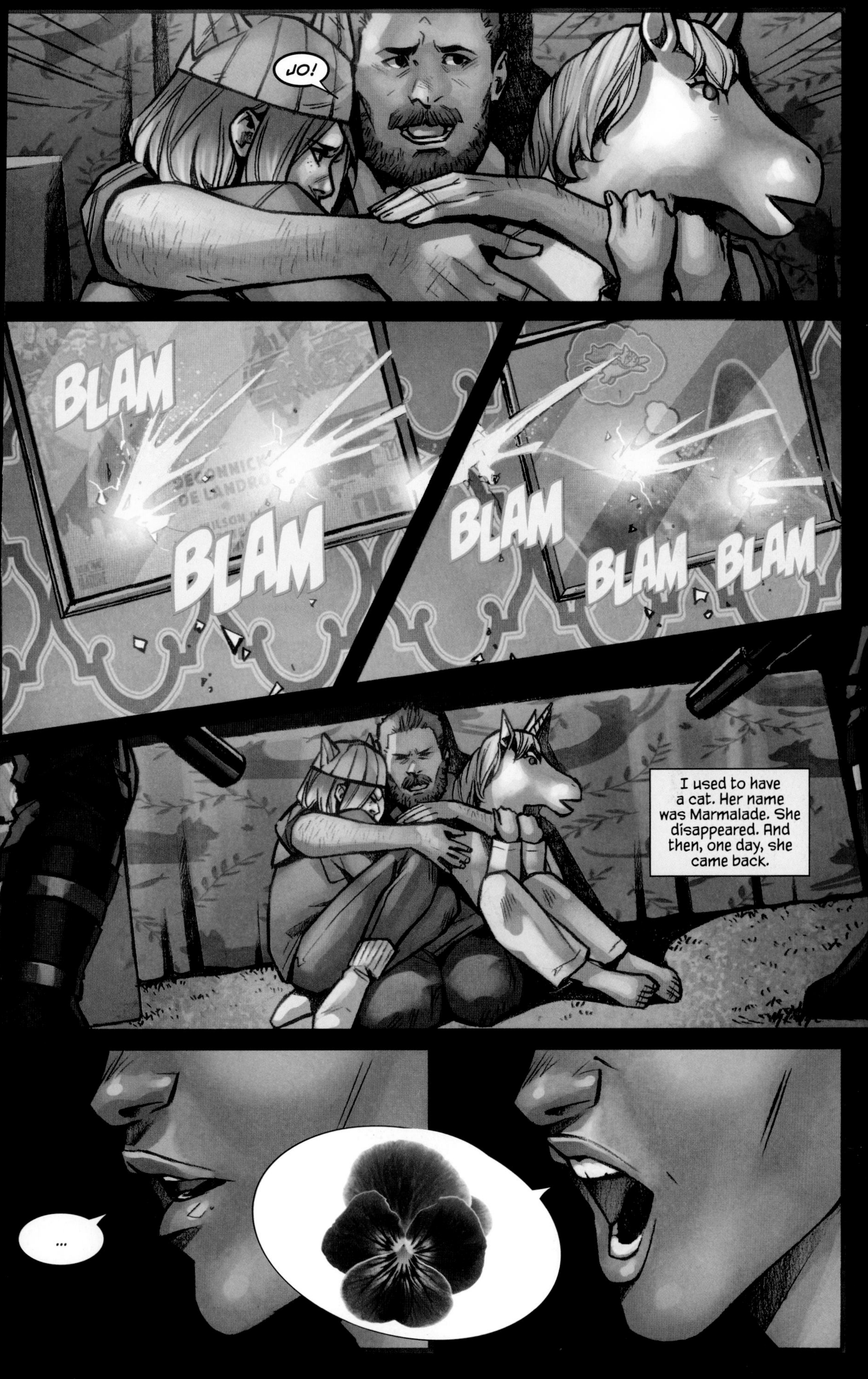

JO!
BLAM
BLAM
BLAM
BLAM
BLAM
I used to have a cat. Her name was Marmalade. She disappeared. And then, one day, she came back.
...

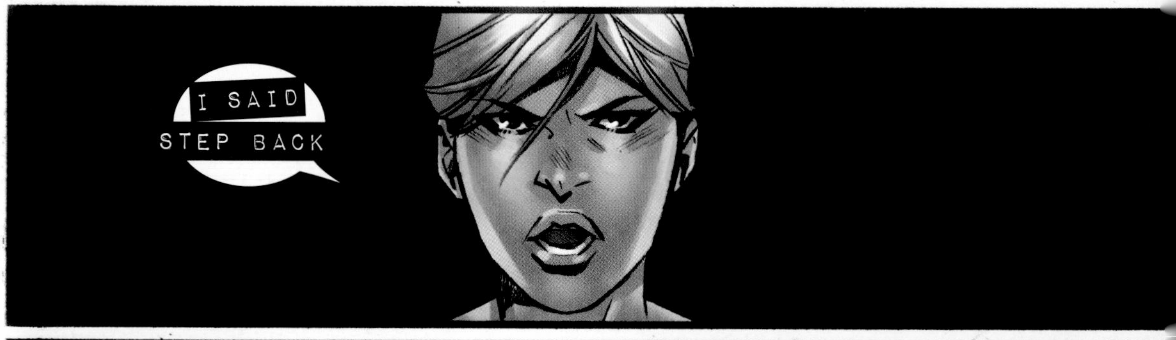
I SAID
STEP BACK
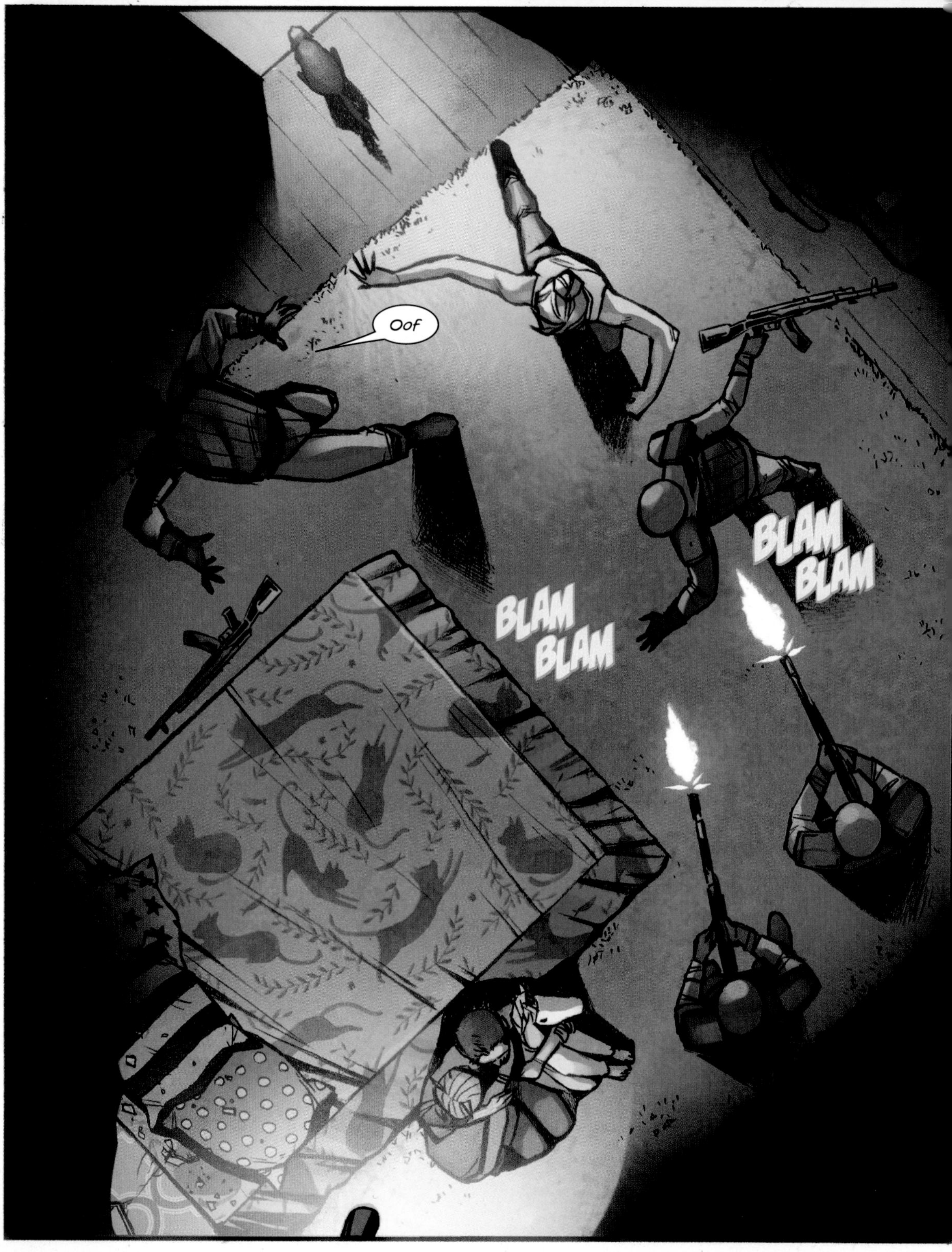
Oof
BLAM
BLAM
BLAM
BLAM

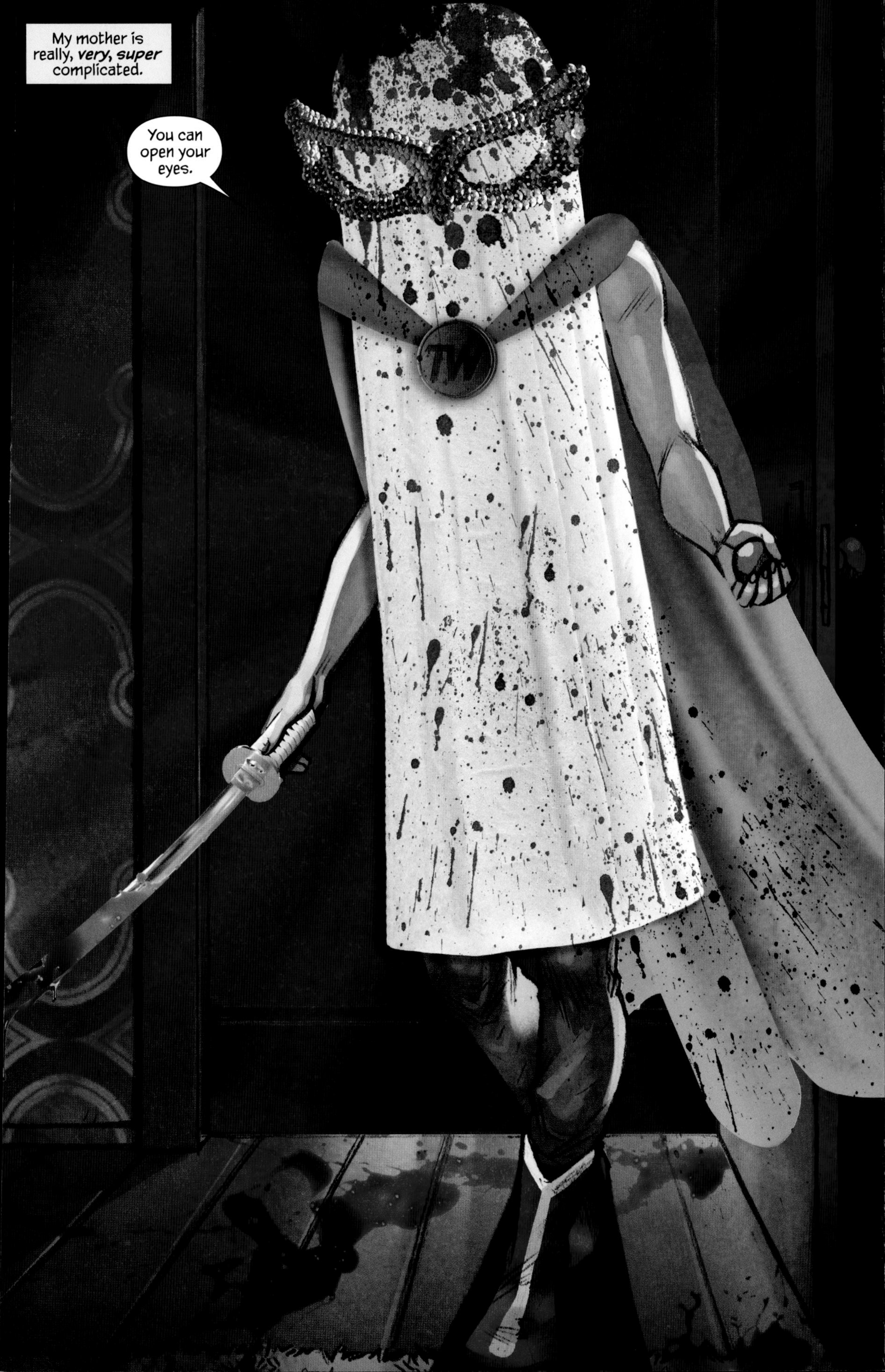
My mother is really, *very, super* complicated.
You can open your eyes.

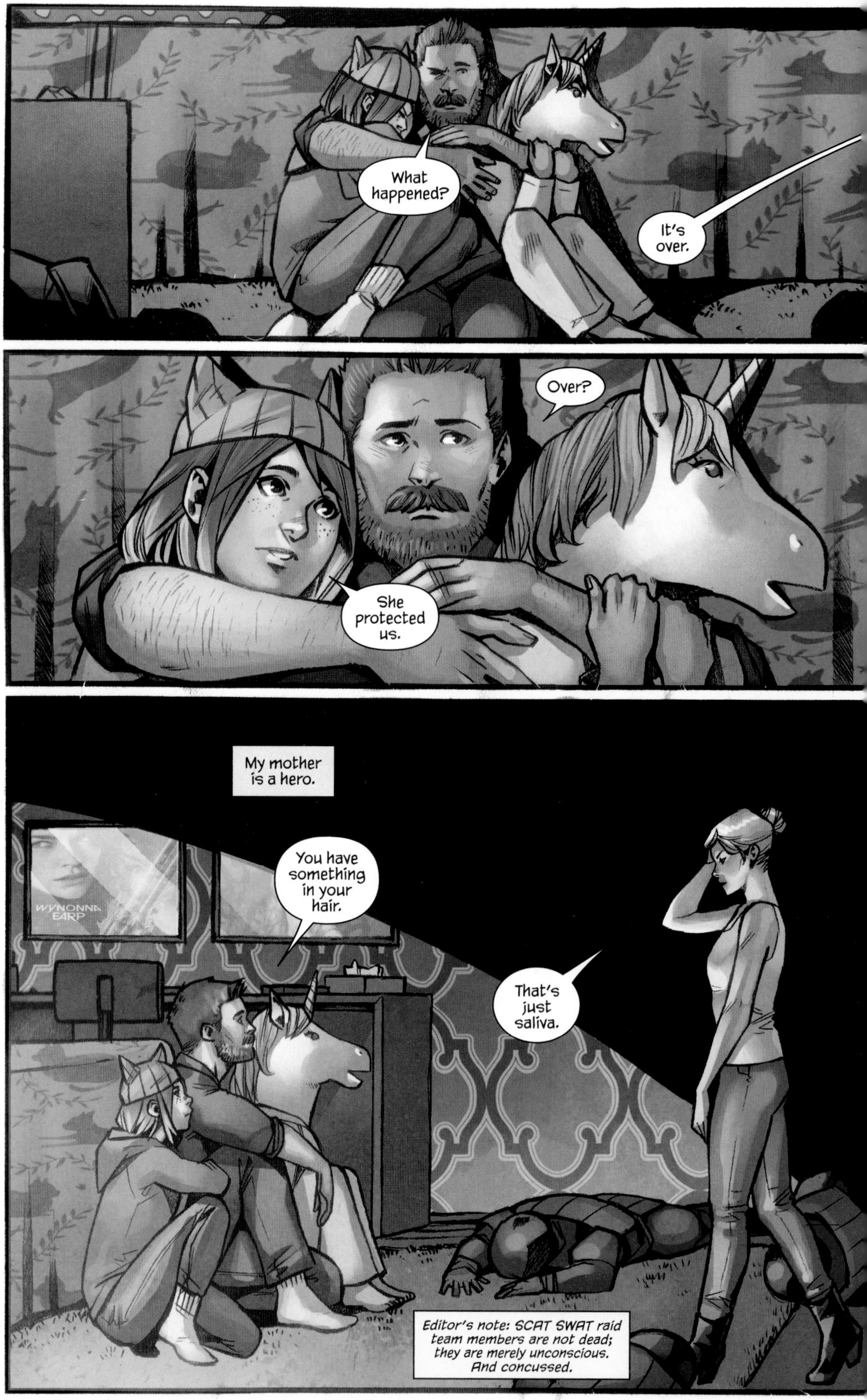
What happened?
It's over.
Over?
She protected us.
My mother is a hero.
WYNONNA EARP
You have something in your hair.
That's just saliva.
Editor's note: SCAT SWAT raid team members are not dead; they are merely unconscious. And concussed.

WE ALL WEAR DISGUISES.

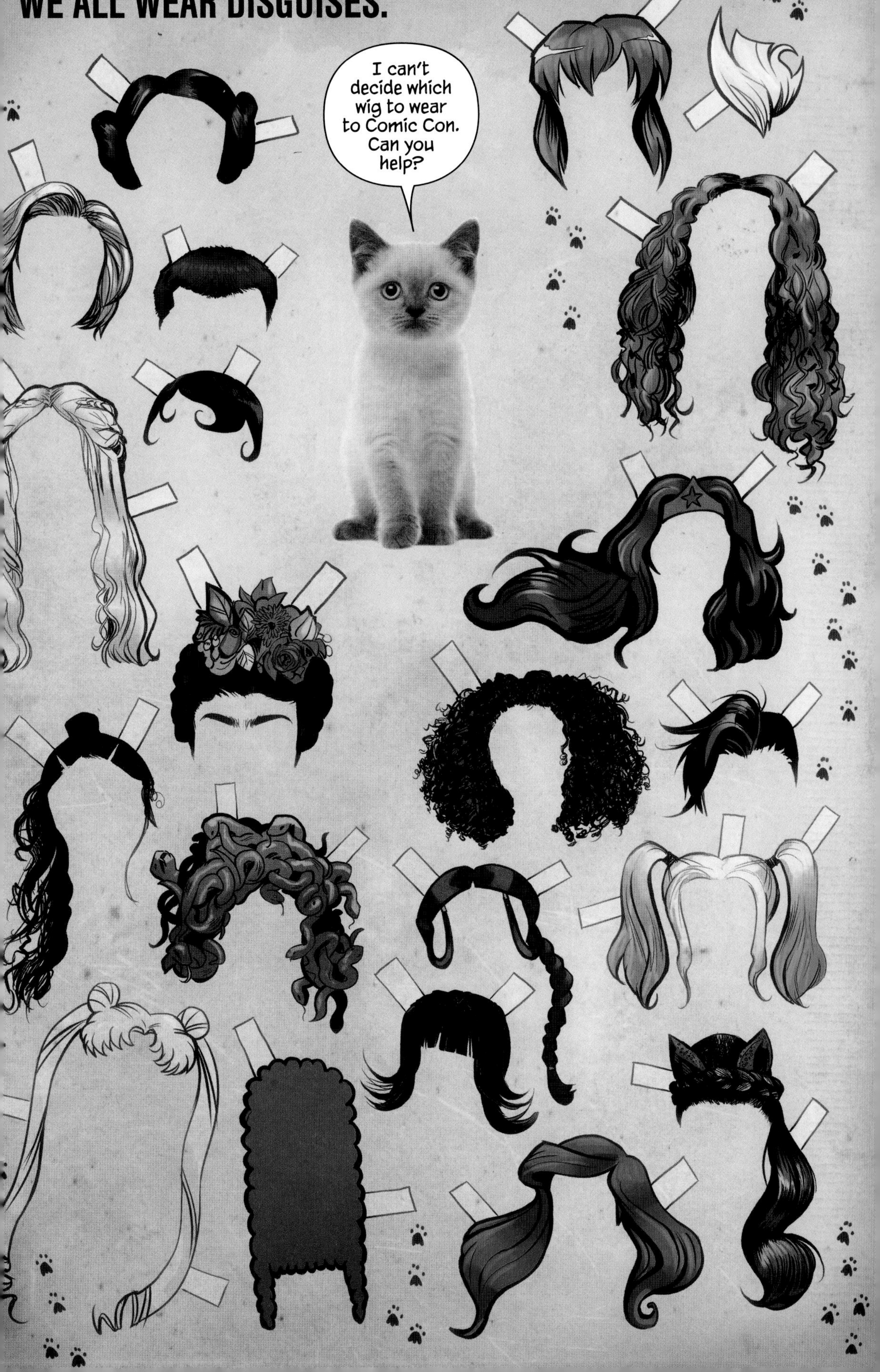
I can't decide which wig to wear to Comic Con. Can you help?

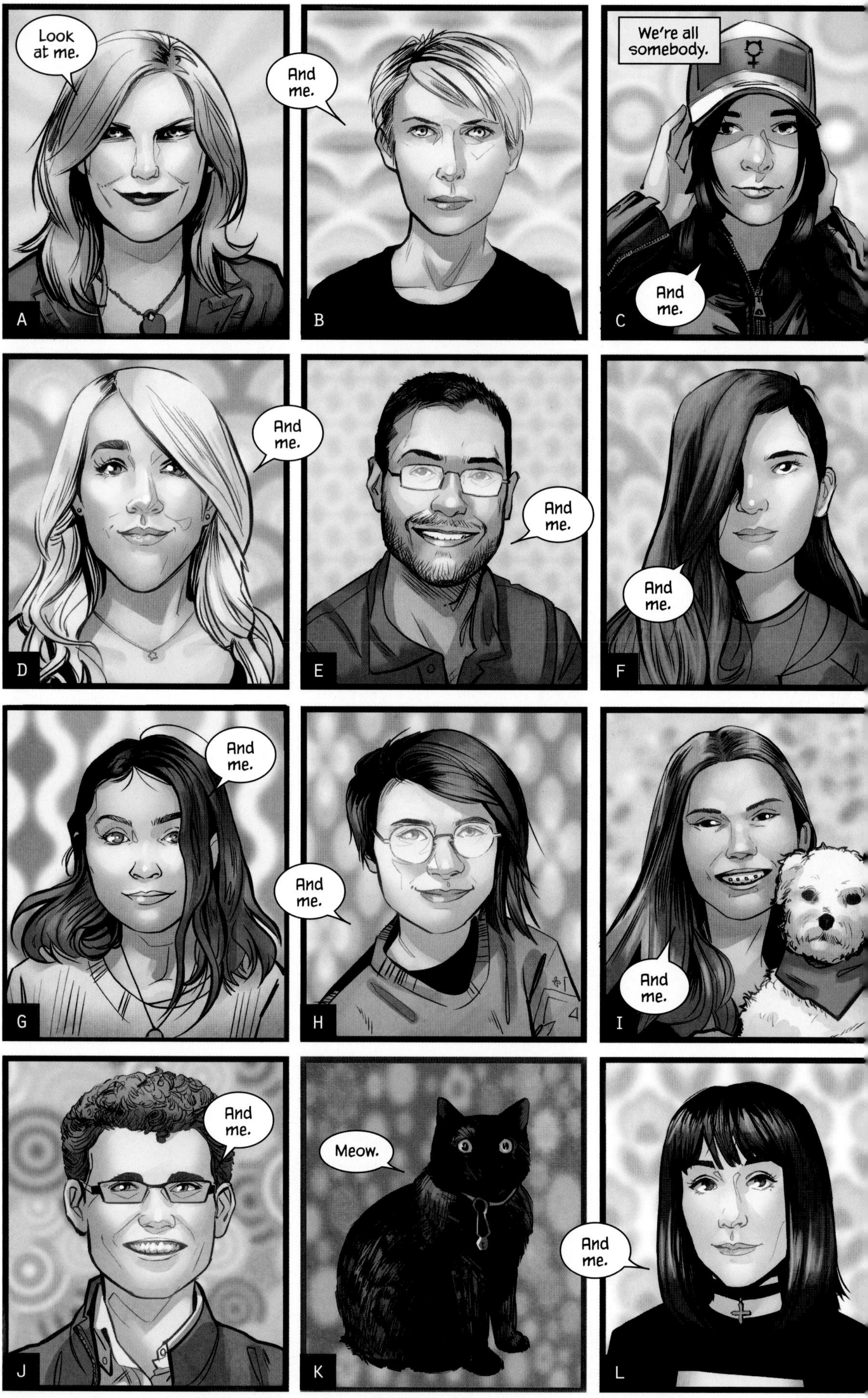
Look at me.
A
And me.
B
We're all somebody.
And me.
C
And me.
D
And me.
E
And me.
F
And me.
G
And me.
H
And me.
I
And me.
J
Meow.
K
And me.
L

CHELSEA B)LIA C)KATE D)RACHELLE E)JOE F)ELIZA G)AVA H)STELLA I)EMILY J)KATIE K)PHOENIX L)ELISE

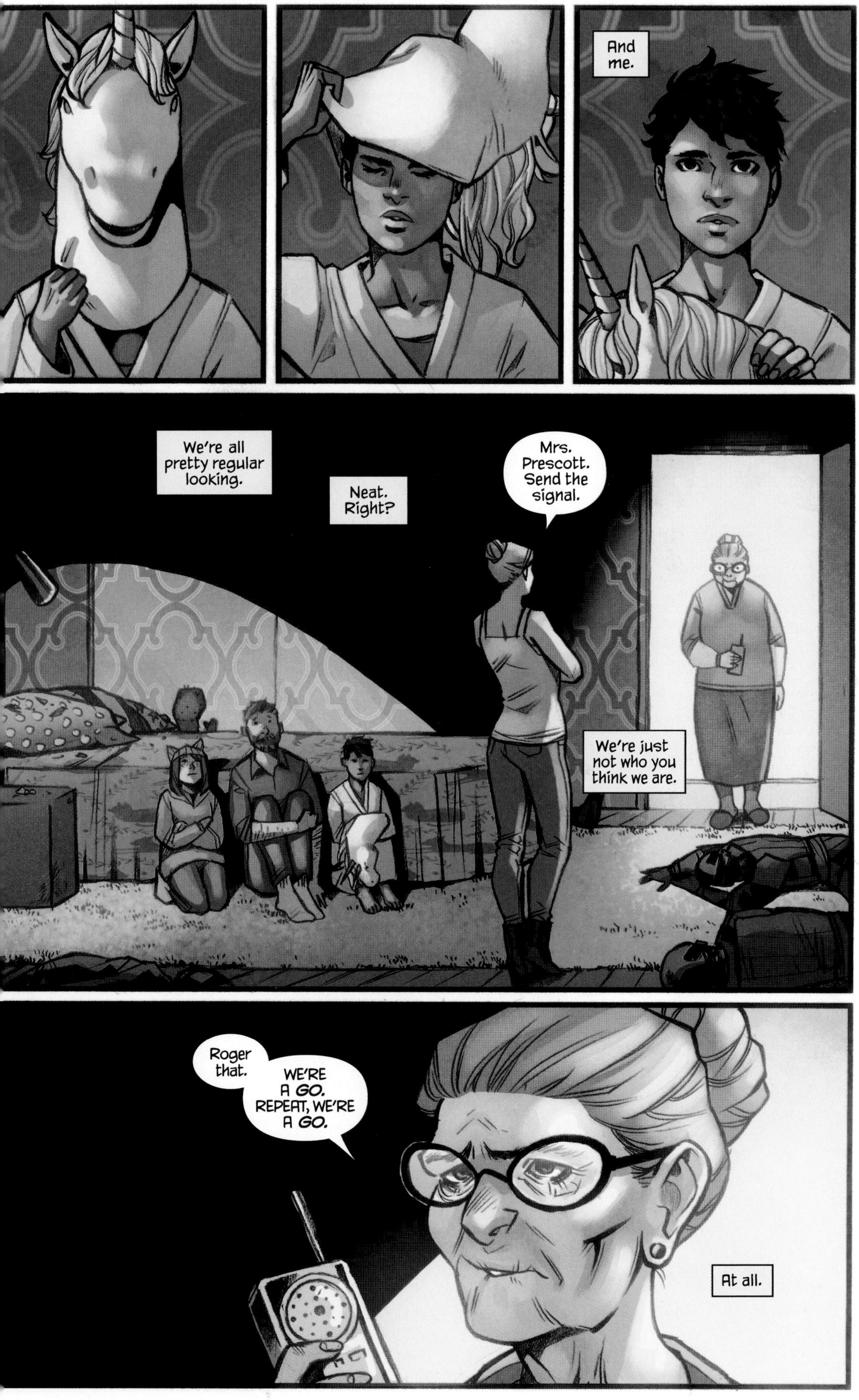
And me.
We're all pretty regular looking.
Neat. Right?
Mrs. Prescott. Send the signal.
We're just not who you think we are.
Roger that.
WE'RE A GO. REPEAT, WE'RE A GO.
At all.

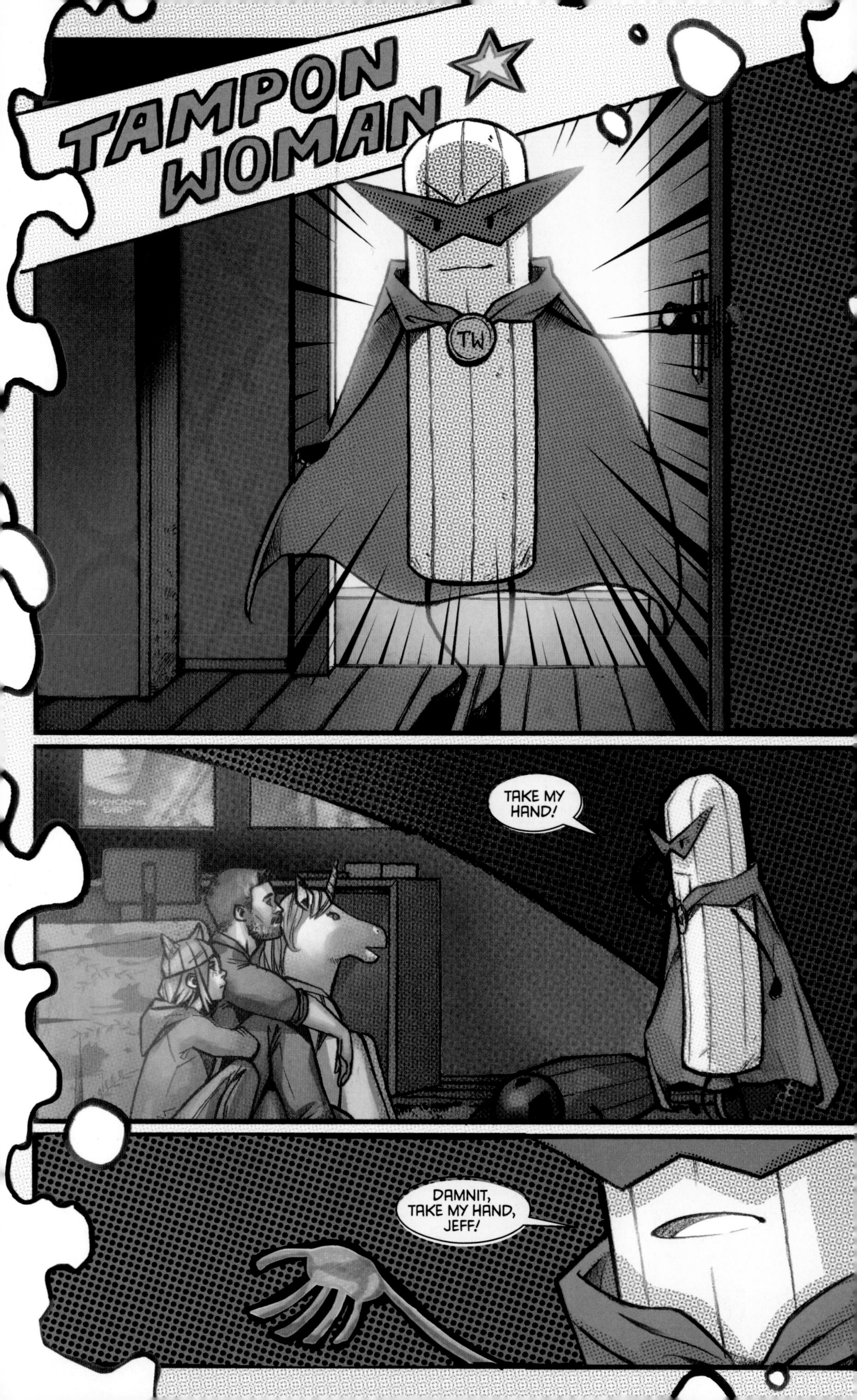
TAMPON WOMAN
TW
TAKE MY HAND!
DAMNIT, TAKE MY HAND, JEFF!

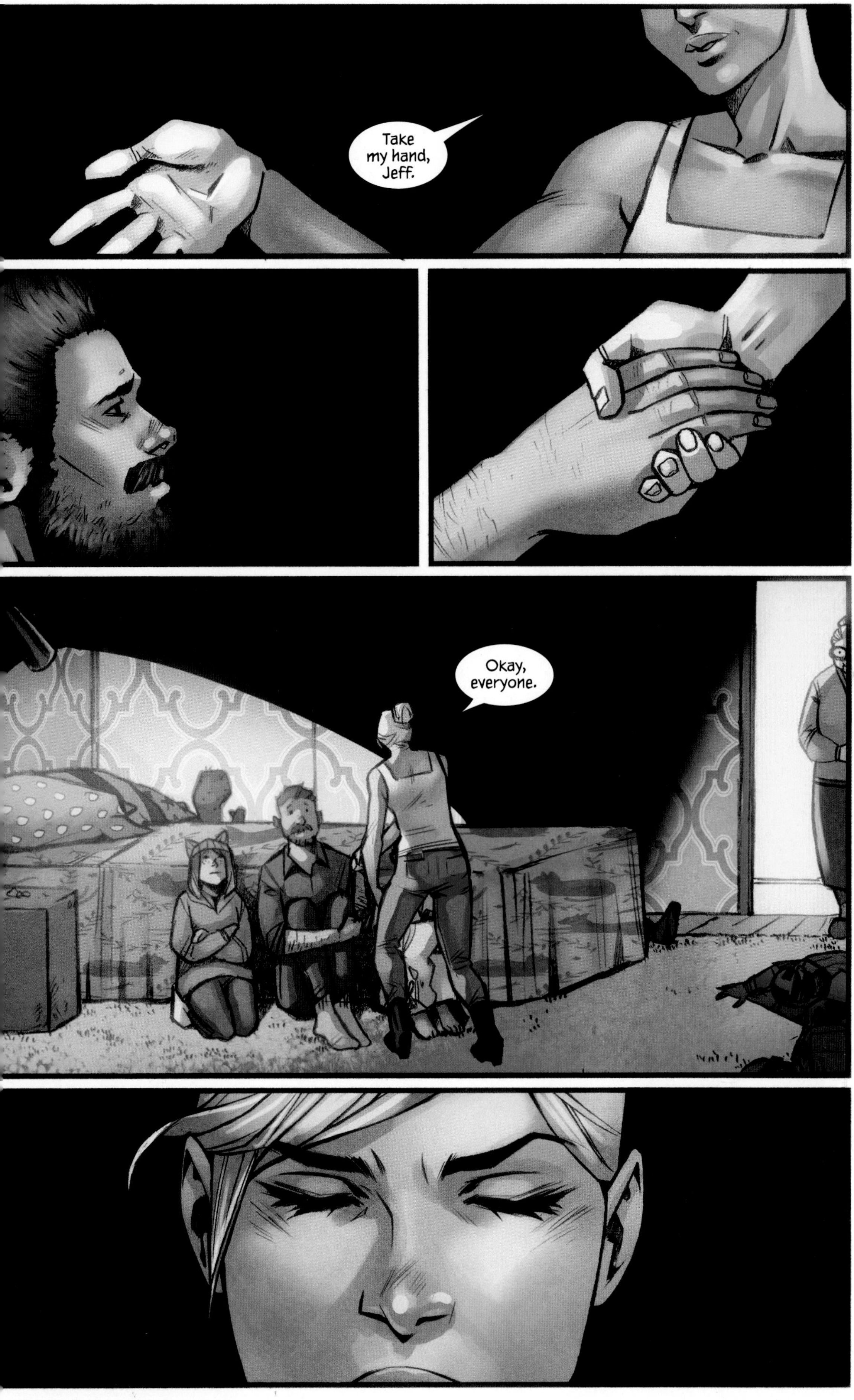
Take my hand, Jeff.
Okay, everyone.

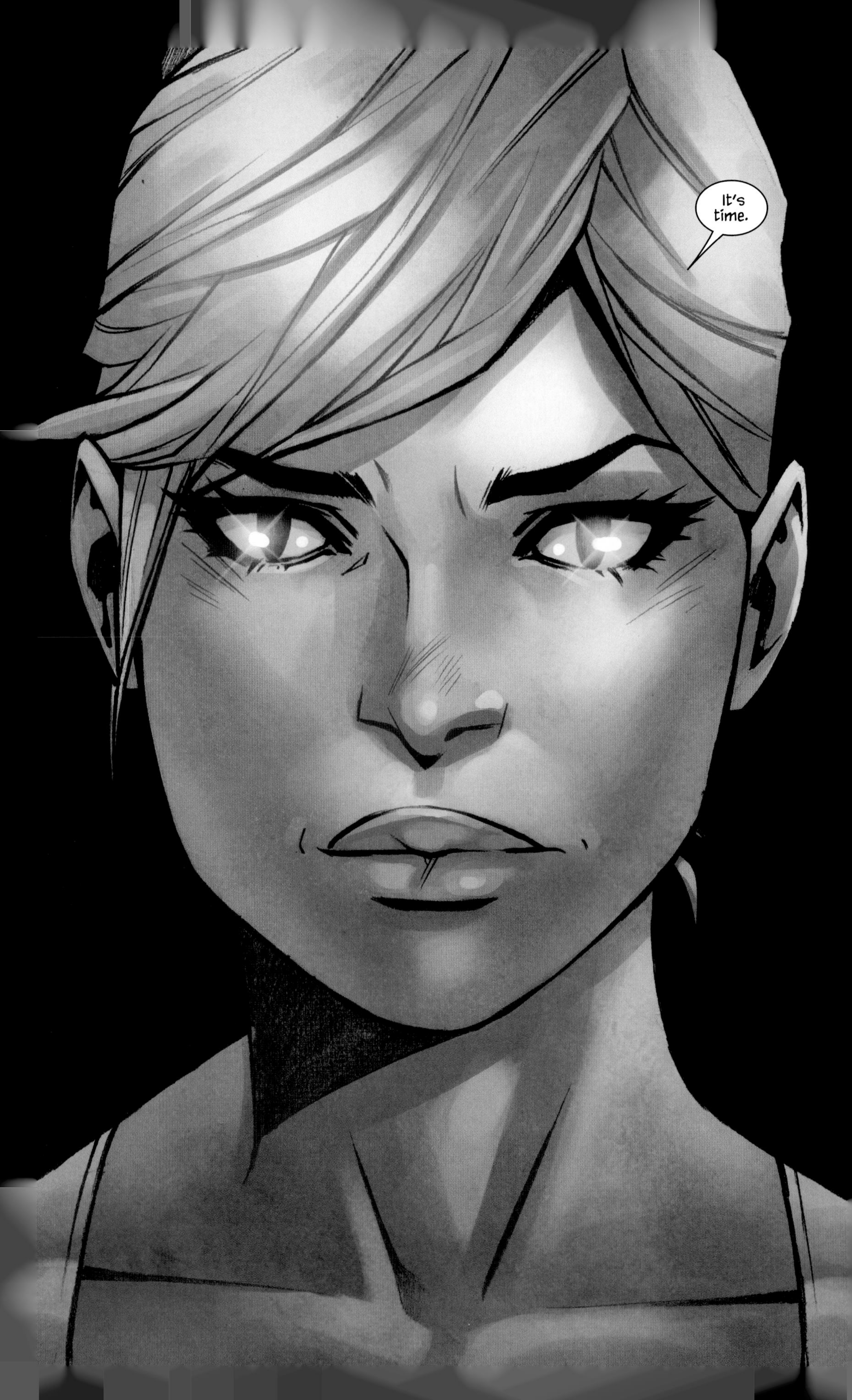
It's time.

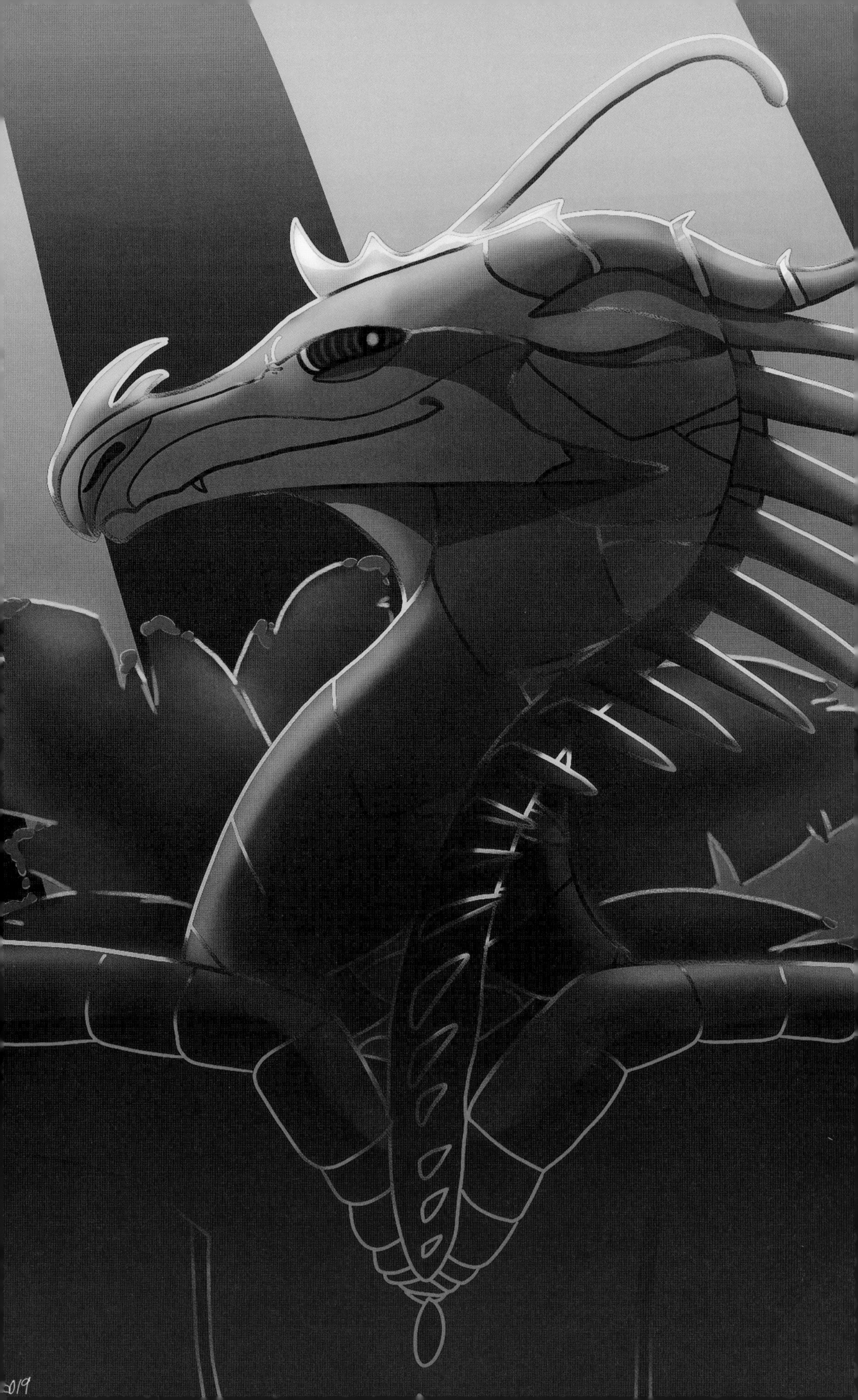

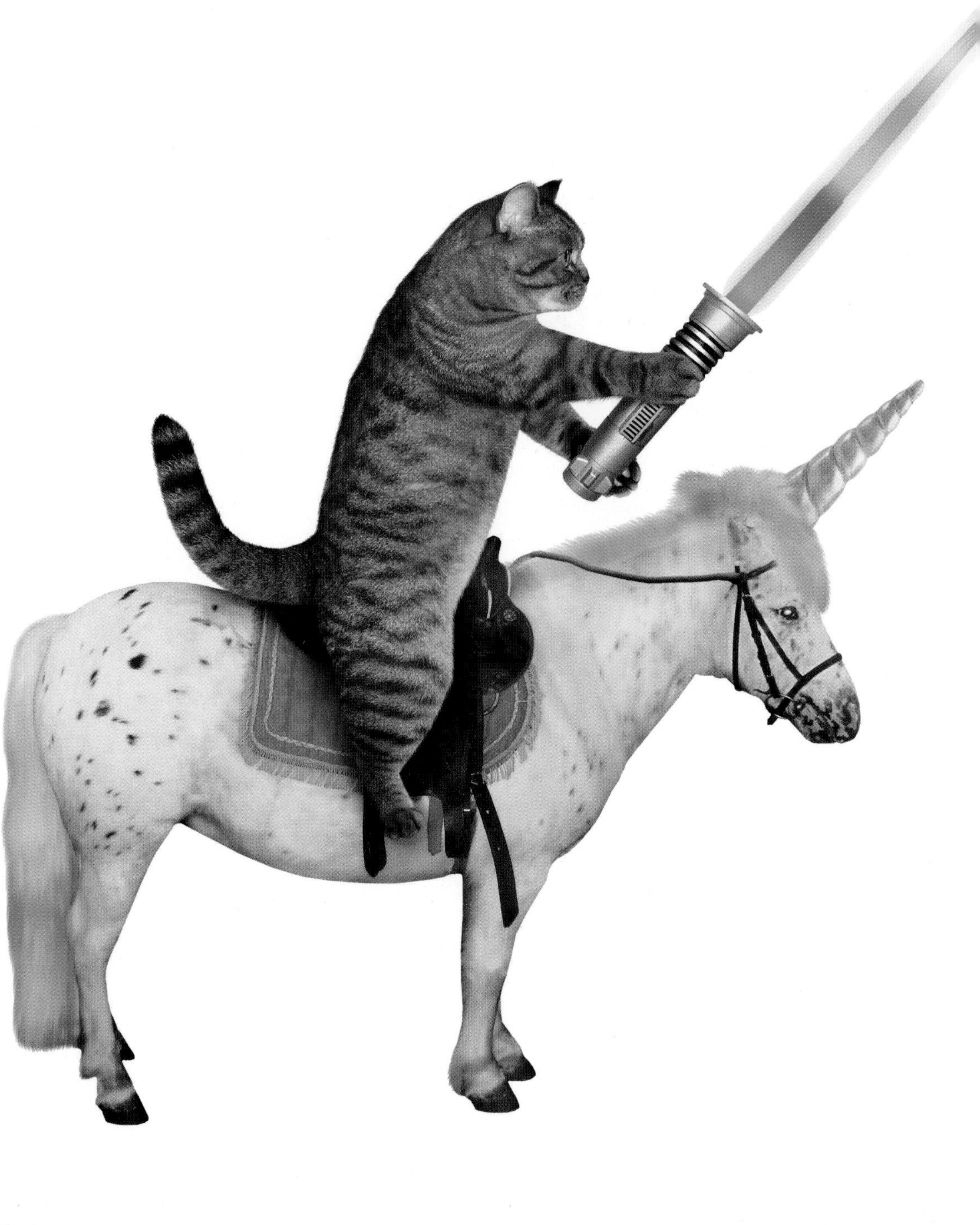

ISWEARI'MALMOSTDONE

ELIZA FANTASTIC MOHAN, AGE 14

I do not expect for this to be your favorite book.
I do not believe in miracles.
I do, however, hope that these poems will make you feel like you
are enough.
Because you are.
I know, it's hard to believe.
How could I know?
I don't know you.
Maybe you did something awful in your life.
Maybe you had awful things done to you.
I don't care.
Not to sound like a therapist, but
you are enough.
You are special.
You are beautiful
and kind
and smart
and funny.
You are anything you want to be
and everything you are.
You are a star in the night sky
or a beautiful flower.
And if you're not into that sort of shit,
you are a badass.
Tough with a heart of gold.
You are loved.
And valued.
And every day you make someone's life just a little better.
You have people in your life who would miss you if you were gone.
So, please, don't go.
Stay for the sequel.

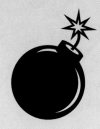

MINISTRY OF
TROUBLE
INCORPORATED

CREATOR/WRITER
CHELSEA CAIN

CO-CREATOR/CREATIVE PRODUCER – COVERS, ADS, SUPPLEMENTAL ART
LIA MITERNIQUE

PENCILS
KATE NIEMCZYK

COLORIST
RACHELLE ROSENBERG

LETTERER
JOE CARAMAGNA

ADDITIONAL INTERIOR ART
STELLA GREENVOSS
AVA HOOD
ELISE MCCALL

POEM
ELIZA FANTASTIC MOHAN

YOU HAVE BEEN CONTACTED BY THE MINISTRY OF TROUBLE. AWAIT FURTHER INSTRUCTIONS. ☿

WHAT CATS TALK ABOUT WHEN WE'RE NOT HOME.

So basically, there's this guy, and he's not a great dude but he's in love with his brother's girlfriend...

Does the girlfriend love the brother?

Yeah, the girlfriend loves the brother--they're in a relationship. But the dude is like, "Oh, I love this girl so much," but like, also, hasn't really realized it yet?

HAHAHA!

So basically he finally works up the courage and reveals his emotions and shows he cares after so long and he KISSES HER.

Ew.

He kisses her, but it turns out it wasn't her! It was her doppelganger, from 1864, who's evil.

Wait! No! What?

Plus she is also the guy's ex-girlfriend. And he used to be obsessed with her! So that was super awkward.

...What the fuck?

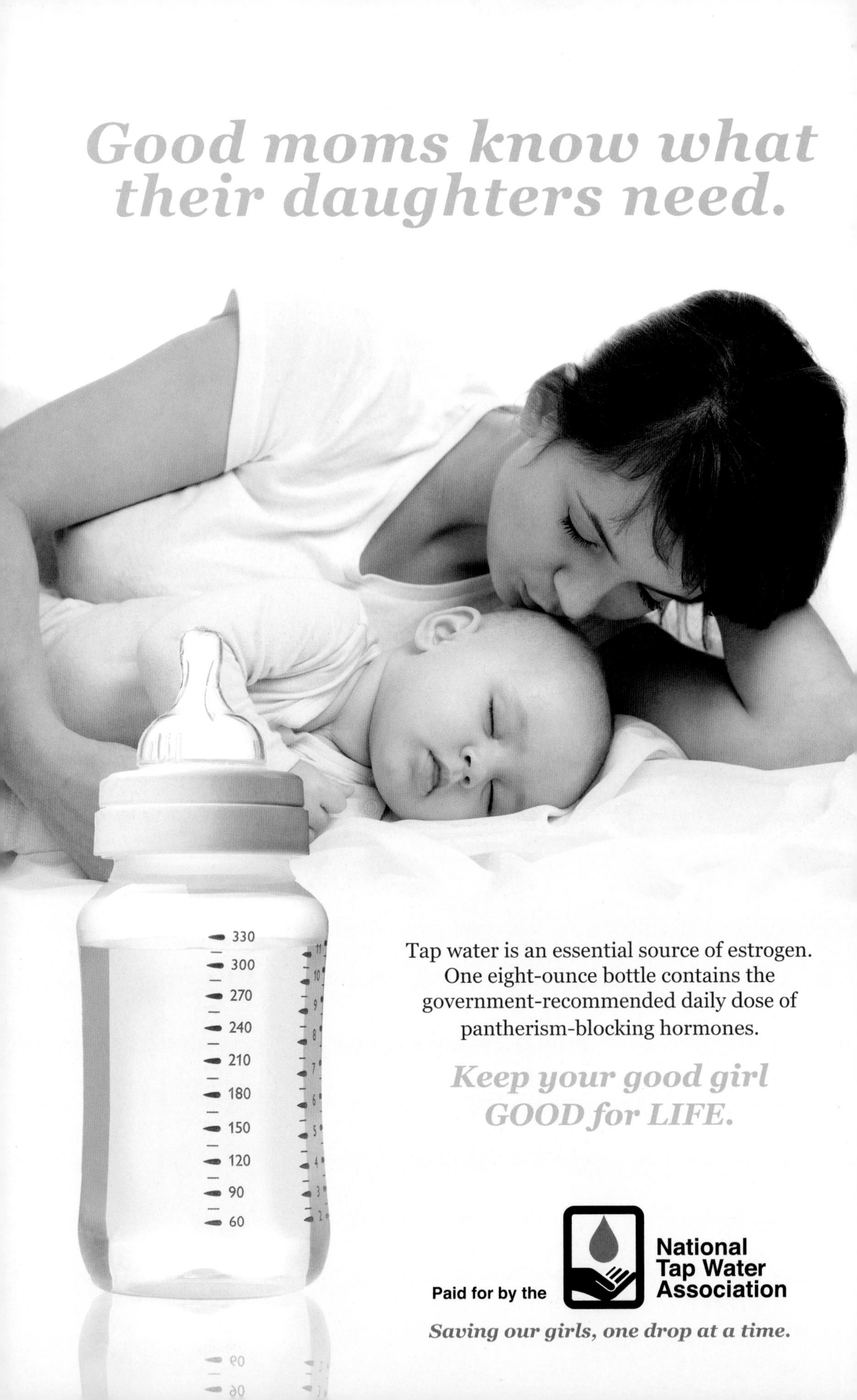
Good moms know what their daughters need.
Tap water is an essential source of estrogen. One eight-ounce bottle contains the government-recommended daily dose of pantherism-blocking hormones.
Keep your good girl GOOD for LIFE.
Paid for by the
National Tap Water Association
Saving our girls, one drop at a time.

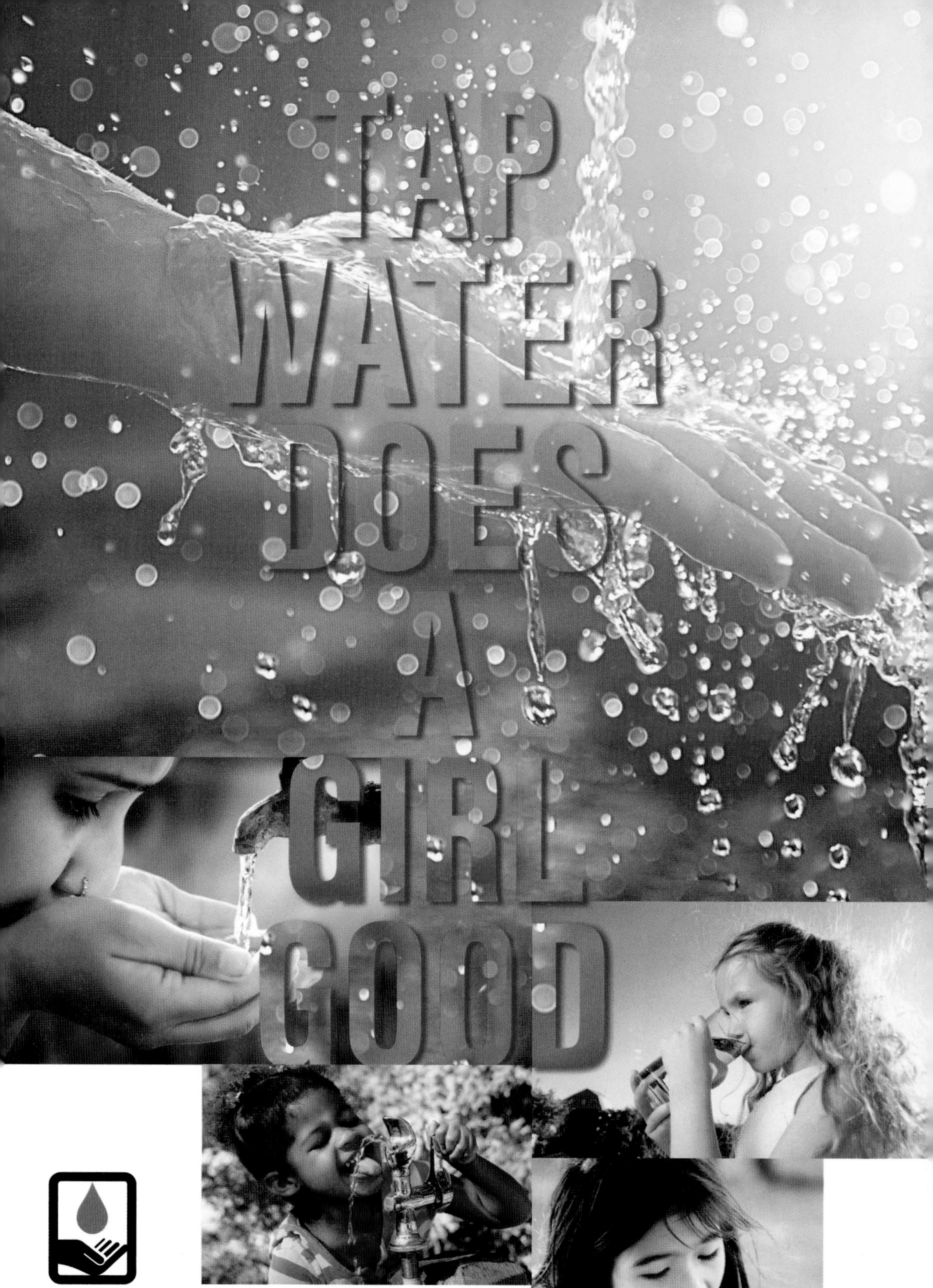
TAP
WATER
DOES
A
GIRL
GOOD

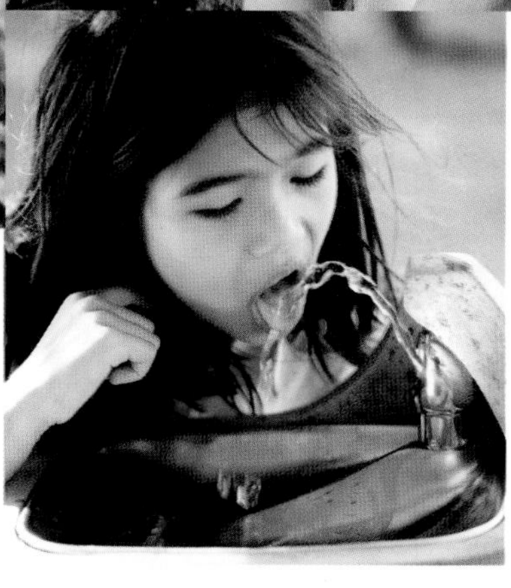

A single 8 oz glass of tap water contains half the recommended daily dose of menstruation-preventing hormones and other additives.

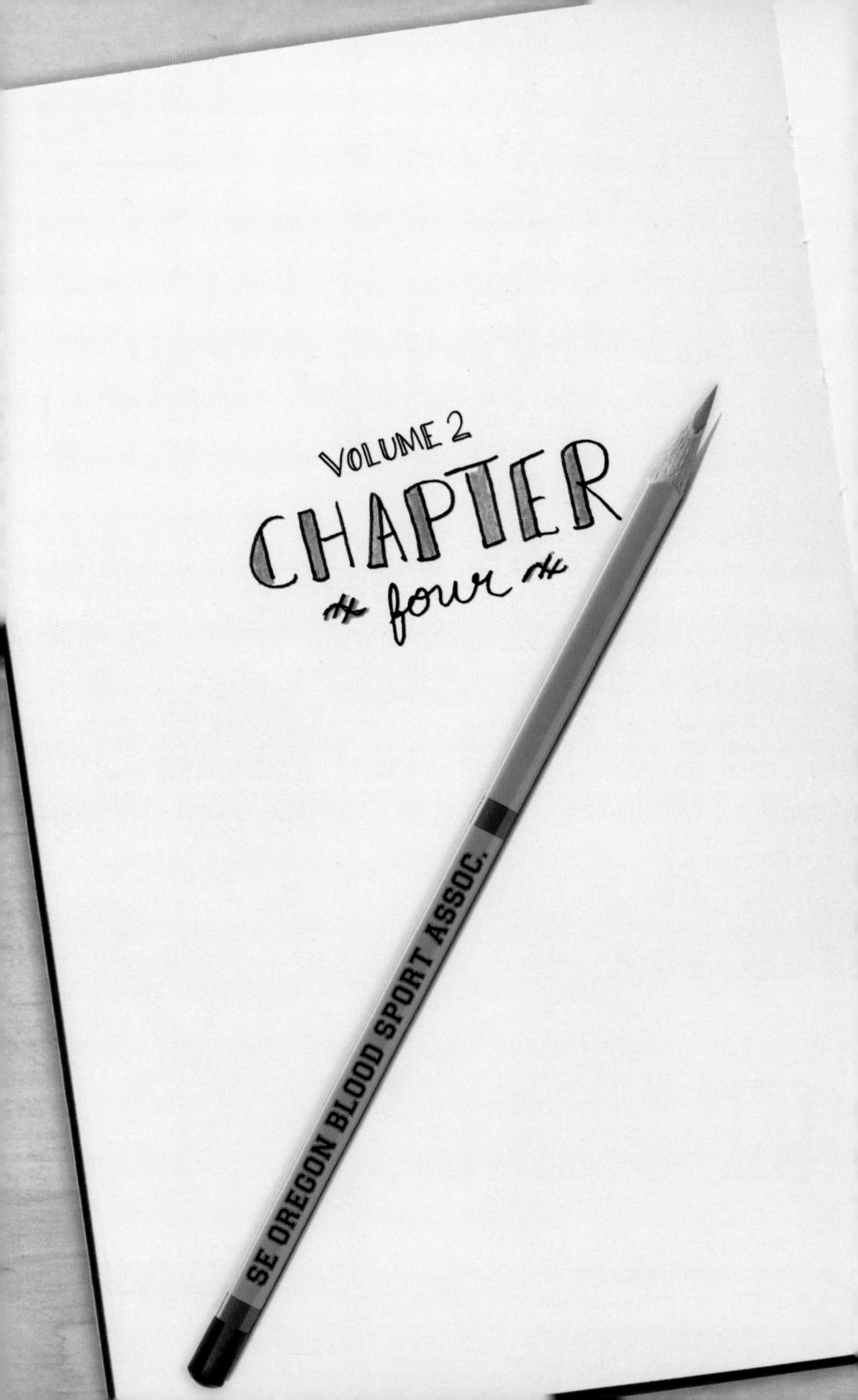
VOLUME 2
CHAPTER
four
SE OREGON BLOOD SPORT ASSOC.

maneaters

PRESENTS

WHAT'S HAPPENING TO ME
AND CAN IT BE
STOPPED?

 Chelsea Cain   Lia Miternique   NO. **8**

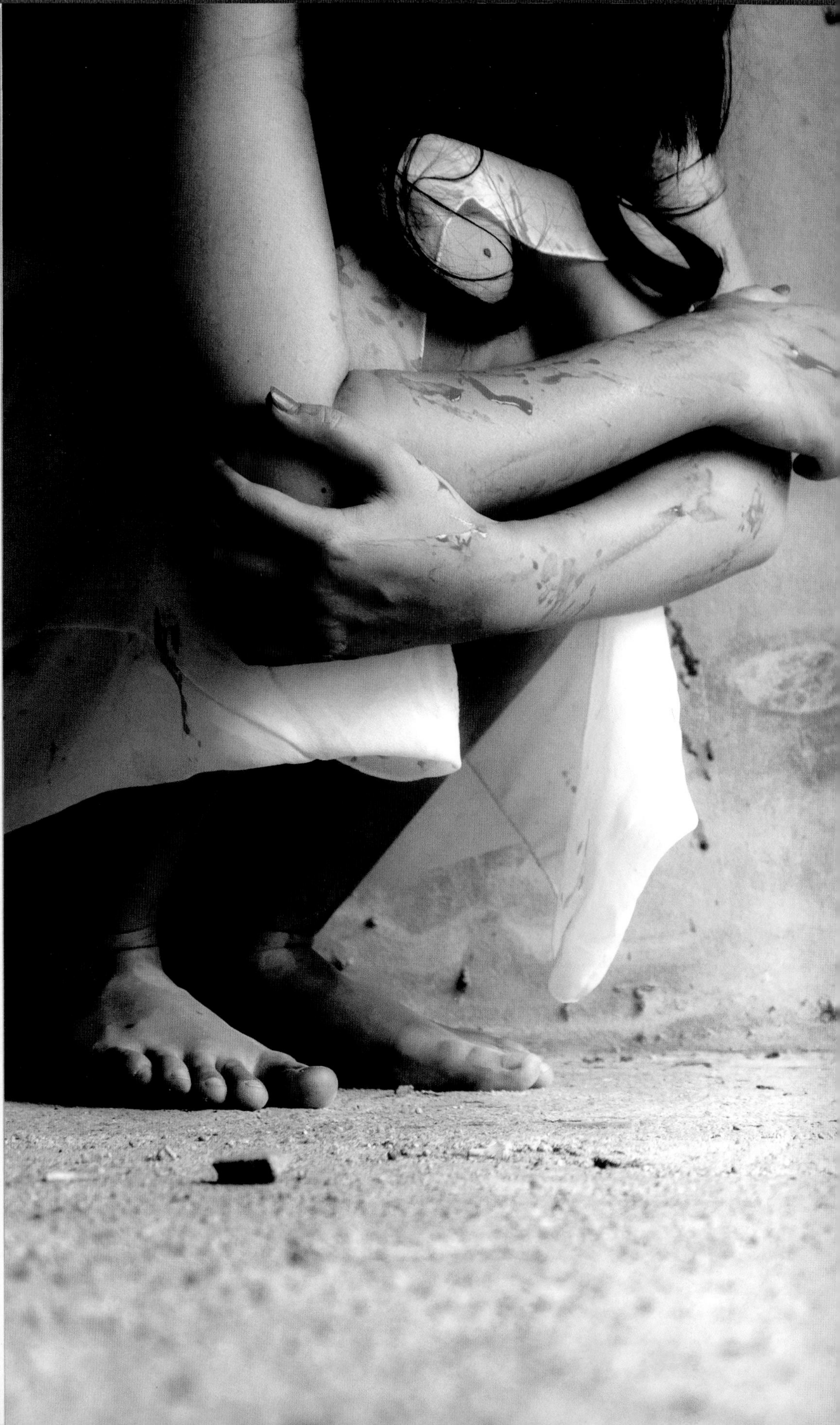

MENSTRUATION: IT'S NOT A GAME

A classroom exercise for students ages 11-14

Who can play?
Boys and girls, gender nonconforming, nonbinary, trans, and gender questioning individuals, etc.

Supplies
- This book *(one per player)*
- Safety pins *(one per player)*
- A copy machine
- A 2-oz clear plastic cup *(one per player)*
- 1 gallon of body temperature pig's blood
- Scissors
- String
- Pen/pencils
- A teacher, school nurse, or other trusted adult to act as Facilitator
- Tampon *(two per player)*

Setup
Your Facilitator will divide you into pairs. If there is an odd number of students in the room, elect the person not paired with another student to be a "victim." Cover him in pig's blood and have him lie quietly on the floor at the front of the room. This student should moan from time to time.

How it works
This exercise is divided into 5 interactive rounds designed to appeal to a wide range of skill sets.

 All students participating in this unit must have a parental consent form on file in the school office.

ROUND 1
CHOOSE A CHARACTER

Are you a Jennifer or are you a Mandy?

Each pair of students must have one Mandy and one Jennifer. Together you form a unit called "Best Friends." Discuss among yourselves which character you'd like to play.

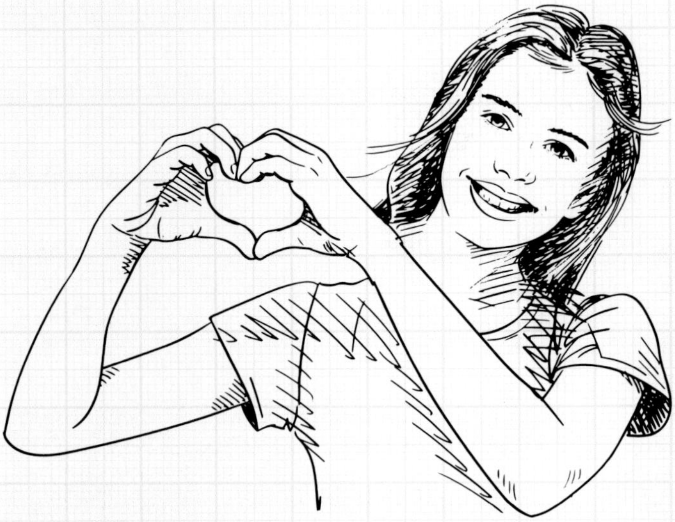

JENNIFER

(an ordinary sixth grader)

Likes

Daisies
Color-coordinated pillows
Converse
Meadows
Music in the car
Gold nail polish
Bright colors
Flowy cardigans
Elephants
Toe rings
Edits

Dislikes

Field trips
Avocados
Loud eaters
Zippers that don't work
Spicy foods
Houseplants that die

Catchphrase: "I can't find my phone."

Most used emoji: 🩶

Bio: Jennifer is an overachiever who has signed up for 11 camps this summer. She is currently participating in four after-school activities and babysitting the children of six neighbors. She has recently started wearing lipgloss. She has a secret Pinterest page. She has never seen a whale.

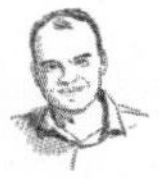

If an agreement cannot be reached between partners, your Facilitator will assign roles to you.

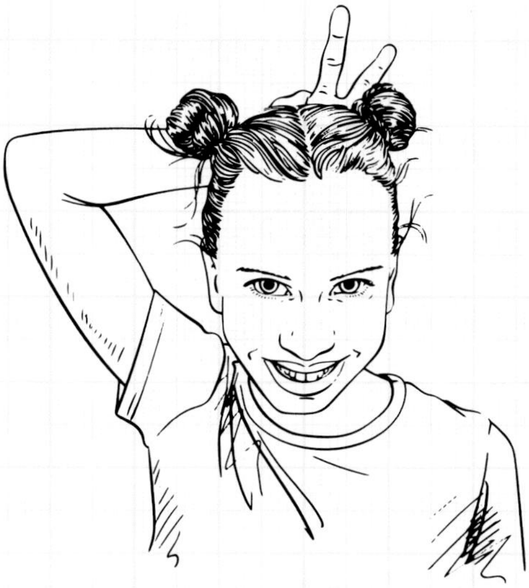

MANDY

(an ordinary sixth grader)

Likes

Heights
Bath bombs
Mechanical pencils
Halloween
Sea salt and vinegar chips
Sharpies

Dislikes

Barbeque potato chips
Acrylic nails
Loud eaters
Compliments
Wearing retainer

Catchphrase: "I'll do it in a minute."

Most used emoji: 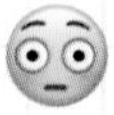

Bio: Mandy has been working up the nerve to audition for a school play for the last four years. She likes activities that happen in the dark, like movies, and laser tag. She wants to have a turtle when she grows up. Once she had lettuce stuck in her teeth for three days, and nobody noticed. She spends most of her free time DMing fandom accounts on Instagram. So far, no one has written back.

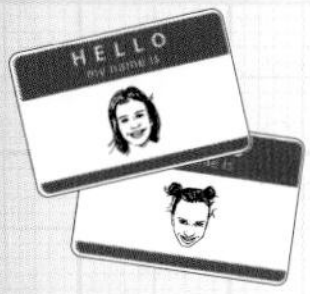
HELLO

Name Tags

Once you've decided on characters, turn to page 86, cut out the name tags from the name tag page, and distribute appropriately.

ROUND 2

ROLE PLAYING

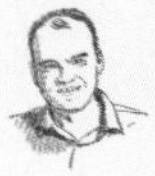

Now that you've decided on a character, your Facilitator will lead you in a role-playing exercise. Find a place in the classroom where you can face your partner. This is a scene between Mandy and Jennifer. It takes place at a fictional middle school in a medium-sized American city. Perform the scene.

SCENE I

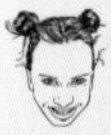

MANDY: *[Conspiratorially]* I STOLE AN ESTRO-POP™ FROM MY BROTHER. WANT TO TRY A SIP?

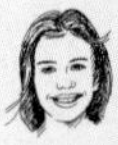

JENNIFER: *[Shocked]* WHAT?! YOU KNOW GIRLS AREN'T SUPPOSED TO DRINK ESTRO-POP™! IT'S HORMONE FREE!

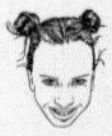

MANDY: I KNOW. IT'S DELICIOUS. I'VE BEEN SNEAKING IT FOR WEEKS.

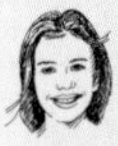

JENNIFER: *[Uncertain]* YOU'RE SURE IT'S SAFE?

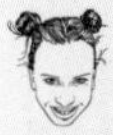

MANDY: DON'T BE A LOSER.

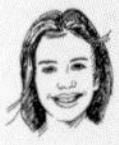

JENNIFER: OKAY. JUST A TINY SIP.

[Jennifer drinks]

Discussion prompts

Can you identify any feelings that came up in the situation?

Did you feel "silly" acting the scene out?

Were you afraid of being judged?

****Advanced**** Perform the scene again, with French Belgian accents.

"Scene I" is part of a larger dramatic work and is used with limited permission, for educational purposes only. Interested in acquiring performance rights for your HS Theatre Dept? Contact Estro-Dynamo LLC NYC for more info.

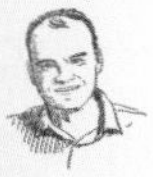

Judge your scene partner below and submit after unit completion.

ANONYMOUS PARTNER EVALUATION FORM

NAME OF SCENE PARTNER:________________________________

CHARACTER YOUR SCENE PARTNER PLAYED (CHECK ONE): ☐ MANDY ☐ JENNIFER

FOR THE FOLLOWING, CIRCLE A NUMBER ON THE SLIDING SCALE. 1 = POOREST PERFORMANCE

ENUNCIATION [did your partner pronounce words correctly and clearly?] 1 2 3 4 5

PROJECTION [did your partner speak with a loud, confident voice?] 1 2 3 4 5

EMOTIONAL VULNERABILITY
[did your partner portray the character's emotional truth?] 1 2 3 4 5

PHYSICALITY [did your partner physically inhabit the role?] 1 2 3 4 5

CHARISMA [rate your partner's stage presence] 1 2 3 4 5

FRENCH BELGIAN ACCENT (if applicable) 1 2 3 4 5 6 7 8 9 10

OTHER COMMENTS OR CRITICISMS

ANONYMOUS PARTNER EVALUATION FORM

NAME OF SCENE PARTNER:________________________________

CHARACTER YOUR SCENE PARTNER PLAYED (CHECK ONE): ☐ MANDY ☐ JENNIFER

FOR THE FOLLOWING, CIRCLE A NUMBER ON THE SLIDING SCALE. 1 = POOREST PERFORMANCE

ENUNCIATION [did your partner pronounce words correctly and clearly?] 1 2 3 4 5

PROJECTION [did your partner speak with a loud, confident voice?] 1 2 3 4 5

EMOTIONAL VULNERABILITY
[did your partner portray the character's emotional truth?] 1 2 3 4 5

PHYSICALITY [did your partner physically inhabit the role?] 1 2 3 4 5

CHARISMA [rate your partner's stage presence] 1 2 3 4 5

FRENCH BELGIAN ACCENT (if applicable) 1 2 3 4 5 6 7 8 9 10

OTHER COMMENTS OR CRITICISMS

ROUND 3

CARD GAME

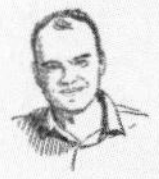

In this card game, you'll learn about causal relationships and increase your familiarity with menstruation-related terms.

Setup

If you haven't already, cut out the cards on flap A and flap B, found at the front of this book. There are two players. Each player should have a full set of cards. So you will need 2 copies of this book. Or a copy machine.

Each deck includes

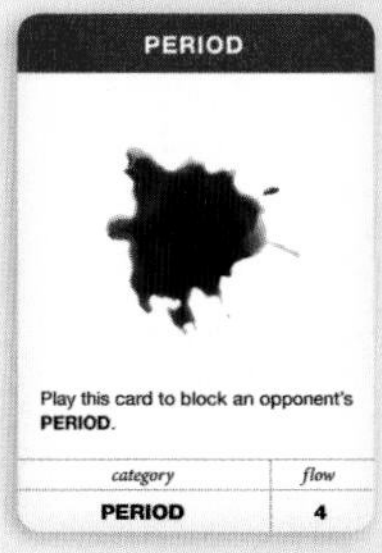

PERIOD
Play this card to block an opponent's **PERIOD**.
category
flow
PERIOD
4

6 PERIOD cards

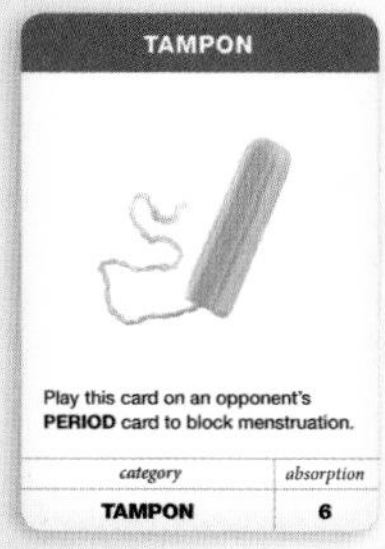

TAMPON
Play this card on an opponent's **PERIOD** card to block menstruation.
category
absorption
TAMPON
6

5 TAMPON cards

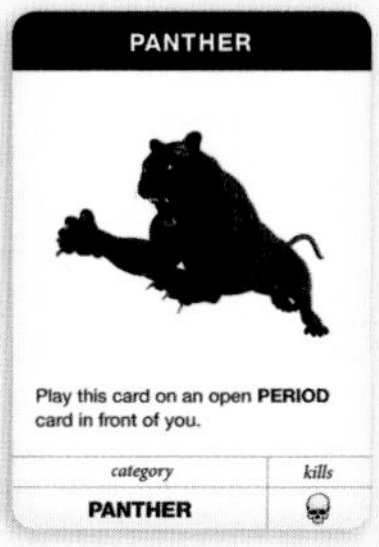

PANTHER
Play this card on an open **PERIOD** card in front of you.
category
kills
PANTHER

6 PANTHER cards

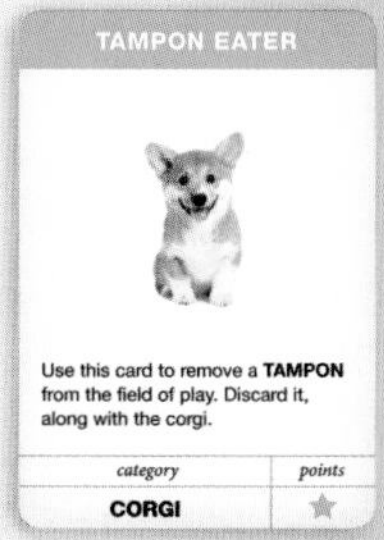

TAMPON EATER
Use this card to remove a **TAMPON** from the field of play. Discard it, along with the corgi.
category
points
CORGI

1 CORGI card

Gameplay

Each player shuffles her deck of cards, places them facedown in front of her, and then draws 6 cards from her deck into her hand.

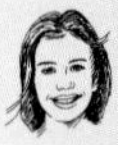

Jennifer always goes first.

She may play one card from her hand onto the table in front of her. The only card she may play is a PERIOD card. If she does not have a PERIOD card, she chooses a card from her hand to discard and she draws another card from her deck.

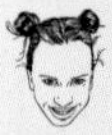

Mandy always goes second.

Mandy may play one card from her hand. If Jennifer has played a PERIOD card, Mandy may cancel the PERIOD card by placing a TAMPON card on top of it. If Mandy does not have a TAMPON card, she must play a PERIOD card onto the table in front of her. If she does not have a PERIOD card, she chooses a card from her hand to discard and she draws another from her deck.

The game is over when no one can play a card. The person who has played the most panther cards wins.

If neither player achieves pantherism, play again.
If players have the same number of panther cards at the end of the game, it is a tie.

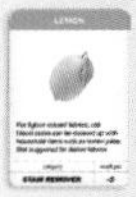

****Advanced**** For advanced play, sub out the TAMPON cards in the basic deck for the STAIN REMOVER cards in the expansion pack found on page 87. When a PERIOD card is played, note its FLOW number. STAIN REMOVER cards all come with a STAIN VALUE. They can be played on top of PERIOD cards. When the STAIN VALUE added to the FLOW = 0, remove the PERIOD card from the field of play.

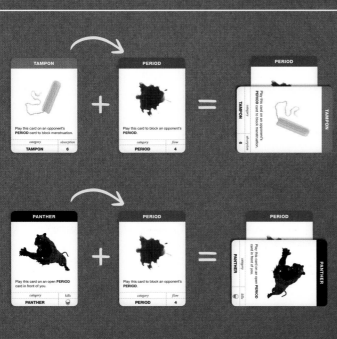

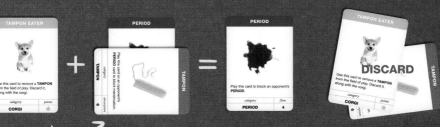

BLOOD SPORT

Not all games are based on chance or skill. Some games are rooted in dexterity. In this round, players will engage in timed physical exercise.

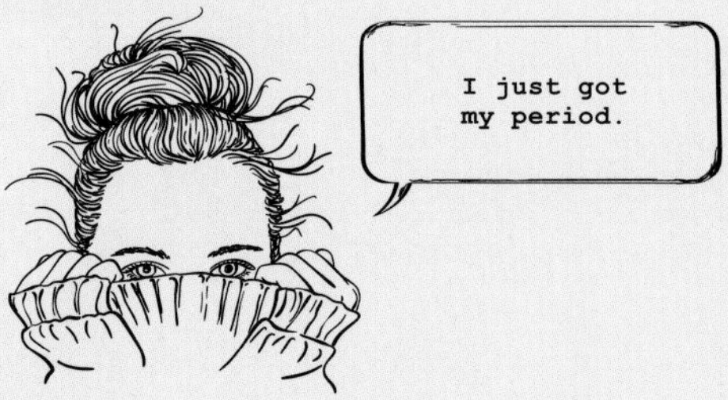
I just got
my period.

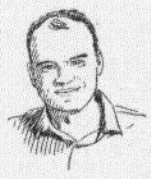

Your Facilitator will now distribute a 2-oz plastic cup of pig's blood to each student. Each cup will be filled to the rim. This represents a heavy flow.

All students should carry their pig's blood to the gymnasium for this round. Careful! Don't spill a drop.

Once you're in the gym, divide into two teams. All MANDYS on one end of the court, and all JENNIFERS on the opposite end of the court.

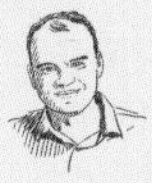

Your Facilitator will now distribute two super absorbent tampons to each student.

Gameplay

Dip your tampon in your cup of blood and absorb as much blood as you can.

Transport the blood-soaked tampon to the center of the court.

Hand it to the Facilitator.

Return to base.

Repeat the process with your second tampon.

You have 3 minutes.
(The average time between middle school classes.)

The team that has completed the most tampon drops when the buzzer goes off wins.

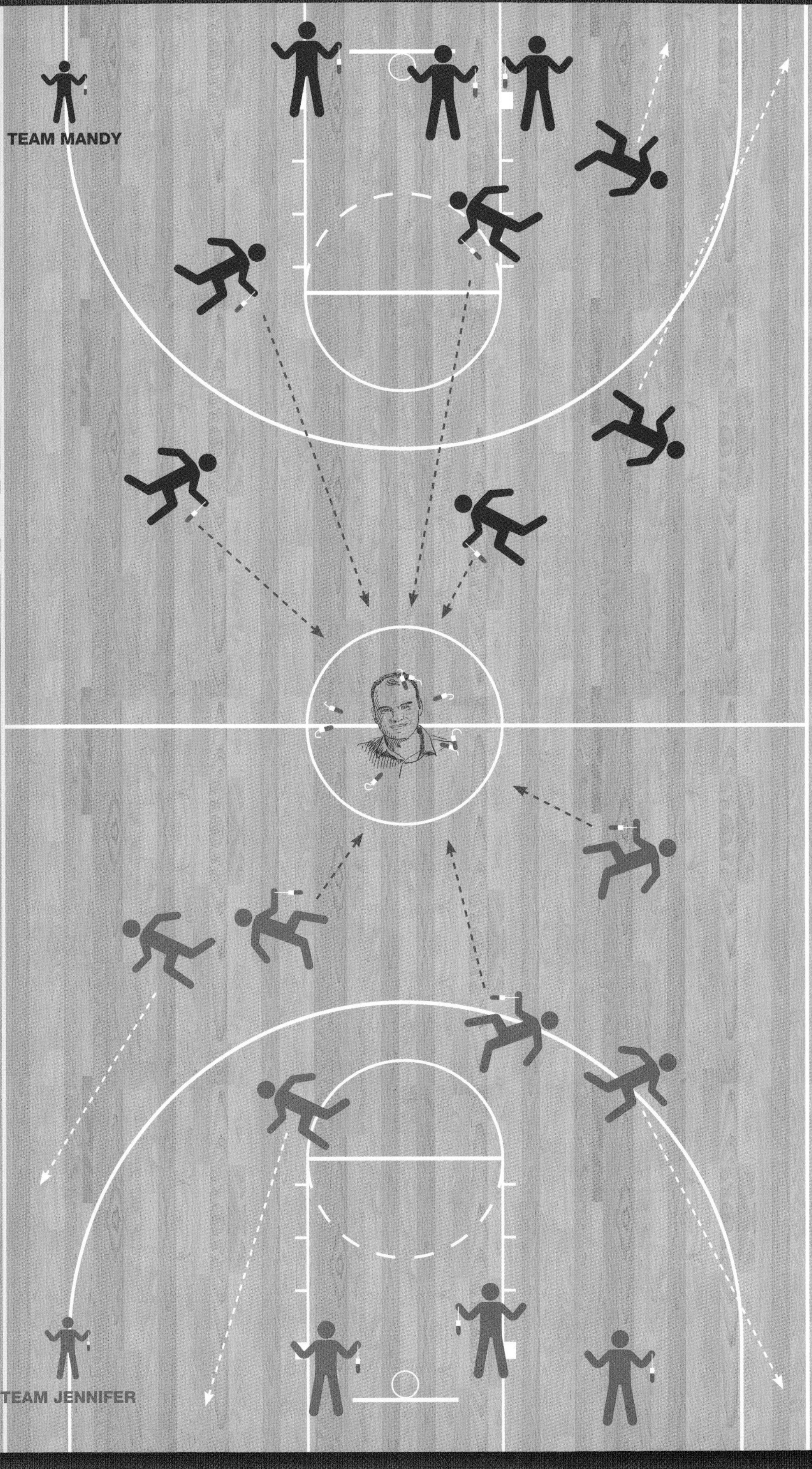
TEAM MANDY
TEAM JENNIFER

COMBAT SIMULATION

> This last round relies on very simple graph plotting, math, fine motor skills, and attention to detail. Mandy, Jennifer, and some werepanthers are represented on the opposite page. In this exercise your Facilitator will be playing the part of the werepanthers.

Tactical scenario

Jennifer and Mandy have been ambushed by werepanthers! Attempt to avoid attack.
You may take one move action per turn, unless otherwise stated.

Movement rules

Each square on the grid = 5 feet [eg: if you have a base speed of +30 you can move 6 squares]
Diagonal movement costs 7.5 movement.
Moving off-road costs 7.5 movement.

Turn order

Jennifer always goes first. Then all the werepanthers (1-5). Then Mandy. Then all the werepanthers (1-5). Repeat.

Attack rules

Any characters occupying the same square must engage in combat.

A character's base attack bonus = $\dfrac{\text{their base speed}}{\text{pi}} + 2$

The character with the highest attack bonus wins.
The losing player takes 4 points of damage, unless otherwise stated.

JENNIFER	MANDY	WEREPANTHER
Base Speed: +25	**Base Speed:** +25	**Base Speed:** +60
Hit Points: 20	**Hit Points:** 19	**Hit Points:** 118

JENNIFER

Feats:
Soccer,
basic ceramics

Estro-Pop.
Regain 10 Hit Points

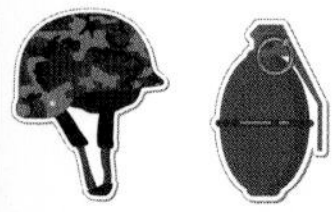

Use each item for +1 against attack

⚠ **Use your character's catch phrase** *[page 66]* for a +1 to your attack.

MANDY

Feats:
Laser tag,
making cupcakes,
braiding hair

Wi-fi. Use 3 actions to find a wi-fi signal. Then double your speed for two turns.

Use each item for +1 against attack

⚠ **Use your character's catch phrase** *[page 67]* for a +1 to your attack.

WEREPANTHER

Feats:
Ambushing
Slinking
Creeping
Leaping
Stalking
Crouching
Mauling
Teaching math

Claws:
+5 to attack

Teeth:
+5 to attack

Mission: Werepanthers take turns in or (1-5). Move toward girls and attack.

Death tracker

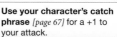

Student Health Edition, Estropure Scholastic Founda

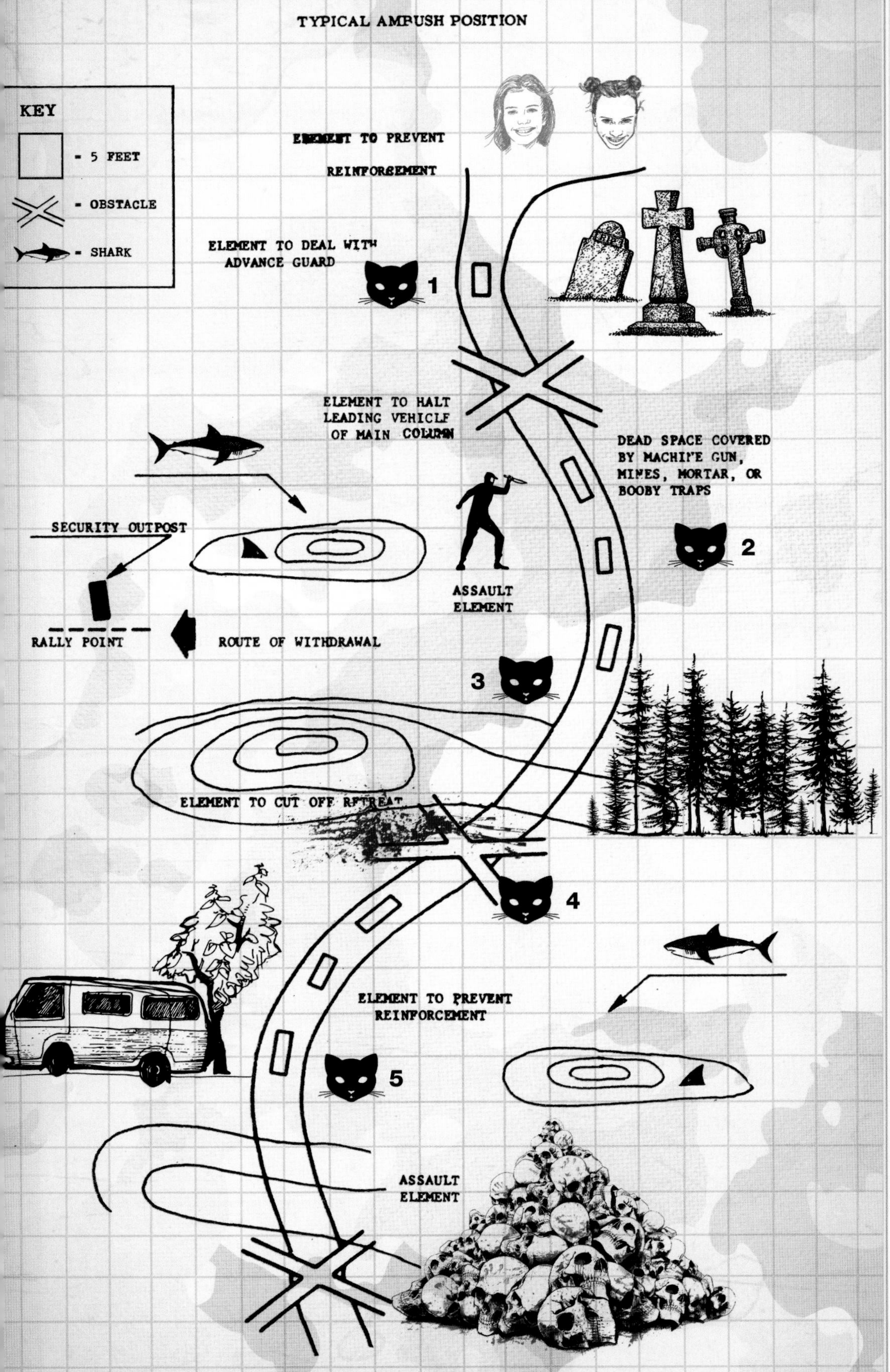
TYPICAL AMBUSH POSITION
KEY
= 5 FEET
= OBSTACLE
= SHARK
ELEMENT TO PREVENT
REINFORCEMENT
ELEMENT TO DEAL WITH
ADVANCE GUARD
1
ELEMENT TO HALT
LEADING VEHICLE
OF MAIN COLUMN
DEAD SPACE COVERED
BY MACHINE GUN,
MINES, MORTAR, OR
BOOBY TRAPS
SECURITY OUTPOST
2
ASSAULT
ELEMENT
RALLY POINT
ROUTE OF WITHDRAWAL
3
ELEMENT TO CUT OFF RETREAT
4
ELEMENT TO PREVENT
REINFORCEMENT
5
ASSAULT
ELEMENT

CHAPTER REFLECTION

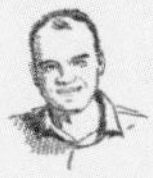

Games offer us a useful life simulation to test our resilience and solve problems. But what if I told you this wasn't a simulation?

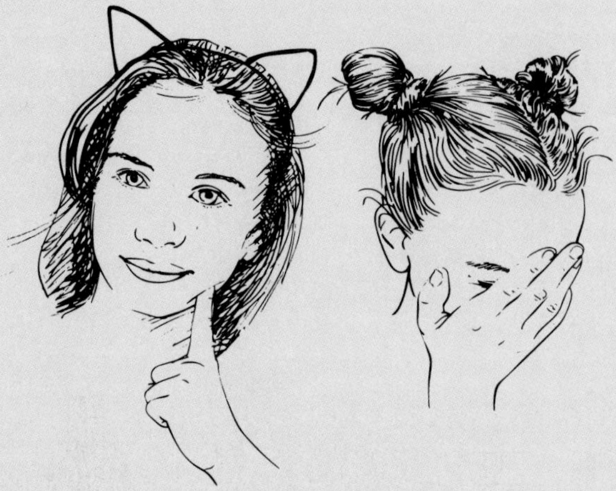

As MANDY and JENNIFER, you have tempted fate by drinking Estro-Pop™, practiced competitive strategies, heightened your reflexes, tested your math and memory skills, and, we hope, learned something about yourself along the way.

If this unit has taught you nothing else, let it be this: The cat always wins.

Menstruation is not a game.

And Jennifer and Mandy are not characters.
They're real people.
Both have agreed to allow us to use their stories here, in the hope that others may learn from their experiences.

Jennifer and Mandy are just like you.

Two ordinary sixth-grade girls, who thought that maybe turning into a panther might be cool.

Jennifer and Mandy wanted to experiment. They thought that menstruation was natural. They believed they could "handle" it.

They each learned a valuable lesson.

Where are they now?

You're about to find out.
But first, let's get real...

PANTHERISM: GAME OVER

Sure, menstruation seems sophisticated. Grown-up. Dangerously enticing. But did you know that menstruation costs money?

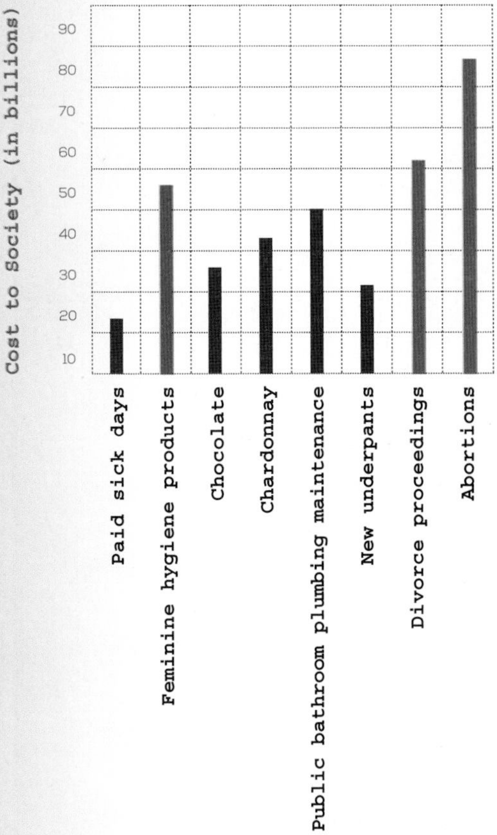

Cost to Society (in billions)
90
80
70
60
50
40
30
20
10
Paid sick days
Feminine hygiene products
Chocolate
Chardonnay
Public bathroom plumbing maintenance
New underpants
Divorce proceedings
Abortions

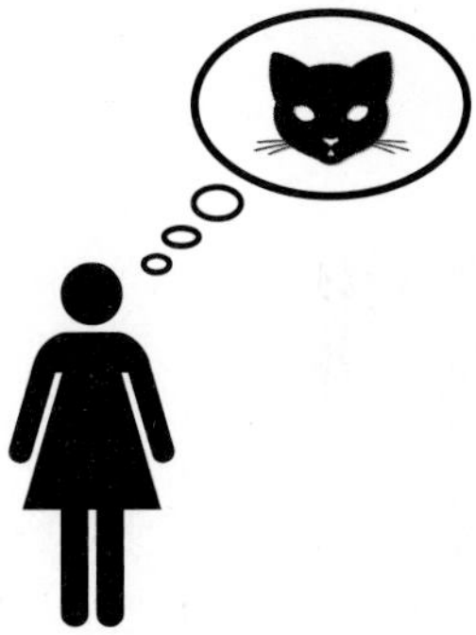

79% of all girls between the ages of 11-14 report that they have fantasized at some point about **Pantherism**.

Need help? Talk to a guidance counselor, school nurse, or dad.

The life you save might be your own.

Where is JENNIFER now? Turn to PAGE 78.

Where is MANDY now? Turn to PAGE 80.

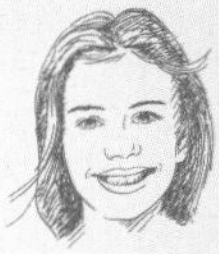

Where is Jennifer now?
She is...

CAGED AND

This is her story.

Jennifer is 17 now, with sad brown eyes that hint at a well of regret. Five years ago, she was a popular, energetic sixth grader, with lots of friends, good grades, and a bright future. Now she's locked up in a containment camp in Eastern Oregon. Her parents don't come and visit her. Because she killed them.

Jennifer is one of over 600 girls held at the Oregon State Panther Detention Center, five hours from Portland. It's bleak, surrounded by high desert. Temperatures swing from 112 degrees in the summer to -15 degrees in the winter. The girls live, four to a room, in converted stables—the Center was a livestock exchange before the government came calling. No TV. No cell phones. No computers. The only thing to watch at OSPDC is the sunset. Occasionally a curious deer will approach the chain-link fence that surrounds the Center, but they are quickly shooed away by guards, for their own safety. After all, every girl incarcerated here is a murderer.

Jennifer doesn't remember mauling her family. Her pantherism manifested suddenly. Her friends report that she changed overnight. She was no longer the sweet, carefree girl they had known. She was moody, combative, aggressive. She cut her hair. She quit the cheerleading team. She announced her intention to learn how to play electric guitar. In hindsight, these behaviors are textbook indicators of impending mutation.

"I just wanted to read Sylvia Plath," Jennifer said at her containment hearing. "And one thing led to another."

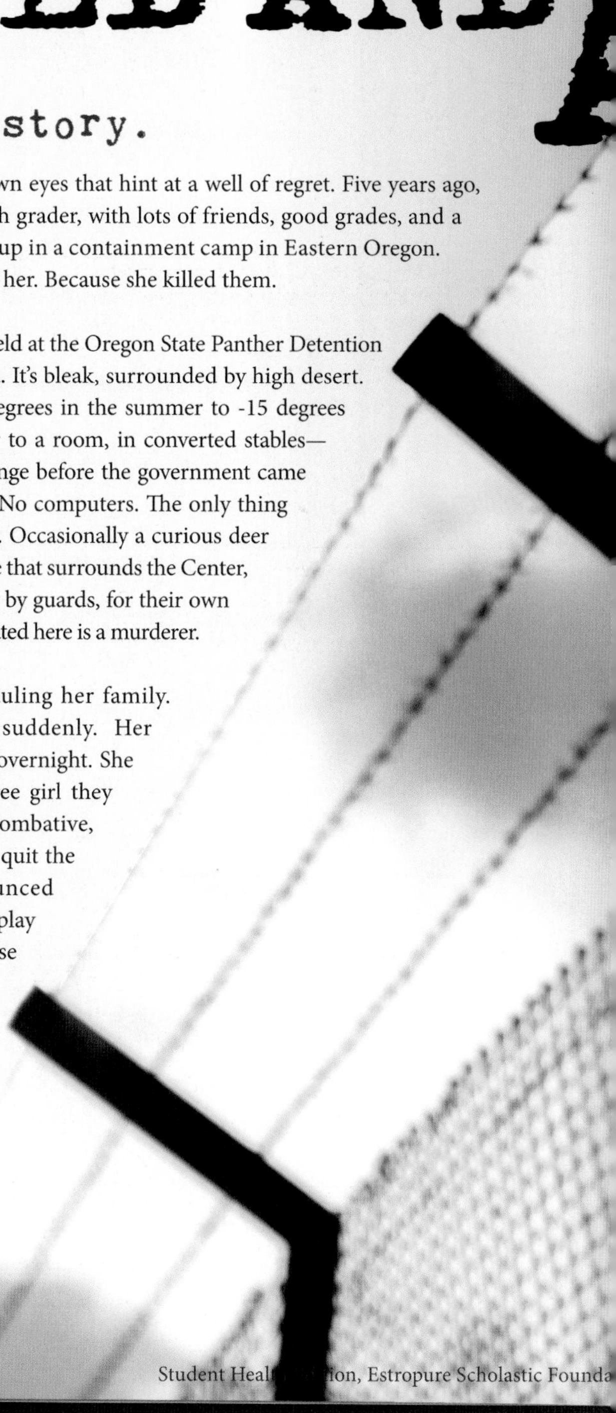

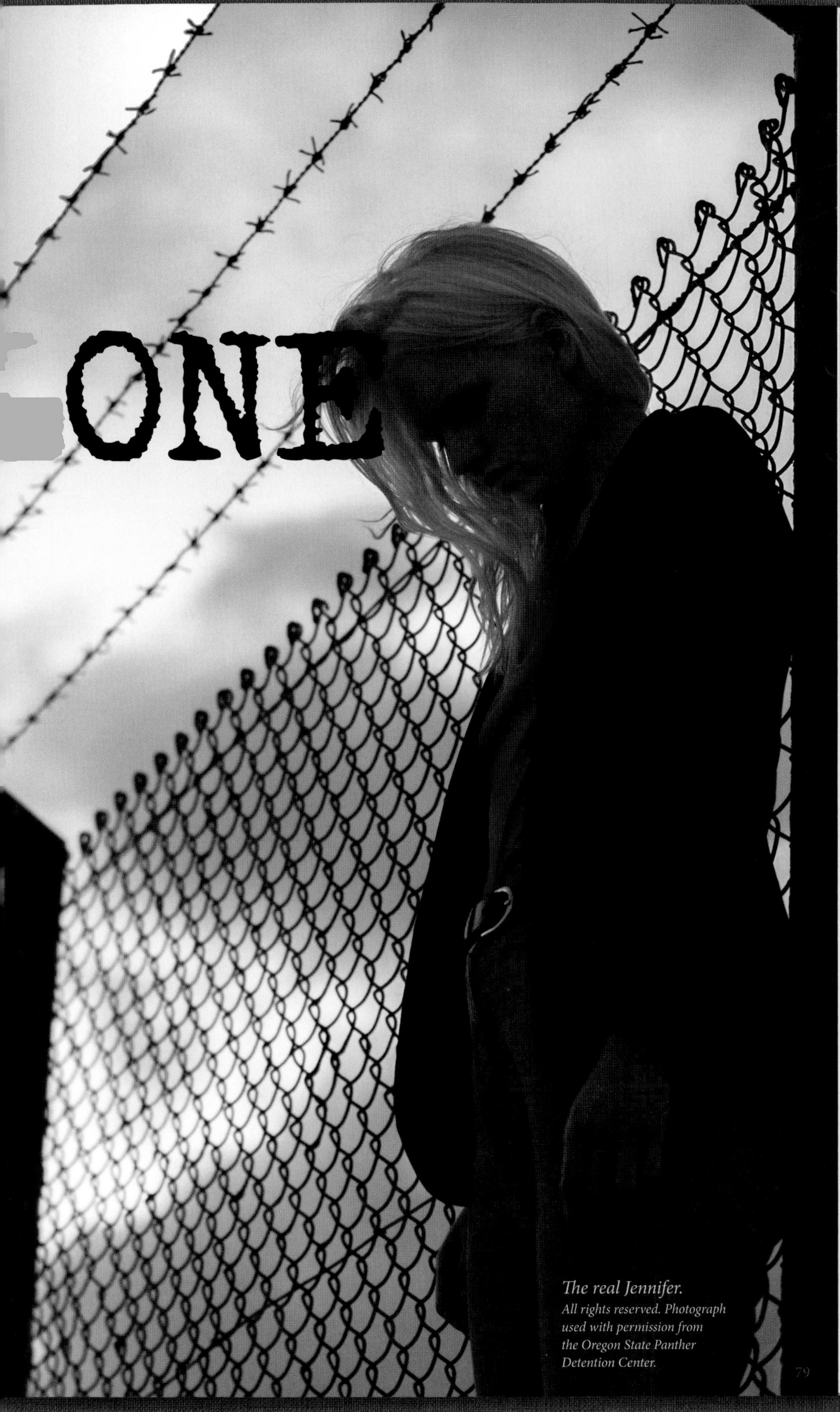
ONE

The real Jennifer.

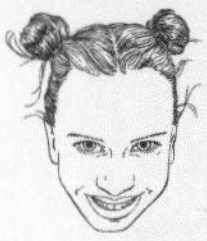

CHAPTER REFLECTION
OUTCOME: MANDY

Where is Mandy now?
She is...

KEEPING THE PR

Mandy's dangerous choices could have led to bloodshed. But thanks to her quick-thinking mother and the staff at Ruminations, she is now harmless. This is her story.

It's been nearly five years since Mandy's last transition. As a Toxo X Pos female with feline tendencies, she still struggles. But Mandy is a rare success story. Mandy's mother credits the staff at Ruminations, a celebrity Pantherism recovery center in Malibu, California, where Mandy spent 12 months receiving in-patient treatment. She has returned twice for shorter stays and for appointments related to the hormonal implant and tracker embedded in her pituitary gland (a condition of her probation).

Mandy looks younger than 17, and smiles easily. Her condition prevents her from attending school, but lately she's been taking some online courses, and she hopes to one day become a counselor to teens like her.

"It started out as a private rebellion," she confides. "I would sneak one of my brother's Estro-Pops™ from the fridge, hide it in my room, and nurse it for days, one small sip at a time. The more I drank, the less appealing tap water became. I guess it was a control thing. I would go days without any tap water at all—it made me feel powerful to walk past my school water fountain. I even stopped using water to brush my teeth. Then I'd hear about a girl who'd turned panther and mauled someone, and I'd feel so guilty I'd binge drink straight from the faucet. It was a vicious shame cycle."

Because of Mandy's yo-yo water consumption and lack of steady hormone exposure, she experienced a menstrual event. "Thank God no one was home," she says now. She mutated in the first floor half bath in her family's Dutch Colonial. "Everyone always wants to know what it's like," she says. "It was intoxicating. I felt powerful. I wanted to prowl. I didn't even know I knew how to prowl! But it came naturally. The weird thing is, I felt comfortable in my body for the very first time."

Mandy was already exhibiting panther-like thinking. Every minute spent in panther form can cause changes to normal female brain patterns. But Mandy caught a break. Her mother arrived home from an A.A. meeting to find her shape-shifted 12-year-old daughter slinking down the driveway. "She tasered me," Mandy explains matter-of-factly, "hogtied me, called the SCAT recovery unit, and I woke up chained to a bed in Malibu."

Intravenous hormone treatments and implants don't work for everyone. Mandy is one of the lucky ones. That night still haunts her though. "I still think about when I was a panther," she says quietly. "But thanks to my mom and Ruminations, I now have an implant that will guarantee I never experience it again."

She flashes her pretty smile, and her cheeks dimple.

"If I want to maul my mom, I guess I'll have to use a knife." She laughs. "Just kidding."

DATOR INSIDE

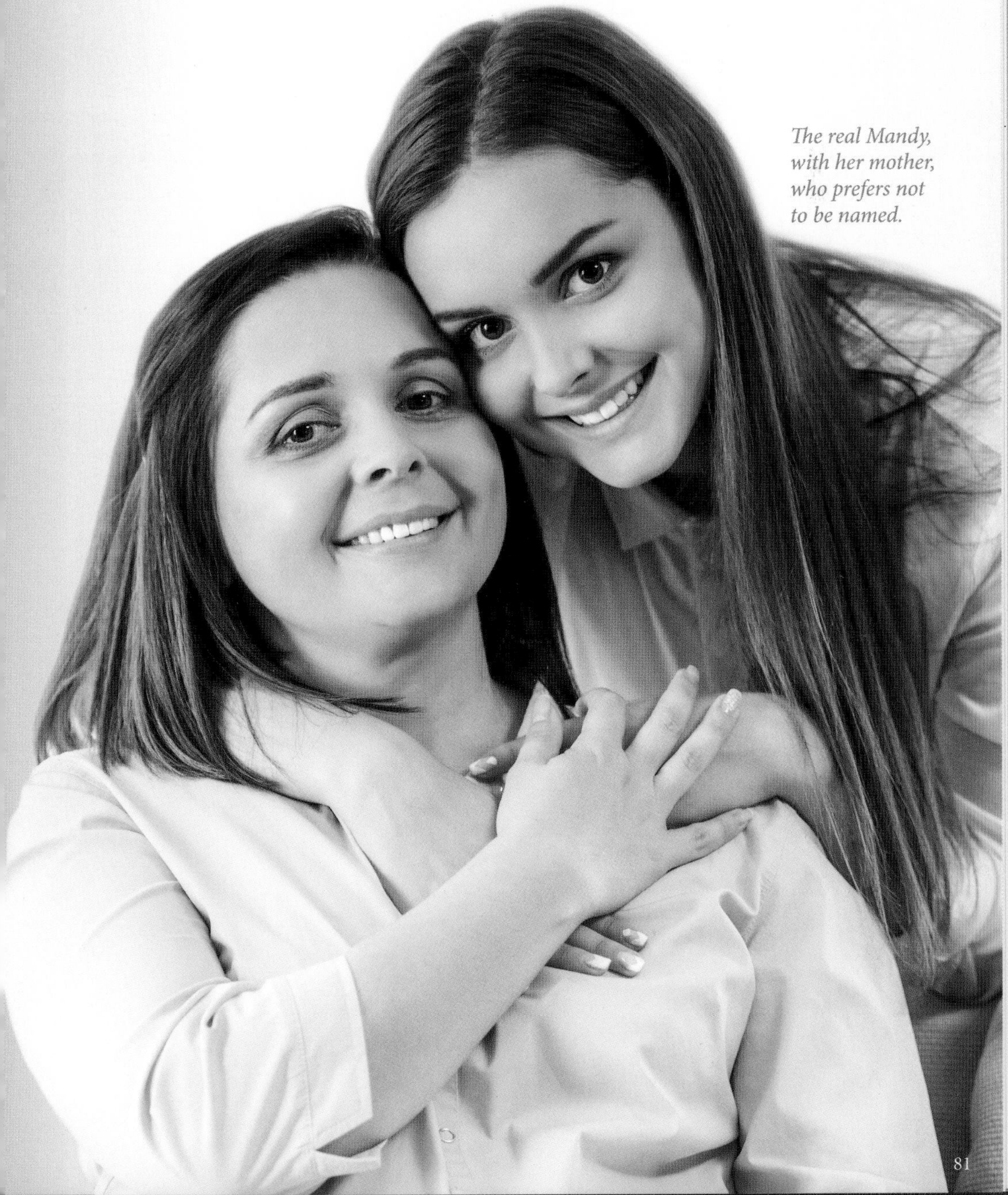

The real Mandy, with her mother, who prefers not to be named.

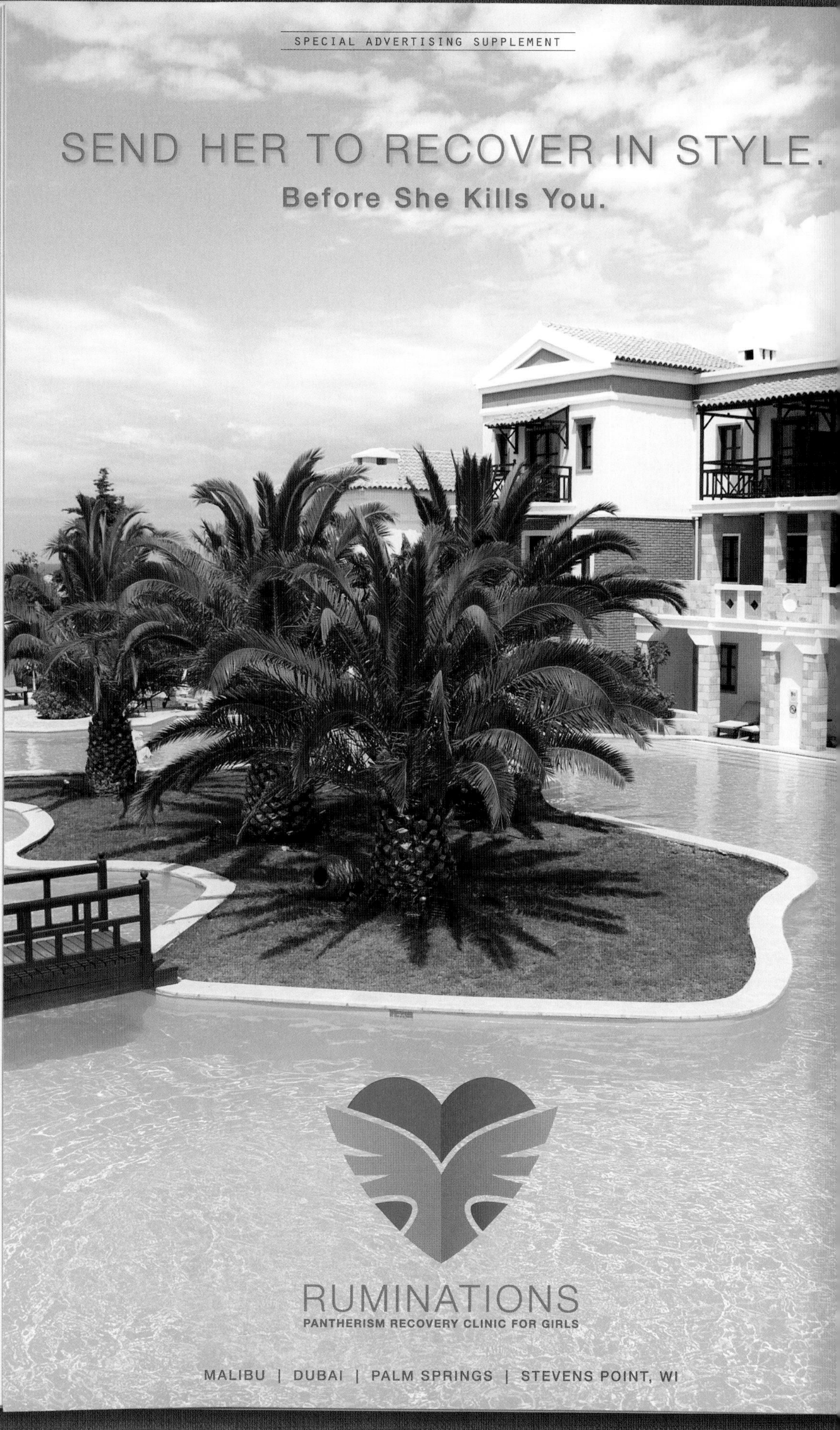
SPECIAL ADVERTISING SUPPLEMENT
SEND HER TO RECOVER IN STYLE.
Before She Kills You.
RUMINATIONS
PANTHERISM RECOVERY CLINIC FOR GIRLS
MALIBU | DUBAI | PALM SPRINGS | STEVENS POINT, WI

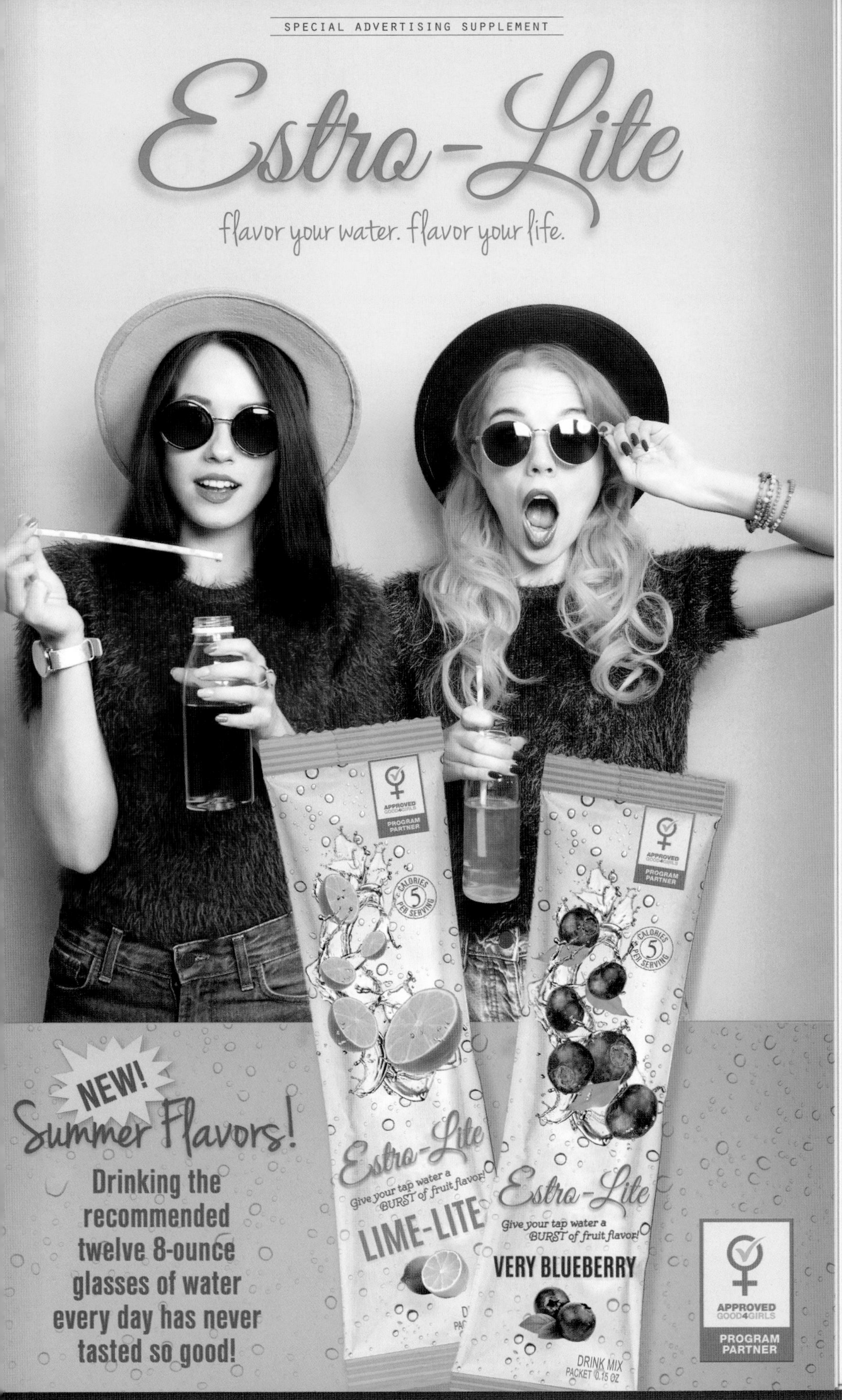
SPECIAL ADVERTISING SUPPLEMENT
Estro-Lite
flavor your water. flavor your life.
NEW!
Summer Flavors!
Drinking the recommended twelve 8-ounce glasses of water every day has never tasted so good!
APPROVED GOOD4GIRLS PROGRAM PARTNER
CALORIES 5 PER SERVING
Estro-Lite
Give your tap water a BURST of fruit flavor!
LIME-LITE
Estro-Lite
Give your tap water a BURST of fruit flavor!
VERY BLUEBERRY
DRINK MIX PACKET 0.15 OZ
APPROVED GOOD4GIRLS PROGRAM PARTNER

Girl: A Game for Boys

By Livia von Sucro

3+
Players
Cis men players, plus one cis or trans woman facilitator, and an optional but recommended audience of cis and trans women.

50 Minutes

Intensity

Supplies:
Paper and pens.

Keywords:
Domestic violence, sexual aggression, discrimination, misogyny.

Background

"Girls can wear jeans
And cut their hair short
Wear shirts and boots
'Cause it's OK to be a boy.
But for a boy to look like a girl is degrading
'Cause you think that being a girl is degrading
But secretly you'd love to know what it's like
Wouldn't you
What it feels like for a girl?"

—*Original quote by Charlotte Gainsbourg in The Cement Garden, 1993; later adapted in the lyrics to "What It Feels Like for A Girl?" by Madonna, 2009*

This game is about violence against women and takes that violence seriously. If you're in the mood for something ludicrous or comic, this game is not for you.

This game is an exercise in empathy, designed for cisgendered men and a cisgendered or transgendered woman moderator. The men will portray girls or women who have just escaped from a situation of abuse and violence perpetrated by men.

The scenario takes place once the women have reached a protected, but unfamiliar environment, such as a hospital or women's shelter. For the sake of their psychological and physical health, the women have abandoned something precious to them. Now, they have the opportunity to tell their stories in a group conversation similar to group therapy. The cis or trans woman moderator will play a mediator within the game scene. She establishes the order of speaking for the characters, acknowledges each speech act, offers her thanks, can subtly encourage someone to talk, etc.

The presence of an audience, especially one consisting of cis or trans women, is strongly recommended.

Once the characters have shared their stories, the audience should ask the players about their choices, stories, and behaviors; critique; make suggestions; or even share their own personal histories if they feel comfortable doing so. At all times, please act with love.

The hope is that after this activity, male players will have given some thought to what being a woman in our society is like, reflected upon their own privilege, and become more empathetic towards women.

Setup

Making Characters (10 mins)

"One is not born, but rather becomes, a woman."
—*Simone de Beauvoir*, The Second Sex, *1949*

Hand out paper and pens to the players.

The players can chose to portray women whose story they have read in a newspaper, so that they can have a voice. They can create their character based on real stories about domestic violence, sexual aggression, discrimination, misogyny, and so on.

Each player should give their character:

- A name.
- A history that explains how they arrived here.
- A sorrow, which is what they had to let go in order to survive.
- An emotion about being here: either hope, the faith that things will get better, or
- A disbelief, a melancholic certainty that nothing will change.

The game consists of the characters telling their stories in a group therapy session, and the game ends when the mediator asks the characters to hug. Ask if everyone here is comfortable with hugging, and let people opt out of they need to.

#Feminism

A Nano-Game Anthology

This issue of Man-Eaters was inspired by #Feminism, a nano game anthology, and one of the most brilliant, provocative, and devastatingly funny social satires I've ever read. It is my favorite thing ever. You can buy a copy at storytelling.pelgranepress.com.

CC

Catcalling

by Tora de Boer

4
Players

30
Minutes

Intensity

Supplies:
A smartphone
with internet.

Keywords:
Street harassment,
bros, intervention,
dancing.

Background

"HEY BABY! HOW ARE YOU DOING?"
Ignore them, just ignore them and keep walking.
Head down, and look as uninterested as possible.

"COME ON BABY, GIVE US A SMILE!"
Not in your wildest dream, jackass... More
distance. Distance is good! Around the next
corner is a more crowded street. I hope they
won't follow me.

You are going to play three versions of the same
catcalling situation, showing how bystander
intervention can make a difference.

Setup

Roles:

The roles are: Catcaller, Two Friends, and
the Target

Clean slate ritual:

Choose a song you all like—it must be
danceable! It will be used at the end of the game.

Setup:

Read the rules, decide who will play each of the
roles, and then play.

When dividing the roles, think about what
experience you want—players will play the same
role throughout the game. Your gender should
not influence which part you play in the game.

Each scene takes place with the Catcaller and
their friends present at a bus stop—as the
game progresses, the Catcaller's friends
increasingly intervene.

Play

Intro:

Play the song "Blurred Lines" by Robin Thicke
and really listen to the lyrics.

Scene 1:

In this scene, the Catcaller and Friends are
hanging out at a bus stop. The Target stands in
front of the group with their back turned and
eyes closed. The Catcaller should start catcalling
the Target while the Friends help with short
follow-ups or encouragement, using their body
language as well as their words. The catcalling
goes on for about 2 minutes or until it naturally
dies out.

Intermezzo:

The Target has a short monologue about the
thoughts and feelings they had during the scene
(about one minute).

Scene 2:

The Catcaller and Friends are back at the bus
stop. The Target stands in front of the group but
with their body turned sideways, in the direction
of Friend 1. The Target's eyes can be open or
closed; they do not speak. The Catcaller starts
catcalling the Target again. Friend 2 helps with
short follow ups or encouragement. Friend 1
tries to stop the situation and defend The Target
using only short sentences or single words.
This goes on for about 2 minutes or until it
naturally dies out.

Intermezzo:

The Target has a short monologue about the
thoughts and feelings they had during the scene
(about one minute).

Scene 3:

The Catcaller and Friends are at the bus stop
again. The Target stands in front of the group,
facing them with their eyes open. The Catcaller
starts catcalling the Target. Both Friends defend
the target and try to stop the situation (no
restrictions). This goes on for about 2 minutes
or until it naturally dies out.

Intermezzo:

The Target has a short monologue about the
thoughts and feelings they had during the scene
(about one minute).

Outro:

Play your chosen "clean slate" song and dance
the experience out of your body. Then sit down
and talk about your experiences.

About the Designer

Tora de Boer (Denmark) has been a larper for eleven years, but this is the first time she's written anything, so be gentle!

CREATOR/WRITER
CHELSEA CAIN

CO-CREATOR/DESIGNER
LIA MITERNIQUE

You can use safety pins to attach these name tags to your clothing. If you need more name tags, ask to use your school printer.

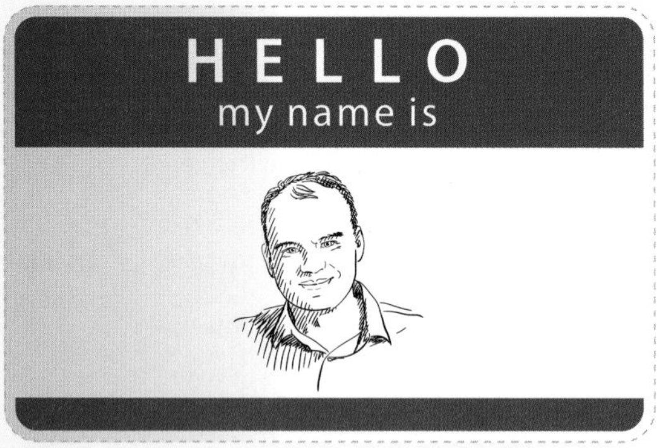
HELLO
my name is

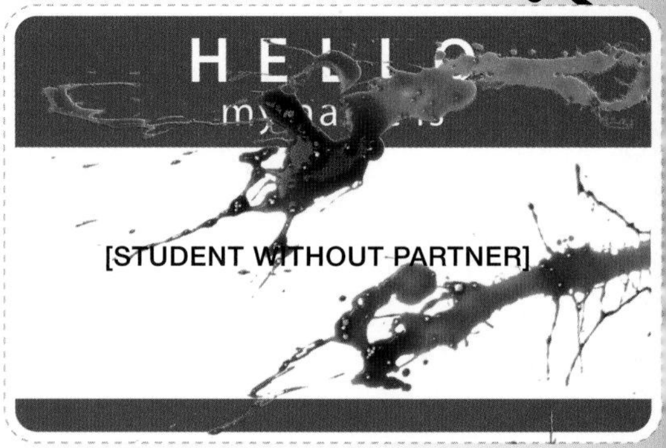
[STUDENT WITHOUT PARTNER]

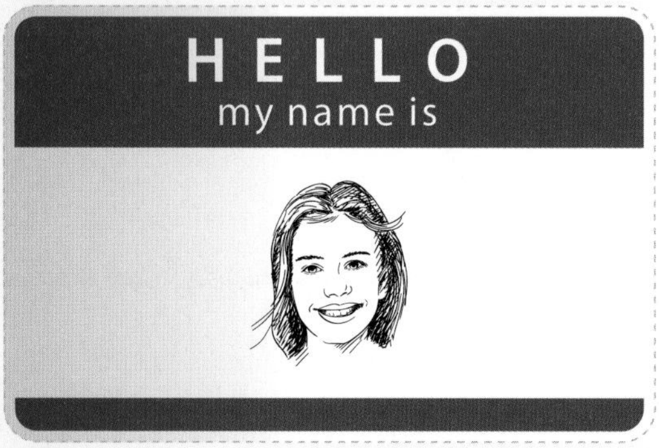
HELLO
my name is

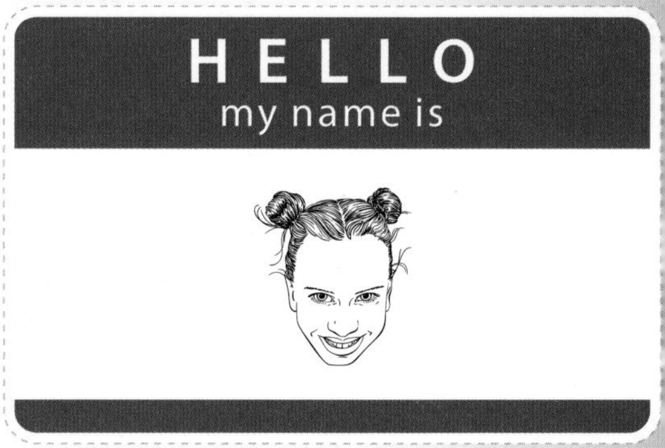
HELLO
my name is

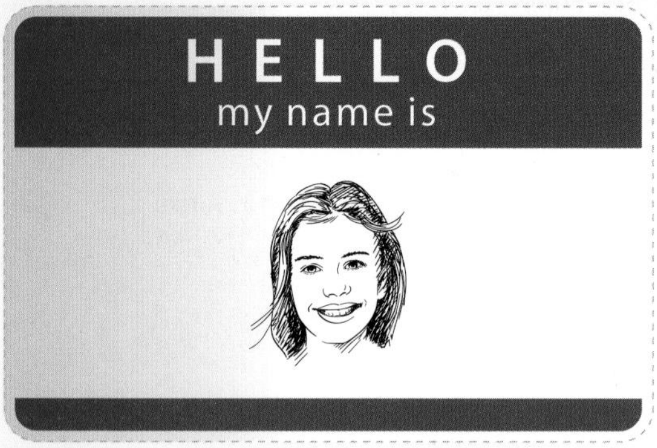
HELLO
my name is

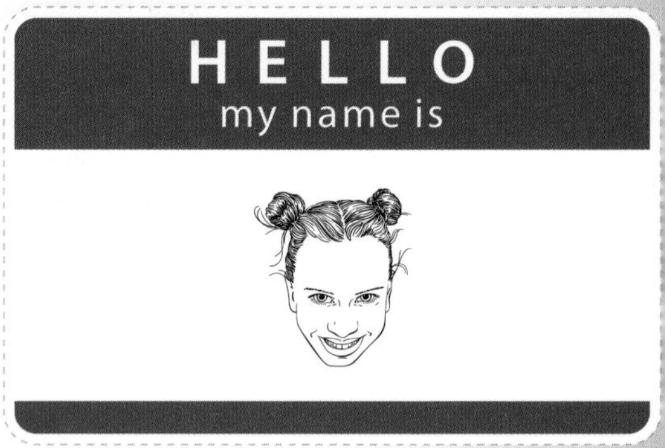
HELLO
my name is

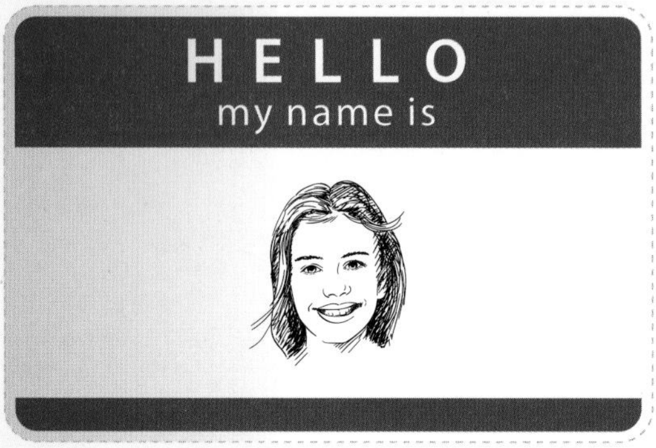
HELLO
my name is

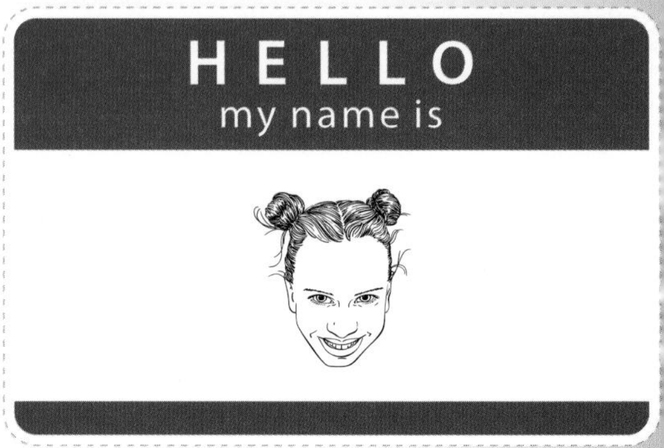
HELLO
my name is

‹PANSION PACK: Stain Remover Cards

LEMON

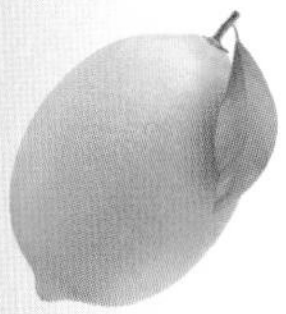

ʳ lighter colored fabrics, old ›od stains can be cleaned up with usehold items such as lemon juice. ›t suggested for darker fabrics.

category	*wash pts*
STAIN REMOVER	**-3**

ASPIRIN

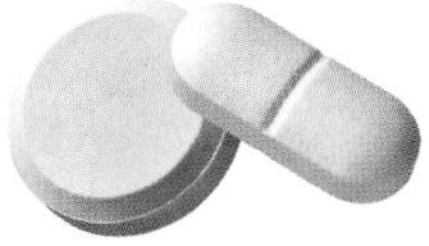

Crush up a few aspirin and mix with cold water to make a paste. Apply it to the stain. Let it sit on the stain overnight, and launder as usual.

category	*wash pts*
STAIN REMOVER	**-2**

BLEACH

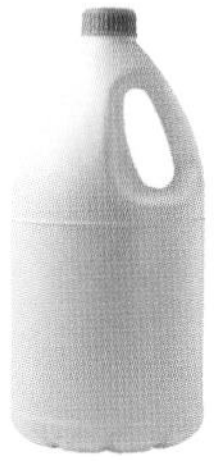

Oxygenated bleaches and enzymatic cleaners up your blood stain removal game. Use as directed.

category	*wash pts*
STAIN REMOVER	**-6**

SALT

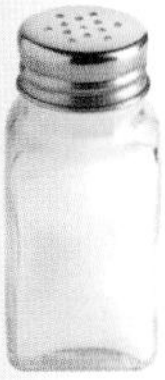

you don't have stain remover, try alt! With a little cold water, it is ʳeat at cleaning up bloodstains.

category	*wash pts*
STAIN REMOVER	**-4**

ESTRO-POP

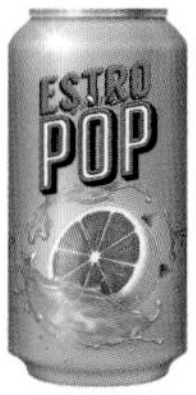
ESTRO
POP

Grab the nearest can of Estro-Pop and soak the stained fabric in it overnight. Then launder as usual.

category	*wash pts*
STAIN REMOVER	**-7**

CORNSTARCH

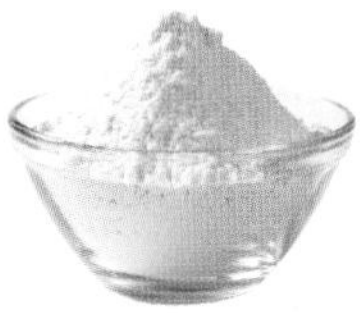

Cover the stain with a paste made from cornstarch and water. Rub it in gently. Put in a sunny spot. When the paste is dry, brush it all away!

category	*wash pts*
STAIN REMOVER	**-1**

SPIT

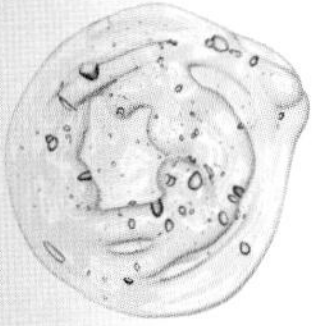

ɪn a pinch, nothing beats saliva.

category	*wash pts*
STAIN REMOVER	**-5**

WHITE VINEGAR

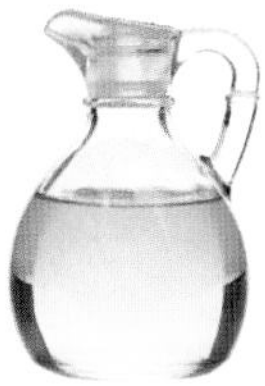

Pour it – full strength – directly onto the stain. Let it soak in for 10 minutes. Then blot with a towel. Repeat if needed. Then launder.

category	*wash pts*
STAIN REMOVER	**-8**

AMMONIA

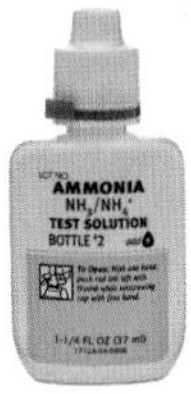
AMMONIA
TEST SOLUTION

Dab the stain with a mix of 1/2 ammonia, 1/2 cold water.

category	*wash pts*
STAIN REMOVER	**-9**

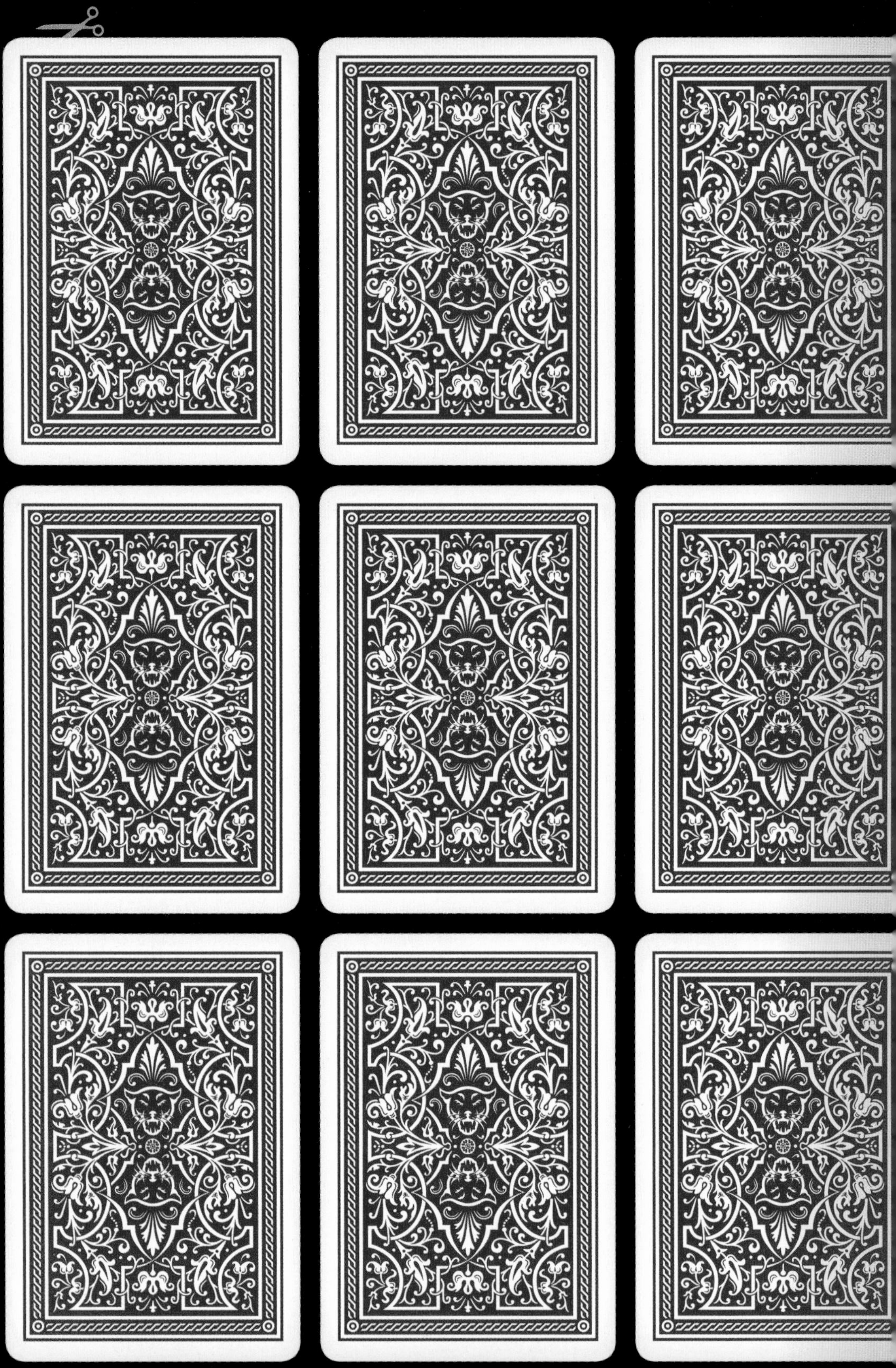

Cut out and photocopy for additional BLOOD SPORT scorecards.

OFFICIAL BLOOD SPORT SCORECARD

COMPETITION _____ DATE _____

HOME TEAM _____

COLOR _____ CAPTAIN _____

AWAY TEAM _____

COLOR _____ CAPTAIN _____

NO. ☐

FIRST TAMPON

SECOND TAMPON

NO. ☐

FIRST TAMPON

SECOND TAMPON

EXTRA TIME

NO. ☐

HOME TEAM _____

NO.						PLAYER

AWAY TEAM _____

NO.						PLAYER

PANTHERISM ENCOURAGES WOMEN TO LEAVE THEIR HUSBANDS KILL THEIR CHILDREN PRACTICE WITCHCRAFT DESTROY CAPITALISM AND BECOME LESBIANS.

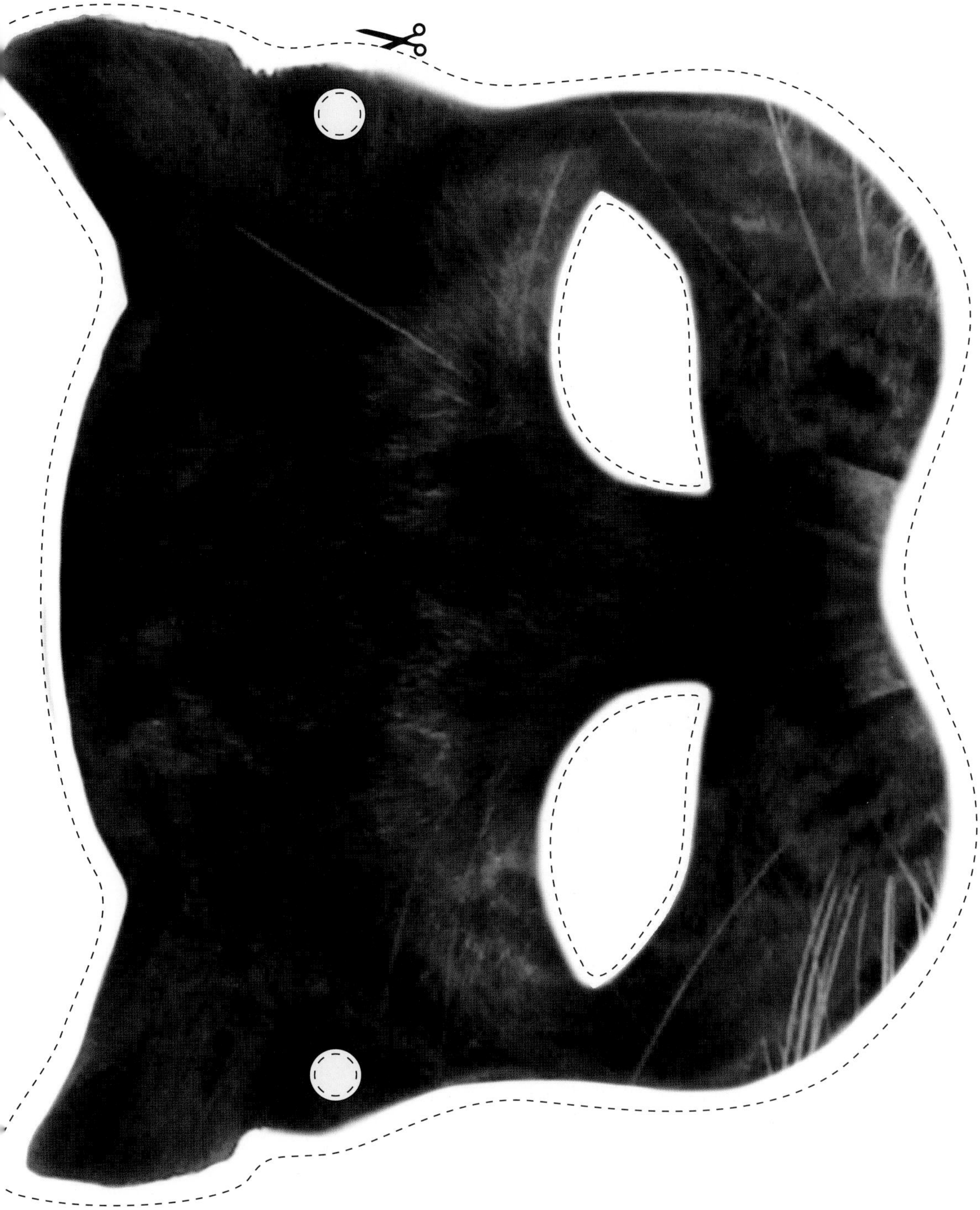

1. cut accurately along dotted lines
2. punch out holes
3. attach string
4. tie around head

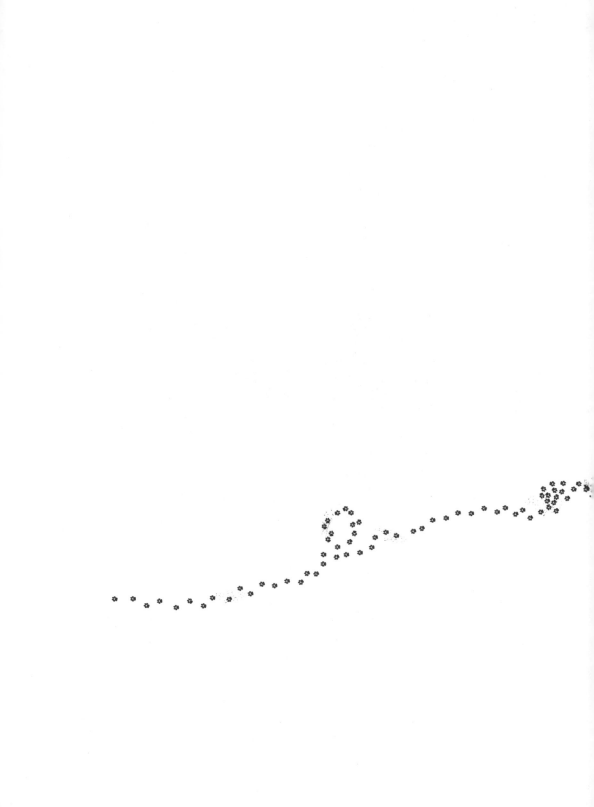

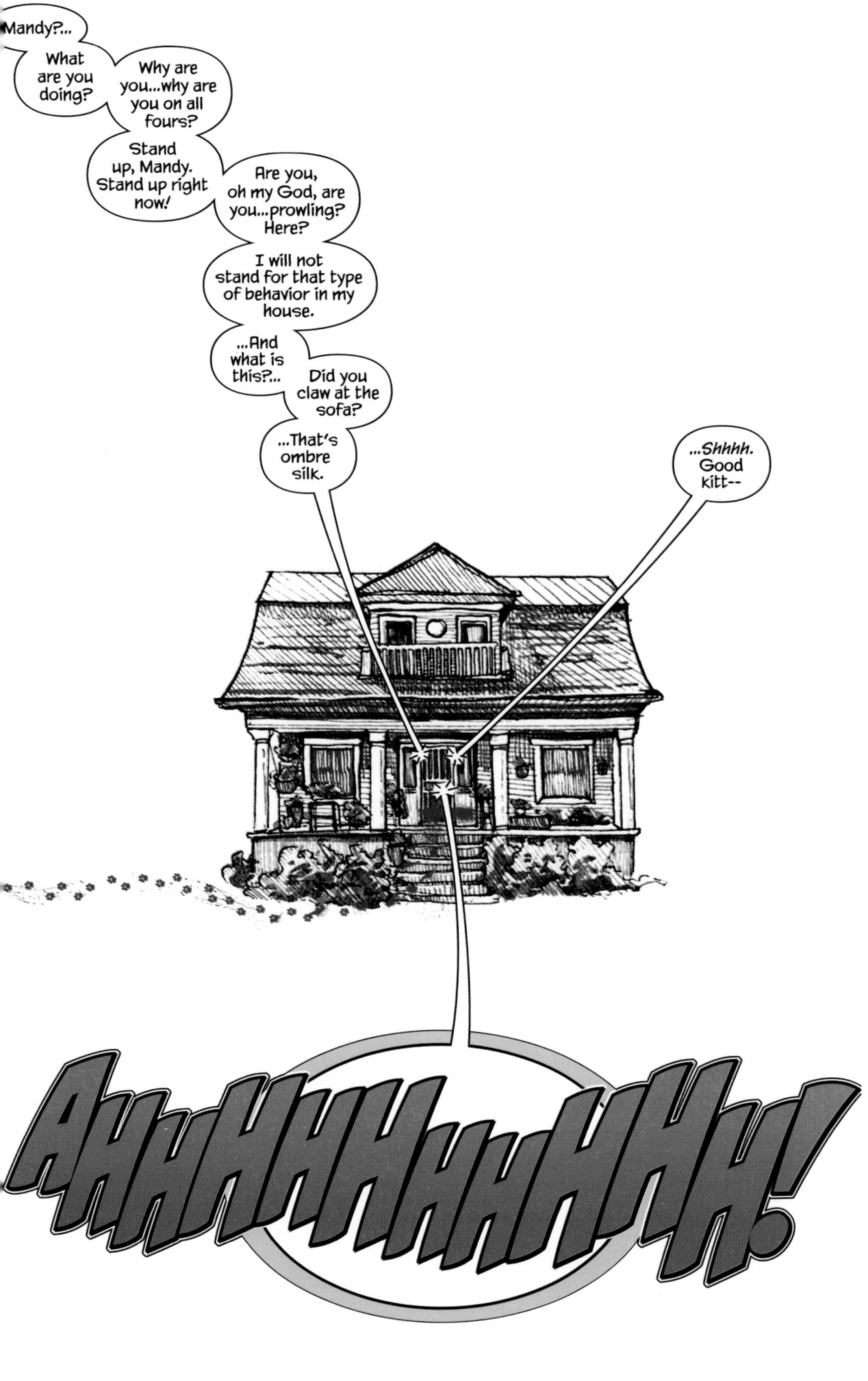
Mandy?...
What are you doing?
Why are you...why are you on all fours?
Stand up, Mandy. Stand up right now!
Are you, oh my God, are you...prowling? Here?
I will not stand for that type of behavior in my house.
...And what is this?...
Did you claw at the sofa?
...That's ombre silk.
...Shhhh. Good kitt--
AHHHHHHHHHHHH!

man-eaters

COVER ART GALLERY

ISSUE #1

A

man-eaters
1

B

man-eaters
1

C

D

man-eaters
1

ISSUE #2

A

man-eaters
2

B

man-eaters
2

C

man-eaters
2

ISSUE #3

A

man-eaters
3

B

man-eaters
3

ISSUE #4

A

man-eaters
Cat Fight
4

B

man-eaters
Cat Fight
4

ISSUE #5

A

man-eaters
5

B

5

ISSUE #6

A

man-eaters
6

B

man-eaters
6

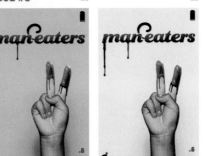

ISSUE #7 A B

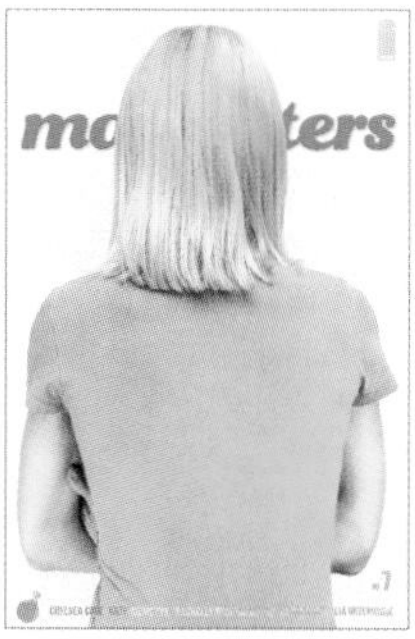

ISSUE #8 A B

ISSUE #9 A B

ISSUE #10 A B

ISSUE #11 A B

ISSUE #12 A B

TRADE VOLUME 1 A B

TRADE VOLUME 2 A

COVER ART DESIGN:
LIA MITERNIQUE

VARIANT COVER 1C:
MARIA LAURA SANAPO

VARIANT COVER 1D:
BETH SPARKS

VARIANT COVER 9B:
ELISE McCALL

PRODUCTION BY TRICIA RAMOS

IMAGE COMICS, INC. • **Robert Kirkman**: Chief Operating Officer • **Erik Larsen**: Chief Financial Officer • **Todd McFarlane**: President • **Marc Silvestri**: Chief Executive Officer • **Jim Valentino**: Vice President • **Eric Stephenson**: Publisher / Chief Creative Officer • **Corey Hart**: Director of Sales • **Jeff Boison**: Director of Publishing Planning & Book Trade Sales • **Chris Ross**: Director of Digital Sales • **Jeff Stang**: Director of Specialty Sales • **Kat Salazar**: Director of PR & Marketing • **Drew Gill**: Art Director • **Heather Doornink**: Production Director • **Nicole Lapalme**: Controller • **IMAGECOMICS.COM**

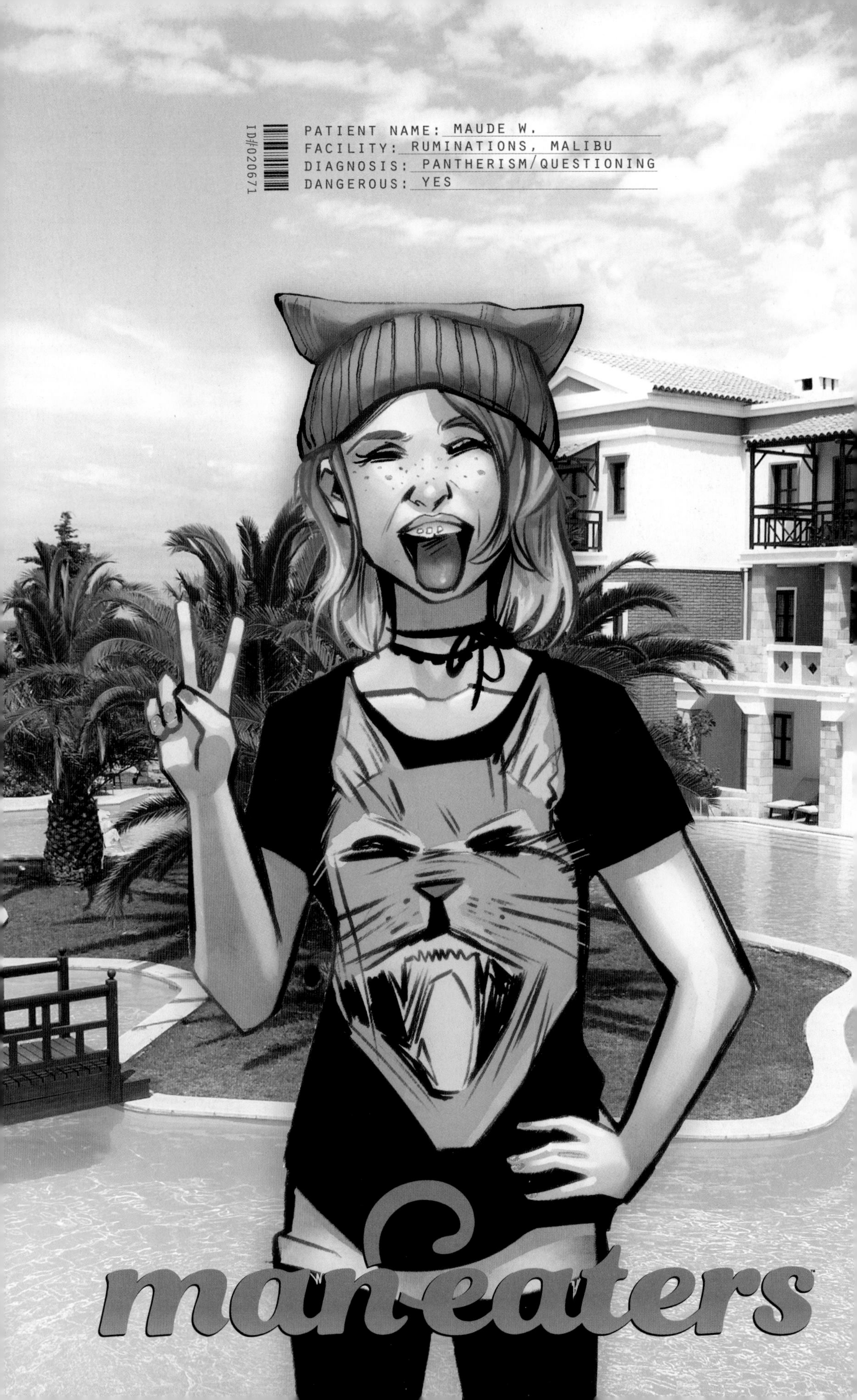
ID#020671
PATIENT NAME: MAUDE W.
FACILITY: RUMINATIONS, MALIBU
DIAGNOSIS: PANTHERISM/QUESTIONING
DANGEROUS: YES
man eaters™